Harold Lloyd

The
Shape of
Laughter

RICHARD SCHICKEL

New York Graphic Society • Boston

There is a moment in childhood that belongs eternally to the great clowns of the silent screen. This book is for my children, *Erika* and *Jessica,* who by sharing that moment with me taught me the most important thing about my subject.

The quotations from Lloyd's autobiography are reprinted with permission from Harold Lloyd, *An American Comedy,* Dover edition, copyright 1971 by Dover Publications, Inc., New York (an unabridged republication of the work originally published in 1928 by Longmans, Green & Co., New York, with the title *An American Comedy: Acted by Harold Lloyd, Directed by Wesley W. Stout).*

International Standard Book Number 0-8212-0595-1

Library of Congress Catalog Card Number 73-89958

Designed by Betsy Beach
Composed by DEKR Corporation, Woburn, Mass.
Printed by Murray Printing, Forge Village, Mass.
Bound by Colonial Press, Clinton, Mass.

Manufactured in the United States of America

Contents

The Shape of Laughter   1

The Films

    LONESOME LUKE, 1915–17   144

    THE EARLY GLASSES CHARACTER, 1917–21   146

    A SAILOR-MADE MAN, 1920   150

    GRANDMA'S BOY, 1922   152

    DR. JACK, 1922   154

    SAFETY LAST, 1923   156

    WHY WORRY?, 1923   160

    GIRL SHY, 1924   166

    HOT WATER, 1924   176

    THE FRESHMAN, 1925   182

    FOR HEAVEN'S SAKE, 1926   188

    THE KID BROTHER, 1927   190

    SPEEDY, 1928   192

    WELCOME DANGER, 1929   194

    FEET FIRST, 1930   196

    MOVIE CRAZY, 1932   204

    THE CAT'S PAW, 1934   208

    THE MILKY WAY, 1936   210

    PROFESSOR BEWARE, 1938   212

    MAD WEDNESDAY   214
      (The Sin of Harold Diddlebock), 1947

Filmography by Eileen Bowser   216

Acknowledgments   218

Photograph Credits   218

Safety Last (1923).

The Shape of Laughter

By the time he died, on March 8, 1971, at the age of seventy-seven, Harold Lloyd had become an obligatory name on the short, nostalgic — sometimes falsely nostalgic — list of the great comedians of the silent screen: Chaplin, Keaton, Harry Langdon, sometimes Laurel and Hardy — and Lloyd. No one dared omit his name. He had been so greatly popular in his time and he was obviously such a nice man, living in prosperous retirement in his legendary home in Beverly Hills, that it would have seemed both anti-historical and unnecessarily cruel not to at least mention him in passing. Besides, no illustrated history of the movies — indeed, of the social history of twentieth-century America — seemed complete without that famous still from *Safety Last* of Lloyd hanging from the hands of a clock, its face itself dangling from the huge timepiece's mainspring, some twelve stories above a busy downtown street. Somehow, better than any other, that picture seemed to summarize the inordinate lengths to which Lloyd and his peers in the great, lost art of silent comedy would go for a laugh. And if few knew exactly how and why Lloyd came to this unlikely and obviously temporary predicament, fewer still cared to investigate the matter. It was difficult to see his films, since they had long since gone out of general release and two compilations of their best sequences, put together by Lloyd himself in the early sixties, had aroused only mild, and certainly not critically acute, interest. There were no calls for a general revival of his work, as there were for that of Chaplin and Keaton. It would have been fair to say that when he died, Harold Lloyd was recalled fondly, and even warmly by those who had grown up on his films in the 1920s. But he was not remembered, not in the fullest sense of the word.

There were two reasons for this. In 1971, when Richard Griffith, former curator of the Museum of Modern Art film library, came to write an introduction to the reprint of Lloyd's reticent, primitive venture into the as-told-to autobiography, *An American Comedy,* he noted the lack of interest in Lloyd, a lack of interest so profound that not a single substantial book had been written about him. This reflected, Griffith commented, "the disesteem in which he has traditionally been held by the movie highbrows. They do not like his optimism. His calculated comedy methods have been labeled 'mechanical' and let go at that. His wealth and success have been held against him. . . ." So far as these remarks go — and Griffith did not live to finish the introductory essay — they are

1

entirely accurate. For example, in *The Comic Mind,* a study devoted entirely to screen comedy, and largely to silent comedy at that, Gerald Mast spared but sixteen pages for Lloyd, and though he gives grudging acknowledgments to Lloyd's skill as a creator of incredibly long and intricate gag sequences, he calls him "deliberate, cold-blooded, and detached . . . superficial." Ultimately, Mast tells us, "Lloyd comedies say nothing about life." The problem, as he sees it, is that Lloyd (and Langdon) lacked "that perfect unity between soul and surface, internal feeling and external gag, comic business and serious implication, subjective reaction to human life and objective depiction of it in the film medium." This bias was even shared by James Agee, whose 1949 piece, "Comedy's Greatest Era," remains one of the few essays in film criticism that combines grace of expression, thoughtfulness of analysis, and judiciousness — and which did more than any single work of criticism to revive interest in the silent comedians. Agee felt it necessary to balance his generally affectionate remarks about Lloyd by remarking, "It great comedy must involve something beyond laughter, Lloyd was not a great comedian."

If the critics found a lack of what we would now call "soul" in Lloyd's films, they found a similar lack of emotional resonance in his life off screen. It seems to have contained only one serious crisis, which (typically) Lloyd himself went to some lengths to disguise, and so far as anyone outside his immediate circle knew, no tragedies, though again, there was more unhappiness in Lloyd's life than met the uninformed eye. Essentially, his road to success — an enormous success in his time, quite comparable to Chaplin's, economically — had been a smooth one. His childhood was apparently emotionally stable, if rather less geographically rooted than most, though, interestingly, all the great silent comics had rather footloose beginnings. Lloyd's struggle to establish himself professionally was both brief and without major frustration. He made the transition to the sound era more easily and more profitably than most of his peers, though without the glorious results that Chaplin, after much creative anguish, achieved in *City Lights* and *Modern Times* — if, indeed, it is fair to call these sound films in the full sense of the term. In any event, he was not ruined as Keaton and Langdon were, not forced into the sometimes humiliating low-budget pictures that Laurel and Hardy had to make in order to keep going. Then, when public taste gently, without rancor or shocking haste, veered away from him, he was able to quietly withdraw, never officially announcing a retirement, and indeed, keeping himself before the public in a variety of dignified ways during the last three decades of his life — as a producer, as the host of a radio show for a brief time, and, most important to him, as Imperial Potentate — the national president — of the Shrine. He was even the star of a Preston Sturges movie, though it didn't come out as successfully as it might have. Later, of course, there were his compilation films to attend to, and the inevitable old man's round of retrospectives, film festivals, seminars, and lectures, as well as

extensive real estate holdings to oversee, and a succession of obsessive hobbies to fill the hours between his public and business engagements.

Of such things legendary status as a cultural hero is not made. What is required is some sort of tragedy. An artist who dies before his time — F. Scott Fitzgerald is the classic example in our era — is in a sense fortunate; if he had any ability at all we mourn not only for the indifference visited upon him by a world which underestimated his mortality, but for the work that might have been. But death is not necessary to achieve tragic status. For example, Buster Keaton was effectively silenced as an artist by drink and by the insensitivity to his gifts of his last employer, Metro-Goldwyn-Mayer, who gave up on him too quickly, too brutally, when his first sound films proved unprofitable. Charles Chaplin, in a sense, produced and directed his own fall from grace. His marital difficulties and his earnest, if innocent, left-wing political views did not jibe with the benign image of "The Little Fellow" (indeed, his compulsion to lecture the world about how it ought to think and behave politically fatally marred his last movies. Unable or unwilling to sue for a renewal of the affection he had once found in his adopted country, he withdrew in bitter exile, and did not return until he could return to the prodigal's welcome that was arranged for him on the occasion of his receipt of a special Academy Award in 1972 — an event that, not accidentally, coincided with the carefully managed reissue of his old films by shrewd promoters. Even poor Harry Langdon, the least conscious of silent comedians, and the one with the briefest period of stardom, came to be seen as a tragic figure. As Frank Capra, who was part of the team at Mack Sennett's studio that concocted a screen character for him — something close to *The Good Soldier Schweik* — and who directed his first independent feature tells it, Langdon was afflicted with a sudden swelling of the head. He dismissed most of the group, Capra included, who had helped create his success, floundered for a bit, and then after the coming of sound sank entirely — into short subjects, then bit parts, then silence. Agee's article did not merely rescue his reputation, it made it, for he had never really established himself in his time, as Chaplin, Keaton, and Lloyd had; without Agee, Langdon would have been almost completely forgotten. Now, if anything, his ranking exceeds Lloyd's in the estimate of many scholars.

Thus the congeries of factors that have condemned Harold Lloyd to the fringe of historical consciousness. And thus the need to re-examine his achievement. In this essay I am not going to argue that received opinion about him is completely wrong. Nor am I going to attempt to prove that there was some hidden psychological wound or some previously unsuspected depth of vision or feeling that only now, at some distance in time, we can perceive, and thereby find new values in his films. Yet it seems to me self-evident that any performer who achieved and sustained over a period of years the enormous popularity that Lloyd enjoyed must have had virtues that his more recent critics

have ignored. It also seems to me, having had the opportunity lately to study the body of his work, that it has, for the most part, an overriding virtue which is so obvious that it is easy to overlook, namely that it is simply and consistently more hilarious than the work of any contemporary other than Keaton. Or, as Agee immediately added after acknowledging that Lloyd, for lack of heart, might not be a "great" comedian, "If plain laughter is any criterion — and it is a healthy counterbalance to the other — few people have equalled him, and nobody has ever beaten him."

It is a point to be borne firmly in mind. And there are others that come to mind as his work unfolds before one, some three or four decades after it was done. For one thing, the world through which Lloyd moved was the "realest" of all the comic worlds of the silent screen, the freest of exaggeration and stylization, both physically and in terms of the other characters encountered by Lloyd's character, often identified in the credits only as "The Boy." There are few freaks or grotesques here, and the streets, shops, and homes he moved through were more often than not locations rented for a few days' shooting, and so far as one can tell, scarcely changed or decorated by the movie-makers. And, because Lloyd himself is usually such a normal, everyday sort of chap, fitting so easily into these ordinary surroundings, one gains from the films now a quite extraordinary sense of the physical reality of a period fast receding from living memory.

One point seems particularly worth emphasizing, if only because Lloyd and his co-workers (probably unconsciously) emphasized it. That is that the decade or so between the end of World War I and the stock market crash in 1929 was a period of contrast between the older, essentially rural America — nineteenth-century America that had, in fact, continued to flourish at least as a repository of values for the first two decades of this country — and the new urban America that was developing. This new nation inside the old seemed nothing less than a miracle to a goodly portion of the citizenry, especially to those who, like Lloyd himself, had been born into rural small-town America, but had been irresistibly drawn to the glamor and the economic opportunities of the growing cities. This all seems odd to us today — oppressed as so many of us are by the ugliness and decay of city life. But to Lloyd's generation everything about the city seemed fresh and enthralling. The automobile, for instance, represented a wondrous convenience, an object of almost indescribable longing, not a source of pollution and, indeed, death. No wonder one of his greatest comic sequences — Harold taking his wife and his in-laws for a first spin in a new car in *Hot Water* — is so beautifully orchestrated and so strangely touching. One understands what the car means to its new owner as a first symbolization of rising status and as a demonstration to his thoroughly awful relatives that he is a more substantial figure than they had reckoned him to be. Thus, its gradual demolition as he attempts to master both the mechanical intricacies of the vehicle and the confusions of the city's traffic regulations is not only suspenseful and funny, but

4

oddly moving. One gains the sense from this sequence that Lloyd's befuddlement and his increasingly desperate attempts to maintain his *savoir faire,* to project mastery in a situation for which he had no training, emotional or otherwise, was instantly and entirely recognizable to his audience — and that it was one for which they had instant empathy. Indeed, one does not have to work very hard to rekindle, some forty years later, a similar emotional response, for there are still complicated objects we long for but which can undo our dignity, our *amour propre,* when we attempt to bring them under our control. Simply replace the *Hot Water* car with something like a camper and place in it an urban American attempting to embrace the outdoor life, from which we are now as alienated by birth and training as Lloyd and his generation were from the city and its tools for living, and the comic point becomes self-evident. Similarly, it seems to me, Lloyd's obsession with high places, his literally nightmarish discovery of himself clinging to the ledges, decorations, flagpoles, clocks of skyscrapers, makes perfect sense for his time — and has a resonance for us as well. *Safety Last* may contain the most famous of these sequences, but he had begun experimenting with similar work in his two- and three-reelers of 1920 and '21, *High and Dizzy* and *Never Weaken,* and he may have topped all these "thrill" sequences with the great one contained in an otherwise indifferent sound film, 1930's *Feet First.* At any rate, they were all products of a period in which the whole nation was mightily impressed by our relatively new-found ability to build upward, ever upward. The skyscraper was perhaps the greatest symbol of the age's technological achievements — a thrilling, yet in some sense a scary, thing. (It still is, only now anxiety outruns pride — witness the interest in the 1974 super-production, *The Towering Inferno,* an adaptation of two best-selling books about the currently lively fear that the great buildings downtown may be firetraps in which hundreds could be killed by accident.) In any event, there is no need to emphasize that skyscrapers almost immediately became a feature of our dream world, as any psychoanalyst can testify. Nor is there much need to stress the dreamy quality of Lloyd's high-rise thrill sequences, the (again unconscious) surrealistic air about them. They afford us, now, the opportunity to reflect on how recently our attitudes toward our environment were diametrically opposed to what they have become, how quickly we have reversed ourselves, and — perhaps more to the point — how Lloyd's always disastrous entanglements with the contraptions of modernism seem to predict the exasperation with them that more and more of us would feel in the years to come. Again, it is impossible to believe that this rather simple soul, always in rather narrow-minded pursuit of the strongest possible gag-line, had anything like social criticism in mind. He was not writing on film an early version of *Future Shock.* But it is all there to see if one has the eyes to see it.

Along this line, it is interesting to note how accurately his pictures reflect the exquisite confusions of a time of vast environmental transition. For example, in

that same sequence in *Hot Water,* one of the things Lloyd, his family, and his car get entangled with is a fire engine answering an alarm. The engine is horse drawn. Yet this encounter with a remnant of nineteenth-century technology follows almost immediately their eluding a traffic cop who is mounted on what appears to be the latest model motorcycle. Similarly, there is a great sequence in the film immediately preceding, *Girl Shy,* in which Harold must stop a wedding before the girl he loves marries a sly bigamist. He must get from city to country, and in the process he uses — or attempts to use — every mode of land transportation then available (including, most spectacularly, a runaway trolley car). The point is not merely that this is as beautifully orchestrated a sequence as anything in Keaton, but that horses and horse drawn vehicles come as readily to his desperate hand as motor-driven conveyances. The confusion of the old-fashioned and the modern, doubtless accepted without thought by audiences of the day, since it is accepted unblinkingly by Lloyd, adds a note of peculiar interest to the movie today — a strange displacing note — that often occurs in other Lloyd movies as well, and gives them a special value on rediscovery. Indeed, there is something of this quality — the familiar made casually unfamiliar by quirks of costume, decor, or what have you, lurking in the corner of nearly every frame of every silent film. It is one of the things that make them so endlessly fascinating to study today.

In reviewing Lloyd's work today, one is also struck by how purely it seems to be the product of the movies and of nothing else. This is often held against him by critics like Mast, who point out that Chaplin and Keaton were "international" stars of vaudeville and music hall before coming to film, that even Langdon served a long — if not particularly distinguished — apprenticeship in the same environs. Aside from the most modest kind of work in amateur theatricals and in some professional stock companies, it is perfectly true that Lloyd had only a small amount of stage training, and no vaudeville background whatever. It is also undoubtedly accurate to say that he knew next to nothing of the comedic traditions, established in the dim reaches of theatrical history, that informed Chaplin's work in particular. Lloyd's schools were the movie comedy factories, mainly Hal Roach's, but also, for a short interval, Mack Sennett's. And as Agee said, "The early silent comedians never strove for or consciously thought of anything which could be called artistic 'form,' " although, as he also says, "they achieved it."

The basic Sennett and Roach films, especially in the early days when Lloyd was apprenticing, consisted of setting up an excuse for a chase or "rally" (as the device was known around Sennett's) and then getting it going — at undercranked speeds, of course, so movement would be (Agee's phrase again) "just a shade faster and fizzier than life." Sennett, in particular, was uninterested in the comedy of character (though perhaps he achieved a comedy of humors

6

from time to time), and though film scholar William K. Everson finds more character development in the Roach films, it remains difficult to advance very elaborate claims for them either in this respect. At any rate, Chaplin left Sennett precisely because the opportunities for his delicate pantomimic characterizations were few and he feared being lost in the general uproar. Keaton also had only brief Sennett experience, taking a cut from his $250-a-week vaudeville salary to learn the craft of film comedy for a starting fee of $40 a week, at first working mainly in the Fatty Arbuckle series. In fact, of the legendary top bananas of the silent screen, only Lloyd worked for any length of time at either of the premier comedy studios. And that may very well account for the fact that it was he who developed to its highest point the comedy of thrills and movement — the "rally" raised to its highest levels — though there is nothing in any of Lloyd's work that would suggest the balletic parallels a number of critics, especially the French, have found in Sennett's rallies.

But that's all right, too. Sennett himself used to reserve his bluntest derision for critics of that school, noting happily that he had never seen a ballet in his life. What's more important is that Sennett in the beginning, then Keaton and Lloyd with greater sophistication, were able to use the first machine capable of capturing and reproducing motion in order to satirize an age of machines that had set the whole society into accelerated motion. It scarcely detracts from Chaplin to say that except for *Modern Times* his films seem scarcely aware of the mechanization of life. The Little Fellow had other fish to fry. Similarly, it seems unfair to criticize Lloyd for his failure to develop a tragic sense of life. He, too, had his eye on other matters. And besides, there do not seem to have been any incidents in his early life that might have set him to brooding about injustice, about the pathetic and the absurd qualities of existence. In his films he did suffer, as Andrew Sarris has acutely pointed out, "terrible humiliation . . . on the social ladder," and these moments can generate more potent shocks of recognition than most critics care to admit (*The Freshman,* for example, is full of them). Still, it is fair to say that Harold Lloyd had every reason to suppose that the most banal of American philosophies — the pluck and luck dream by which a poor but eager youth is elevated above the crowd because he is willing to work hard to develop his God-given talents — actually worked. It had for him, and he had the good fortune to place before the public his best and most carefully developed work at precisely the historical moment when that public as a whole had every reason to share his belief in this most common form of the American dream. He was comedian to the Age of Prosperity, and no more than his audience did he have any reason to suppose that the age would not last, that a moment ought to be spared for the thought that trouble and tragedy are timeless, and, for the individual, quite resistant to the movements of the business cycle. But if, indeed, Chaplin and to a degree Keaton had the depth and

Lloyd relaxes with the men who were the greatest influences on his art —
Charles Chaplin and Douglas Fairbanks. The year was 1934.

sensitivity to comprehend this and to encompass it in their art, one may also note that Lloyd's sublime unawareness of it can be refreshing in its innocence, its naivety.

Indeed, it might even be correct to suggest that Lloyd is rather unfairly lumped with Chaplin, Keaton, and Langdon. They are considered together largely, it would seem, because they were the leading producer-stars of feature-length comedies in the 1920s. But it has always seemed to me that Lloyd's eager youth, slender and well groomed, with nothing but his lensless glasses — themselves a completely natural, everyday sort of appurtenance — to set him apart, to establish his "character," owed more to the early Douglas Fairbanks screen character than it did to stage convention, which insisted on grotesque makeup and costume for "low" comics, and which Lloyd's competitors, each in his own way, adapted to the screen. Fairbanks, like Lloyd, though on a grander scale, had come from legit, where he had been mostly a juvenile, and the character he played in his early movies, before he turned to historical spectacles, was a variation on the kind of youths he had been playing on stage. Like Lloyd's character later, this character was usually introduced either as an inept and wealthy idler who discovers within himself untapped depths of courage and physical inventiveness when he stumbles into some sort of danger, or as a rather dreamy lower-class youth entertaining fantasies of heroism behind his clerkly counter who is given the opportunity to act out those dreams in reality — usually because the girl he loves requires rescuing from some peril or other. These, precisely, are the situations Lloyd found himself coping with in his features, and it seems interesting that Fairbanks made the last of these pictures *(The Nut)* in 1921, a year after he had made the first of his swashbucklers, *The Mark of Zorro,* whose success determined his new direction. For in that same year Lloyd, who had begun in 1918 to experiment with his "glasses character," as he liked to call his only enduring screen persona, made his first feature, *A Sailor-Made Man,* which is astonishingly close to the early Fairbanks formula. In other words, consciously or not, Lloyd saw a niche in the process of being vacated and nimbly hopped into it.

It did not take him long to make it his own. Fairbanks had never been averse to getting a laugh, but he also fancied himself, quite correctly, as a considerable romantic figure, and his stunts, thrilling as they were, were primarily designed to show off his graceful and dashing athleticism. Lloyd, however, depended on looking as comically awkward as possible when he was confronted by difficult circumstances, and, of course, he was required to draw out his chases to the point where an audience's fears for him were converted first into nervous laughter, then into the pure boffo thing. This, obviously, left but small space in which to build up the romantic side of his screen character, which also had its ridiculous side — this shy, pale four-eyes, the kind of kid who plays clarinet in the high school band, has trouble getting a date for the prom, and hopefully takes

9

the business course (though it is hard to imagine him mastering the courage to sell anything except from behind a modest notions counter). Still, Lloyd's relationship to the Fairbanks character, who was also an all-American optimist, a four-square believer in what amounted to Rotarian values, is clearer and closer than his relationship to the creations of the screen figures we more generally regard as his closest competitors and to whom we most frequently compare him, mostly invidiously.

To summarize the matter briefly, then, Harold Lloyd's relatively undramatic personal life, its lack of obvious tragic overtones, has led to a regrettable lack of popular interest in his creative output; also, his work is more bound to his times than the work of most silent comedians, although that begins to seem something of an advantage now, as his films, because of their naturalistic air, help us to gain a historical purchase on his age; his films also owe less to literary and theatrical tradition than those of the other great silent comedians, but that may mean that they have a pure "movieness," a significance in the establishment of a film aesthetic that owes less to the other arts than some critics would like; his work is less "universal," more "American," in its underlying values than that of other actors, Chaplin in particular, though this lack of pretension can be refreshing and something of a value in itself; and in any event, it is unfair to overstress his relationship with the other masters of screen comedy, because his work seems to have grown out of a tradition quite different from the one which informed them. Finally, and this may be the most significant point of all, Lloyd's personal history led him inescapably to the kind of art he created, and was thus responsible for its virtues and its defects. Indeed, one could say that the linkage between Lloyd the man and Lloyd the primitive screen artist was closer, more direct, than that of any other comedian, any other screen personality one can think of. One could say, in fact, that Harold Lloyd's early life — his later life was far darker than most people know — reads very much like the script for a Harold Lloyd movie.

2 Harold Clayton Lloyd was born, of Welsh descent, in a modest frame house in Burchard, Nebraska, on April 20, 1893. He was the son of James Darsie Lloyd, whose family had come west from Pennsylvania to open a general store in this very small town (population: approximately three hundred) at some unspecified earlier date. His mother was Sarah Elizabeth Fraser Lloyd, who was raised in Toulon, Illinois, at least according to her son. (Mrs. Lloyd herself claimed she was born in Colorado to a family that was "a pillar of society.") At any rate, she met and married Darsie (or "Foxy" as he was later nicknamed)

The father of the man: Harold at one-and-a-half (1894). A cheerful three year old, and looking less than happy to be sharing the frame with elder brother Gaylord.

P.M.P. 6023

when she was visiting relatives in Burchard. They had another son, Gaylord, five years Harold's senior, and he also in time became a motion picture actor, one whose career was certainly launched by his successful younger brother and, some say, cut short by him, when Gaylord's good looks and attractive presence began to seem a threat to the star. This, however, is a dubious speculation, as Gaylord's career was never very distinguished.

There is no doubt, though, that Lloyd's childhood was a restless one. Darsie Lloyd had a small patrimony and he invested it in a photographic studio run by a man named Bennett in nearby Humboldt, some four times larger than Burchard. The venture failed and the elder Lloyd took a job as a shoe clerk in Denver, an occupation to which he would periodically return when nothing grander was available. There is considerable family disagreement as to the sequence of the moves thereafter, but it was probably something like this: "Denver to Fort Collins, back to Denver, thence to Pawnee City, returning to Denver; next to Beatrice, thence to Omaha, once more to Denver and back again to Omaha." This is only one of the itineraries Lloyd suggests in his rather premature (1928) autobiography, but in a later interview he settled for it as probably the most accurate. The matter is not important. What is significant is Darsie's inability to sink roots in prosperous soil anywhere. According to Lloyd, other members of his family thought he exaggerated the frequency of their moves, but it seemed to the child that they were forever upping stakes and moving on. It may well be that the elaborateness of the home he finally built when he had money — a home wildly out of character for this modest-seeming man — was a reflection on his childhood. It would seem that he was more disturbed by this moving about than he generally let on, that he wanted to root himself so firmly that he would never again be threatened, or even tempted, by movement.

There were sound enough reasons for the elder Lloyd's restlessness. As Lloyd himself wrote: "The same dissatisfactions and optimisms that sent the pioneers across the Mississippi in search of a promised land kept many of them moving when the grass turned out to be not so green as it first had seemed. The population was in a constant state of being shuffled and reshuffled." Moreover, it should be borne in mind that in the nineties as well as in the first decade of this century the plains states suffered a prolonged agricultural depression. Lloyd grew up in an atmosphere of pervasive economic discontent, and his father, it seems, lacked either the will or the imagination to break out of this distressed region until 1911, when the elder Lloyd and his younger son moved to San Diego. There is also some possibility that the Lloyd marriage was none too stable, though their son was always extremely discreet on this point, and that the move to the west coast represented a final rupture. Anyway, Harold remembered being sent to stay with relatives at various times during his childhood, always, he claimed, for economic reasons. Nevertheless, Mrs. Lloyd did not make the move to San Diego, and it appears that later, when Harold began to prosper and was able to

buy her a home in Los Angeles, she did not rejoin Foxy, who was also there, serving as a kind of personal manager for his son. At any rate, if the comedian was not the product of a broken home, he came from one that showed a number of chips along its genteel edges.

But genteel it was; Lloyd was quite insistent on that point. "There are two kinds of poor boys in America — the Tom Sawyers and the Huckleberry Finns. . . . I was a good example of a Tom Sawyer." That is to say, there was nothing of the truant or outlaw *manqué* about him. He was, by all accounts, mannerly, well spoken, obedient and generally well thought of by his elders. Indeed, as he and his family paint it, he was something of a classic small-town boy. He was freckled. He loved marbles (as an adult he kept the collection of aggies he had won as a boy in a plush-lined box and sometimes added to it when he found a particularly handsome new one in a toy store). He loved dogs (as a child he was nicknamed "Yabble," the sound he made when trying to call his dog: "Hey Bill." When the dog was poisoned, Harold felt the loss deeply, and much later, when he could afford it, he kept a large kennel devoted to raising prize-winning dogs).

It would seem that he had the younger sibling's traditional difficulties in keeping up with an older brother and his gang. Lloyd recalled going ice-skating with Gaylord and friends, not being allowed to join their game of shinny, and lacking both the gumption to keep the bonfire going or to go home on his own. He whined a lot and received a brotherly licking — and a good deal of satirical baby talk — when he got home. The following summer, however, Gaylord had to save Harold from drowning when the latter proved too ambitious in his assault on a swimming hole where he had accompanied the older boys. Harold also remembered being a camp follower in a juvenile gang battle in Denver, in which the kids from Tenth Street (his block) launched an assault on a rival crowd operating on the other side of the arroyo created by the Platte River. In particular he recalled a retreat by his gang that turned into a rout so frightening to him that he ran into the Lloyd home and locked all the doors against invasion. He would also remember, from the Denver days, a baptism by immersion after a revival meeting, an uncharacteristically emotional religious experience. More typical of his boyhood in Denver, and more fondly remembered, was a natatorium where on given days the management would throw a few dollars' worth of coins into the pool and allow the boyish clientele to dive for them, a watery activity more to Harold's liking. Denver also offered trolley cars you could ride free if you were daring enough and adroit enough to catch hold of the rear end as it was moving past.

Of course there were odd jobs almost from the beginning. Lloyd would remember waiting up all night for the circus to come to town in order to be first in line for the small tasks that were rewarded with passes to the afternoon's performance. Then, too, you could collect discarded bottles and turn them in for

13

their deposits to make enough money to buy admission to that swimming pool, where you could dive for still more money. Later on, Hal (as he was generally called) would become a popcorn vendor working the trains when they stopped over in Beatrice. He would make the stuff on his mother's stove and pay her back for the raw materials and such labor as she invested in the enterprise. And of course there were the paper routes, in both Omaha and Denver. Harold would remember that he converted his Denver route from a marginal enterprise into one of the most profitable such businesses in the city, in part because he was particularly adept at finding ways to make deadbeats pay up. At the same time he also mowed lawns and took care of furnaces, depending on the season. He wrote that by the time the Lloyds moved on again, he had two other boys working for him and that he sold the paper route at a handsome profit.

It is all Norman Rockwell stuff. And as kid brothers from time immemorial have learned, young Harold came to understand that guile and charm could overcome strength. Once forbidden to tag along with his brother and his pals to the swimming hole, Hal skipped ahead and was waiting for them when they arrived — not strictly in violation of the parental admonition which had specifically enjoined tagging along. He also remembers a visit to a relative who asked Hal to weed his vegetable garden for him. He used a variant on Tom Sawyer's ploy for whitewashing the fence, agreeing to show neighborhood kids one new magic trick for each row they finished. His mother, in a dreadfully pious article about Harold's boyhood which someone helped her draft for a movie magazine, recalled that young Hal used this technique more than once, often conning boys quite a bit older than he was into fetching and carrying for him. "Don't blame him, Mrs. Lloyd," she remembered one of them saying. "We like to do things for Hal. He gives us value received."

And it does seem that he had a way with him. Mrs. Lloyd remembered one time encountering an astronomer on the street. The man was selling peeps through his telescope, and having chatted briefly with him, she passed on her way, thinking her son was still at her side. When she discovered he wasn't, she hurried back to find him deep in conversation with the astronomer. "He's a right big question box, that lad of yours, Ma'am. He asked so many things I just found myself liking to tell him what I knew."

Probably Harold looked upon the telescope as something akin to the magical, and magic was something he had cared about from the time his hands were big enough to manipulate a deck of cards or a patented trick you sent away for. The tricks, in turn, were akin to practical jokes, which were about the only form of humor Lloyd was known to indulge in off the screen. He claimed his interest was first whetted by the tricks and puzzles he found described in various newspaper columns, and this interest certainly served to reinforce his precocious absorption in the theater. At any rate, he was particularly fond of a contraption consisting of a long tube with a squeeze bulb at one end and a deflated bladder at the other.

14

This last could be placed under the tablecloth at a point where one might expect a dinner plate to be placed. By squeezing the bulb the prankster could then make the diner's plate dance alarmingly. Lloyd also had a deck of marked cards with which to amaze and mystify his friends, and working as an assistant to itinerant magicians, he acquired some knowledge of hypnosis — or at least enough so that with the aid of a confederate he could flimflam his chums at basement and backyard performances. Even as an adult, even as a star, he generally carried a trick or two in his pocket, by this time probably as a ready-made defense against the kind of people who expect comics to be comical outside of working hours. At least he could disarm them with a stunt and prove himself a regular guy.

As for the theater, neither Lloyd nor his relatives could ever recall a time when he was not interested in it. As an extremely young child he was wont to line up all the hats he could find, invent a character for each, and sit cross-legged before them, carrying on long, imaginary conversations. Then, too, his mother could remember thinking she heard the voices of several children playing out of sight on a porch and, upon investigation, find only little Hal, talking to imaginary friends.

Among his earliest memories was a medicine show that played Pawnee, Nebraska, when he was extremely young. He also remembered seeing *The Great Train Robbery,* often regarded erroneously as the first American story film, but quite correctly recalled as the first such film to achieve genuine popularity. Indeed, with this film many a nickleodeon opened its doors, and with the coming of these first small, inexpensive people's theaters, movies finally established themselves as a business to be taken seriously, as an enterprise with more future than a fad and more potential for money-making than anyone had dreamed possible. Lloyd, however, was not unduly impressed. Pictures, he said, "were just another form of something to do, falling somewhere between the Sunday comic sections and running to a fire." They had, he said, no reality — and no romance comparable to that of the theater. As an adolescent, Hal invariably had a job as doorman whenever the local opera house was playing some touring company. In return he was permitted to stay and see the show — *Mazeppa, Uncle Tom's Cabin, Peck's Bad Boy, The Old Homestead, The Flaming Arrow, The Round-Up* — all the melodramatic and comic staples of the popular theater from which the movies, in the beginning, would draw many of their basic plot devices (if not whole pirated stories) as well as characterizations. Because the camera could accomplish spectacular tricks of stagecraft so much more efficiently and effectively than stage designers could, shows such as these were the first commercial victims of the movies. Not that Lloyd's early exposure to the theater was confined entirely to drama. He recalled seeing minstrel troupes and dialect comedians, especially of the Dutch and Swedish variety, since the Germans and the Scandinavians dominated this portion of the Middle West when he was growing up.

As the years wore on, Harold grew into bigger and better theatrical jobs — candy butcher, usher, head usher, call boy, grip, stagehand. Once he was even recruited for one of the children's roles in *Macbeth* by a touring company playing a one-night stand in Beatrice. Lloyd was to recall that he managed his on-stage cries for help — he was one of the witnesses to Banquo's murder — but that he dried up when he ran off, though he was supposed to continue the cries off-stage. He thought it was having to carry on so in front of professionals that caused the lapse.

It was around 1906, in Omaha, that he was able for the first time to establish a regular connection with the theater as an actor. An astrologer — or phrenologist (Lloyd was unsure about this, as he was about many details of his childhood) — had set up shop in a vacant store window, and Lloyd, never one to pass up an opportunity to investigate the magical, joined the crowd listening to his spiel. A fire truck rumbled by and drew everyone but Lloyd and a man named John Lane Connor away from the con man. When the latter had finished, his two man audience introduced themselves and Lloyd was delighted to discover that Connor was a member of the Burwood Stock Company, which had set up in a downtown theater for the season. When Connor confessed that one of the problems of the theatrical life was the theatrical hotel, Lloyd suggested that he might find it more comfortable lodging with his family, for the Lloyds were apparently not above taking in an occasional boarder — in those days something middle-class families did only reluctantly, since it amounted to a public confession that they needed money. But it was done, and Connor got Lloyd jobs as a super, and small parts whenever his company required the services of an adolescent.

Indeed, some of the parts weren't so small. Lloyd would recall playing Tess's younger brother in *Tess of the D'Urbervilles,* a role with some sixty sides. Nor was the company an undistinguished one. Frank Bacon, very shortly to go on to enormous popularity as the star of *Lightnin',* a play he developed from a vaudeville sketch and in which he would perennially tour, was the leading man. Lloyd Ingraham, an extraordinarily prolific film director in later years, was also in the company. Bacon, in fact, thought so highly of Harold that he asked him to join him when he began touring the sketch version of *Lightnin'.* Mrs. Lloyd refused permission, but the actor told her (she said), "You're going to hear great things of that boy someday."

Interestingly, the youth was able to teach some members of the company, notably Connor, a good deal about makeup. As part of his endless fascination with the magical — that is, the process by which the ordinary can be transformed into the extraordinary — Harold had meticulously studied the subject, both by reading and by closely questioning every veteran character actor who passed through the theaters where he hung out. A set of sample photographs he had made up to demonstrate his prowess soon after he arrived

in Hollywood still exists, and there can be no doubt about his ability to deeply disguise himself. The desire to do so is, of course, some sort of clue to his character.

While his introduction to the professional theater was being effected, Lloyd was deeply involved in amateur theatricals as well. The family lived in two houses during their longest stay in Omaha, and in both of them Lloyd's father — encouraged and helped by Lloyd and his pals — constructed basement stages on which his son could mount his own productions. Lloyd vividly recalled the move from the one house to the other. A friend from his old neighborhood accompanied him, and both rode in the moving van with their feet dangling from the tailgate. Arriving at the new address, they dug out two old clown costumes Gaylord had given Harold, and the latter applied the classic white clown makeup to each of their faces. Before nightfall they had put on a front yard show for the kids of the new neighborhood. Lloyd would later recall that it was the least painful move he had ever made, his little performance helping him avoid the twin perils of being the new boy on the block — loneliness or a get-acquainted fight.

Once the stage was ready in this new house, young Hal put on a number of productions. In 1921, two young women who had been cast in several of these shows fondly recalled Lloyd's obsession with the theater. They remembered filching curtain rings from their mothers' draperies, cutting the tag-ends off neighborhood clotheslines in order to support the theater's gunny-sack curtains, and carrying boxes into the basement in order to support the slats that served as seats. They said Hal once confiscated a number of laths from houses being built in the neighborhood and from them fashioned swords. "They were white and slick and dangerous," one of the girls remembered. "Why, we used to fence with the boys til our sides were sore, because we knew if we didn't Harold wouldn't let us play." But, they claimed — unknowingly supporting his mother's contention about Harold's charming ways — "we would have done just anything Harold told us to."

Mostly the young actor-manager-director-writer charged pins, literally, for his plays, but for one super-production, *Tom Morgan, the Cowboy of the West,* he charged three cents for first row seats, two cents for ones in the row behind, and a penny for last row accommodations. Before a largely "far-sighted" audience, as he put it, he staged what appears to have been a near-classic western drama, one in which the heavy (played by Lloyd himself, who already knew a showy part when he saw one) forces the tenderfoot hero, fresh from the East, to dance by firing a revolver at his feet (a device borrowed, of course, from *The Virginian*). He then abducts one of the two girls in the cast, who, finding herself threatened by the other young woman, confesses herself to be "insanely jealous." The performance was marred by the failure of a cap pistol wielded by Lloyd to fire on cue, but on the whole, according to the quite possibly biased reports that survive, audience reaction was extremely positive.

17

"Speedy" and "Foxy."

The young pugilist, circa 1910–12.

Mrs. George Ketcham, mother of the youth who played the title role of the tenderfoot, recalled young Harold's theatricals with enormous enthusiasm. She remembered Harold and her son coaxing dimes out of her so they could buy cocoa butter as a makeup base for those who played "greasers" — the word is hers — and other dark-skinned characters. She also recalled Lloyd soliciting her opinion as to how the braces he wore on his teeth were working, and remembered that her encouraging words were generally rewarded by a private preview of some new trick he was working up.

What one sees developing in these years is, obviously, the basis of Lloyd's screen character, and a major facet of his own adult personality as well. There was a powerful quotient of ambition in his makeup, but that was common enough in young Americans of his generation. What was not so common was his practical-mindedness and his determination. Lots of boys have worked at odd jobs, but few have had such a consistent record of success as Lloyd appears to have compiled. Lots of youngsters have dreamed of the theater as a way to escape humdrum small-town lives; indeed, most of the first generation of movie stars were escaped provincials, very often from pinched circumstances, and astonishingly often the products of marriages in some measure unhappy, if not totally disastrous. Very few — unless they were cursed (or, who knows, perhaps actually blessed) by stage mothers — so persistently and at such an early age partook of so many opportunities to try the stage, to learn the profession from the bottom up. All of these traits were evident in "The Boy" who was to capture such huge audiences so easily. More important, perhaps, was Lloyd's often laughable, but never contemptible, eagerness to please, his desire to ingratiate himself with everybody he encountered. It was there in his childhood — this strange likableness that made him an acceptable leader to kids both younger and older than he, and to adults, whether they were neighbors indulging his taste for the theatrical or professional theater people giving him a boost toward competence in their line of work. Again, these traits would mark his screen characters. Nor should one fail to remark the young Lloyd's competitiveness. In time he would become a competent player of nearly every game and sport to which he set his hand, and his estate would boast facilities of country club quality for just about every non-team sport regularly played by Americans. Even as an adolescent he boxed competitively, and Lloyd would recall that once in an amateur bout in Denver he knocked out an opponent who eventually knocked out the state champion in his weight class.

Obviously economic necessity drove him, at least part of the time. Obviously, too, his perpetual sense of being forever the new kid on the block accounted for his eagerness to ingratiate himself with everyone. Perhaps, also, he sensed that even though his family often passed for middle-class, it had to continually scramble to maintain its tenuous footing. That may have made Lloyd ape even more assiduously the good manners and the pleasing, "peppy"

personality so highly valued by that class's social arbiters. Finally, one gets from his own memoirs, and from those of the people who knew him at this time, a feeling of distance. Lloyd was liked, all right, no question about that, but there is no intimacy either in his recollections of others or theirs of him. In his memoir he quite deliberately presents himself and his world in stereotypical terms — and that is how most people seem to remember him, too. There were no jagged edges on his personality, nothing that really caught in anyone's mind. There is a blandness about everyone's memories of him in these early years that is, in the end, rather unsettling in its effect.

No one seems to recall an angry moment or even a genuinely awkward one. He was . . . "nice." It is the highest word of praise in the lexicon of the middle-class Midwesterner, and categorizes those amiable, ambitious young men who cause no one any trouble, surprise no one when they prosper, and are — then and ever — the backbone of the nation. Yet they are people who somehow always seem to elude us as characters, slipping deftly away from us whenever we try to make genuine contact with them or try to discover what makes them tick. It has always been a nice question: are they the most deceptive of people or is there actually something missing in them, some inability to love and thus to be loved? Why is it that, for all their cleverness, all their talent, all their energy and ambition, they seem never to elicit from us either the depths of affection or the sudden outpourings of outrage that we lavish on other people with whom they sometimes share public life? Is some element missing from the air or earth of the region? Are they victims of the repressions, the inhibitions about touch, expression, and feeling, that are about all the thin-blooded, unfervent Protestantism of the place seems to create? Is their frequent economic success the result simply of crude Freudian sublimation in which libidinal energy is poured recklessly into the pursuit of success, yet hoarded in miserly fashion when it comes to human contact?

It is a matter, perhaps, of little consequence. But there are an awful lot of these people in America, perhaps more of them than of any other sort, and they form the largest part of the great audience. They may briefly embrace with a wild enthusiasm someone like Chaplin — just to keep our comparisons within bounds — yet never express their feelings for someone like Lloyd with anything like the openness that they allow themselves for a more alien temperament like Chaplin. But, for a Lloyd, they are always there, always pleased to be played to. For him their affection may never seem to burn as bright as it does for others. But for him it would never burn out, either. This Lloyd would soon begin to learn.

3 "Secretly I longed for him to go to college," Harold Lloyd's mother would later say, "but this was too much to hope for in our moderate circumstances." Still, opportunity managed to knock in a rather peculiar fashion. During most of the time the family was in Omaha, Darsie Lloyd worked for the Singer Sewing Machine Company, first as a salesman, then as an assistant state manager. (It was in the latter capacity that he acquired his colorful nickname, for he proved to be particularly adept at collecting back payments. One day he even succeeded in recovering two machines the company had long since given up hope of ever seeing again. "Oh, you foxy Lloyd," cried a delighted supervisor when Darsie turned up with the machines, and the name stuck.) Sometime in 1911, Foxy was involved in an accident with a brewery truck, and because its driver had been sampling his wares, Lloyd was able to win a damage suit. Suddenly he had $3,000 in cash, enough to grubstake a move. He proposed taking Harold with him — there was no mention of Mrs. Lloyd. Her story is that her son went to live with "relatives" around this time — which is the truth, but obviously not the entire truth. Father and son disputed where to go. Foxy was thinking of New York, which he imagined would offer opportunities suited to his gifts, or Nashville, where a relative published a religious journal of some sort. "Speedy," which is the nickname father laid on son around this time — it was later the title of one of his best movies — held out for San Diego, where his old friends from the stock company, Connor and Ingraham, were now working. They decided to flip a coin — heads they did what Foxy wanted, tails they followed Speedy's lead. The coin came down tails and they headed westward, where, with his apparently unerring instinct for poor business opportunities, Foxy invested the proceeds of his court settlement in a pool hall–lunch counter, just far enough from the center of downtown San Diego to be, at best, a marginal enterprise. Indeed, Foxy was able to keep it going for only a little more than a year.

Mrs. Lloyd had approved the move to San Diego on the condition that Harold finish high school, and true to his word, he continued school there. He also: "relieved my father in the pool hall and lunch counter; played leads in high school shows and aided Connor in staging them; acted as assistant in fencing, dancing, and elocution in Connor's dramatic school; played in and helped Connor stage lodge and club entertainments; played characters in four local stock companies and was assistant stage manager of one; gave Shakespearian readings before high school English and elocution classes; worked as stage hand at the

Spreckels, the road-show theater." Speedy obviously required the quality his nickname implied.

His father, who was perhaps beginning to sense the chance to live out his dreams of success through his son, strongly encouraged him. And sensing — or hoping for — posterity's interest, he kept the program of the plays in which Harold appeared during the San Diego period. Anyway, they show that Harold was gaining a solid background in the theater, often playing in adaptations of best-selling novels — a very popular genre of the day — things like *Dr. Jekyll and Mr. Hyde, The Little Minister, The Count of Monte Cristo, The Sign of the Four, Strongheart,* and so on.

This was a transitional time for Lloyd, who was now in his late teens. According to him, dramatics was a major activity at San Diego High School, "nearly on a par in student esteem with football," and he was warmed perhaps more than he should have been by the laughs he got on stage and the congratulations he received afterward when he appeared as the lead in a college farce called *Going Some.* The next day, however, Connor took him to task, mostly for stepping on his best laughs, not allowing them to build to the heights they might have obtained. Connor pointed out, quite rightly, that Lloyd had a great deal more professional experience than his classmates and that he should have been much better than he had been. Lloyd took this criticism, much of it carefully detailed and quite technical, in good part and afterwards seemed to regard it as a significant part of his theatrical education. Perhaps more importantly, he was making the transition from child actor to juvenile, from bit player to supporting actor, essaying long roles with increasing confidence. One summer, when Connor organized a little touring company to play the smaller cities of the area after the stock season closed, Lloyd found himself doing major roles in *Trilby, Oliver Twist* (playing, at different times, both Fagin and The Artful Dodger), *Little Lord Fauntleroy,* and *Ten Nights in a Barroom,* as well as stage managing. The latter often involved him in difficult enterprises.Once he had to rouse the manager of a furniture store and get him to unlock his shop in order to lend the company the stuff it needed for its setting. Another time the company arrived in a town on the Fourth of July and found all the natives had gone to the beach, and Lloyd had to tear down the set, find another theater in a town where the inhabitants felt the need for some holiday cheer, and set up all over again. Again, there is a forecast of the willingness and the practical-mindedness of Lloyd's later screen character.

By the spring of 1913 things were not going well in San Diego. Foxy had lost the pool hall and decamped for Los Angeles to look for work, the stock season was running out, and the market for lodge entertainments was drying up with the onslaught of hot weather. Lloyd moved out of his room and into a tent on the roof of his apartment house — cheaper accommodations and not at all uncomfortable in the early summer in salubrious San Diego. Down to his last

nickel one day, he spent it on doughnuts and got a night's work as a stagehand for a touring company of *Ben-Hur* — pay $1.50. There was also a day's work with the Edison Motion Picture Company, on location, a scene in which Lloyd stripped to a breechclout and appeared as a Yaqui Indian, serving dinner at a white man's table. A little later he was able to catch on as stage manager with another touring show, but it was clear to him that there would not be enough theatrical work in San Diego that summer to keep him going. And by this time there was no other work he wanted to do. So he joined his father in Los Angeles, where the latter was shoe-clerking again. They lived in a theatrical boarding house, populated mainly by small-timers, and Harold began making the rounds of theatrical companies, buoyed mainly by Foxy's unfailing encouragement, which included making dinners for his son's theatrical friends — he was famous for his spaghetti.

Harold got a spot of work almost immediately with the Morosco Stock Company, perhaps the leading theatrical troupe in town, which steadily employed such stars as Florence Reed, William Desmond, and Charles Ruggles. Lloyd, however, got just three small parts, and though they paid $25 a week, the system required rehearsing for a week with no pay, thus cutting the actor's take by a third. Even so, one imagines Lloyd would have hung on, but after a few weeks there were no parts at all for the young actor. Consequently he looked up the Edison people he had worked with in San Diego and got extra work and even a bit part or two with them before this unit of the New York-based company returned home. Lloyd went to see himself in one of the pictures, and he didn't like what he saw. It is a familiar problem with movie players, based, as Lloyd said, on the fact that we don't photograph as we think we look. That was especially true in those days, because orthochromatic film required the players to don a heavy white makeup, which was anything but naturalistic in its effects. By the time the Edison people departed, it is probably fair to say that Lloyd saw little future for himself in movies and had gained no love for the medium comparable to his feeling for the stage. He may well have partaken of the disdainful attitude toward movies that people from legit generally adopted toward them.

Still, that's where the work was for actors in Los Angeles at this time. Movie-makers, heavily dependent on a reliable source of sunlight in those early days, had started exploring Southern California a half-dozen years previously. They found it especially convenient in winter, when outdoor shooting around New York was nearly impossible. By 1913 a permanent movie colony had been established. It was in this same year that the acknowledged master of the American film, D. W. Griffith, spent his longest season ever on the coast, occupying himself with, among other things, his first near-feature length movie, *Judith of Bethulia.* He was shooting it in the San Fernando Valley and at Biograph's Hollywood studio at the same time Lloyd was doing extra work for the Edison company. That fall, when Griffith returned to New York, he would

break with Biograph over the company's refusal either to release *Judith* all in a piece (they wanted to put it out one reel at a time, as if it were a serial) or to promise to let him make more films of its length (four reels) or longer. Within weeks Griffith would sign a contract with Reliance-Majestic and return to the coast to continue making shorter films while preparing *The Birth of a Nation.* This epochal film would establish, finally and forever, the right of the movies to be taken seriously — not because it ran for two hours and cost over $100,000, but because it would be the subject of intense social controversy, demonstrating the power of film not merely to entertain but to deeply stir vast audiences intellectually and emotionally.

Griffith himself was responding to larger developments. The Europeans had begun the fad for longer pictures, notably with *Cabiria* and a production of *Queen Elizabeth* starring Sarah Bernhardt. Adolph Zukor had imported *Queen Elizabeth* and done so well with it that he had organized Famous Players (". . . in Famous Plays," to complete the slogan that summed up the new company's policy, which was to adapt stage successes, utilizing the talents of well-known stage actors). The company would become mighty Paramount. Meantime, Thomas Ince, a one-time actor, had opened his studio and was beginning to pioneer a factory method of production which would become in a few years the standard method of turning out film in large volume. In short, the outlines of the "industry" that was very shortly to emerge were being sketched in while Harold Lloyd was seeking employment during his first months in Los Angeles.

Most immediately relevant to Lloyd was the fact that Mack Sennett had left Griffith and Biograph the year before to set up his own company, Keystone. Having assembled the basis of his comic stock company (Mabel Normand, Ford Sterling, Mack Swain, Chester Conklin, and Fatty Arbuckle being among its leading figures), Sennett had begun turning out at least one short movie a week. His first few releases were rather crudely frenetic, but before long he had created something like a craze for comedy. The summer Lloyd hit town, Sennett signed up a promising young comedian who had been touring America with one of Fred Karno's comedy companies, which was offering American audiences a taste of English music hall entertainment. The comedian's name, of course, was Charlie Chaplin. By early 1914, after Chaplin had made only a handful of films for Sennett, both the reviewers and the public were beginning to single him out of the Keystone crowd. A year later he would be a star, producing and directing his own films for another company, and in 1917 he would sign his famous million-dollar contract with First National, making him, with Mary Pickford, the screen's highest paid star.

Chaplin made $150 a month during his first three months with Sennett and $175 thereafter. In this period Lloyd counted himself lucky to make five dollars a day on a highly irregular basis. Mostly he worked at Universal, but even getting on the lot was difficult. An extremely crabby gatekeeper was employed to keep

unknowns out of the bullpen, where extras assembled every morning at eight hoping that some assistant director in charge of casting these tiny roles would notice them. This system was common at most studios at the time, and at Universal the extras were expected to wait around until midafternoon on the off chance that one of the four companies operating on the lot might need some extra bodies for its last shots of the day. At first Lloyd could get by the gateman only after the lunch hour, by donning makeup and mingling with the employed extras as they reported back in from the snack bar across the street. He got very little work this way, since not much casting was done this late in the day, but he did become a familiar figure around the lot and he was able to establish contacts among the upper echelon of this low caste — the guaranty players, those who were paid the going rate for extra work but had agreements with the studio assuring them of a minimum of four or five days of work each week. Once again he ingratiated himself with people who could do him some good; in time the guaranty players began letting him on the lot through a window in their dressing room, and from then on Lloyd began to work fairly regularly.

Eventually he attached himself to a unit run by J. Farrell Macdonald, the man largely in charge of turning out J. Warren Kerrigan westerns. Lloyd found himself playing a few character bits and achieving guaranty status — five dollars a day, five days a week. He remembered *Samson and Delilah,* a four-reel epic, as the high point of this stage of his career. During almost two straight weeks of work on the picture he also served as a makeup man, slapping crepe paper beards on mob extras (the lowest of the low, they were recruited from the hobo class and paid a dollar a day with lunch) on a production-line basis, so they would look like hirsute Philistines to a camera kept at a goodly distance.

Shortly thereafter, however, Universal expanded and bureaucratized. A casting director was appointed, which meant that contacts built up with assistant directors were now worthless. Worse still, it was decreed that only those with what we would now call speaking parts would receive five dollars a day. More minor roles would rate only three dollars. A group of the guaranty players struck, refusing to accept the proffered three-dollar jobs. Of course, as soon as their strategy became obvious, they were offered nothing but such parts. Most surrendered, but Lloyd did not, and neither did a sometime mule-skinner, saloon swamper, cowboy, and gold prospector named Hal Roach. Roach, whose manly skills were quite useful in westerns, though he was not much of an actor, had become friends with Lloyd when both were cast as minor gangsters in some forgotten crime film. Before long he was to become an important factor in Lloyd's career.

For the moment, however, the two went their separate ways. Allan Dwan and Christy Cabanne, both former Griffith assistants who were then beginning their own careers as directors, turned Lloyd down. Cabanne went so far as to suggest that he wasn't really a "picture type," whatever that was. Lloyd

Extra days: Lloyd seems to have specialized in slippery characters. Top, he is seen at far left bothering a pretty girl. Next, he's a city slicker in a western. Finally, he is seen in *Samson and Delilah,* on which he also served as a makeup assistant, bearding (with crepe paper) the Philistines.

retaliated by hauling out his sample pictures of himself in sundry makeups and Cabanne had to admit that he might have something — but the director still did not offer him a part. Eventually, Lloyd found a job with an independent outfit making short films out of L. Frank Baum's *Oz* stories. It was there that he again encountered Hal Roach, who surprised Lloyd one day by announcing that he had acquired a few thousand dollars of capital from the scion of an oil-rich English family living in California and that he was going to set himself up as an independent producer of comedies. He asked Lloyd to come in as his top comedian.

So far as one can tell from his reminiscences, Lloyd had never until this time thought of himself as a funny fellow. Neither, it seems, had Roach. "He got to the studio on time, he worked hard, but . . . he had no say whatever," Roach told a reporter recently. "We didn't have scripts until we had two-reelers," he added. "Everything came out of my head. He had no idea what he was going to do until I told him." In these remarks we perhaps get a clue as to why Roach would risk his minuscule capital on an untried youth with no apparent gift for or ambition toward comedy. Roach, whose ego was — and through the years remained — a powerful one, wanted an actor who would merely be a projection of the new producer-director's ideas. And as we have seen, Lloyd was a youth who was extraordinarily eager to please. In short, it seems that Roach's decision was not an aesthetic one, he did not recognize in the actor a previously unsuspected talent; Lloyd was simply cheap, available, and unlikely to be troublesome.

Roach rented space in the Bradbury mansion, once the seat of a prominent early Los Angeles family, but now run down to the point where it was rented out to shoestring movie operators for production offices. Even as a remnant it had considerable grandeur, with turrets, bay windows, and fine wood carving. And its site, atop the Court Street hill in downtown Los Angeles, was impressive. But the first pictures Roach made there were not. He thought that a troupe of child actors doing a comedy series — a sort of midget variant on Sennett's stock company of adult zanies — could be popular as well as novel. Ultimately, the *Our Gang* series would prove his hunch correct. But the first such film — no one seems to remember its title — in which Lloyd appeared as a chauffeur-chaperon to two mischievous boys, was not successful. Neither was another comedy in which Lloyd played a relatively straight, light role opposite an actress named Jane Novak. Roach then hired an eccentric comedian who made four pictures which were apparently even worse than the first two. Roach fired him and abruptly appointed Lloyd the low comedian. "Think up some funny get-up and let's get busy."

Lloyd improvised a one-reeler that Roach liked well enough to offer him a raise — from three dollars a day to five — and told him to devise a comedy character who might sustain a series. By this time Chaplin had achieved his first success, and Roach and Lloyd were by no means alone in attempting some sort

27

of imitation of his developing character. Lloyd would later insist that "Willie Work" was not a tramp character, though it appears he had neither fixed abode nor a regular livelihood. Still, his makeup and costume were different — a cat's whisker moustache, a heavily padded coat, and a battered top hat. Nothing much came of this creation, however. All Lloyd chose to remember about him was a gag Roach once thought up: There was some sort of cable car that hauled pedestrians up the hill where they were working, and Roach thought it would be hilarious to have Willie stumble and roll down the length of this vehicle's tracks. Lloyd was game, but an inexperienced cameraman placed his instrument at the bottom of the hill and tilted it up to follow the action. The camera angle, of course, duplicated precisely the angle of the hill, and so on film Lloyd appeared to be rolling down a track in flat country — no laughs or thrills in that. And many bruises for the fledgling comedian. A second attempt at the shot was made, with the camera properly angled, but this one was taken from such a distance that Lloyd was barely discernible. They did not try again. This film and similar successors failed to find a buyer among the distributors back east and Roach decided to try another tack.

He hired a man named Roy Stewart, a heavy in westerns, and teamed him and Miss Novak as the leading characters in a thing called *Just Nuts*. Lloyd supplied the low comedy. Miraculously, the film sold to Pathé, which then offered Roach a contract for a series of films if he could sign his three leading players to long-term contracts. Stewart asked for, and received, a ten-dollar-a-day agreement. When Lloyd heard of it, he asked for the same and Roach poor-mouthed him. He could afford only the same old five dollars for Lloyd. This, despite the fact that Lloyd was expected to play as many as three character bits in each of the two-reel Novak-Stewart dramas as well as the leads in the one-reel comedies that would alternate with them on Roach's schedule. The producer promised Lloyd a raise if he would just be patient a little longer, but Lloyd, who had after all been on the scene the longest, was hurt and departed. He was replaced, but Pathé canceled the contract after seeing three more releases and Roach was forced to shut up shop.

Roach then took a job as a staff director at Essanay, where his career and Chaplin's briefly crossed. The latter had finished his year with Sennett, and desiring greater control over his own films, had accepted an offer from Essanay, which was half-owned by Broncho Billy Anderson, the portly early western star. Though Sennett had come to admire Chaplin, he was not sorry to see him go, especially when the actor rather grandly told Mack, "The public doesn't line up outside the box office when your name appears as they do for mine." At any rate, Chaplin's opportunity was also Roach's. Essanay hired a number of fine comics to support Chaplin, but since he has always been a slow worker, someone was required to keep them busy between times. Roach did so, and

apparently learned something in the process, for he was never again to have much trouble marketing his films.

Lloyd, meantime, reported to headquarters — Sennett's Keystone Studios. These were at the time part of Triangle, a distribution scheme which linked Sennett with the other two leading independent producers of the moment, Griffith and Ince. Lloyd's association with Sennett was not to be a long one, but if nothing else it taught Lloyd mastery of an important element in the comic's trade, the "Brodie" (named after the celebrated Brooklyn Bridge leaper). The artists who accomplished Brodies were known as "bumpers," and there was an even more arcane argot for subspecialties. For example, the fall that is preceded by a little leap into the air and ended by a landing on one's neck was known around Sennett's as a 108. (Ben Turpin, the great cross-eyed comic, was generally regarded as a peerless maker of 108's.) It was by doing a 108, when a motorcycle crashed into a fruit cart manned by Lloyd, in Italian costume, that he won acceptance at Keystone. There, a nice distinction was drawn between "stand-up actors" and those willing and able to do inventive Brodies.

Even so, he was perhaps a little too straight for Keystone. Lloyd worked some with Ford Sterling and some with Fatty Arbuckle and there was even talk of a contract at a higher-than-usual price. But after only a few months Roach was beckoning again, with an offer of $50 a week. When Lloyd told Sennett's business manager that he had decided to move on, the manager warned him against shoestring outfits and mentioned that the proposed Keystone contract would escalate quite nicely over a period of time. Lloyd replied, however, that he thought he was doing "the wiser thing. You have Conklin, Arbuckle, Sterling and other good comedians and I would be a long time getting anywhere against that competition. Why pick out the highest wall to jump when there are plenty of curbstones around?"

Ford Sterling, when he heard that Lloyd was leaving but planned to continue doing comedy, was dismayed. "You're foolish to bother with that stuff," he said, perhaps still bitter over Chaplin's easy ascent over him to the top banana's rating at Sennett. "You will never get anywhere in cheap comedies. I think you can act. If you want my advice, get in with D. W. Griffith and do the Bobbie Harron sort of thing. There's a future there and Griffith can make you."

Actually, it wasn't bad advice. Harron, whose career was cut short by suicide, was a popular and gifted juvenile, and it's likely that Lloyd, a slender 5'10" with dark hair and pleasantly regular features, might have done well enough in Harron's sort of roles. Or perhaps not. Harron had a youthful sexual appeal — women seemed to want to mother him — which is hard to detect in Lloyd, who may well have sensed this defect in himself. On the other hand, Lloyd had so far failed to be very funny — no one had figured out just what this amiable, ambitious youth might be good at.

A selection from the portraits in make-up which Lloyd had taken to help him break in after he came to Hollywood. Pictures were probably taken in 1914.

Lonesome Luke vs. The Little Fellow.

Still, Roach had another offer of a contract from Pathé, again contingent on his reuniting Novak, Stewart, and Lloyd. Amazingly, when it turned out he could not recruit the first two, the distributors agreed to go ahead with a program of releases featuring Lloyd alone. This time Roach had taken on a businessman as partner, Dan Linthicum, and the combination of their names created a corporate name, Rolin Comedies. Now it was up to Lloyd — or, more likely, Lloyd and Roach — to create an ongoing comedy character with a steadily salable appeal. It seemed at the moment that it had to be some variant on Chaplin's Tramp. Distributors and exhibitors, then as now, preferred imitations of proven success rather than dangerously original material. Lloyd claimed that from the first he was uncomfortable with his character — named Lonesome Luke (and often called Luke de Fluke in titles) — because although he worked hard to differentiate him from Chaplin's Little Fellow, he was obviously inspired by the great man's creation. But as he said, he had only "vague yearnings" toward originality at this point and no concrete ideas in that direction. So he was stuck with Luke.

Roach has flatly claimed that "Lonesome Luke was my idea," but Lloyd long ago disputed that notion. It was his father, according to Lloyd, who created the figure's costume, and since no one ever talks about Luke except in terms of apparel, Foxy deserves at least some of the credit for his creation. Wardrobing began with a pair of size 12AA shoes Foxy spotted in a shoemaker's store and for which he paid five dollars to be given over to the owner who had left them for resoling. The black and white vertical striped shirt came from a haberdashery, the coat from a woman's tailored suit. To this was added a pair of too-short, too-tight pants, an undersized vest, a collar and a top hat. For makeup, Lloyd darkened and arched his eyebrows and wore a moustache waxed and curled — which Chaplin's was not. The differentiation between Luke and The Tramp was obvious: They both might wear oversized shoes, but whereas all of The Tramp's clothes, except his bowler, were too large, all Luke's were too small.

Oddly enough, the films Lloyd started making in January, 1916, were successful, though it is impossible to say why. Most of the Lonesome Lukes, all one-reelers (Lloyd and Roach didn't risk a two-reeler until the spring of 1917), were uncopyrighted and their negatives were not preserved. Thus there was no definitive list of their titles, let alone a sound sampling of the work created in this period. William K. Everson, who has seen a few Lukes, disputes Lloyd's assertion that he tried to avoid Chaplin's mannerisms. He found the latter's gait, his little skid of alarm, the disdainful twist of the moustache, all very much present in Lloyd's pantomimic repertoire. Luke also had, according to Everson, the casual cruelty of The Tramp in his early days before Chaplin began sentimentalizing him. He even found that Roach and Lloyd were imitating, as quickly as possible, plots and situations that had worked for Chaplin. For example, Chaplin's *The Fireman* was quickly followed by Lloyd's *Fireman, Save My Child;* the tonic water and gym episodes in Chaplin's *The Cure* were taken

over in the Roach-Lloyd *Pipe the Whiskers;* and the first Luke two-reeler, *Lonesome Luke on Tin Can Alley,* was, according to Everson, "the most blatant steal of all."

There were excuses for this derivativeness that went beyond the problem of needing to make pictures acceptable to the distributor and his customers. Production pace was the most obvious one. If you are obliged to make one movie a week, however short, you are bound to grab material from any handy source. Then, too, everyone was working within highly stylized limits. In 1916 Chaplin had said, "All I need to make a comedy is a park, a policeman and a pretty girl," and such combinations of two or three low paid actors and a free setting formed the economic basis of the movie comedy business in those days. Out of them grew the artistic conventions — if that is the proper word — that audiences came to expect in these little films. The central character, TheTramp or Lonesome Luke, was well known as a result of constant exposure so no time needed to be wasted in introducing or developing his character. And since the point of the exercise was to establish as quickly as possible a situation that was dangerous or embarrassing to the central comic figure and rig it so that it could be resolved by a chase, there was bound to be some duplication between the efforts of the rival comedians. There is probably a finite number of settings and situations that can be employed in the inexpensive manner required of these films. The creativity came, of course, in figuring out innovations within the basic stylizations of the genre — which is why, for example, the Keystone people placed such emphasis on mastery of the Brodie. A novel fall was money in the bank. So was a chase that — literally — covered new ground.

In the beginning, Pathé sent out four scenarios it had bought from a sports cartoonist in New York. Roach and Lloyd were puzzled by them as neither had ever worked from a script before in comedy and it didn't seem to them that the writer back East had the slightest idea of their problems — such as a $1200 budget for each picture. The fellow had invented situations it would have cost thousands to realize. Roach and Lloyd went ahead and made versions of these scenarios, but cut out material that would have sent them over budget (Lloyd has said that two basic gags were generally considered sufficient to carry a one-reeler anyway) and then turned to the established practice for this kind of movie. Since Griffith's earliest days at Biograph and before, the practice was to discover a likely location and then improvise, using whatever it offered to suggest comic ideas — a Chinese laundry, a hotel, a roller-skating rink, a delicatessen, a tailor shop, an amusement park, all were grist for their fast-grinding mill.

In the meantime, Rolin Comedies was building up a little stock company. After the first half-dozen pictures Bebe Daniels, a dark, large-eyed girl of about fifteen from a theatrical family, had come on as the ingenue. She turned out to be not only an attractive comedienne, but a girl friend for Lloyd. They were both expert dancers, and after a day's work at the studio or on location, they liked to

search out dance contests and enter them as a team. They frequently won prizes. Around this time Snub Pollard (his real name was Harry) joined Rolin as second comedian to Lloyd. After securing the moustache (or "mo," as it was known in the trade) that every comic felt he needed as a trademark — Pollard's was modeled after the Kaiser's — the vaudevillian from Australia was launched on a long and varied career as a familiar secondary figure — and occasional lead — in silent comedy. He once gave an interviewer a nice insight into what a career in low comedy meant in purely physical terms: "You know," he said, "I guess I've been bathed in no less than ten tons of very wet cement. I figured up once that I'd caught about 14,000 pies in my puss and had been hit by 600 automobiles and two trains. Once I was even kicked by a giraffe." He may have exaggerated some of those figures, but there is no disputing the toughness and good spirits a career like his demanded. In the early days, even the klieg lights were a problem. There is scarcely a reminiscence of silent-picture making that does not include a reference to the extraordinary intensity of these lights and the phenomenon of "klieg eyes" which they produced. It was like having a huge cinder lodged permanently in each eye, according to Lloyd.

Despite these occupational hazards, despite the imitativeness of his character, despite the low budgets and the fact that Roach kept moving his studio from place to place, a Roach-Lloyd style was beginning to emerge in these films, especially in contrast to the style of the reigning figure, Chaplin's Little Fellow. Lloyd was beginning to slow down the pace of his films so that he could concentrate on character — and not only his own — and create slightly more complex stories. At this early stage The Tramp, as an individual, was already pretty much all he was going to become. The quick, anarchical cruelty of the early films was now being blanched out, and if The Tramp was still something of an opportunist, still somewhat corrupted by his contacts with a society that insisted on his marginality, he had also become gentler in his relationships with the innocents of the world — children, young women, animals. The end of a Chaplin film now often showed him, if not reformed, uplifted in some way by loving one of God's creatures, however briefly and hopelessly. This may have represented an advance in his art — though it was certainly not an unmixed blessing — but it caused a decline in the sheer humor of his films. With his mind on other, higher matters, Chaplin was becoming parsimonious with his gags, though of course the ones he essayed were still of extremely high quality. This represented an opportunity of sorts for Lloyd, Sennett, and Chaplin's other competitors. By sacrificing characterization and reference to those loftier matters that now preoccupied Chaplin — and which were to make him, off-screen, such a tedious fellow for the rest of his life — they were able to offer audiences more humor, more action, than Chaplin. The people in Sennett's comedies "zipped and caromed about the pristine world of the screen as jazzily as a convention of water bugs," as Agee so nicely put it. And Sennett's pace was something Roach

and Lloyd could easily emulate. Finally, since Lloyd was as much an eager beaver as ever, he could be commanded to engage in harum-scarum activities that the increasingly dignified Chaplin would only occasionally resort to.

There is a more or less common critical consensus that in the 1915–16 period Sennett had moved past his early, fumbling stage, in which sheer movement often substituted for genuine inventiveness. Roach and Lloyd were also developing. And being noticed. A trade paper ad referred to Lloyd as "the Human Rubber Ball" because of his endlessly bouncing ways, and a trade reviewer speculated that he "must be made out of India Rubber. The way he suffers himself to be kicked all over the map, hit on the head with a mallet and fall down a dizzy flight of stairs is marvelous."

Still, both Lloyd and Roach were unhappy with what they were doing, though in different ways. And moving to the two-reel format midway through 1917 did not really improve matters for them. It was true that the greater length gave them, at least theoretically, opportunities to build longer, crazier, more inventive gag sequences. And with two weeks to make each one, they could occasionally afford the luxury of planning, leaving themselves less at the mercy of improvisational inspiration, which when it didn't work often gave the endings of silent films a frantic air, with everyone scrambling madly about in search of a topper for the picture. When they came up with one, the effect could be sublime. When they didn't, audiences were left feeling flat, denied the resolution of the comic chords strummed earlier. Lloyd would later recall that Roach, as a director, seemed insecure. "Hal had a very excellent mind, a very fertile mind for thinking of comedy ideas," Lloyd would tell a student audience late in his life. "But because he hadn't had the experience, he wasn't quite as good at setting up a scene. There were many times, even in the very early days, Hal would say, 'How would you do *this*, Harold?' Now he was the boss, and it was his company and I was working for him. Sometimes we'd be working on a beach where we maybe had two or three hundred people watching us and Hal, in those early days, would be a little embarrassed because he just didn't know how to set it up. So I more or less took over and helped him." Lloyd would also remember that Roach's inventiveness did not seem to exceed the one-reel length. When he had worked a week on a film — roughly the amount of time required to make a single reel — he had a way of asking his assistants how much film he had yet to shoot. The answer was usually something like another reel. Whereupon, according to Lloyd, he would say, "Well, boys, let's finish her up," and then shoot the rest of the picture "as if he had a train to catch." This haste, Lloyd wrote, "would let the picture down with a soggy thud. It brought my discontent with Lonesome Luke to a head."

Lloyd, it should be noted, was not the only one to sense a certain restiveness in Roach when he was serving as a director. George Stevens, the director who began his career as a Roach cameraman, would later recall that

even when a film seemed to him to be proceeding nicely, Roach would cry, "This is going badly," and assign someone else to finish the picture. It is possible that he became bored with the sometimes tedious mechanics of picture-making. It is also possible that in the essentially creative role of director he was insecure in a way that he was not in the essentially critical role of producer. It is also possible that in some way Roach envied his performers, either for their fame or for the fact that they were often credited with an inventiveness that was frequently his. At any rate, his comments about Harold Lloyd, a half century after their collaboration ended, are streaked with meanness. He was similarly graceless about his next great discoveries, Laurel and Hardy. Charley Rogers, who frequently directed them, told their biographer, John McCabe, that though Roach wanted their films to succeed and seemed to like them personally, "there was something odd occasionally in his feelings about the pictures. . . . sometimes it seemed that he would unconsciously do little things which harmed them. Or maybe he just didn't understand. Maybe it was because he had a first-rate comic mind but never had a chance to learn the business of putting comedy on celluloid himself. It always puzzled me."

Well it might have. Still, if there was a certain tension between Lloyd and Roach on the set, there was no disagreement between them about the quality of the work they were doing. It was simply not satisfying to them. Lloyd would occasionally drop into theaters to see how his pictures were playing only to discover youngsters misidentifying him as Chaplin. Even more depressing was hearing the scorn with which adults corrected them. Gradually he had discarded Luke's too-tight clothes — "an offense to the eye" — and turned him into more of a dude, but there was just no escaping the fact that Luke was indelibly Chaplin-inspired, and that Lloyd would not begin to move out of Chaplin's shadow until he created a character that reflected his own spirit and sensibility. As for Roach, he was reaching toward a more realistic style of comedy than that turned out by the primitive surrealist Sennett. There would be no lions in *his* hotel lobbies — unless of course there was some reasonable explanation for their being there. The implication here, borne out by his films, is that Roach devoted more effort to story than he did to inspired gag-making. And if his films of this period rarely attained the moments of divine lunacy that Sennett's films achieved, there may well have been more consistency to them, a more reliable standard of comedy. Later, of course, when Lloyd hit his stride, and after that when Roach teamed Laurel and Hardy, Roach would finally surpass Sennett, and he remained active as a producer for more than a decade longer than his old rival.

Both Lloyd and Roach, in their minds, were competing against someone — Lloyd, the actor, against Chaplin; Roach, the producer, against Sennett — but both came to believe that the answer to their needs was a more realistic central figure. It was some time in late 1917, Lloyd would later say, that "a hazy idea"

began to form in the back of his mind. "I had been feeling around for a youth, possibly a boy who could be carried along through a college series, a comedy Frank Merriwell . . ."

Simultaneously, Roach was groping in the same direction. "I was of the opinion that a guy playing straight could be just as funny as a guy with a lot of makeup," he told one recent interviewer. To another, he elaborated:

When I broke into this racket, all comics dressed as comics — baggy pants, monkey jackets, big floppy shoes, freak hats, self-cocking eyebrows, trained performing facial muscles. I had an idea, and with Harold Lloyd as my raw material, I experimented with it. I took away his comedy moustache and his grotesque wardrobe and dressed him instead as a regular human being, but wearing a pair of over-sized horn-rimmed glasses which gave him the slightly owlish appearance of an innocent-minded, guileless young fellow. Then, when something devastating befell him, it had the precious quality of the unexpected, and for audience reactions was infinitely funnier than if ho'd worn a zany makeup.

Roach has been, through the years, less than generous about the invention of Lloyd's quite possibly immortal screen persona. "Harold Lloyd didn't have anything more to do with inventing this character than you do," he said to one interviewer. "Earl Monahan, who played drunks for us, came on the set one day wearing glasses without glass and that gave us the idea to put horn-rimmed glasses on Harold. He thought he did this . . ."

And so he did. Lloyd's version of the creation was that he had seen a movie — he never could remember the title or the star — about a fighting parson, "tolerant and peaceful until riled, then a tartar. Glasses emphasized his placidity." He thought they could be adapted into a trademark for his "hazy idea" of a new character. He mulled over the idea and talked it over "night after night" with an actor named Mortenson who lived in his apartment building. And came to essentially the same conclusions Roach had reached, or was about to reach. The glasses, besides being a trademark would "suggest the character — quiet, normal, boyish, clean, sympathetic, not impossible to romance. . . . I would be an average recognizable American youth and let the situations take care of the comedy." This, he thought, would be the better for not depending on "a putty nose." And, he said, "funnier things happen in life to an ordinary boy than to a Lonesome Luke. Exaggeration is the breath of picture comedies, and obviously they cannot be true to life, but they can be recognizably related to life."

In his autobiography Lloyd admits that perhaps this was not as clear to him at the moment as it became in later years. Roach, of course, insists he had to make the whole idea clear to Lloyd in the first place. "We did exactly the same things we'd do with Lonesome Luke, except he'd do [them] straight," he said.

"The Glasses Character" in an early incarnation. Flowing tie was last odd element in costume and was soon discarded for a more realistic four-in-hand.

Star and producer: Lloyd and Hal Roach use a running board as a conference room on the set.

The whole argument may be feckless — it is after all a fact that in late 1917 a new Harold Lloyd appeared on the screen. In any case it is an insoluble one. No third party is now alive who was present when the two men decided to dissolve through Lonesome Luke to "The Boy." And there is no objective record of what happened around the Roach offices in the summer and fall of 1917. Lloyd does, however, credit Roach with talking their distributor, Pathé, into abandoning the still-profitable Luke and letting him try the new character. Characteristically, though, the modest Lloyd thought they would let him go and put another comedian into the makeup he had created. Roach, in New York, convinced the Pathé people that Lloyd, who was by this time making $100 a week, was going to leave if they insisted on his continuing as Luke and that, anyway, the time was ripe for a new, more naturalistic comedian. It appears that Lloyd suggested that the new character be introduced in a series of one-reelers, partly so that his identity could be quickly established through a steady drumfire of new releases, and partly so that if they turned out some turkeys, the audience's memory of them would be quickly wiped out by new, better pictures. Nonetheless, Luke was not dropped cold. Lloyd introduced the glasses character in *Over the Fence*, a baseball story in which Foxy Lloyd appeared in a bit as an umpire, and though in his autobiography he claims Luke was never heard from again, the fact is that Lonesome Luke two-reelers (perhaps taken from a stockpile) more or less alternated with one-reel glasses character releases until the end of the year. After the last week of 1917, however, Lonesome Luke was heard from no more. For the rest of his career, Harold Lloyd would never appear in public as any other character but the boy in horn-rimmed glasses.

4 The first set of horn-rims came from a little occulist's shop on Spring Street in Los Angeles. The first pair Lloyd had tried on were too heavy, while the second, too large, obscured facial expression. The final choice was made from a tray containing at least thirty sets of glasses which Lloyd scoured through in search of the perfect pair. He kept these glasses for a year and a half, repairing them again and again — he was a very superstitious man — until finally nothing more could be done with them. When he shipped them off to a manufacturer in the East for duplication, he received twenty pairs — and his check was returned. It seemed he was responsible for an enormous jump in the sale of tortoise shell rims. Indeed, the new series of one-reelers were successful right from the start. They played better theaters than the Luke shorts ever had, including first-run downtown houses. And though Lloyd was not really aware of

it, and wouldn't be until he made a visit to New York in 1920 and actually saw his name in lights, he was in the process of becoming a true star.

Not that all the problems were solved. For one thing, Roach seemed preoccupied at the time with developing other talent. Whether this was done as a threat to Lloyd, in order to keep him from making impossible monetary demands on the fledgling corporation, or simply out of an expansionist urge, it is impossible to say. At any rate, Roach was mostly unavailable as a director now, and though Lloyd filled in from time to time this did not prove very satisfactory. A succession of directors including Lloyd's old boss, J. Farrell Macdonald, failed to work out. Finally, Snub Pollard suggested Alf Goulding, a member of his old vaudeville company, and by the end of the year Goulding and Roach were alternating in the director's chair. Lloyd liked this arrangement, since Goulding had a broad style, while Roach's was more realistic. He felt this gave him a range that permitted him to appear to the widest possible audience.

Goulding was a fast worker. He and Lloyd could sometimes finish a one-reeler in three days and once they even finished one in a day and a half. It may be that Roach somewhat resented their speed. At any rate, one afternoon Goulding told Lloyd that he might as well take the next morning off, since he had a number of scenes to shoot that didn't require his presence. Lloyd was grateful for the extra sleep — he was, after all, a hard-working fellow. At nine, however, he was awakened by a call from Roach insisting that he turn up at the studio forthwith. It was, he claimed, bad for morale for the star to absent himself when everyone else had to be there (Roach's pettiness is an ongoing theme in their relationship — and a mystery of sorts). Lloyd refused; Roach carried on without him. Dwight Whiting, who had been the original source of financing for Roach, and who had by this time decided to take an active role in studio management, replacing Linthicum, tried unsuccessfully to mediate the quarrel, and both men remained adamant. But when Roach made a picture starring Bebe Daniels and Pollard, it elicited a query from Pathé about their absent star. They sent an emissary westward and it was he who patched up the difficulties between Lloyd and Roach. Indeed, it would seem that it was Pathé who kept them together for the next five years.

Roach has insisted that "the only fighting we did was over the quality of the pictures we made," but that does not square with Lloyd's memories. He seemed to think that their chief bone of contention was money. When he introduced his new character, Lloyd signed a contract calling for a raise from $100 to $150 a week for the first six months of its term, $300 thereafter. When the time came for the raise to take effect, however, Roach and Whiting insisted that it could not be done. While Pathé had increased its advance on each film from $1200 to $1500, that just about covered higher production costs. Since Roach and company might expect to realize something in the neighborhood of $2600 from

their share of box office receipts, Lloyd readily admitted that that left them only a very thin profit margin. On the other hand, he pointed out that he had no percentage of his pictures, and that by asking him to continue at his low salary with promises of more to come if the films started turning larger profits, they were, in effect, asking him to share the risks of the business without permitting him to share in its potentially large winnings. He held firm; so did Roach, and Lloyd struck. Though one of his films was playing Sid Grauman's "Million Dollar Theater" in Los Angeles, the kind of booking Roach pictures had never attained previously, Lloyd discovered that Roach had turned down a similar booking for another of his pictures, in order to support his contention that Lloyd was not yet a big moneymaker.

Lloyd decided to go to New York and confer with the Pathé people personally. When he called the Pathé office he was delighted to discover that the woman at the switchboard immediately identified "Mr. Lloyd." More meaningfully, Pathé treated him like a true celebrity, picking up the tab for a week of excellent wining and dining. Perhaps just as important for his future, Roach tried putting the glasses on Alf Goulding during Lloyd's absence and the experiment was a disaster. There was something inimitable about Lloyd.

The result was another intervention by Pathé, which again offered its good offices to bring the parties together. Most significantly, the company agreed to guarantee the star's salary. Any time Roach couldn't afford to pay it, Pathé would make up the difference. And under the terms of this new agreement, $300 was just a starting salary. If all went well, Lloyd would soon be making a good deal more than that. Higher salaries could not, in fact, be denied him or any other actor, for it was no longer possible for the proprietors of this new industry to pretend that it was still in its infancy, requiring the indulgence of a newborn babe. It is likely, though records were somewhat vague, that *The Birth of a Nation,* released four years earlier, had grossed something like $100 million. Chaplin and Mary Pickford had by now signed million-dollar contracts, and William S. Hart and Douglas Fairbanks were scarcely less important stars. Cecil B. DeMille was turning out highly profitable westerns and historical spectacles, while Erich von Stroheim was making *Blind Husbands,* the first of his memorable studies in perverse sexuality, a film which would prove that there were enormous profits to be made in titillating the public with a heretofore unimaginable sexual intensity. It might be that a star of short comedies could not command the profits and thus the salary of those making features, but Lloyd simply could not be kept at his old salary level in a prosperous time, when everyone in the industry (with the possible exception of D. W. Griffith) had recognized that stars were the basis of its profitability and its stability, guaranteeing the public that when they put their money down to see a favorite player they would get what they expected and wanted.

Moreover, Lloyd was getting better. Some of the one-reelers of the 1918–19

period contained sequences every bit as well constructed and as hilarious — if not as elaborate or as long — as the more famous sequences of physical comedy in his later features. Roach claimed many years later that he and his gag specialists had had to teach Lloyd how to take falls, but the fact is that Lloyd had been introduced to the art at Sennett's and he was, on the record of his films, an extraordinarily apt pupil.

Take a more or less random example, *Why Pick on Me?* Here Harold plays a rather effeminate young man out for a stroll on the pier at Santa Monica trying to pick up girls — who are naturally more interested in the muscular lifeguards. He pays particular attention to Bebe Daniels, who is walking out with a much burlier male. When the ice cream her boyfriend has been licking falls off his cone and onto Harold's cone, the boys get into a fight. Harold shrewdly cons his opponent into holding his — Harold's — coat. Whereupon he hits him a smart blow and takes off. Encountering him again, Harold taps him on the shoulder, the man whirls and swings and, of course, slugs a policeman, which starts the chase. This leads to a fight on one of those whirling platforms which were such a familiar feature of old-time amusement parks, throwing people into hilarious tangles. Up to now, the picture has been well made but not particularly original. Then Harold is thrown off the centrifugal wheel, followed by what appears to be a very large woman, who lands on him. Grotesquely, she turns out to be a he. In drag. It is startling to find this kind of humor in a comedy made in 1918. No wonder that nice people were often shocked by it. Now comes the climactic chase, a beautifully timed thing, with Harold easily vaulting, among other objects, an oncoming bike, a midget, a rope, and a fence (he is helped through the latter by a furious ram). He uses a teeterboard to gain the second floor of a building and a neat back flip to get down from it. The whole business ends with him taking a flying leap off a bridge and landing in a boat containing a fat lady. She hastily decamps, permitting Harold to escape the policeman who is by this time firing at him, so great is his frustration.

Now, one could say that the basic situation, miscreant vs. befuddled cop, had already passed through the cliché stage of silent comedy and become a kind of classic. It is also true that, aside from Fairbanks, no one had put together a chase superior to this one in terms of the sheer number of times the gag we believe must be the topper is topped. Indeed, Lloyd himself would stage more elaborate and dangerous exercises of this kind, but none would be superior or more satisfying in terms of movement. Watching him at work, one derives the same sense of pleasure in seeing a series of beautifully orchestrated movements, each leading logically yet surprisingly to the next, that one derives from seeing an expert trapeze or tumbling act at the circus. Moreover, there is a wit about these movements that often seems every bit equal to the wit one finds in Chaplin's quite similar attempts to elude the minions of the law. The difference is that Lloyd expressed his wit exclusively through his supple body; all

41

Hit Him Again (1918). Bebe Daniels is the anxious corner assistant.

his ideas were kinesthetic in nature, while Chaplin's were only partly so. Heaven knows, The Tramp had a wonderfully expressive body, but its vocabulary was derived not from sport or acrobatics but from the pantomime and ballet. Moreover, he was a shrewd judge of human nature and he was entirely capable of offering his pursuers all sorts of false scents — sudden appeals to cupidity or laziness, for example — which in the end, of course, worked to The Little Fellow's advantage. In this sense, Lloyd was more straightforward and, if one may say it, more American. One can't help but think that Lloyd's posthumous reputation might be higher had not the intellectuals, who so early took up Chaplin's cause, been less interested in promoting the potential of movies as high art and more inclined to recognize their possibilities as something new — a mechanized but (at their best) authentic folk art. Part of the trouble was that the thinking community did not yet include sports among the subjects worthy of thinking about (that is actually a development of only the last ten years or so), and thus it had no basis for appreciating what Lloyd was doing. Another factor was simply snobbery. As Vachel Lindsay, the poet who took it upon himself to be the first aesthetician of the movies, was to say a little later, "Writers whom I will not mention have learned to speak the name of Charlie Chaplin with a sigh . . . and then have no more to do with the movies."

Not that Lloyd achieved such satisfying results every week. The release immediately following *Why Pick on Me?,* called *Ask Father,* is the tale of a shy but plucky young man who approaches a rich man's office to ask for his daughter's hand. The film has its charms, but it strains rather too hard for laughs. Dad, for example, has a treadmill to slow down unwelcome visitors and a trap door to dispose of them if they're too persistent. Down the hall, by an excessively nice coincidence, there is a costume agency from which the repulsed Harold gets a series of disguises to help him penetrate the mogul's security system. He finally gets a suit of armor, and as with the treadmill and trap door, one recognizes — despite the laughs — an exaggeration that pushes satire over into a farcicality too broad for comfort, one that deteriorates into mere silliness. This is especially unfortunate because there are some clever gags in the film. Bebe Daniels, for example, cast as the rich man's receptionist, is attracted, in a perfectly understandable way, to Harold's good-natured persistence. Whenever it appears he is about to be thrown out of the office, she carefully arranges pillows so he can make a soft landing. This leads to love and to a happy ending which, even if it arrives too suddenly (in the manner of one-reelers), is nevertheless satisfying in a minor sort of way. The entire film certainly has a higher level of inventiveness than something like *Billy Blazes, Esq.,* where Lloyd essays a parody of the western. There, except for one or two isolated gags which are not developed, the film consists mainly of a lot of aimless running around. After one has absorbed the basically funny inconsistency of a cowboy wearing horn-rims, it's no longer very amusing.

Thus consistency was not a hallmark of the Lloyd-Roach product during its first year or so of work with the glasses character. On the other hand, consistency was not a common virtue in the world of silent comedy, whatever tricks nostalgia plays on people's memories. Indeed, comedy being the difficult art that it is, it is hard to name any comedian who has had to sustain a large output and who has managed to be consistently funny — think of what has happened to every television comic who has tried to sustain a weekly show. The point is that in nearly two years of making one-reelers on an almost one-a-week schedule, Lloyd managed to create a number of high moments sufficient to establish his credentials with the audience. And, funny or not, he gained the kind of regular exposure that is vital to building any career in mass entertainment. As a rule, if a performer has any ability at all, familiarity breeds not contempt but acceptance. People begin to think that if a man or woman is being booked regularly, other people must think he or she is good — and they begin to come around to that point of view, no matter what their initial reaction was. But of course the performer must have something — otherwise the Vera Hruba Ralston syndrome evolves.

By April of 1919, all concerned had reason to be content with the way things had worked out since Harold had donned his glasses. The films were profitable and he was being noticed by the public. In fact, it is probably fair to say that he had attained by this time the ranking he would hold with the public for the rest of the silent era — that is, second only to Chaplin among the comedians. In any event, in the spring of 1919, Pathé was willing to commit itself to a new contract, calling for Lloyd and Roach to produce nine two-reel comedies in the next months. Lloyd was to receive for them $1,000 a week in salary, plus a twenty-five percent share of the profits on each film. Pathé, for its part, was to raise the rental fee from the $300 per week per picture that it had been getting for the one-reelers to $3,000 apiece for the longer films. The rise, Lloyd said, was explained "solely by demand." The pictures themselves — though now costing between thirty and forty thousand dollars apiece to produce — were not, he felt, that much better or different than the one-reelers.

Certainly *Bumping Into Broadway,* the first of the two-reelers, was not superior in terms of story or individual gags to Lloyd's better one-reelers. A romance between a struggling playwright and a musical comedy chorine (Bebe Daniels) who live in the same boarding house, the film has some good moments — Lloyd getting his finger stuck between the keys of his typewriter and throwing the offending machine out the window (where it strikes a passing policeman, of course), or an inventive sequence where Lloyd tries to avoid a landlady bent on collecting his overdue rent (among other things, he hides by hanging himself on a coat rack, disguised by a coat, and smuggles himself out of the building in the dirty laundry).

Twice as long did not necessarily mean twice as funny. It did mean,

44

however, twice as attractive in some other ways. The principal gain was in what might be termed a sense of repose. One feels a certain relaxation in the actors, perhaps as a result of having more production time, hence more retakes and less tension. One also senses that they may have been creatively stirred by the fact that there was room in the longer pictures for inventive bits of business. If the actors wished to contribute to the films, the results would not necessarily end up in the cutting room trim barrel. And of course, increased budgets meant larger casts, which meant that items like the chase could be extended because more people could be employed to create more problems for Harold (*Broadway* concludes in a well-populated gambling house that is raided by a corps of cops as large as any normally employed by Sennett). More important, Roach could now hire locations if he needed to, instead of having to depend on the kindness of the parks department. He could even afford to build fairly elaborate sets when he wanted to.

So as of spring, 1919, things could not have been going better for Lloyd. Then, however, Bebe Daniels decided to leave. Lloyd in his autobiography says merely that she wanted to find greater dramatic opportunities, and that since she had a long-standing offer from DeMille, she decided to take him up on it when her contract with Roach ran out. There may well have been some truth in this, but it is surely not the whole story. For one thing, Lloyd's career was obviously on the rise and it was a strange moment for her to leave an actor with whom she was so closely associated. More important, the two had been great and good friends almost from the moment she had joined the company. Lloyd's reminiscences of these years take on a warmer coloration when he speaks of their nights together trying to win prizes at the dancing competitions. (Their leading opponents were the tragic Wallace Reid — the movies' first famous drug addict — his wife Dorothy, and Wallace Beery and Gloria Swanson, then featured players with Sennett.) As his salary had risen, so had the quality of the conveyances which took Harold and Bebe to and from the dance halls. First there had been a stripped-down fenderless flivver, which looked like a racing car, though it lacked real speed. After that there was a powerful touring car, which Lloyd had painted cerulean blue with white wire wheels, in imitation of Beery's car. This, however, was the extent to which Lloyd "went Hollywood" in these early years. Some time in 1919 though, he decided to move out of his apartment and into his first modest house. Now, suddenly, there was nothing between Harold and Bebe. And a larger explanation is required.

Bebe apparently loved Lloyd, and it seems likely she wanted to marry him. The trouble was that Lloyd, like his screen character, was quite insecure around women — at least at this time. He behaved toward Bebe as he behaved toward everyone else who was important then in his life — ingratiatingly. "He was in love with Bebe Daniels," Roach has flatly said, "but he so kowtowed to everything she wanted that she thought there must be something better."

45

Actually, it seems that Harold would give her anything she wanted, except a wedding ring. One can't but think that he was concerned, as are so many ambitious but close-fisted men, that the responsibilities of marriage might burden him too soon. Certainly he wanted to be free to concentrate on the great opportunity that now lay before him. And, oddly enough, events almost immediately proved his caution to be well grounded. For on August 24, 1919, a Sunday, Harold Lloyd suffered the only major setback — it came close to being a tragedy — of his young career.

5   He had no difficulty in replacing Bebe Daniels, either in his professional or his personal life. He and Roach decided his next leading lady should stand in sharp physical contrast to Daniels so they started looking for a petite blonde. The casting agencies turned up no one suitable. Then Roach noticed a young woman playing the lead in a film opposite Bryant Washburn, a popular leading man of the day, and they agreed that she seemed just right. They discovered that her name was Mildred Davis, but also that she had since moved to Tacoma, Washington, where her father, a newspaper circulation promotion man, had taken a new job. When they finally contacted her, they found that her parents were reluctant to let her return to Los Angeles alone. She had yet to finish high school, and besides, like most middle-class people, her parents were leery about those wicked movie people. But somehow she prevailed on them to let her at least appear for an interview with Roach and Lloyd. Not realizing that they were seeking an ingenue, she bought herself a sophisticated wardrobe, including a plumed hat, so that Lloyd and Roach found it difficult to believe that this was the fresh young thing who had made such an impression on them in the Washburn film. For her part, she found Lloyd, who appeared in makeup for their meeting, something less than an exciting figure. Things were soon straightened out, however, and in June she made her debut opposite Lloyd in his third two-reeler, *From Hand to Mouth.* From there she went immediately into *His Royal Slyness,* and she would continue to appear opposite Lloyd until *Safety Last,* in 1923, when they married and she withdrew from the screen.

Mildred Davis would be an agreeable though hardly a striking presence in these films. She had none of Bebe Daniels's quiet flair for the delicate business of playing opposite a comedian, which required suggesting credible romantic attraction to a figure both the other players and the audience must find absurd. Miss Davis solved the problem largely by being quiet as a mouse, seeming perhaps a trifle dumb. The Daniels's characterization was not for her — that edge of kookiness that implied some need for, or at least tolerance of, the comic's

Mildred Davis is seen with Lloyd in an obviously posed
portrait used in publicity for *Grandma's Boy* (1922).

strange ways, which attracted adventures not normally available in the essentially dull bourgeois world they inhabited. Miss Davis was sweet and pretty in a vapid way, and if she didn't add much to the festivities on screen, she at least did not detract from the star's turn.

As they worked on their first picture together, Pathé prepared a new advertising campaign designed to build Lloyd up both with the public and in the trade. The latter would be addressed first. In a letter sent to Pathé branch offices by headquarters, attention was called to a national advertising campaign to begin in the fall, built around space in the *Saturday Evening Post.* In part, the letter said:

Charlie Chaplin, Douglas Fairbanks, Mary Pickford and other big stars whose pictures to-day command big rentals, all had a turning point in their careers — a period in which their pictures jumped from small rentals to prices to which they legitimately are entitled. And the turning point in Harold Lloyd's career now has arrived. You know as we know that in the past the Harold Lloyd comedies were being sold at ridiculously low prices; so low that when on the first of March this year we started raising the prices on one-reel Lloyds, inside of nine days all our branches combined showed an increase on collections for these subjects of 400 per cent without receiving one cancellation.

Noting that because of the one-a-week release schedule, Lloyd had become the most widely circulated of all comedians, this optimistic announcement implied that there would be great anticipation for each new Lloyd release, since they would now come along only once every twenty-eight days. Pathé obviously believed that its buildup of Lloyd, along the lines he had shrewdly suggested, had paid off handsomely and that it was now time to cash in.

Lloyd and Roach concurred, and in order to help the program along, Lloyd agreed to spend Sunday, his one day off, posing for a new set of publicity photos at the photographer's downtown studio. The photographer was a man named Witzel, with whom Roach players often worked. Witzel was first going to take some straight portraits and some gag shots, and while Lloyd was making up at the studio, he would occasionally glance out the window to the stable yard of the old Bradbury mansion — Roach had moved back there again — where Frank Terry, a property man, held up various objects he felt might help make funny shots. Among them was a round black bomb of the sort that the conventions of political cartooning insist anarchists and other radicals carry. Terry mimed the use of the bomb, its fuse smoking, as a cigarette lighter, and Lloyd nodded approval of the notion.

At Witzel's, a handful of propless pictures were taken, the last of which Lloyd recalled as a mock tragic one, when the photographer decided it was time to take some more amusing shots. Terry picked up the bomb, lit it, and handed it

to Lloyd. It was equipped with a long, smoky fuse, meant to enhance the humor and suspense of its use on the screen. The smoke, however, turned out to be excessive, obscuring Lloyd's expression, and, as the fuse burned down, of course, Lloyd had to bring the bomb closer and closer to his face in order to touch fuse to cigarette. Witzel still couldn't get the shot he wanted, and Lloyd lowered the bomb to his side, saying it was time to insert a new fuse. At this point the bomb exploded. It tore a hole in the ceiling, sixteen feet above, shattered every window in the room, and split Terry's upper plate from end to end. Witzel fainted.

Lloyd was terribly wounded. His face was badly seared, he was temporarily blinded, and he was in excruciating pain. Terry, also hurt and badly shaken, guided him to the sidewalk outside and hailed a motorist, asking the man to take Lloyd to the nearest hospital, where he was immediately placed under sedation. He awoke to find his eyes bandaged; now, to his fear that his face was too scarred ever to allow him to appear on the screen again, there was added the fear that he might be permanently blinded. He was told what had happened. The bomb had been made for a stunt designed to enliven an outdoor gathering of something called "The Uplifter's Club," an organization to which Lloyd and several other people at the studio belonged. It had been charged by a property man who didn't know much about explosives, and when another bomb, its twin, shattered an oak table, the club members decided to return this one to the studio. There it was carelessly mixed with the comedy bombs, but no one ever did explain how it came to be equipped with the comedy fuse that completed its innocent disguise.

Lloyd was naturally depressed by what appeared to be the abrupt ending of his career just as he stood on the threshold of major success, and he did admit to a brief period of gloom as he lay on his hospital bed. But that does not seem to have lasted long. Within a few days, the doctors were able to tell him that the sight in his left eye would be unimpaired, though they were worried about the right eye, which some of them believed had been punctured by a shard from the bomb. Reassured that he would have at least partial vision, Lloyd began planning a new career as a director, and he reported, "Visitors and the hospital staff were startled by the cheerfulness of a man who had just seen a career blow up in his face with heavy damage to both. When I fretted, it was mere impatience, more often than not, at the delay in being up and at it."

What Lloyd did not report in his autobiography was that he had suffered one permanent, unredressable injury, and friends and co-workers formed a benign conspiracy to keep knowledge of it from the public. He had lost the thumb and forefinger of his right hand. Indeed, so well kept was this secret that even Hollywood insiders didn't know it. Jack Benny, for example, only learned of it many years later, when he asked Lloyd, by this time retired, to appear on his television show and do a few mild stunts, and Lloyd had to refuse because the

prosthetic device he had worn on screen had long since rotted. Even then he would not appear on any screen without it.

It is Roach, to be sure, who claims to have designed the device to disguise the deformed hand. He says he found a firm in New York to manufacture it, and that "by the time [Lloyd] was well and out of the hospital we had the whole thing ready for him." About this point, the truth will probably never be known, since Lloyd was so reluctant to discuss the matter. Indeed, typical Midwesterner that he was, his relentless cheerfulness in the face of adversity was probably just a way of avoiding any deep thought about the matter. When he was doing his more difficult stunts on the screen, it was Lloyd's unconscious habit to mutter to himself, "What the hell, Bill, what the hell." And that's what he kept saying to himself as he lay recuperating, first at the hospital and then in his new home.

Whoever designed the prosthetic device, it was elegantly simple and effective. A rubber company took a mold of his left hand, reversed it, and cast replicas in soft rubber of the missing right thumb and first finger joined together. The rubber index finger was connected by a flap to Lloyd's second finger so that the two could move in unison. The rubber thumb was immovable. On this hand, on screen and in public appearances, he wore a thin, flesh color leather glove of the finest grain. High on his forearm he wore a rubber garter from which elastic bands ran to the top of the glove, keeping it in place when he was performing highly acrobatic stunts. The fact that he did these often dangerous tricks without the full use of one hand — and he was right-handed — makes them the more remarkable. Lloyd was a braver man than his public of the time suspected. And it was characteristic of him that he even increased his participation in sports after the accident. He swam, played tennis and golf, and bowled — with a specially drilled ball. In later years he would roll a perfect game (300) and he often wore a pin attesting to his membership in the 300 club. He was also capable of breaking par occasionally at golf.

Lloyd's favorite game was handball, and he would eventually have his own courts both at his studio and at home. At work his employees were dragooned — most of them not too unwillingly — into playing with him, and at home he often played host to tournaments in which players of national rank participated. For this game, Lloyd had himself fitted out with a special glove with a small wooden striking surface the size of his palm, and if anything his skills improved. The only sport at which he was handicapped was tennis, where a proper grip of the racket is so dependent on the use of the thumb.

Lloyd would later claim that he knew he could return to the screen the day he received a visit from John McKeon and Hiram Abrams of United Artists, the new operation of which the shrewd Abrams would soon be president. Lloyd's accident, according to his attorney, had freed him of all obligation to Roach and Pathé — apparently because it had occurred in line of duty and it could be proved that proper care in protecting his safety had not been exercised. The UA people,

in the process of recruiting more performers to join Pickford, Chaplin, Fairbanks, and Griffith in an arrangement that promised both greater artistic freedom and higher profits from their work, offered Lloyd a five-year contract worth $500,000. He was still dubious about his ability to return to the screen, he reported in his autobiography, though by this time his doubts must have been nearly minimal.

Indeed, one suspects his talk about his moral obligation to inform Roach of this offer and give him a chance to meet it was a ploy to set the rival companies bidding against each other. In any event, Lloyd wired Roach in New York with details of the UA offer. When he got back to the coast, Roach offered to increase Lloyd's participation in his pictures' profits to fifty per cent. Lloyd believed he remembered talk of a partnership in the studio, which he refused, not wanting to be a drag on the operation if it turned out he could not function effectively before the cameras. Roach says he never made any such offer. Whatever the truth, the fact remains that Lloyd had sailed through the great crisis of his career with astonishing ease. It was not a tragedy because he would not let it become one. It was simply not in his nature to entertain for long any thoughts profound enough to qualify as tragedy. What he learned from the experience merely reinforced what he already knew — that an ambitious and determined man could overcome any obstacle if he confronted it optimistically, in good faith and good cheer. Another man might have chosen a different, more difficult way of surmounting a shock such as this one, perhaps taking away from it something that would, in time, deepen his understanding of life, and thus deepen his art. Not Harold Lloyd. It was a matter to be disguised and forgotten as soon as possible.

So Lloyd had converted disaster to advantage. And when he went to New York to sign his newest agreement with Pathé, he had the supreme thrill of seeing his name in lights on Broadway for the first time. Out for a stroll, he happened to glance at the marquee of the Strand Theater, then the city's leading movie house (it was the first Broadway theater to be built exclusively for showing films). Pauline Frederick in *Bonds of Love* topped the bill. But just beneath her name he found his — spelled in red, white, and blue lights — and the title of his first two-reeler, *Bumping into Broadway.* He would remember walking back and forth in front of the theater, staring at the magic sign, struck by the happy coincidence of title and locale. A few blocks later, at another house he saw Dorothy Gish's name above the title of something or other. Once again, just beneath, there was his name, again above the movie's title. Afterwards he could remember nothing else about this day. And why should

he, for in four years he had gone from a five-dollar-a-day nonentity to a star with his name in lights on show biz's main street.

At the time of his accident, Lloyd had been in the midst of a two-reeler called *Haunted Spooks*. He had just completed a hilarious segment in which, as a spurned suitor, he attempts to commit suicide and fails miserably: he steps in front of an oncoming trolley and turns his back, grimacing in painful anticipation of the impact — but at the last minute the trolley switches off the track on which ho's standing; he ties a huge rock to his neck and leaps from a bridge into a stream — which turns out to be no more than ankle deep; he puts a revolver to his temple but it turns out to be, naturally, a water pistol. Obviously, a splendid work. Because of the accident, the film was not finished until March, 1920, some seven months after it was begun, but the public discerned no discontinuity between material shot in 1919 and that shot in 1920. For the rest of this year he would make two-reel films, but the following year he increased his standard length to three reels. Finally, late in 1921, Lloyd would make the first movie he considered a feature, *A Sailor-Made Man* — though it just barely deserves this designation, being but four reels long.

As the films grew longer another pattern began to assert itself, an alternation between what Lloyd would call "thrill" comedies and those he would call "character" comedies. The distinction was important to him, and there is an implication running through his later interviews with journalists and film historians that he preferred the character pieces. Perhaps this was because through the years he had grown increasingly resentful of the view that his art consisted largely of clinging perilously to the ledges of tall buildings. And in truth, such sequences do not bulk large in the body of his work, though they loom large in people's memories. Then, too, it must be remembered that Lloyd had been a juvenile and a character actor in stock at an impressionable age, and had drawn his early friends and mentors from that milieu. It would be surprising if there were not some corner of his ego in which he believed he might have been an excellent straight actor if the right opportunities had presented themselves. And he may have absorbed from these early friends a belief that acting, the creation of a variety of characters in a variety of plays, was intrinsically a higher calling than that of being a comedian, locked forever into a single, predictable persona. Lloyd must have felt that the character comedies gave him more opportunities to satisfy these ambitions and ideals. In any case, this basic alternation of roles would be a constant of his career from this point onward, and it should be stressed that he generally made two or three safely grounded films for every film in which he sought the heights.

For example, he would follow *Haunted Spooks* with *An Eastern Westerner*, his last parody of the western genre, then make *High and Dizzy*, the first of the major high-rise "thrill" pictures — though not his first experiment with the idea of obtaining laughs from on high (this occurred in *Look Out Below*, one of the

first one-reelers featuring the glasses character, early in 1918). He would then make several other "character" pictures in 1920 and 1921 before returning to a succession of lofty and dangerous perches in the marvelous *Never Weaken*, which contains what is in many respects the wittiest of all his climbing sequences.

There is, obviously, something naively arbitrary about Lloyd's definitions. As a general rule there was scarcely a "character" comedy that did not include a thrill sequence of some sort. Nor could it be said that he entirely neglected character in the thrill films. Although he never said it in so many words, it would seem that his definition of a thrill picture was one in which the character gets involved in escapades where death, not merely a serious accident, was a very lively possibility.

By this definition, *High and Dizzy* certainly qualified. Lloyd plays a not very prosperous doctor who is engaged to cure Mildred Davis of her habit of sleepwalking. However, by the time he is summoned to her hotel room to observe her in action, he has been sampling some bathtub gin distilled by a neighbor across the hall from his office and he has some difficulty gaining entrance to the hotel. There are some good minor gags here — buttoning a house detective to a pillar with his coat, and confusing an elevator floor indicator with a clock. There's also a bit where a puppy gets under Lloyd's hat and he takes the hat's erratic movements across the floor as a warning of incipient D.T.'s.

Things don't really get going, however, until he gains access to Mildred's room, and Mildred, in her sleep, heads out the window and starts walking a ledge. Ever gallant, the still spifficated Lloyd follows, hoping to guide her to safety, but carelessly locks the window behind him so they cannot retreat the way they have come. The comedy arises out of the casual confidence with which, drunk, he essays the ledge. It is not until he sobers up and realizes where he is (at which point his hair stands straight up) that the situation becomes dangerous, sobriety leading to knowledge which leads to clumsiness. Somehow they manage to regain safety, and the film ends with their wedding ceremony on the ledge where they discovered, through mutual peril, true love.

Lloyd would later do more complex sequences involving lofty dangers that were both scarier and funnier; the significance of this little sequence, which lacks the development Lloyd and his gagmen would lavish on its descendants, is mainly as a sketch for more elaborate thrill sequences to come. Still, it is certainly not without its modest merits. And it has a certain historical significance as the last picture directed by Hal Roach.

Around this time Roach had ceased his roving ways and settled into a studio he could call his own in Culver City. The organization was growing, for Roach was an ambitious man, with hopes of turning his highly personal operation into a major production company (something he never quite managed, though he was,

at least until the early forties, one of Hollywood's most important independents). Moreover, he did not want his fortunes tied entirely to Lloyd, whose contract was on a fairly short-term basis and who was fast achieving a status that would insure him a welcome at competing studios that could easily outbid Roach. Therefore, he concentrated his energies on finding and developing other comedians and other comic series. Around this time he gave Snub Pollard his own series, which proved fairly popular though rather too mechanistic for most critical tastes. He also gave Gaylord Lloyd a chance. Gaylord's films were reportedly well made, but he did not photograph well or have the natural gift which permitted another comedian's relative — Chaplin's half brother, Sidney — the modest success he enjoyed while trading on the family name. Lloyd's name was not, in fact, strong enough yet to generate much interest in his sibling. More successful for Roach was Stan Laurel, also from the English music hall tradition — indeed from the very Karno company that had brought Chaplin to America. Not yet teamed with Oliver Hardy, and at first employed as a gag man, Laurel was launched in 1918–19 in a series of satires on well-known popular stories and legends. (Among his titles were *When Knights Were Cold, Under Two Jags, Wild Bill Hiccup,* and *Rupert of Hee-Haw,* the last a takeoff on *The Prisoner of Zenda*.)*Also around this time, Roach hired Charles Parrott, like Laurel a trained performer who wanted to retreat behind the camera to write and direct. He was responsible for many of the better Pollard films, and under his stage name of Charley Chase he would become a much-admired, though never hugely popular, star of two-reelers a little later in the decade. Finally, in 1922, Roach would launch his long-cherished idea for a series of kid comedies, the *Our Gang* pictures. These, along with the Laurel and Hardy series, would be among his most profitable productions and would later enable him to manage a smooth transition to the sound era. Both the kids and the great comedy team became, if anything, more popular when talk was added to their routines.

Clearly, then, Roach was a busy man, and since he had little liking for the role of director, he was pleased to be able to give up some of his directorial chores — though for the rest of his career he would return to them from time to time as if trying to solve a mystery. As for Lloyd, Roach's withdrawal from their collaboration opened the way for the highly competent man who, either alone or working with others, would direct all of his films through 1925. His name was Fred Newmeyer, a former minor league pitcher who had drifted into extra work at Universal, where he first met Lloyd and Roach. He worked for the latter as a property man and learned his craft directing one-reelers featuring the other Roach players.

Newmeyer and the other Lloyd directors were self-effacing workers with a

* Laurel recorded an opinion of his contemporary at Roach's. Of Harold Lloyd he said, "He hardly ever made me laugh, but I admire his inventiveness. A smart comedian. The best of the straight comedians."

special gift for unpretentious camera placements. These placements either quietly set up a gag, allowing the audience to savor the knowledge of an impending disaster which was withheld from Lloyd, or, conversely, disguised the gag, by keeping such knowledge from the audience — without seeming to cheat it — in order to enhance its shock value. As much as anyone, the comedy directors of the silent era established the basic American movie style — objective, efficient, unpretentious, with the eye-level camera relatively stationary and set up so that it can record a maximum amount of action with a minimum number of angle changes. This relative immobility and the longish time individual shots were allowed to remain on the screen emphasized the movement of the players and the inventiveness of what they did. So did the fact that movement tended not to be into the depth of the screen but across it, enhancing the illusion of speed. It was all deceptively simple, and it remains, for some anyway, a classic film style, the essence of the action picture, whether comic or melodramatic in intent.

Fortunately, no one was thinking along these lines at the time. They were simply trying to solve the practical problems of making pictures in time to satisfy the release schedule, to remain within the budget, and to please audiences as often as possible. One gains above all from the pictures of Lloyd's transitional period a sense of generosity. Short as they are, they are packed tight with gags. Indeed, toward the end of 1920, Lloyd and his staff ceased to concern themselves with squeezing everything into two reels, and despite the fact that the Pathé contract specified this length, fell into the habit of allowing their wealth of material to dictate length. This now meant expansion to three reels. Under no obligation to pay more for these longer films, Pathé did so anyway — though not as much more as Lloyd felt they might have paid. However, as Lloyd gently put it, even if the extra money was "not so much as we could have forced from them by balking . . . we preferred to keep faith and to build our future rather than immediate profits." Or, to put it another way, his patience was the product of a growing realization that he was acquiring the only power a performer ever acquires — star power, which is based on the ability to withhold oneself from the public, secure in the knowledge that one will be missed by them and, more important, that the profits to be derived from their favor will be even more sorely missed by producers and distributors. In a very short while Lloyd would outstrip anyone's ability to hold him to a mere salary and percentage arrangements. Distributors would be happy to accept a percentage from him in order to secure the privilege of distributing his films.

In 1920, however, he was still a year or so away from the big money of feature film production. The first two films he would do with Newmeyer would be humble two-reelers. But the films themselves looked toward the future. Newmeyer's first film, *Get Out and Get Under,* now seems almost a sketch for later, more elaborate productions that would also feature sequences involving

55

automobiles driven at high speeds and with only the most casual regard for both the speed laws and the laws of Newtonian physics. Again, the situation is simple enough. Lloyd wakens from a bad dream in which Mildred, his girl friend, seems to be marrying another man. He is so shaken by the dream that he decides to visit her and heads for his garage and his handsome new Model T. There are various contretemps involved simply in getting the thing started and moving out of the garage — the door keeps blowing shut on him, and he puts the car into first instead of reverse and exits the garage through a back wall. Then something goes wrong with the motor and Lloyd opens the hood to see what's wrong. He leans farther and farther in searching for the trouble until eventually he is swallowed up entirely in the innards of the car.

In later years, Lloyd would single out this gag as quite out of the ordinary for him. "As a rule," he told Kevin Brownlow, the devoted collector of early movie people's reminiscences, "when I put on the glasses, I never did anything you couldn't believe in. It may be a little improbable, but you could figure it could happen." This routine, of course, was totally without realistic base, since the audience had already seen the car moving smartly along, implying that it was equipped with a motor. Obviously there would be no way for the comedian to disappear completely under the hood unless it were motorless. But, as Lloyd said, it was of no importance, since the idea itself was so deliciously funny. Moreover, he pointed out, Model T's were held to be such elegantly simple and rugged machines, requiring so little maintenance, that people often said that it seemed they had no motors. The sequence, therefore, had an agreeable satirical overtone.

Nor did Lloyd linger over the gag. He was off and running again before anyone had time to think very long about this break with realism, or allow it to spoil their fun. The motorist gets himself tangled up in a parade; finds himself atop a railroad flatcar (and is doused as the train passes under a water tank); and then acquires pursuing motorcycle cops, whom he further infuriates by heading up a street closed for repairs. He makes a temporary escape by hurtling into a moving van which carries him away in secret for a while. Before he finally arrives at his destination he manages both to drive his car into a tent (the tent then moving off under the eyes of his befuddled pursuers), and to get his car hooked to the back of a streetcar — which hauls him off in the opposite direction from the frustrated cops.

As we will see, the whole notion of Lloyd attempting to control an automobile that seems to have a will — almost a life — of its own would reach its highest development in *Hot Water* in 1924. And the tent gag, greatly elaborated, would reappear in *Professor Beware*, Lloyd's second-from-last film, in 1938. Sometimes when he returned to material he had used before it is difficult to say whether he was trying to perfect his work, like a writer revising his works for the collected edition, or whether he was falling back on the tried and the true.

Perhaps it does not matter. Silent comedy relied so heavily on familiar conventions — whether a runaway motor car or a busybody mother-in-law — that there was almost no way to avoid repeating certain situations, and Lloyd was more successful than many comedians in keeping such conventions from turning into clichés. Indeed, one of the most obvious things about these transitional films is their fecundity of invention. Lloyd's growing staff of writers was obviously learning to work well together. No one at the time gave the audience more jokes, more intricately linked, than they, and as the decade grew older, only Keaton and Laurel and Hardy offered serious competition in this respect.

Not that all of Lloyd's films required getting the comedian into some exotic predicament in order to draw laughs. He and his staff were capable of making a quite satisfactory film within extremely tight and highly naturalistic situations. For example, there is the 1921 two-reeler, *I Do,* which involves the comedian in nothing more complicated than a night's baby-sitting for his brother-in-law. In it he gets good laughs out of the simple business of trying to pour milk from a dairy bottle to a baby's bottle without a funnel. After making a fine mess of the job, he satisfies the younger of his two charges by painting the bottle white, creating the illusion for the baby that he's sucking at a full bottle. The picture's second reel is largely devoted to a limited-means chase. A burglar is reported prowling the neighborhood and Lloyd mistakes the creakings of the house for the sounds of a break-in. A balloon with a face painted on it floats by and spooks him; so do the erratic movements of a cat who gets tangled in a stocking (see the dog in the hat in *High and Dizzy*). In the end he manages to set off his older charge's toy rockets and wake everyone up. His misadventures so frighten the prowler that he is grateful to fall into the arms of the waiting police. That was the way of things when "The Boy" was around. Like Lloyd himself, his obvious desire to please, no matter how clumsily he went about it, excused his lapses. In fact, awful as the problems he created for himself were, they had an uncanny way of turning out not just happily for him, but also in some unexpected way, happily for others. In an eager, optimistic time, he proved, in his cockeyed way, many of our unspoken assumptions about the world.

It is well to bear in mind Stan Laurel's characterization of Lloyd as a "smart" comedian. He may have worked only four variations on his basic screen character (poor dreamer, go-getter, idle fop, and later, absent-minded professor), and he may have made only two basic types of films (thrill comedies and character comedies), but he utilized a rich variety of settings for The Boy, and he would eagerly enter any situation, be it exotic or humdrum, if his gagmen could convince him that within it he could find what he needed to cram a film with comedy. More important, as he proved with *I Do,* Lloyd was an extremely disciplined craftsman. If not a creative gagman himself, he was a shrewd judge of his own strengths and weaknesses, in effect an expert managing editor of the

diverse talents he employed and an intelligent critic of his own capabilities and limitations.

There were some who believed it was Lloyd who introduced the practice of previewing films, since he would take them to an outlying theater in the Los Angeles area to see how they played before an ordinary audience and then make additions or cuts based on its response. He was not, in fact, the first to do this (Griffith, in 1915, previewed *The Birth of a Nation* at Riverside, California), but he may have been the first to preview short — and by industry standards, unimportant — comedies. Like all his other 1921 films, *I Do* had been intended as a three-reeler and it was at this length that it was previewed. As it received only a mild reception, Lloyd took the film back to the studio and cut it by a third, leaving no internal evidence in the surviving film that such a radical cut had been made. He thus turned *I Do* into a success comparable to that of the other Lloyd films of the time. He would repeat this process many times in the future, as would many of his peers. It may be, in fact, that one of the hidden secrets of the success of silent comedy lay in the tightness of construction that everyone from Sennett onward insisted upon. All, with the possible exception of Chaplin in his later years, preferred too little exposition to too much.

Lloyd's manner of making a film, however, may have required more previewing and more editing after judging audience response than most. And there lies a paradox. For such a shrewd and careful man, he tended to structure his pictures in a rather haphazard way. Often he and his writers would evolve a central comic scene — for example the thrill sequence in his next picture, *Never Weaken* and then figure out a plot of some sort that would logically lead Lloyd into the situation. "We'd have a certain number of pieces of business, gags, that we knew we were going to do," he explained later. "They were called 'islands.' We knew we had to go there. But whatever we did between those was up to us. We would ad-lib, and make it up as we went along."

As he recalled, he never worked with full scripts until sound pictures forced them on him. When he started a scene he and his writers would, of course, have "made minute notes of the particular sequence we were going to shoot. We would even suspend work for three or four days to work out exactly what we wanted. But when we finished shooting, the result might be completely different from our original idea. We allowed ourselves to remain open. If something came up that was better than what we'd conceived on paper, well, we did it. If you were working to a set script, you could get yourself completely fouled up. After you've changed it a few times, you might have to throw the script away, because you'd lost yourself. This way we built as we went along, like building a house. Building was of great importance."

Indeed, Lloyd thought it was everything, and one tends to agree. He complained that later comedians didn't seem to understand this method of work. Locked into a script, they would pass up the opportunities that present

58

themselves only on the set or the stage, where one can begin to see, in practice, how one bit of business — especially physical comedy — can suggest another, which in turn suggests another, until a bright chain reaction has been created.

There were naturally hazards in this method, and they may partially account for the discounting of Lloyd's abilities in later years. For one thing, large groups of gag writers, bouncing ideas back and forth, concentrating all their attention on a relatively constricted problem — a comic sketch lasting three or four minutes, for example — can turn inspiration up to a very high pitch. But as a rule such groups are much less effective than one or two men when it comes to the more sober business of creating a long, sensibly sustained plot line. Here, wild leaps are not a virtue, and quiet, subtle analysis of characters and their interaction is required. Chaplin, as the years went on, could have used some gagmen. Lloyd, on the other hand, could have used (since he lacked the skill himself) a character man to deepen and broaden the figure he played, to help him fill out the sketchy itinerary that generally took him from "island" to "island."

Or perhaps what he and his people needed to develop — and which might not have been beyond them — was a sense of what Buster Keaton called "the mathematical calculations required to work out a gag." It was this ability to fine-tune a film that Keaton, who placed tight, unifying limits on his basic situations, possessed in much greater measure than any of his peers and that lies at the center of his superiority to Lloyd. His films, Simone de Beauvoir has recently and rightly said, "give the same aesthetic pleasure as the elegant solution of a mathematical problem." Lloyd could achieve this elegance in an occasional sequence, rarely, if ever, for the length of an entire picture; his "islands" too often possessed radically differing climates and topographies.

It is all too clear that his pictures were built backward most of the time. The gags did not flow out of some controlling central idea, but rather this idea — when it could be said to exist at all — was an afterthought, a flimsy vehicle used to get from one "island" to the next. Or, to employ a different metaphor, one could say that the heart (sometimes hearts) ticking away at the center of Lloyd's pictures was a mechanical thing, sometimes an inspired contrivance, but always a contrivance, offering none of the rich satisfaction either of well-observed psychology or of a comedic new math. Hence, much of the lack of favor he has found with posterity.

Judging Lloyd's work, therefore, involves a frustrating trade-off. Given the inspired quality of his best gag sequences, it is hard to say that he and his team should have worked less improvisationally or thought a little more about plot in the larger sense and character in the deeper sense. There are only so many hours in the day, and one would hate to have missed the magnificent flights of humor they often managed in their single-minded concentration on the isolated gag. Yet something is missing here, some warmth, some more powerful sense of identification with Lloyd that one sometimes yearns to make, a final closing of

59

Never Weaken was only three reels long, but it was among the best of Lloyd's high-rise comedies. Note the glove.

the distance between the figure on the screen and those of us watching him in the audience.

But one must resist too facile a judgment of a film like *Never Weaken,* the immediate successor to *I Do* and the last of Lloyd's shorts. It is perfectly true that its genesis was simply a desire to do another film in which Lloyd found himself clinging perilously to some dangerous perch. It is perfectly true, as well, that he and his people knew they were imitating themselves. And it must be admitted that they were obviously straining to find a suitable motive for getting Lloyd — and the picture — off the ground. Nonetheless, it ranks among his most brilliant movies.

The film begins with Lloyd and Mildred mooning at each other from adjoining windows high in an ofice building. She works for a chiropractor with an extremely mediocre practice. He thinks he might ingratiate himself with her — that need of his again — if he can improve her boss's practice. So with an acrobat as an assistant, he starts working the streets, the acrobat taking horrendous falls, Lloyd hurrying up to "cure" him and then passing out the chiropractor's cards to bystanders (a variation on the gag in *High and Dizzy*). Finally, some soap chips get mixed up with a rush of water loosed by a street cleaner, making the roadway extraordinarily slippery and causing enough accidents to crowd the quack's waiting room. Alas, it seems to Harold his efforts are for naught, for he gains the mistaken impression that Mildred loves another and he decides to commit suicide.

One may pause to wonder at this optimistic young man's predilection for self-destruction. It is a great gag setup, naturally, but also, without laboring the point, one should note that a cheerful exterior often masks dark impulses, especially among middle-class Americans, even when they are impersonated by Harold Lloyd. Surely it is worth remarking that audiences accepted this without cavil, as a perfectly realistic impulse. The fact that Lloyd always rendered it as an absurdity helped, of course. In this instance, he finds himself comically blocked in his efforts to write a poetic farewell note. "Without you," he scribbles, "life would be a hollow. . . ." The word he wants is sepulcher. But he can't spell it.

Oh, well. On with the job. His first thought is poison, but even after he's added sugar to it, he finds the taste unbearable. He then tries to run himself through with a paper spindle, but that's impossible. Finally, he strings the trigger of a revolver to the door handle, places himself, blindfolded, in a chair facing the gun (which is, in turn, secured to another chair), and awaits fate to knock and then try the door. Instead, a nearby photographer fires off some flash powder, and he faints at the noise of the explosion, convinced he's gone to his reward.

Just at that moment, however, some workmen are hauling an I-beam into place on the skyscraper being built across the street. Inadvertently it swings in through Lloyd's window, inserts itself under his chair, and swings him, still unconscious, out over the street. There he awakens, and the first sound he hears

is an angelic harp. He is convinced that he has ascended to Heaven, though the audience knows he is merely overhearing a music lesson going on in an office above his. Whereupon he works his blindfold off, only to confront the face of an angel — in actuality one of the decorations on the building.

The sounds of a jazz band rehearsing finally convince him that he is still among the living and alert him to his peril. The crane operators swing the beam on which he's perched back to the construction site, and there follows a glorious thrill sequence. Lloyd is so frightened that he closes his eyes while walking the girders, and steps off into space. Luckily he catches another beam that is being hauled into place just as he falls. But when he tries to catch a girder already attached to the building's skeleton, the beam he is riding swings away again and he is caught in the position of a man trying to hold onto a dock while the boat he's standing in drifts away. And so it goes for an excruciating ten minutes. If there's a red hot rivet around, you may be sure Lloyd will sit on it. If someone has left a wrench lying about, you may be sure he will slip on it. And if there is a funnier short comedy in the history of the American screen, one would like to know about it.

Lloyd finally makes it back to terra firma. There he discovers that the man he thought was his rival is in fact Mildred's brother — and a clergyman to boot, so he can marry them. That is a neat topper, the perfect end to a logical nightmare.

The picture may have little to say about the human condition, but it has a tensile strength as sturdy as the girders that figure so prominently in it. The introductory sequence is strong in itself and neatly sets up the character and the situation that are shortly to be developed. And the almost classic unity of the final sequence, combined with the incredible number of variations Lloyd works on the basic situation — a frightened man in a business suit unaccountably forced to contend with high steel — is a little miracle of comic ingenuity.

Never Weaken was not planned as Lloyd's farewell to short films — it just turned out that way. Nevertheless, it was an appropriate ending to this phase of his career. His character was now fully formed and he had developed a comic style that manifestly had the potential to extend itself and sustain longer films. Finally, in this last of the three-reelers he had put everything together in a masterful orchestration that builds and builds and builds, without letup, yet without frenzy, pulling us gently but firmly into a little world at once mad and logical. We are then released at just the right moment, the moment just prior to the one in which pleasure turns to pain.

Truth to tell, Lloyd's next picture, and his first feature, was not nearly so fine as *Never Weaken*. *A Sailor-Made Man* was in no sense tailor-made. It is the story of an idle youth ("It's too hot to play croquet, let's get married . . .") laying suit to an heiress (see the one-reeler *Ask Father* for precedents). He is required by her tycoon father to prove himself capable of holding a steady job. He

wanders into the nearest Navy recruiting station and, in the movie's funniest sequence, offers himself to a not very grateful nation. In his insufferable way, he attempts to lay down a number of conditions which the Navy will have to meet if he is to favor it with his presence. Infuriated, the recruiters decide to teach him a lesson by enlisting him despite his obvious uselessness.

Much else of small consequence and little comic tension follows as Harold gains his sea legs. In the end, his ship puts into a Middle Eastern port just as his fiancée — played by Mildred Davis — and her father pull in on their yacht. The local rajah has her abducted for his harem, and Harold rescues her, in a rally not much advanced from those of the early Sennet days. The careful buildup of the previous picture is entirely missing and all that one recalls are one or two isolated gags — Harold using a eunuch's spear as a pole vault to gain entrance to the palace, Harold using the pipe from a hookah as an underwater breathing device when he hides from a small army of pursuers in a harem pool.

The film shows its casual method of construction. Forty-five years later, responding to a question from a student at a seminar, Lloyd would recall, "We started out for two reels but we seemed to have so much material that we were loath to stop, so Roach said, 'Why the hell don't we just let it go and see where . . . and it turned out to be a four-reeler." Roach, to his credit, backed his hunch that he had a near-feature in the making by spending heavily on it. The harem is an extraordinarily decorative one, at least in comparison to what one had come to expect from the economy-minded Roach studio, and it is very well populated with both odalisques and guards. One suspects Roach saw in these scenes an opportunity to ape Sennett's bevies of bathing beauties and hordes of cops. Then, too, comedy films, like almost all American movies of the time, had been spurred on by De Mille's opulent example and were growing more lavish. The money was there to spend and the prosperous era of the 1920s was at hand. People were simply more in a mood for lavish entertainments than they had been before, especially at the movies.

In any event the film was a success. And it had its admirers. Gilbert Seldes, the pioneering critic of popular culture, did not like Lloyd, whom he called "a man of no tenderness, no philosophy, the embodiment of American cheek and indefatigable energy." Writing sometime before 1924, he went on to say, "There is no poetry in him, his whole utterance being epigrammatic, without overtone or image." One cannot forbear to remark that one of the troubles with silent movies was that too many people perceived in them opportunities for poetic statement and too many film-makers believed them, resulting in a cloying pretentiousness that makes many of the movies most highly respected in their time nearly unwatchable today. But let that pass. The point is that Seldes exempted *A Sailor-Made Man* from his strictures about Lloyd precisely because he saw glints of the old Sennett madness in it. "Here the old frenzy fell upon him, the

weakling won by guile, and instead of fighting one man he laid out a mob from behind; something excessive, topsy-turvy, riotous at last occurred in his ordered existence.''

Maybe so. Certainly it did well enough to establish beyond doubt that Lloyd could carry a feature picture. But the basic fact remains that the rally — which is all Seldes was praising in the film — was held in exclusive patent by Mack Sennett. The Lloyd-Roach team never did achieve the divine lunacy with this device that its originator did — or that Keaton achieved, for example in *Cops,* where hundreds of policemen pursue him through the dreaming streets. The long, climactic scene in *A Sailor-Made Man* was just not as intricately mad as the works of Sennett or Keaton when they explored this vein.

And, it would seem that Lloyd never really liked the device. Maybe Seldes was correct when he remarked, ''I figure him as a step toward gentility.'' Surely he was possessed by the desire to do something with more character, or at least more ''acting'' in the conventional sense of the term, than he had been doing. His next two movies prove it so.

The first of them, *Grandma's Boy,* was based on an idea Lloyd said he'd had for many years and which he claimed he had tried and failed to make as a one-reeler some years earlier. The story is simple — a brutal vagabond is terrorizing a rural neighborhood and Lloyd shows himself to be the most cowardly of all the locals in dealing with the threat. His grandmother tells him that his grandfather had been similarly afflicted when he was a youth fighting in the Civil War. He, however, had a talisman which gave him the courage to be a great hero. As she tells the story, there is a flashback and we find Lloyd playing the grandfather, wearing square horn-rims to suggest antiquity. She then gives Lloyd the talisman and he goes out and proves himself. Only at the end does he discover that the talisman is nothing but an old umbrella handle and that his grandmother was practicing home-remedy psychology on him.

The picture was more difficult to craft than any Lloyd had attempted, or perhaps would ever attempt. Again, he had begun with something quite modest in mind — two reels perhaps — and again the work had grown on him — unhealthily at first. ''Never mind the footage,'' he would remember saying. ''Let's just go as long as we want to . . . we'll develop it the way we think it should be developed.'' It came out at five reels, and he and Roach, bringing Mildred and Roach's wife with them, took it to Pasadena for a preview. It was, in Lloyd's recollection, ''a great disappointment,'' in Roach's, ''a flop.'' They stood outside the theater (or perhaps they sat in one of their cars — their memories don't square on this point) arguing about what to do. Roach complained that Lloyd had ''put into it — while I was busy with an Our Gang picture — a lot of drama about the Civil War,'' and argued that the picture could be saved simply by excising this material and putting in some gags. Lloyd agreed, but did not want to go as far as

Roach in cutting out what he regarded as the picture's very reason for existence. As Lloyd was to reconstruct their discussion later, it went like this:

Hal said, "Look, Harold, we are making comedies. We are doing things to make people laugh. Let's get back to the kind of pictures we should make."

I said, "Hal, this has got heart. It's different from what we've ever done. It's much finer. It's really got feeling."

"But it hasn't got any laughs."

"Hal, you're absolutely right. Maybe we'd better go back and build a lot more laughs into this picture."

"I'll say we'd better," he said.

And it was done, painstakingly and over an extraordinary length of time. The entire production required some six months, an unheard-of schedule for a five-reel comedy running around an hour. There were, of course, some further mistakes. They tried a little animated figure called Icky, who was to represent the voice of Harold's good and bad conscience, but that seemed strained as well as unfunny. And there were many more previews. Robert E. Sherwood, later playwright and Presidential advisor, then a movie critic, went along with Lloyd to one of the last ones. He reported that Lloyd told the theater manager that he wanted the film run with no advance announcement and with no muscial accompaniment. "I want it to be cold turkey. If they like it this way, I'll know it's pretty near right."

The film went well that night, but Lloyd, who impressed Sherwood with "how keenly and intelligently he can criticize his own work," found flaws and took it back to the studio to work on it further. The result was an enormous success, perhaps the greatest Lloyd had achieved to date.

Sherwood evaluated the finished product and set the line that has been followed ever since in discussing Lloyd. "This buoyant, bespectacled comedian is an apostle of the American faith: he represents the personification of pep, spontaneity, and determination. He is a natural-born world-beater." He also praised his humor as being "as native to these United States as George Ade's, as opposed to the 'continental' style of Chaplin and the English Music Hall style of Keaton." In New York, *The Times* greeted the film as "amusing nearly always and hilarious a good part of the time," though it perceptively noted that Lloyd was blending Chaplin and Fairbanks to create his character. Roach was less reserved. When all was said and done, he felt *Grandma's Boy* "was the best picture we ever made."

So did Lloyd, possibly because he thought that despite "sorting" some twenty new gags through the film, "we never lost any of our theme. I wouldn't let go of one inch of it." Why, he added, "it could have been a drama just as

easily as a comedy,'' for ''if you wanted a tragic picture of a coward, you could do it just as well with this theme.''

Possibly. All one can say is that the picture obviously satisfied some of Lloyd's ambitions in a way that is not readily apparent on the screen. As the reviews of the time testify, it was received as an intelligent, well-made comedy, though one of no extraordinary significance. And there is nothing in it to make one think today that the critics of the time missed something. Lloyd would go on to make at least four or five films that seem superior to it, and it is hard to understand why he thought so highly of it. His characterization of the cowardly youth is, to be sure, a minor departure for him, because though he had often registered fear upon discovering himself in some tight or tricky spot, he rarely posited cowardice as a full-scale character defect. On the other hand, one cannot say that he presented cowardice in a particularly subtle or original way. The idea of the historical flashback was, of course, relatively novel at the time — particularly in a comedy. But again, it is really just an occasion for a rather amusing rally, with Lloyd as a Confederate spy intent on stealing some plans from a Union headquarters and in the process befuddling a number of staff officers and sentries. When, inspired by the talismanic umbrella handle, he leads the pursuit of the villain, there is a wonderfully comic intensity in his activities. There is also good suspense as he sneaks up on the isolated shack where the itinerant has gone to ground. But Lloyd was always determinedly sober in such situations. That was, in fact, The Whole Joke about him, the fact that he was so concentrated on his goal, however ludicrous, that he never sensed how absurd he seemed to others.

In evaluating the film it must be noted that the best sequence is one so limited in intention and in comic material that it could easily have stood alone as a Lloyd one-reeler a few years previously. In it, a shy and inept Lloyd comes courting at Mildred Davis's house. He has gone to some pains for the occasion, having taken his grandfather's old Sunday suit out of mothballs and shined his shoes with goose grease. His odoriferous pains, of course, merely attract all the kittens in the house, and Lloyd's attempts to keep his cool while carrying on a spirited conversation with his girl and fend off the animals is a brilliant little study in embarrassment. The embarrassment grows more profound when his rival, who is also the sheriff (played by Noah Young, the most reliable heavy in Lloyd's little stock company) turns up. Lloyd discovers several stray mothballs in his suit pocket and gently deposits them in a candy box from which both he and his rival partake. The result is simply gorgeous. Large laughs grow from just such tiny acorns in the world of silent comedy, and somehow they are often more memorable than the effects people labored more expensively, more expansively, upon.

Still, if Harold was pleased to think *Grandma's Boy* deeper and more psychologically acute, than his other films, if in his own mind he perceived the

film as — perish the word — "Chaplinesque" and therefore perhaps an instrument to silence critics who insisted on contrasting their work, then who cared to dispute him? For the picture was an enormous success, and since his old contract for three-reelers with Pathé had run out, he went back to New York to make a new deal. It called for Lloyd to make six films of five reels or more in length. Production funds would be advanced by Pathé and Lloyd would receive eighty percent of the profits. With the remaining twenty percent split between Roach and the distributor, it is clear that Lloyd was very close to being master of his own destiny.

Certainly the trip to New York convinced Roach, if he needed any convincing, that Lloyd was at last a star of the very first magnitude. "The news photographers were everywhere," Roach recalled. "They used to set off those flashes that made a great smoke. They followed us into the Biltmore Lobby and filled the lobby with this choking smoke until the hotel people ran them out. Then we went up to our suite and the photographers sneaked up to Harold's room and began firing flashes again until the room was full of smoke and somebody opened the window to let the smoke out. Across the street somebody saw all this smoke . . . and called the fire department. Now, instead of the photographers, they threw us out of the hotel. We went over to the Ambassador."

In some ways Lloyd was lucky in his celebrity. He was such an ordinary looking man that without his spectacles — which of course he never wore off-screen — he could generally pass unrecognized in a crowd. He once made a bet that he could stand outside the Rivoli Theater in New York when one of his pictures was playing and never be recognized by the audience filing out. He took his stance — and everyone brushed right past him. In fact, it amused him to recall an incident that happened when he and Doug Fairbanks, with whom he used to pal around, were in New York and went for a stroll on Fifth Avenue. Crowds immediately collected and swarmed all over Fairbanks while the equally famous Lloyd retired quietly to the sidelines to observe with considerable amusement his friend's difficulties. It should be recorded that Fairbanks had his revenge. Once he and his wife, Mary Pickford, went to a Hollywood premiere with Lloyd and as they exited the Fairbankses were mobbed. When they reached the safety of their limousine, Fairbanks looked out the window for Lloyd and found him swallowed up by the crowd, yelling and making faces at his beleaguered friends. Fairbanks rolled down the window, held up his hand for silence and cried: "Ladies and gentlemen, I should like to make an announcement. That man right there" — and he pointed dramatically — "is the famous Harold Lloyd." The crowd deserted the Fairbankses for Lloyd, and Fairbanks gave the signal to drive off — laughing uproariously.

But that is the only recorded moment of public difficulty for Harold Lloyd, the celebrity. Mostly, he went his way quietly. The comedy studios of the 1920s

67

were a world apart from that larger world apart, Hollywood. The films made on these tiny lots were not generally high-risk ventures. Costs remained relatively low, and so long as a Chaplin, a Lloyd, a Keaton, were present in the feature-length pictures, they were guaranteed profitability. As for the short comedies, they involved almost no risk at all since their bookings were almost automatic in those days prior to the double feature. As a result, they inexpensively absorbed a lot of overhead. The result was a low-pressure atmosphere. The leading producers and stars kept their creative teams around them for years and required no vast armies of technicians to create the huge sets and glittering costumes that the historical and romantic dramas of the day needed. Nor did they have to hype the product with excesses of publicity, which meant that the leading players had no need to venture forth to places where their pictures would be taken. They were, indeed, among the last people in the motion picture business who could go about it in the old way — quietly, economically, concentrating exclusively on the job at hand.

This was particularly true of the Roach operation, where the hard-driving, tight-fisted leader insisted on dedicated work and no fooling around. This policy was beginning to pay off in unexpected ways. By 1922 Hollywood had been grievously — some feared mortally — wounded by scandal. It had been revealed that the beautiful Wallace Reid was a junkie. Worse, Sennett's leading comedian, a man many felt would have rivaled the great comic stars of the era had his career been allowed to develop, was undergoing the public humiliation of three trials for manslaughter in San Francisco. The first two ended in hung juries, and it was not until the third public recital of a sordid incident that Roscoe ("Fatty") Arbuckle was cleared of any wrongdoing. The case involved the strange death of an extra girl named Virginia Rappe, who died of complications following injuries sustained in a sexual orgy. Arbuckle was ruined. Everyone's worst suspicions about Hollywood were further confirmed when, a little later, Mary Miles Minter, an ingenue in Chaplin films, and the beloved Mabel Normand, Sennett's girl friend as well as his leading comedienne, were implicated — the latter quite innocently — in the death of director (and possible dope dealer) William Desmond Taylor. All of this contributed to the decline of Sennett's reputation, which had always been, at least locally, a rather raffish one. (Producer Walter Wanger once remarked that at dinner parties at Mack's home if you didn't take the girl on your right upstairs between the soup and the main course, you were considered a homosexual.) The clean, non-anarchistic work of Roach appeared attractive in contrast, and Lloyd's seemed particularly so. That gentility Seldes had complained about obviously had its uses.

Gentility — combined with his ongoing desire to give greater character depth to his comic roles — led Lloyd in his next film to an unprecedented dullness. *Dr. Jack* is the story of a small-town doctor, a man not especially well versed in the latest medical theories but with a lot of common sense. He is introduced making

an emergency call at a mad clip — to aid a patient who turns out to be a little girl's broken doll. Which he patiently mends. He later applies psychology to get a freckle-faced truant out of bed and to school, uses more of the same to cheer up an old lady whose only ill is loneliness, and is glimpsed encouraging old men to take an interest in life by engaging them in rather violent sports. Never was Lloyd's basic optimism, his belief in a positive approach to life, more in evidence. However, there is something busybodyish about him, as when he breaks up a poker game in which one of his patients seems about to lose his rent money. The scene is good, with Lloyd slyly stacking the deck (while it's in play) so that everyone comes out with identical hands. But there is also a not very subtle pandering here and elsewhere in the film to small-town moralism, a sense of the comedian reinforcing the puritan and anti-cosmopolitan values of a portion of his audience.

This is particularly true when he is called to the city to consult in the case of the "sick little well girl," played by Mildred Davis. She is an heiress who has fallen into the hands of a quack, one Dr. Ludwig Von Soulsberg, who is deliberately making an invalid of her so that he can continue collecting huge fees from her father. "Excitement" is what Lloyd prescribes for her, and he proceeds to provide it by pretending that an escaped lunatic has gained access to the family mansion. He both plays the lunatic and participates in the chase for him (which requires some incredibly quick changes at full gallop). This climactic sequence has an undeniable excitement, but it is also more strained in conception and frenzied in execution than was generally true of the endings of his feature films. It is almost as if he were overcompensating for the softness of the film's first half. As frequently happened in his lesser films, there is an inability to bridge the difference in mood between the parts of the whole, and the overall result is unsatisfying. The picture, however, was apparently every bit as popular as its predecessors; *The New York Times* called it "an exceedingly bright and engaging comedy."

Lloyd's next feature, *Safety Last,* is also rather patchy in construction, and takes a long time to get going. Again one has the sense of Lloyd and his gagmen in possession of only one basic gag and trying to stretch the material around it to feature length. That one gag, however, is so brilliant, and so magnificently developed that it quite blots out the *longueurs* that precede it. It is his famous "human fly" routine, in which he found his immortality — as the man hanging from the face of a clock a couple of hundred feet above the street.

There seems little question that Lloyd felt at the time that he had been earthbound long enough. With the relatively danger-free *Grandma's Boy* and *Dr. Jack* behind him, it was time to reassert his greatest claim to originality, as the most physically daring of comedians.

The specific idea occurred to him one afternoon in downtown Los Angeles when he stopped to watch Bill Strothers, who made his living as a "human fly,"

crawl up the face of an office building in aid of publicizing something or other. "The higher he climbed, the more nervous I grew," Loyd was to recall, "until, when he came to a difficult ledge twelve stories up, I had to cut around a corner out of sight of him and peek back to see if he was over the ledge." A rather obvious question then occurred to him. "If it makes me this jumpy, what would it do to a picture audience, I asked myself. The more I thought about it, the better I liked it."

So he set to work in the gag room, building a story that would somehow get him out on the highest limb of his career. It was simple enough. He is a small town boy who comes to the city to make good, that is, to make enough money to send for the girl he leaves behind (Mildred again). Unfortunately, the only opportunity that presents itself is clerking in a department store, where his career is comically undistinguished. One of his best bits involves being late to work and having to sneak by a supervisor, which he does by dressing himself to resemble the manikins that a workman is bringing into the store, and then being carried in past the floorwalker. There is also a funny sequence in which he is forced, single-handed, to serve a yard goods counter besieged by bargain-hungry matrons.

Alas, his letters home are so optimistic that Mildred decides to come to town for a visit and sample his prosperity first hand. This leads to a scene in which Lloyd takes over the store manager's office while he is out to lunch, pretending to Mildred that he is in charge of things. It is while lurking in the precincts of the executive suite that he proposes to the boss that a human fly be engaged to generate publicity for the store, and he is taken up on the offer.

Strothers himself, cast in the picture as Lloyd's best friend and roommate, demonstrates his skills by employing them to elude a policeman he and Lloyd have annoyed. When the day of the great climb arrives, the same cop is on duty in front of the store; he spots Strothers and gives chase. With a crowd already gathered and the store officials impatiently eyeing their watches, Strothers signals to Lloyd to begin the climb, indicating that he will replace him on one of the higher floors as soon as he eludes his pursuer. Needless to say, he never does, and Lloyd must go all the way to the top.

His trip is one of the most famous sequences in movie history and there is little point in describing it in detail. Suffice to say that the topper to the clock gag is delicately ingenious — an exhausted and by now thoroughly frightened Lloyd, clinging to a ledge and trying to get hold of himself, finds a mouse running up his pants leg. The gagmen, sensing the impossibility of doing anything more spectacular than the business with the clock, very sensibly went for the most vivid imaginable contrast, placing Lloyd in too-close conjunction with one of nature's smallest and most familiar annoyances. It brings the whole sequence back into scale. After all he's suffered, to be assaulted by this most mundane of creatures is just too much.

70

A belief has grown that Lloyd did these and other dangerous stunts without doubles or safety equipment of any kind. But as he was always quick to admit, that was not strictly true. Strothers, for example, doubled for him in a few long shots of the climb and there was a platform some three stories below him when he was doing the more dangerous stunts in the sequence. Still, as Lloyd said, "who wants to fall three stories . . . ?" He noted as well that the safety platform was quite small and that when as an experiment a dummy was dropped from Lloyd's position, it bounced right off and continued on a sickening journey to the street below, just as a stunned man might have. Perhaps the most telling comment on the whole enterprise came from a palmist who undertook to read Lloyd's hand not long after he had finished the sequence. Feeling the calluses he had built up while making it, she guessed that he made his living at manual labor.

Lloyd understood that much of the scene's effectiveness was the result of the camera set-ups arranged by Newmeyer and his new co-director, Sam Taylor (a one-time student for the priesthood at Fordham). They were careful to stress the height at which Lloyd was working in almost every shot, avoiding close-ups and frequent changes of angle that would have encouraged speculation about the whole thing being done with mirrors or some trick. The strategy worked brilliantly — still does, for that matter.

Despite the brilliance of the one sequence, the friendly Sherwood judged Safety Last "a mechanical effort which lacks the usual spontaneity and buoyancy of a Harold Lloyd comedy," though he admitted that it was "marvelously ingenious" and "brimming with tricks that are calculated to tickle the ribs and chill the spine at one and the same moment." Later critics, like Nelson E. Garringer, who did the career article on Lloyd for Films in Review, says, "By general agreement, including Lloyd's, it is his best picture . . . for the combination of screams and laughs is hard to beat."

Sherwood's original judgment is doubtless closer to the mark. Once Lloyd is high enough on the building to be in genuine danger, there are almost no gags as such, only ineptitudes. Though they pull laughter from us, their primary purpose is to enhance our sense of his peril. There is nothing of the satirical quality of the angel and harp bits in Never Weaken, for example. Perhaps one feels more for Lloyd in the earlier film because he is so clearly an innocent victim of a string of unfortunate coincidences. Here, he is largely the victim of his own ambitions, with the option of giving them up at any time and extricating himself from his predicament. No such option exists in Never Weaken. Not only does it have — to risk a rather grand phrase — an element of existential absurdity and terror that is missing from Safety Last, but it has a greater resonance for modern audiences, who are familiar with the way the modern world and its great works (the skyscraper across the street in Never Weaken is a fine symbol in this regard) can impinge on our privacy, force us to cope with its presence as well as we can, without assistance or even sympathy from the institution that has caused our

Harold and Mildred Davis. as they appeared in their last
film before marriage, *Safety Last,* made in 1923 · The Bridge and Groom .

anguish. Finally, looking forward, one could say that simply in terms of complexity and sustained perils, the building climb in *Feet First* of 1930 is superior in invention to the *Safety Last* sequence.

Still, *Safety Last* strikes one as by far the best of Lloyd's features to date, the patchiness of its construction overwhelmed by the humor and excitement the great climb generated. In fact, it is possible to see the film as the beginning of the golden period of Lloyd's career. In the next five years he would complete seven more movies, only one of which was without some merit, three of which would rank, each in its own way, among the finest of his creations. Moreover, this would be the time of his greatest personal happiness, his greatest prestige and popularity. And, incidentally, in this time he would transform himself into one of the wealthiest men in show business, the only performer in *Variety's* list of the top twenty in 1927, which otherwise drew its membership from the entrepreneurial class.*

7   This new phase in Lloyd's life began with his marriage, included the birth of his first child, final breaks with Roach and Pathé, the establishment of his own studio, and the creation of the legendary hilltop home on Benedict Canyon in Beverly Hills, perhaps the greatest of show-biz's showplace estates, infinitely more elaborate — if not as socially prominent — as Pickfair. The period would end with the coming of sound, which Lloyd, unlike many of his comic peers, found himself capable of unhesitatingly, and for the most part profitably, embracing.

Lloyd's story of his marriage to Mildred Davis bears, up to a point, a suspicious resemblance to the story of the last phases of his relationship with Bebe Daniels. With *Safety Last,* Mildred completed her contractual obligation to Roach; according to Lloyd, she was entertaining offers from other studios and, like Miss Daniels, looking forward to working in dramatic pictures. Once again Lloyd and Roach felt they could meet the financial terms of their rivals, but not the opportunity they presented for a wider range of roles. This time, however, Lloyd was awakened in time to the prospect of a loss greater than that of an inoffensive leading lady. "It needed the prospect of losing her," he said dimly, "to bring home to me the fact, apparent for months to everyone else from the increasing ardor of my devotion, that I loved her." So he proposed, she accepted,

---

* John Ringling, the circus magnate, headed the list, with such theater owners and movie moguls as Adolph Zukor, Marcus Loew, Lee Shubert, William Fox, and Jesse Lasky ahead of Lloyd, whose net worth was estimated at fifteen million. Below him, interestingly, ranked such industry heavies as Joe and Nicholas Schenck, Carl Laemmle, and Klaw and Erlanger, the theater chain owners.

73

and they determined to marry in the quietest possible way, with only Mildred's mother, her bridesmaid (nameless in Lloyd's account), and his brother Gaylord as best man in attendance. (Note the absence of Foxy and his wife.) Unfortunately, however, his press agent, Joe Reddy, discovered their plans — or so Lloyd preferred posterity to believe — and reporters were at Mildred's home when the great day arrived. She hid on the floor of the car Lloyd had sent for her and instructed the chauffeur to drive her to Lloyd's house. A little later, when they approached the church, the newsmen were waiting. They drove away, returned later, found the press still present, and then made a deal with them. The bridal couple would pose after the wedding if the photographers would agree not to violate the ceremony. And so on February 10, 1923, it was done. The Lloyds took an extraordinarily modest wedding trip, ten days in San Diego followed by four days at a bungalow at the Ambassador Hotel in Los Angeles — before Harold reported back for work on his new picture. A week thereafter they moved out of his old home on Hoover Street, the one he had moved to when he had first begun to make a little money in the movies and which he had apparently been too preoccupied to vacate in the intervening years. The new house was on Irving Boulevard and was somewhat grander than the old one — though not grand enough to detain him for long.

For it is fair to say that at this point Lloyd was virtually alone at the top of his profession. It is perfectly true that no one ranked him as an artist with Chaplin, but Chaplin's pace had slowed considerably. He had made *The Kid* in 1920 and was now about to bring out two films, *The Pilgrim,* not one of his best or most popular comedies, and an austere drama of betrayed love, *A Woman of Paris,* which he directed but in which he appeared only in a bit role — a *flop d'estime.* A year later he would make *The Gold Rush,* perhaps the finest of his long films, but then he would wait four more years before making *The Circus.* Meantime, Stark Young, the highly respected drama critic, was advising him that "you have finished your creation" of The Little Fellow, that the character was "perfect long ago" and now showed "a falling off in invention and zest." Mr. Young advised having a go at *Liliom, He Who Gets Slapped, Peer Gynt* — in short, to do something for "culture" as it is traditionally defined. Worse, Chaplin was beginning to listen to the intellectuals, to look for new worlds to conquer. Within a couple of years he would be confessing an ambition to attempt a life of Christ — the sure sign of a movie-maker either far gone on himself or in desperate need of inspiration. "Christ had charm and a sense of humor," Chaplin would tell an interviewer. "He was what we call a mixer; yet He was always alone. . . . Nobody understood Him. . . . That is the supreme tragedy. . . ." Perhaps things were worse with him than one likes to imagine. Perhaps, always prey to the belief that no one really understood him, he had managed to identify himself with Jesus. In any event, Chaplin was manifestly beginning that long process of withdrawal into arrogant isolation that would take up the rest of his life.

As for Lloyd's other rivals, Keaton was coming on wonderfully, but his masterpieces, *Sherlock, Jr., The Navigator,* and *The General,* were still a little bit in the future. And in any event he would never be quite as accessible to the mass public as Lloyd. That frozen face. . . . What lay behind it? How could he permit some films to end with his character dead or his dreams shattered? What were we supposed to think about him? What, indeed, did he think of us? Why did he not confess, by some gesture, that need for approval which it so pleases an audience to give if it can, if only the performer will ask for it? His gags were, of course, irresistible, but the man himself was too much the enigma to attract the kind of open affection Chaplin had commanded and the comfortable familiarity Lloyd now could command. And the others? Langdon was still doing small parts. Laurel and Hardy had not yet been teamed; Charley Chase was not yet established; the French comedian Max Linder had never really made it here; Arbuckle was wiped out. In short, Lloyd was now the dominant comedian — if not in the hearts of critics (though he was certainly doing all right with them), then assuredly in the theaters, where it counted most.

Why Worry?, the picture he interrupted for marriage, could only confirm that position. He and his staff had decided it was time once again to vary his character. He had, in order, played a coward, an ordinary nice fellow, an extremely ambitious youth. Now it was time, perhaps, to do his fatuous young heir, basically the same character he had played in *A Sailor-Made Man.* This time, however, he is far gone in hypochondria, and he is introduced taking ship for "Paradiso," an island off the coast of South America renowned for its healthful climate. He is accompanied by a nurse, played by his new leading lady, Jobyna Ralston. She had been working in Roach one-reelers and was rather in the Bebe Daniels mold, both in looks and in spirit, and thus frankly an improvement over the new Mrs. Lloyd.

When Harold and friend land in Paradiso, a revolution is in progress, and Lloyd is mistaken for a counter-revolutionary whom the insurrectionists are expecting. Lloyd, of course, is sublimely oblivious to all this and strolls serenely through the final stages of the revolution, thinking all the running, shouting, and shooting he observes are simply odd local customs, perhaps part of some quaint native festival.

Once the revolutionaries are in command, they escort him to jail — not without difficulties, since Lloyd is under the impression they are a guard of honor and believes they are taking him to a hotel: he even sends their captain back to retrieve a suitcase he has forgotten. At the jail he signs what he believes is a register, but which is, in fact, a list of prisoners to be shot at dawn.

Thus far the picture had proceeded nicely, and with more pace and humorous absurdity than Lloyd had generally managed to get into the early reels of his films. Now the plot required that Lloyd's cellmate be a giant, whom the comedian would enlist to help him break out and who would become his ally in

rescuing his nurse (who had fallen into the lascivious hands of the revolutionary leader) and in restoring normalcy to the island. Unfortunately, the Ringling Brothers giant who had been engaged for the role died suddenly, and the picture was suspended while a search for a replacement was launched. There was no lack of applicants, but they were all merely big men, not truly giants. Finally, someone read a newspaper account of a huge pair of shoes a cobbler in Minneapolis had made for one of his customers, shoes only a giant could fill. They traced their purchaser, and on his way to New York on business Roach took the northern route, interviewed the man, and discovered he was, if anything, larger than the late Ringling star. His name was Johan Aasen and he was signed. And his presence is a major factor in making the film remarkable.

For he supplies the brawn to go with a brain that Harold begins to develop under the press of necessity. The giant, it seems, was captured by the revolutionary forces only because he was suffering from a terrible toothache and therefore not in fighting trim. In order to restore him to full fettle, Lloyd must yank the offending tooth. To do that he rigs a block and tackle to gain sufficient purchase on the huge molar. He ends up tying himself to one end of the rope that is attached to the tooth, running the rope over a tree limb, and leaping — a living counterweight — from a balcony. Giganticizing the delicate art of dentistry is a splendid comic notion, and the pains we recall from our own experiences in the dentist's chair inform our wincing laughter as Harold goes crudely to work on a man whose anguish we imagine must match his huge size.

There are other delights in the film: the giant using cannonballs like bowling balls to knock down enemy troops, while the still-hypochondriac Lloyd, midst shot and shell, carefully dries his feet so he won't catch cold; the giant with a cannon strapped to his back, allowing himself to be used as a human firing platform; Lloyd duelling with several soldiers at once while studying a book on sword fighting in order to rescue Jobyna; the three of them — Lloyd, the giant, and the girl — holding off an army after their ammunition has run out by poking the empty cannon over the parapet of the fort, beating on a drum to simulate the sound of its firing, blowing cigar smoke out the mouth of the cannon to simulate the sight of its being fired, and heaving coconuts at the advancing soldiers to make them think shot is landing among them.

Described, this last does not sound believable, let alone terribly funny, but it is on film, and it provides as good an opportunity as any to demonstrate how the silence of silent films worked to their advantage. There has always been much talk about the poetic nature of this cinema, how much more important gesture and symbol were in conveying — imagistically — ideas and emotions in silents than they are in sound films. More often than not the self-consciously poetic films of the silent era have not stood the test of time very well. But simply because of the absence of voices, the audience, without being consciously aware of it, was instantly disabused of any realistic expectations the minute they took

Rehearsing The Great Toothache. Harold the human counterweight, takes heroic measures to conquer a giant's giant pain in *Why Worry?* Below, one of Lloyd's new co-stars got a special chair for relaxing on the set; the other had her name misspelled.

their seats. Therefore they could accept events and characters that in sound films, or on the stage, they would not have accepted. This humble gag of Lloyd's is a perfect example of this. There is no problem in believing that his silly ruse might actually work. Since we cannot hear the unreality of the drum substituting for the cannon's report, we are free to imagine its being an exact duplication. Since we cannot hear the menacing sounds of the advancing army — drums and bugles sounding, officers exhorting their men — we are free to imagine that the noise and activity created by Lloyd and his cohorts can actually be heard by the troops and that it could actually panic them.

Perhaps one need look no further than this for an explanation of why the great silent comedians could not survive the coming of sound. For the majority of their gags — and certainly most of their best ones — depended entirely on the fact that they were believable only within the stylized world of the silent screen. They were careful to lure us into this world with great gentleness — which may account for the slowness of the early reels of their films and the care they expended on building gags — so that we weren't too rudely forced to accept their more outlandish fancies.

Certainly *Why Worry?* was the most outlandish fancy Lloyd ever attempted, and though it was profitable, one has the impression that of the films of this, his major period, it was the least appreciated in its time, that it was dismissed as a slightly regressive work. Now it seems anything but. Indeed, it seems to look forward, more than any silent feature one can think of, to such great Graustarkian lunacies of the sound period as the Marx Brothers' *Duck Soup* and W. C. Fields's *Million-Dollar Legs,* both of which took place in countries of the mind, dream worlds where creatures like Lloyd's giant and the rapid movement of large bodies of men chasing madly about seemed completely believable. Lloyd seems inspired in some new way. In *Why Worry?,* decked out in straw skimmer and saddle shoes, and sporting a ludicrous cigarette holder, he is funnier in appearance, funnier in himself, than he was in any other feature film. It is a relief that here he is selfish, self-absorbed, a thoroughgoing goof; the earnestness, the reflection of the star's desire to be liked, so evident in past and future films, is for once set aside. "Now that I think of it, I really enjoyed protecting you," a subtitle has him saying to Miss Ralston after he has rescued her from the villains, and that tells the whole story. In every other Lloyd film that thought would have been uppermost in his mind, a basic premise for much of his activities; here it comes as a surprised afterthought. One can't help thinking that his reputation with posterity might have been higher if he had allowed himself more films in which he was less determinedly sweet, in which he had permitted audiences to see that he too had, if not a dark side to his nature, at least a side that could be victimized by the self-serving and anarchical impulses of the unconscious. Even Chaplin, in the midst of his most sentimental exercises, permitted The Tramp to give into these impulses — to indulge in a whimsical cruelty here, a tweaking of

authority's nose there. Lloyd, except for this one time, could never free himself from boyhood warnings that sugar catches more flies than vinegar.

When it came to business, however, he was all business — there was no longer any need to ingratiate himself with anyone in that realm. With *Why Worry?* safely and profitably launched, he resolved to sever his ties with Roach at last. Doubtless it seemed foolish to the comedian to continue to share profits with the producer, who by this time was contributing almost nothing, personally, to the Lloyd productions. All Roach was providing was studio space, and that Lloyd could rent, or build to suit himself (which is what he decided to do). Roach claims his Our Gang comedies were the chief "bone of contention with Lloyd. Every time he saw a good gag in an Our Gang picture he'd say it was his; and if he saw a good gag in one of our other pictures he'd cry and complain because I hadn't given it to him." Lloyd implied in his autobiography that he had a contractual right to first call on Roach's time, that he was not getting it, and that he used this deficiency on the producer's part as a loophole to wriggle completely free of him.

Both sides suggest that whatever their differences, the parting was reasonably amicable. Roach's percentage in the Lloyd films was now so modest that he probably felt no great financial need to hold on, and, it seems fair to suggest, the lot was no longer big enough to comfortably contain a major star and an increasingly important — or at least self-important — producer. In any event, they agreed to continue splitting future profits on the pictures they had made together on the basis of the contracts under which the films had originally been produced, and Lloyd would claim that as of 1928 his one-reel glasses character films — in which he had no percentages — had trebled their original grosses in re-release for Roach and Pathé. At some later date he bought up his shorter films, save the Lonesome Lukes and the few he had made prior to them, and his estate now has full ownership of them all.

8 In late 1923, Lloyd was in the real estate market. He needed both a new home and a new studio, the land for both of which he acquired at this time. He could easily afford it. He was once asked: "How long did it take you to make your first million?" "Ten years," was his reply. "And your second million?" "Three months," doubtless the three months after he had made his first feature under the 80-20 split of the profits guaranteed by his third Pathé contract. By late 1923 he surely had several millions more to play with.

He did not put an enormous amount into the studio he acquired. A silent picture studio required very little in the way of elaborate equipment (sound, among other things, required a quantum leap in this regard), and the land he purchased, well out on Santa Monica Boulevard, where the Mormon Temple now stands, was not, in those days, expensive. The acreage was large enough so that Lloyd could indulge his boyhood fondness for big dogs, and probably at least as much space was devoted to kennels for the sixty or so prize-winning Great Danes that were his hobby at the moment as was set aside for picture production.

Around the same time, his mother's brother, William R. Fraser, a former forest ranger who had become his business manager in 1922, found what seemed to him an excellent piece of land on which Lloyd could build a house suitable to his station, and one day he took the star out to see it. They turned up a dirt road off Sunset Boulevard and into a canyon in which stood the old Benedict home and bean farm. It was dry and dusty in the late fall and not very appealing to Lloyd. "What do I want with that gully and rock hillside?" he asked Fraser. "Besides, Beverly Hills is too far out."

Fraser, however, was not to be dissuaded, and backed by the other officers of Lloyd's new company (which was managed by John R. Murphy, like Newmeyer a graduate of Roach's prop department), he finally got Lloyd to agree to the purchase — with impatient indifference. "All right, all right. But leave me out. Let it be a corporation deal purely and simply." The property that was to become unquestionably the love of his life did not begin to exert its spell on him until the winter, when the rains came and the streams and arroyos ran full of water, turning the hillside green and bringing out the color in the wild flowers. Now Lloyd began to fancy the place. He had the old Benedict homestead remodeled as a home for his mother, and she lived there for two years while Lloyd and his wife, who bore their first child, Gloria, on May 22, 1924, planned the remarkable residence that was soon to begin rising on this spectacular site.

Harold and Gaylord.

Lloyd and his co-directors, Sam Taylor (left) and Fred Newmeyer on the set of *Girl Shy*. Taylor was a one-time seminarian, Newmeyer a one-time minor league ball player. Both were graduates of Lloyd's gag room.

Over at the new studio, meantime, things were going swimmingly, with a new project that would eventually be known as *Girl Shy.* No doubt Lloyd and his team, most of whom had come with him from Roach, worked on it as they had on all his other pictures. At any given moment he might have as many as eight gagmen working for him at higher wages than they could command anywhere else — $750 a week, some say as much as $1,000. They were top talent, too, many of them having credits on Buster Keaton's best pictures as well as Lloyd's. As Lloyd once described the process, at the beginning of a film they might have agreed "upon a story or have five more or less hostile plots, and I may like them all or none, or parts of this and that. The result usually is a compromise so scrambled that no one and everyone can claim the authorship." There were always fights over what would work, what wouldn't, what was a believable situation, what was a totally unrealistic one, but once a choice was made as to which variant Lloyd would work on as his basic character, and what the broad outline of the story was likely to be (the detailed hooking up of incidents was the last thing to be done on the movie, usually after the major sequences were filmed), Lloyd would divide up the work as the spirit moved him. "Sometimes I felt fit to send them out alone, to work by themselves, or in pairs." It didn't matter. In the end, all their work was funneled back to the star sitting more or less as chairman of a committee of the whole. "Maybe they'll come back with one [fully developed] idea we can use, but very seldom did it happen that way. Generally, they produced an idea, and we sat in there and worked it out."

No matter. Three things were certain. The first was that the writers would produce — and Lloyd would film — more gags than the finished picture could possibly hold. The second was that plenty of room would be left for on-set improvisation. The third was that cutting and reshooting would take place after previews with a paying audience of strangers. As for the direction of the movie, Lloyd would claim, especially in later years, that however the credits read, he was his own maestro. "I never took credit for direction, although I practically directed all my own pictures. The directors were entirely dependent on me. I had these boys there because I felt they knew comedy, they knew what I wanted, they knew me — and they could handle the details. When you're acting in front of the camera you can't see yourself, and these boys were able to say, 'Harold, don't you think it would be funnier if you did so-and-so?' "

Probably no one will ever be able to sort out just where Lloyd's contribution to the direction of his pictures ended and where that of the men who received on-screen credit for them began. But it seems fair to say that like Keaton and Chaplin — and like Harry Langdon at the end, with disastrous results — he was senior officer present at every stage of the work, and that that was the way it had to be for a silent comedy star. Lloyd was not, however, a terribly stern taskmaster. Once you were part of the team, whether as writer or technician, you were likely to stay with Lloyd a long time. He kept the men on salary all year

long, whether a production was under way or not, and stoutly insisted, in later years, that they were far better off under his paternal patronage at his shop than they were later when the unions came in and set up work rules.

The atmosphere seems to have been loose, but Lloyd always remained the "smart" comedian. For example, he had a gagman named Frank Terry who was a strange case. "He was one of the best, but he was also one of the worst," as Lloyd told Kevin Brownlow. "He'd give you ten ideas, and only one of them would have a germ in it. The others were horrible. He had an original mind, but no judgment at all." One time when Lloyd wasn't using him, he sent Terry over to Fox so he could make some extra money, warning his superiors there that the point about Terry was to listen carefully for the good idea that would inevitably be buried among the bad ones. In a couple of weeks they sent Terry back, because "they couldn't pick that little wheat out of the chaff."

"Our lack of method is deplorable," Lloyd said at the time, "but somehow it works." And it seems probable that it worked precisely because Lloyd, being reasonable and well-organized — compulsive might be the most accurate term for him — could afford to encourage all the anarchical creative ferment that his employees cared to churn up. It was reported in a fan magazine at the time that during production Lloyd was anything but confident in demeanor: "There is one thing about Harold that is always amusing. . . .If you ask him how his picture is going, his face falls, he looks utterly downcast and miserable. 'I'm afraid of it,' he says." But besides being a common enough defensive attitude among creative people, this is probably simply a reflection of his preoccupation with the details of getting things right. He claimed that he was always the one to call for one more retake, even after he had done seven or eight on a scene, trying to get it just right. His lead was needed especially in the all-important business of timing, which when wrong will ruin a perfectly good laugh and of which Lloyd was the only proper judge, since only he could hear the ticking of his inner clock. Even Roach had to admit that. "He couldn't write or think of funny things, but you put him in a scene and give him something to do and if it wasn't funny he'd know and squawk until it was changed and was funny." Indeed, so objective was Lloyd about work that, according to Roach, "He never said, 'Do I do this or that?' He said, 'Now what does *he* do?' " — meaning his character.

The one thing he evidently could not and would not tolerate around him was a domineering, or potentially domineering, creative figure. That surely was responsible for the testy quality of his relationship with Roach, as well as for the fact that none of the men who worked with him during the glory days ever succeeded outside his orbit. Even the best of them, Sam Taylor, didn't last long once he left Lloyd's shadow (although he picked up a few credits — including the famous "additional dialogue" credit on Shakespeare's *The Taming of the Shrew,* which actually is just an inept way of indicating that he had adapted the play for the screen for Fairbanks and Pickford). Lloyd just didn't want strong men around.

83

Indeed, he told an interesting story to Kevin Brownlow about Frank Craven, the playwright, who wondered why Lloyd had so many high-priced writers on his payroll. After all, Craven said, one or at most two men had written all the classic stage comedies. Why should movies be any different? And why should Lloyd pay all those salaries when he could probably get just one man — someone like Frank Craven, say — to do the whole job? Lloyd decided to give him a chance, though not as a single. Instead, he threw him in the pool with the other writers. Craven lasted just three days; then he came to Lloyd and said, "... I sat in there for three days and these fellows were throwing ideas all over the place, and I couldn't think of one damn thing. It really hurt my pride. I would have liked to help you, but Harold, it's your medium."

And so it was, but perhaps precisely because Lloyd had rigged a situation that would guarantee his control over his creations. There was, simply, no other power center but the star on the Lloyd lot — only a jumble of amiable courtiers preoccupied mainly, it would seem, with seeing that their best-loved gag ideas got into the finished film. None had the prestige of even a Frank Craven to challenge the boss's judgment or, perhaps more important, to make a claim for significant creative credit in public. But one cannot say definitely that Lloyd would have fared better with stronger people around him. In sound films, in fact, he worked with several distinguished directors — Leo McCarey, Elliott Nugent, Preston Sturges — and his pictures were not noticeably improved by their presence (though McCarey did very well with him). All one can really say is that the absence of a strong story man, someone who could make Lloyd and his pals in the gag room create a firm line for his pictures and then make them hew to it, would have been enormously helpful. And Lloyd might have given Craven a fairer chance by asking him to work alone, in the manner he was used to, to create the outline for a picture before letting the gagmen at him.

This story problem was emphasized in Lloyd's first independent production, *Girl Shy*. It contains one of Lloyd's greatest sequences, but like so many of his pictures, the several reels it required to reach this marvelously perilous gag island were no more than mediocre. Lloyd's character is a tailor's assistant named Harold Meadows, in Little Bend, a town, one of the titles informs us, so small and backwards that pitching horseshoes is its only form of dissipation. He is a stutterer and a fantasist, occupying his idle hours by writing a book on how to make love, though of course he is too shy ever to have kissed a girl. However, when an heiress (Jobyna Ralston) is passing through town, her car breaks down and she is forced to take the same train Harold is taking to the big city, where he is going to present his manuscript to a publisher. She has a dog with her and Harold gallantly helps hide the animal from a conductor bent on enforcing the line's rule against pets in the passenger section (at one point he is forced to nibble dog biscuits in order to fool the fellow). Once he gets to the city, he loses the girl, gets laughed out of his publisher's office, and retreats to Little Bend in

despair. The girl, meantime, makes a point of passing through the town again, hoping to see him. There is a rather poignant moment when, sitting beside a stream, dreaming of her, he sees her image in the water and dismisses it as imagination, when in fact she is standing behind him. There's also a funny moment when, shyly courting her, he sits down on what he takes to be a rock and it turns out to be a somnolent turtle.

Alas, it appears she is committed to marry another man, a rather greasy-looking fortune hunter. But then the tide of events begins to turn in Harold's favor. The women in his publisher's office start reading his manuscript and laughing over it, and the house decides to bring it out as a comic work, a satire on the love manuals of the time. At the same time he discovers that his love's intended is already married and is therefore a potential bigamist.

But the wedding is to take place within hours. He must warn her. Here his stammer frustrates him. He cannot make himself talk clearly enough to buy a railway ticket or to place a phone call to her. Which sets up the masterful concluding chase of the film, worth describing in some detail. He leaps on the back of a passing car. It turns into a garage a half block later. He hitches another ride — and this time he has chosen a student driver out practicing turns, who takes him around and around in circles. He manages to get another ride, but then encounters a detour which takes him over a perilously bumpy mountain road. Thrown out, he steals a car belonging to some bootleggers and ends up with both cops and crooks chasing him. Then at a point where there's room for just one car to pass on the road, he encounters a truck. He talks the driver into trading vehicles, but promptly drives the truck over the cliff.

Now the pace picks up. Harold somehow grabs a ride on the back of a police car that is still chasing about looking for the bootleggers. He swings off that onto a passing truck, then drops off onto the back of a horse. The frightened animal promptly runs away, Harold clinging precariously to any part of its anatomy on which he can gain a purchase. Finally knocked off, he lands on a fire truck, then is knocked off it by a passing auto. Now he tries hanging onto a jammed streetcar, which pulls away leaving Lloyd, for it turns out he merely had hold of another rider who was also trying to cling to the outside of the car. Harold promptly steals an empty trolley, and it just as promptly begins to career along the tracks, completely out of control. Finally, the trolley loses contact with the overhead wire that provides power and Harold climbs to the roof to recouple it. The minute he does, the car takes off and he finds himself clinging desperately to the pole. Going around a curve, the pole swings wildly out over the street. Harold lets go and drops through the roof of a passing convertible. Its startled driver sideswipes a passing motorcycle cop and when the latter stops the car to lecture the driver, Lloyd steals the cop's bike and takes off again. When the motorcycle finally runs out of steam, he grabs a horse-drawn wagon and gallops away again, only to lose a wheel as he pounds along. Undaunted, he cuts the

wagon free and mounts one of the horses, and it is on this steed that he finally reaches the front gate of his true love's mansion to which, all along, we have been cross-cutting as the wedding ceremony has proceeded. He manages to blurt out his somewhat incoherent objections to the match, and then simply sweeps the girl up on his shoulder and makes off with her — rather as Dustin Hoffman would do in a similar scene in *The Graduate* almost a half century later.

This sequence is surely the greatest chase Lloyd ever produced and is, arguably, the greatest chase in film history (the train chase in Keaton's *The General* being one candidate for comparable rank). It offers, in fact, just the aesthetic satisfactions of an elegant solution to a mathematical puzzle that Mme. de Beauvoir attributes to Keaton, while at the same time providing a very pleasing transformation of the shy stammerer into a hero — both without sacrifice of frenzied suspense. Again, the conclusion of the film quite wipes out one's impatience with the slower — though certainly not unpleasant — reels that preceded it, and with the thin simplicity of Lloyd's characterization.

The film was enormously successful. By and large, Lloyd's work, like that of the other great silent comedians, was virtually review-proof. People would have gone to see their films no matter what the critics said. But the critics tended not to take comedy very seriously. Comparisons were few and vague, and generally each man was treated as if he were a genre unto himself. Thus, *The New York Times,* while generally praising the picture, would say, ''We do not think that this effort is quite as subtle fun as 'Why Worry?' '' — which says nothing at all about the distinctly different moods and intentions of the two films. *Time* thought better of it — ''Not only the funniest picture that Harold Lloyd has done, but pretty nearly the funniest that anybody anywhere has done, including all of California'' — but that statement, though doubtless welcome to the producer, was an exaggeration and not much help to anyone, including the historian. It does, however, emphasize the isolation from the mainstream of the industry in which the comics worked. They were expected to be funny. This expectation conditioned people, critics as well as the public, to assume that what they were seeing was funny — in toto. No one seemed to draw any very fine distinctions between one film and the next, to note differences in quality between one part of a movie and another. The critics were, in fact, lazy about comedy as they were not about films with more obvious pretensions to art. The anonymous man from *The Times,* for example, devotes almost no space to the masterful chase sequence, nattering on about the love scenes preceding it, probably because they are, in a way, more literary, more within the traditional range of culture reference available to him. *Time* at least stressed the chase, and more important, mentions in passing a key point about Lloyd, the thing that was responsible for much of his prosperity. He might not be as ''humorously subtle'' as Chaplin, the magazine said, ''but nowadays he is snappier.''

Ever the smart comedian, Lloyd worried that perhaps an excess of concern about story and character could cost him popularity. In the 1920s he was heard

to say, "I like the story pictures as well as anyone, yet I am a little afraid of overdoing them and forgetting one of these days that we are makers of comedies. Critical approval is pleasant but heady stuff. A teaspoonful after meals, say, will aid the digestion. In larger doses it has been known to set up delusions of grandeur." It was in a mood like this, having just completed what he fondly believed to have been a study in character (and perhaps the Harold Meadows of *Girl Shy* was indeed the shyest version of his basic screen character), that Lloyd and friends decided to do what they must have thought would turn out to be a plain old laff riot — *Hot Water.*

In a sense he may be said to have succeeded. There is less attempt to establish any sort of individuality for Lloyd's character in this film than in any feature picture he made. He is seen simply as a young husband, profession unknown, background unestablished, who in the film's first section attempts to bring home a load of groceries, in the second takes his wife and her awful relatives for a spin in his new car, and in the third tries to silence his excessively talkative and meddling mother-in-law when she decides to stay over at his house for a very long night. In the course of these activities he reveals nothing about himself that is extraordinary. He is neither remarkably shy nor confident, neither markedly brave nor cowardly, nor anything else. The movie is, for two-thirds of its length, one long mother-in-law joke, depending entirely on universal acceptance of the fact that mothers-in-law are inevitably a terrible trial to their sons-in-law.

Just as there was less interest in sketching in a character for Lloyd, there was less interest in creating a proper story line for him to follow. Essentially what we have is morning, afternoon, and evening in what might properly be called "one of those days," as in the rhetorical question, "Did you ever have one of those days?" The film might be called three variations on a theme, the theme being Harold frustrated — frustrated in his modest desire to accomplish a few simple tasks, enjoy a few simple pleasures.

Lloyd never thought very highly of the picture and it is certainly unpretentious. Yet except for a fatal flaw in the final third of the film, it is also a quite enjoyable bit of pure farce. Indeed, the first portion of the picture is worth outlining because it shows a facet of Lloyd's talent that he did not often choose to demonstrate in his longer movies, that is, his skill as a comedian in a limited, everyday sort of physical setting. The picture begins at an outdoor market where Lloyd has stopped to pick up a few groceries for his wife. Having neglected to bring a shopping bag, he is making his way homeward juggling six or eight packages of widely divergent shapes and sizes when he unwittingly wins a turkey in a raffle. The beast is live and his disposition is not a happy one. Gamely, the already heavy-laden Lloyd tucks him under his arm and boards a crowded streetcar. His difficulties begin when, trying to keep his balance on the swaying car, he keeps reaching for a cord; the cord summons the conductor, who keeps re-collecting Lloyd's fare from him, in itself a dreadful problem for the poor

87

fellow, since each time he must reach into his pocket he must unburden himself of his packages. He blandly hands them over to the increasingly irritated conductor, and finally, when the latter is fully laden, Lloyd pays him by extracting a nickle from the change-maker attached to the conductor's belt — which is fair enough and funny enough. This matter settled, Lloyd turns his mind to surviving the trip without loss of groceries or dignity, not observing that two little boys have brought a spider on the car with them. Needless to say, it escapes and immediately scurries up Lloyd's pants leg. Trying to shake it loose, he repeatedly kicks another straphanger, who, of course, retaliates. Whereupon the spider reappears on the top of Lloyd's shoe, from which point the comedian slyly transfers it to his tormentor's shoe, so that, inevitably, it heads up the stranger's pants and Lloyd has the pleasure of seeing him go into a St. Vitus's dance. In the world of the silent comedian such victories are bound to be brief. For at this point the turkey gets loose and disappears. Lloyd soon finds himself down among the legs of his fellow passengers searching for the creature. It has taken refuge under a lady's skirts and she, predictably, assumes Lloyd to be a masher when he pursues the bird with an excess of zeal. By this time, the passengers are united in their demand that he be expelled from the car, and the sequence ends with Lloyd sitting in the middle of the road, his packages strewn about him, fashioning a leash for the turkey out of his necktie.

One cannot speak too highly of the sequence. It is like an early one-reeler in construction, in its ability to discover the raw material of comedy in an extremely limited and completely ordinary environment, and in the brilliantly simple linkage of one small disaster to the next, all leading to the final large humiliation of the protagonist-victim. One also likes the lack of blandness in Lloyd's response to his difficulties. Usually he did not show much irritation, and if he did, he did not allow it to spill over into acts of revenge against those who were not clearly identified as villains. Here, however, his fellow riders' lack of understanding and helpfulness toward a man who obviously is a victim of unlikely circumstances, their unfair assessment of him as a common nuisance when manifestly he is doing his best not to be one, finally riles him, so that by the end he is (as well as he can) returning unkindness for unkindness. In this sequence, more than anywhere else one can think of, he approaches that which was best and funniest in the Chaplinesque mode — The Tramp's feistiness when, despite his innocence, he found himself put upon by an indifferent or hostile world. There is here an innocence, perhaps not entirely conscious, in the conception of the role that is more attractive than his go-getter or idler characterizations, and more winning, because more austere, than his more obvious attempts to play upon audience sympathies (as in *Grandma's Boy* and *Girl Shy*). Neither Chaplin nor Keaton, it will be recalled, ever offered histories or psychologies for their characters. They simply — and triumphantly — were. And that is what Lloyd is in *Hot Water*.

This mode also sets the tone of the movie's second, perhaps even more triumphant, section, another little masterpiece of farcical contrivance. Arriving home, he finds that his wife's family — her ne'er-do-well brother, her kid brother, and, of course, her mother — have dropped by for a visit. Without meaning to, Lloyd manages to offend all of them. The mood changes, however, when his new car, a Butterfly Six (the name is a nice touch), is delivered. It is a surprise for his wife and, we come to understand, an important symbol for him, a visible sign to his in-laws that he is doing well — better, no doubt, than they predicted he would.

Off they all go on a trial spin. At the first left turn Lloyd fails to go around a traffic button set in the middle of the road and is lectured for his sin by a traffic cop. He then finds himself behind some uniformed World War I veterans on their way to a patriotic function. One of them loses his tin pot helmet; it falls to the street where it precisely resembles a traffic button, though it is nowhere near the center of the road; following his previous instructions, Lloyd attempts to go around it and ends up on a neatly tended lawn.

This is only the beginning of Lloyd's troubles. Glancing around, he sees a motorcyclist approaching and looking in the mood for a race. Lloyd presses down on the accelerator and signals him to come on. The cyclist, however, turns off and is replaced by a policeman on a cycle, who speeds up, gets in front of Lloyd's car and waves him over to stop. Instead, he speeds up and pursuer becomes pursued — until Lloyd chases him through a gas station's plaza and bumps him smartly into a stream in a park — where a child eyes the dripping cop and points solemnly at a nearby sign that prohibits swimming.

Meantime, Lloyd and family are once again on their merry way, his mother-in-law's scarf blowing in his face obscuring his view as she shouts instructions to him out of the owner's manual. The upshot is a tangle of fenders at a busy intersection. The cop guarding it approaches, ticket book at the ready. Mom, of course, proceeds to tell him off — and Harold gets the ticket. Whereupon, the traffic backed up in all directions, he attempts to extricate himself — and backs straight into the majesty of the law, who rewards him with another summons. Now, on top of everything else, he finds he can't get his car started. The snarl of traffic by this time has reached Gordian complexity, and the cop orders him to push the car out of the way — of course it rolls down a steep hill no one seems to have noticed before, Lloyd trying to hold back the vehicle by grasping a leather strap attached to the rear luggage compartment. When he finally gets back in behind the wheel, he finds a horse-drawn fire engine hard on his heels. Trying to outrun it, he swerves onto a sidewalk to avoid a van parked in the middle of the road, and finds himself resting atop a service elevator in the sidewalk, which immediately begins to rise. Desperate signals from mid-air bring some children to their aid, and the car is returned to the ground with a shattering thump. At which point Lloyd backs it out, directly into the path of an oncoming

trolley. The sequence ends with a disconsolate Lloyd, his car a wreck, sitting down on the running board — which breaks under his weight.

Obviously a sequence like that is hard to top. As it turned out, alas, it was impossible. The in-laws all decide to stay over at Lloyd's, and for some reason Lloyd has a chloroform-soaked handkerchief in his pocket which he offers to the mother-in-law when she accidentally inhales too much pepper at dinner. Lloyd believes he has killed her — an impression reinforced when he hears his brother-in-law calling the police, though he is actually only attempting to fix the day's harvest of traffic tickets. There follows further confusion — with the mother-in-law sleepwalking, the cops in the neighborhood searching for a burglar, and so on. It is essentially a reworking of the not-very-funny ghost sequence in the two-reel *I Do.* After the superb naturalistic comedy of the first two parts, the strained invention of this sequence looks particularly feeble and it seems astonishing that Lloyd would let the film go forth as he did. In its defense it might be noted that following the Broadway success of *The Bat*, the Mary Roberts Rinehart thriller about a seemingly haunted house, there was a flurry of imitations (even the great D. W. Griffith, desperately needing a hit, tried one) and Lloyd doubtless hoped people would accept this small sequence as his contribution to a pop-cultural fad. Or maybe he hoped that the fine first sections of the work would blot out memory of its feeble conclusion. In any event, it is the only silent film in the Lloyd *oeuvre* in which he violates the basic law of his art, which is that the end must be funnier than the beginning.

Still, *Hot Water* by no means fared badly with the critics, though none seemed to have thought it one of his finer creations. They were by this time prepared on the basis of past performance to give him the benefit of the doubt. And, indeed, so should we. The early sequences are much anthologized and the film as a whole benefits from something quite rare in Lloyd's work — a memorable supporting performance, this one by Josephine Crowell, the veteran character actress, in the role of the mother-in-law. In her cloche hat, her large frame swathed in clothes of matronly dignity, her extraordinarily mobile lips twisting alternately into expressions of rage and outrage beneath her prominent nose, she presents a memorable image of middle-class propriety undergoing acute pain, and like Margaret Dumont in the Marx Brothers films of the next decade, she succeeds in transcending type, becoming one of our most vivid memories of the silent era.

As for Lloyd, he preferred not to remember much about *Hot Water.* It was, after all, quite short (five reels), and writing only four years after its release, he was able to say that "coming as it did between two longer, better films, it is little remembered." This is perhaps fair enough, though not entirely just to the good work it contained. Still, there can be no denying that the second of those two "longer, better films" was infinitely its superior, perhaps infinitely the best of all Lloyd's work. It was called *The Freshman.*

Success, as they say, has many authors, and many were to claim *The Freshman* as their own. Hal Roach was one of them. Before Lloyd left him, the producer claimed he had seen a newsreel of a football game played on a muddy field. "A guy'd hit the ground and slide ten yards. That gave me the idea . . . but. . . ." Soon thereafter the rules of the game were changed so that the ball was declared dead and the play over at the point where the ball carrier's knees touched the ground. End of gag. But not, Roach believed, the end of the idea of having Lloyd play an eager-to-please college neophyte, literally tripping over himself to win friends and become a campus hero like the much-publicized, much-admired stars of the game in those years when it was the most glamorous sporting spectacle the nation had to offer. Roach's only doubt, he now says, was that Lloyd might be too old to be believable as a college boy (he was thirty-one in 1925, when *The Freshman* was made). As it turned out, this was not a problem; Lloyd was ever-youthful in appearance, even when he was quite an old man. (Lloyd's last film, *The Sin of Harold Diddlebock/Mad Wednesday* opens with footage from *The Freshman*. And though it was made two decades later, Lloyd looks uncannily like the boy in the earlier film.)

A more serious problem, and a more serious claimant to the authorship of the movie, was one H. C. Witwer, a writer of popular fiction for the mass magazines who had also sold a couple of stories to the studios. In February, 1926, after the film went into release, he sued Lloyd for $250,000, claiming the film's idea was lifted from "The Emancipation of Rodney," a story (it is unclear whether it was written originally for the screen or as a magazine piece) he had submitted to Lloyd. Witwer died soon after, but a Los Angeles court enjoined further distribution of the film until the matter was cleared up; this is said to be the first such injunction in movie history. And even though that injunction was set aside, a U.S. District Court awarded Mrs. Witwer a share of the profits for the period of 1926–31, and it was not until 1933 that a U.S. Circuit Court of Appeals finally disallowed the Witwer claim. It is the only blot on the Lloyd organization's record of generating its own material during the silent period, and one would not take it too seriously — it will be recalled that Lloyd had originally thought of his glasses character as potentially the hero of a series of college stories — except for one rather striking bit of internal evidence that lends some credence to the Witwer claim.

This is the fact that the picture is extraordinarily well constructed. It is perfectly true that it contains "islands" of merriment, just like its predecessors;

but these grow organically out of an extraordinarily well-knit, and (for Lloyd) quite poignant story. It is easy to imagine the gagmen working, for once, from a carefully organized outline of some sort. On the other hand, it might well be argued that the Lloyd team was growing in skill, for it is also true that from this time onward all Lloyd's movies give evidence of sturdier, much less improvisational, construction. Against this interpretation one can set the possibility that the enormous success of *The Freshman* was carefully analyzed by Lloyd and his cohorts and that they discovered that it was the story that made the difference, and they determined that thereafter they would pay more attention to it. One can come to no definitive conclusion.

What one can and should say is that *The Freshman* — which has remained the most popular Lloyd work on the film society circuit and thus the one modern audiences have had the best chance of seeing — is surely his masterpiece, the one Lloyd feature no one seems to dispute as belonging in the same class as the best of Chaplin, Keaton, Langdon, and Laurel and Hardy — one of the comic screen's indisputable masterpieces. The movie contains two famous sequences. The first is one in which Lloyd goes to a college dance (at which he is the host) in a tuxedo that is merely basted together, and must take his tailor with him to make instant repairs. Lloyd's efforts to act the smooth college Romeo while keeping his suit from falling off, and arranging to back himself up against curtains and screens behind which the tailor lurks, needle at the ready, are simply brilliant, the more so since the tailor keeps nipping at his "medicine," which renders it impossible for him to ply his trade in anything but haphazard fashion. The second sequence is, of course, the big game. One after the other of the Tate College football team is put out of commission, but Harold, as the substitute of last resort, must finally be permitted to enter the game (still wearing his spectacles — under a nose protector). And he wins it with various imaginative, occasionally illegal strategies (unlacing the football and letting it lie seemingly unattended on the field; then when the opponents attempt to pick it up, jerking it from them by a single lace he is quietly holding and sauntering casually up the field with the ball hidden behind his back).

These are delicious conceits and would have been enough to assure any previous Lloyd film of a warm reception, no matter what happened in between. But in this film he finally achieved — without apparently noticing it — a true comedy of character. Moreover, and again without seeming to be entirely aware of it, he achieved a subtle satire on the values so many commentators blithely insist he always upheld — American optimism and go-getterism, the drive to be popular at any cost. In fact, it may be said that this is the only Lloyd film that is constructed around a desire to satirize a contemporary fad — the inordinate public interest in college life.

The opening scenes show Harold Lamb (as the character is called here) in his modest, lower-middle-class home in a room decorated with a huge poster

advertising a movie about a Big Man on Campus. Lloyd, gotten up in a ridiculous freshman beanie and Tate letter sweater, is assiduously studying material on the dress and slang appropriate to a youth aspiring to be a social success among his peers. Worst of all, he is practicing a handshake that involves a complex and absurd little jig before extending the hand of friendship. Already there is something pathetic about him, as well as comical.

And his arrival on campus — having fallen in love with the first girl he meets on the train to Tate (Jobyna Ralston again) — is a disaster. He mistakes a crowd at the station as a welcoming committee for him, rather than for a returning football hero; he assumes an elaborate car into which he hops is intended for him, instead of the college president; he stumbles into a student assembly and makes a ridiculous inspirational speech, its ludicrous quality enhanced by a kitten which insinuates itself under his sweater, sending him into itchy paroxysms while trying to maintain his dignity.

In short, he is a marked man. And the students, led by a sneaky bully, decide to play to his BMOC fantasies, allowing him to believe that he is as popular as he wants to be, the while mocking him behind his back. In fact, trying to glad-hand his way into his fellow students' regard, he runs through his allowance buying sodas and the like for mobs of them at the campus sweet shop, reducing himself to odd-jobs and penury in order to make ends meet. There is, to put the matter simply, a malice at work here that is not present in any other Lloyd film, and that malice can only be interpreted as a comment on the meanness and hypocrisy of the middle class, simultaneously exploiting and ridiculing a youth whose only crime is a lack of subtlety in his attempts to ape their manner and thus win their acceptance. Considering Lloyd's own strenuous efforts in this regard as a youth in the early stages of his career — indeed, considering the modest, moral, permanently cheerful face he ever turned toward the world — one can't help but speculate that in this film he permitted himself the luxury of unburdening himself of some secret feelings.

Perhaps the movie's most powerful statement in this respect occurs during one of the football team's practice sessions, when Lloyd, the water boy, is allowed to suit up and serve as a living tackling dummy for the team, which batters him nearly unconscious. Yet after each brutal mauling, he comes up smiling, encouraging the club to do its worst to him, until at the end he is clutching pathetically at the coach's ankles. Whereupon he is ordered to revert to his original role as water boy and gather up all the practice equipment. Even then Harold, happy that he has been able to contribute to the team's success in some way, assures that brute (so tough he shaves with a blow torch, a title informs us) that it has really been a great practice.

This display of true grit wins him his uniform and the opportunity to become a last-minute hero in the big game, thus also winning the opportunity for the heroic role he has so long coveted. Far from being false, this ending comes as a

The Freshman: Extras help Lloyd rehearse the headstand that drew a good laugh in the finished film. Visiting Iceman Red Grange gets a carefully posed lesson in camera operation.

relief; emotionally we require that all this pain be rewarded. And it is handled smoothly, logically — there is no sense of its being tacked on to satisfy the audience's conventional expectations for the end of a comedy. It could be argued that the film's climax simply supports a Horatio Alger sort of moral. Certainly a good deal of pluck and luck is involved in Lloyd's transformation from figure of fun to campus hero. But this is too simple a reckoning, for it ignores, to begin with, the implicit stupidity of the methods by which the student body chooses the figures it admires. And it ignores, more significantly, the tone of the entire film, in which Lloyd is seen to cut a more feverishly foolish figure than he does in any of his other movies — surely a comment of sorts on the false values he works so desperately to embrace — not to mention the mass cruelty at work in the endless hazing to which he is subjected. (A scene in which he discovers he has been made a fool of and turns on his tormentors is second only to the conclusion of the tackling dummy sequence in poignancy.)

Interestingly, several early reviews of *The Freshman,* though generally favorable, stress the fact that the movie is not as funny as some of its predecessors, which indeed it is not, Lloyd and his team having transcended their precedents. It was, however, dim of the critical fraternity not to see that something unusual was taking place here, though at that time the very idea that a comedian might actually be growing, or at least attempting to grow, in his art was not one that readily occurred to the vast majority of people who made it their business to review movies regularly. Only a handful of those who concerned themselves with movies — usually on an occasional basis as writers — even understood that movies were, in themselves, an art form. The regular reviewers tended to patronize the generic movie forms, spoke of art only when a film's director (preferably, in this era, a Russian or a German) was careful to present his subject in such a manner that there could be no mistake about his high intentions. So the extraordinary qualities of *The Freshman* passed without comment in the press, though it was outstandingly successful with the public at the time and remains the title most people most readily associate with Lloyd's name.

Oddly, Lloyd got a better press with his next film, *For Heaven's Sake,* which was the first to be released by the new distributor, Paramount. Lloyd chose Paramount to replace Pathé after the latter had passed into the hands of a Wall Street brokerage firm that refused his demands for an improved contract. It is his weakest silent feature, though it begins, as many Lloyd films do, with a superb short gag sequence. Lloyd, back in his role of an idle, well-to-do idiot ("who is probably as rich as Mr. Lloyd himself," as *The New York Times* put it), is being driven somewhere by his superstitious chauffeur, who swerves the car to avoid crossing the path not of a black cat, but of a truck with a black cat painted on it, and wrecks the vehicle. "That will be all right, James," says Lloyd, stepping serenely out of the debris. He thereupon enters the first automobile showroom

he sees, buys another car, then manages to stall it on a train track, where a passing express demolishes it just after Lloyd steps out to crank it.

Thereafter, alas, the film runs downhill rather rapidly. Lloyd chances upon a mission in a slum section of town, falls for the minister's daughter, and undertakes to rescue the financially imperiled church. (There is a good quick gag when, entering the mission for the first time, he hands his hat and cane to a derelict thinking he must be the butler, and the bemused drunk wanders off wearing Harold's finery). Among his other activities, he attempts to recruit a group of toughs for the congregation, and after firing a gun in their pool hall hang-out, gets them to chase him to the mission. The cops join the rally; there is another nice moment as director Sam Taylor pans the beatific faces of the yeggs, singing hymns while they quietly divest themselves of hot merchandise, the cops, too, joining in the chorus. Still, this chase, on foot, is hardly among the most inspired of Lloyd's career and a subsequent, more elaborate rally is worse. The millionaire members of Lloyd's club in effect kidnap him, hoping to prevent his marriage to the mission lass, and the members of her congregation mount a search and rescue mission which climaxes with them riding wildly through the city streets aboard a double-decker bus they have commandeered, and which is part of the time driverless. The swaying of this contraption at high speeds is alarming, especially since Lloyd and friends are all riding on the open upper deck (the bus was mounted on huge rollers before a rear-projection screen to obtain the effect), but the sequence is curiously made. Throughout Lloyd is uncharacteristically passive. Even on the bus, the most perilous stunts — including a drunk tightroping along the upper deck rail as the bus seems to lurch wildly around curves — go to other members of the cast. As a result, there is very little audience identification with Lloyd's character, and the thrills in the sequence are rather empty ones. Moreover, the entire motivation for this climactic chase seems feeble. One just doesn't believe that the class sense of his clubmates is so exquisite that they would go to these lengths to prevent his marriage.

The Times thought the film "a comedy of gags" with "the story itself . . . of little consequence," but that is not strictly accurate. The romance is a bit more complex than was customary in Lloyd's films and the minor characterizations are a bit more fleshed out. In fact, Lloyd and Taylor explored the story's setting in more leisure and with more interest than ever before in a Lloyd film — making it something of a sketch for a later, much better film about the life of the poor in the big city, 1928's *Speedy.* Nor can one deny that involving Lloyd — or any other silent comic for that matter — in a story about religious life was novel and intrinsically interesting. The problem, contrary to *The Times's* reviewer, was that the gags weren't strong enough to satisfactorily enliven these other admirable qualities. Perhaps one's final, patient judgment ought to be that the

lessons of *The Freshman* had been learned but not fully digested, so that the virtues of that film were not yet easily repeated.

During the year *For Heaven's Sake* was in release, a small studio in large financial difficulties, Warner Brothers, decided to stake what was left of its resources on a novelty known as sound pictures. In that year they released a John Barrymore movie, *Don Juan,* with its musical score recorded directly on the film. They also prevailed upon Will H. Hays, that model of middle-western rectitude brought in as the industry's so-called czar to improve the movies' image after the scandals earlier in the decade, to record a prologue for *Don Juan.* In it one could plainly see that the words one heard were perfectly synchronized with his lip movements, and the public was mightily intrigued. Warners quickly released two more features with a recorded score, as well as a series of shorts of well-known concert artists singing popular arias. Meantime, *The Jazz Singer,* essentially a silent film that broke into synchronized song whenever Al Jolson did one of his numbers, went into production, to be released October 6, 1927.

The other studios felt that if they ignored sound it would probably go away, and, indeed, it is interesting that some of the greatest silent films were made after it was technically feasible to make talkies. Among them were *Wings, Underworld, The Wind, The Last Command,* F. W. Murnau's masterful *Sunrise* and King Vidor's no less impressive *The Crowd,* not to mention the late Garbo movies, *Love* (a version of *Anna Karenina*) and *A Woman of Affairs* (adapted from that great period best-seller, Michael Arlen's *The Green Hat*). Chaplin made *The Circus,* which was totally silent, and Keaton was not heard from in *Steamboat Bill, Jr.* or *The Cameraman.*

Similarly, Lloyd was not interested in sound. In 1927 and 1928 he went ahead with two silent features, seemingly oblivious to the technological revolution, and as late as 1929 he had virtually completed a silent film before deciding to roll with the wave of the future, expensively scrapping some of the film and re-shooting much of it in order to accommodate sound sequences.

It could be said that, taken together, his last two silents, *The Kid Brother* and *Speedy,* stand as a sort of summary of his career as a silent comedian, with the latter — virtually unremarked by later critics — coming especially close to *The Freshman* in quality.

The Kid Brother is a rural comedy, with Lloyd back in his role of the bumpkin dreamer, beset by large people who misunderstand him as an impractical dope, perhaps a coward. The plot's business is to reveal not only his intelligence, but an admirable courage when something worthwhile is at stake. *Speedy,* on the other hand, presents an urban Lloyd, somewhat hampered in his ability to make a living by the large chunk in his imaginative life that is preoccupied by baseball fandom. There is no undertone of cowardice in this characterization, and, refreshingly, little personal ambition. In fact, one of the best qualities of this last

The Kid Brother shyly woos the girl from the medicine show. She was played by Jobyna Ralston, who was Lloyd's leading lady in six of his most important films of the 1920s.

silent film is Lloyd's willingness to sacrifice himself in order to help out friends. More important, as he neared the apex of his career he succeeded in making two films that (again like *The Freshman,* but unlike *For Heaven's Sake*) satisfactorily melded imaginative gags and thrill sequences with stories of some complexity. In short, with these movies Lloyd made a contribution to what one has come to think of as the "high silent" period, the two or three years in which it became increasingly obvious that the very nature of film was about to be changed — talking pictures are not just silents with sound added, but a whole new art form — and during which movie-makers created a sort of collective apotheosis of the dying form.

The Kid Brother is a kind of male Cinderella story, with Lloyd as the frail Harold Hickory, much put upon by his hearty father, who is sheriff of a backwoods town, and his muscular elder brothers. Lloyd was never more appealing than in those films where the quick guile of his character was set in opposition to the blundering brutishness of the world and was employed not for material advancement but simply for survival. There is a purity of motive in these pictures that renders them, and their leading man, peculiarly attractive.

From the beginning, Lloyd's cleverness in his role of household slave is wittily established. For example, he mechanizes his chores of clothes and dishwashing. To wash the clothes, he ties them to a rope, sticks them in a butter churn and uses it as his washing machine; when the wash is clean, he simply runs the whole line through the wringer and attaches it to a balloon which floats aloft to expose the clothes to the quick-drying upper airs. Similarly, when it comes to the dishes, he puts them in a net bag, sloshes them about in sudsy water, places them neatly on a shelf which, in turn, is placed on the stove. When its heat has dried them, he simply lifts the whole shelf, with its neatly stacked burden, back on its wall brackets.

The plot revolves around Harold, wearing a borrowed shirt with his father's badge on it, issuing a permit for a medicine show managed by Miss Ralston to play in town. The father forbids such foolery in his Calvinistic precincts and he orders the youth to close the show in the middle of its performance. There is a melee, a fire destroys the show, and Lloyd invites the girl to take shelter in his home. This leads to a bright sequence in which, next morning, each of his brothers attempts to pay court to her by serving her breakfast in bed. Harold has already sent her away, but his rivals don't know it and he is not averse to a little luxury himself. Hidden behind a blanket curtain he has rigged for her privacy, he slips a curtain ring over his wrist to imitate a bracelet and reaches a sly and fluttering hand around the curtain to receive a double breakfast.

His chance to prove his true worth finally arrives when the con man and the strong man from the medicine show, learning that Harold's father is holding the money the town has saved in order to build a dam, steal it. The older Hickory is accused of thievery, and Harold is barred from the posse organized to recover

the money. The girl inspires him with uplifting slogans ("You can be what you think you can be," etc.) and he sets off on his own to clear his father's name. Almost immediately he runs afoul of a bullying neighbor who also has eyes for Miss Ralston. He knocks Harold out and into a rowboat, which drifts downstream into a bay where the hulk of a grounded freighter rests. It is here that the thieves have hidden with their swag, and in a scene quite reminiscent of Buster Keaton's adventures on a derelict ship in *The Navigator,* Harold invades the vessel to confront the crooks.

The chase within its dark confines is beautifully managed, with two high points. The thieves have brought a monkey from the show along and Lloyd uses it to convince the strong man, his chief menace, that he has a posse with him. He equips the monkey with heavy shoes and sets him to clomping around the deck above, almost convincing the thief that he is surrounded by large numbers of vengeful rustics. The other memorable moment occurs when Lloyd is cornered and the strong man repeatedly hits him on the head with a huge iron bar. Miraculously, Lloyd does not go down — because, it is suddenly apparent, he has taken refuge under a jutting piece of iron, on which the villain's club has been banging ineffectually. Harold's wrap-up of his nemesis is also tidy; he uses life preservers as giant quoits, ringing the strong man with them until he is immobilized, then hoisting him aloft in a cargo net and dropping him overboard into a rowboat, which he then paddles ashore with a broom. Needless to say, he wins both Miss Ralston and, at last, the respect of family and neighbors.

The most obvious parallel to this movie in Lloyd's previous work is *Grandma's Boy,* but *The Kid Brother* is in almost every way superior — the story is both more complex and more naturalistic, providing believable gag situations from which the humor of Lloyd's efforts at high-speed problem solving seems to arise naturally. More important, perhaps, his portrayal of a cowardly nature is infinitely more subtle. He does not, certainly, go out of his way to look for trouble, and in the early part he spends a good deal of time skittering nervously away from his menacing relatives and the next-door bully. On the other hand, right from the start, he shows a spunky quality suggesting he has more courage than he perhaps admits to himself. His last-reel transformation is thus prepared for, easily accepted. And the avoidance of an easily humorous explanation — there is nothing like the umbrella-handle talisman in *The Kid Brother* — is a great advance. Finally, Lloyd offers a much more textured and critical look at small-town life in this film than anywhere else in his work — obviously the views of such literary figures as Sinclair Lewis, Sherwood Anderson, and H. L. Mencken had begun to penetrate even Lloyd's small world. His kin are mean-spirited in every sense of the phrase, and so are their neighbors, who are hypocritical about the medicine show (they have passed a law against entertainment, but are glad enough to go to it once it is set up), quick to substitute outrage for trust when their money is discovered to be missing, and generally lead dark, closed lives

Monkey business in *The Kid Brother*. To make his antagonist (Constantine Romanoff) think he's surrounded by a posse, Harold equips a pet monkey with a pair of shoes and sets him to clomping around the ship.

there in the backwoods — which is, of course, why Lloyd is so attracted to the girl from the ever-roaming medicine show. Indeed, this would be Lloyd's last extended use of a rural setting in his films, and he would never again pander to rural values (as he had in *Dr. Jack,* for example). In the 1920s the world had turned — fast — and throughout the culture, from this time on, celebrations of bucolic virtues would become increasingly difficult to find, exposés of them increasingly familiar.

But Lloyd was not without a certain nostalgia for the past, for values he imagined had been more readily visible in times gone by. He was, after all, an American, and Americans — particularly of this century — have commonly believed that they are living on the residue of some Golden Age, that somehow they just missed enjoying a historical moment of amazing grace. Something like that feeling underlay *Speedy,* Lloyd's last silent film, which was among the most touching and sweet-spirited of his movies.

He appeared here in his basic characterization, neither rich nor cowardly, but as a dreamily ambitious youth who persistently allows his dreaminess to get in the way of getting ahead. He is introduced as a soda jerk far gone in a passion for baseball, too preoccupied by radio accounts of ballgames to serve his customers adequately, and enlivening his job whenever possible by turning it into a mock ballgame. He posts the line score of the day's game as he gets it off the radio by using doughnuts, pretzels, and appropriately shaped pastries as numerals, placing them so the kitchen help can keep abreast of the game. He also keeps a catcher's mitt handy so he can field the fresh fruit his fellow workers toss him to adorn his sundaes.

He very shortly loses this job but then he takes a job as a taxi driver, at which he is no less dreamy, but perhaps more dangerous to the general public. By this time he is also preoccupied by the problems of his girl friend and her father (she is played by an actress new to Lloyd, Ann Christy, her father by the expert Bert Woodruff). The father is proprietor of the last horse-drawn trolley line in New York, which runs along some quaintly realized Lower East Side avenue. The traction magnates are eyeing his franchise, though he is loathe to sell, not only because he has devoted his life to the line, but because he, his horse, and his car are a beloved neighborhood institution. The old man's position is weak: his franchise specifies that he must run his route at least once per day, and if the traction people can prevent him from so doing, they can take over.

Lloyd, meantime, has his adventures as a cabbie, notably a wild ride to Yankee Stadium, attempting to get a very important passenger out to the ballgame on time. The passenger is Babe Ruth, played by himself, registering no more than bemusement. The addition of his star value to Lloyd's made *Speedy* a movie unique in the actor's career, since in no other did he appear with any star, professional actor or not, of a magnitude comparable to his own.

The traction people, meanwhile, have determined to stage a riot on the old

VIPs: Harold poses with his father, Darsie ''Foxy'' Lloyd, chief cook, cheerleader and consultant when he was breaking into films. Later such celebrities as Babe Ruth (who co-starred with him in *Speedy*) and heavyweight champion Jack Dempsey, were available as publicity-generating companions.

streetcar to prevent its completing its franchise-dictated rounds. The neighborhood rallies round to protect the car, and the fight between this rabble armed with improvised weapons (one man wears a baseball catcher's protective gear, another a football uniform, the Chinese laundryman wields a red hot iron, others bear pots and pans from the housewares store) and the toughs recruited by the traction magnates is a glorious rally. It was inventive and touchingly staged by Ted Wilde, a gagman promoted to the director's chair for this film and nominated for an Academy Award for his contributions to it.

This plan foiled, the would-be monopolists now resort to horse-and-trolley napping. Lloyd's only clue to the whereabouts of the purloined rolling stock is supplied by a faithful dog who has nipped the seat out of the pants of one of the thieves. Following this rather obviously marked man, Lloyd finds the crooks' hideout and makes off with the horse and car. A wild chase follows, with Lloyd galloping the contraption through the streets, free of any tracks. At one point the horse loses his shoe and Lloyd must cut him loose. Motive power is then supplied by an automobile to which he quietly hitches the streetcar. When the auto's occupants look around, the streetcar appears to be bearing down on them, about to crash into them from behind, which of course makes them drive still faster. Lloyd expertly cuts loose from the car at just the right moment, acquiring a new team by stealing horses from a distracted teamster. Much of the film was shot on location in New York, an unprecedented thing for Lloyd to do, and at one point, as Lloyd was wheeling around a corner at top speed, he crashed into an El support; this footage of a totally unplanned thrill was kept in the final cut of the film. The streetcar is all but wrecked when he tries to make it hurdle a ditch uncovered by the crooks, but Lloyd triumphantly drives the battered, now wheelless cab the length of the route, maintaining Pop Dillon's franchise.

Like its immediate predecessor, this film titled with the star's youthful nickname is extraordinarily well structured, the story line and gag sequences smoothly integrated. And, like *For Heaven's Sake*, it warmly explores a cut of life with which Lloyd did not ordinarily deal. Moreover, his relationship with the young woman and her father, his involvement in their life, gives a rootedness and a complexity to the romantic relationship that was also unprecedented in Lloyd's work. (There is a comical courtship scene at Coney Island that ends with extraordinary poignancy. Having lost their money, they must hitch back to the city in a friend's moving van. On the way, they rearrange its contents, turning the inside of the van into a model of the living room they hope some day to share.)

Setting aside the honorable failure of *For Heaven's Sake,* and regretfully noting the passing of the lunatic spirit that animated *Why Worry?,* these pictures seem to prove that in the eight years since he began making features, Lloyd had, through diligent trial and error, achieved mastery of a comic form that suited his gifts and his audience admirably. He made few great claims either for that form or that audience. ''I think my character represented the white-collar middle class that felt frustrated but was always fighting to overcome its shortcomings,'' he

would say many years later. "We had a big appeal for businessmen. They're always telling me they loved that boy because he was good for a laugh — you came away refreshed and you didn't have to do any heavy thinking."

Yet it was no small thing he had accomplished in a short span of years, something only a handful of people accomplished, though many tried. He had created an immortal screen icon, and he had found a way of mounting that icon that was inventive, widely appealing and satisfying to him. And — unlike Chaplin — he was entirely content to live with that persona for as long as anyone wanted him to do so. He had even found, in most of his last silent features, a way of giving that figure some of the warmth and roundedness he had been criticized for lacking. There is reason to suppose that if the silent era had lasted a few more years, he might have gone still farther in that direction, struck some of the pathetic notes he tentatively plucked in *The Freshman* and, indeed, in *Speedy*. There his desperate efforts to save the streetcar line have no crass motivation whatever, but appear to stem from a real regard for a little institution that performs a valuable service in giving a sense of identity, of continuity, to a polyglot community.

Speedy is among the most overlooked of Lloyd's features, though it was quite successful in its own moment despite the competition from sound films. Hollywood had now overcome its initial hesitation about sound movies and was rushing headlong into a future it did not understand and had not planned for. In fact, it could not have planned ahead, for so much would be conditioned by the great economic disaster of the 1930s. Lloyd, too, would be borne along on these currents, and he would not be able to consolidate the artistic growth he had made at the end of the silent era. As an artist he would be forced, hereafter, to grope for handholds on a slippery precipice, and he would not again make a film as quietly assured, as thoroughly pleasing, as this last of his silent films.

10   Through 1924 Harold Lloyd made two pictures a year; thereafter he made one a year, and since they were handcrafted products, the work of a small creative group whose activities he had to oversee daily, and since he took such an active interest in post-production work, including their exploitation, he was an extremely busy man. One finds in the archives no detailed record of his life as a family man and one must assume that most of his free time was devoted to overseeing the construction of his new home. Considering its lavishness, and the fact that he demonstrated as a homeowner the same devotion to detail that he exercised on his films, one must imagine him not only busy, but happy, since he always seemed to prefer pouring his energy into projects rather than into his relationships with people.

105

Greenacres

In his autobiography, written just before the house was completed, he reported that initially "we wanted no formality," but that their architect designed a home in the Italian Renaissance style, "formal and growing progressively more so." But a friend, also an architect, advised him: "Don't build a monument to your architect; build a home for yourself," and he claimed that after a year's work the initial plans were scrapped entirely. This seems an exaggeration, for Lloyd confessed that his architect-friend "failed to impart" the secret of non-monumental construction to him, and the finished project resists any other description. Of course, Lloyd had a unique problem. He had determined to build a house out of current income, and the fact was that the income was nearly unlimited. Over the four years he was building his showplace, he was able to divert something like two and a half million dollars to the project.* With that kind of funding available it would have been impossible, probably, to keep any architect within the bounds of prudence. In any event, Italian Renaissance the house started out and Italian Renaissance it ended up — more or less. Southern California Eclectic would probably be a better term for it.

The first construction on the sixteen-acre estate was a play area for Gloria, so she would have something to occupy her while her parents inspected progress on the thirty-two-room main house and the extensive gardens and sport facilities surrounding it. The central feature of Gloria's preserve was a small scale half-timbered, thatch-roofed English cottage, complete with electricity, running water, heat, and small-scale furniture. This was set on a small lawn enclosed by a hedge, and there was a stable, in the same English country style, for Gloria's Shetland pony. Naturally she had her own playground, which in addition to the standard equipment contained an aviary, a monkey cage, a small clock tower, and an incline down which she could race in a miniature car, making a figure eight and ending up at a wishing well. One wonders what she could possibly wish for when she tossed a coin into her well.

Indeed, inspecting the estate today, one's impression is that she had all the best of it. Her playhouse is much closer to human scale than her father's cavernous, gloomy, rather dully appointed mansion. Moreover, the things that remain impressive about the house are things that would most delight a child — the garden and game area, and perhaps the basement and sub-basement full of the lavish equipment that made it function smoothly. We are assured that all the furnishings and decor of the house were personally selected, or at least approved, by the master, but they are impressive only for their obvious

---

* The very idea of having a half million or so yearly to spend on building a house seems incredible. Even in these days when some movie stars can command a million dollars a picture, most would be hard-pressed to duplicate this profligacy. But taxes were extremely low in the 1920s and Lloyd was in a unique position. The most he had to spend on his shortish, modestly mounted films was $750,000, and he was known to have grossed as much as three million in the initial domestic release of his comedies, with foreign rental doubling the U.S. take. Since he was the sole owner of the Harold Lloyd Corporation, and thus the sole recipient of its profits, it was not hard to amass money faster than he could imagine ways to spend it.

108

costliness. Nothing has any true distinction, and nothing — aside from some personal memorabilia in the library, some remnants of the hobbies Lloyd pursued in his later years — expresses anything of Lloyd's personality. Everything seems to have been bought merely to demonstrate the wealth of the owner. The spirit of the house is close to that of the Robber Barons' "cottages" at Newport — a somehow distressing comparison.

The home, which Lloyd christened Greenacres, is most memorable from the outside. Entering from Benedict Canyon Drive, one passes a guard house and a chain link fence slipcovered in plants, then winds up a tree-shaded driveway. The left branch of the drive takes one to a seventy-foot lath house, the top floor of which was used as servants' quarters, the bottom as a seven-car garage. In this area are greenhouses which supplied the plants for the estate's twelve formal gardens as well as workshops in which almost everything used on the estate could be repaired or improved. The right fork of the driveway leads to the main courtyard, where it circles around a fountain. There is a small garage here, housing the two Rolls-Royces Lloyd liked to keep handy. The setting of the house, as seen from this elevation, is extremely pleasing. The roof is red-tiled, the color of the stucco a pinkish pastel (now, alas, looking a little dirty), and the house seems to grow naturally out of its hilltop site. Out of view, to the left as one faces the house, is the Olympic-sized swimming pool and pavilion, and beyond that is the four-wall handball court, with accommodations for spectators, that was Lloyd's special pride. Above the driveway to the right is a long formal garden with reflecting pool and beyond it is a walkway leading to an observation point. This is above the 110-foot waterfall that drops sheer to the canyon floor, emptying into a portion of the canoe course, which doubled as part of the drainage system during the rainy season. Down there, too, are ponds and a hole or two of Lloyd's nine-hole golf course, now flattened out to improve drainage. (Lloyd's neighbor, Jack Warner, also had a nine-hole course, and they sometimes erected a stile over the fence separating their properties and invited guests in to play a sporty eighteen.) From the look-out above the fall Lloyd could look across the canyon and see the gables of Pickfair and of his rival Chaplin's home. From other vantage points he could see some of the other showplaces of Hollywood — Carl Laemmle was a neighbor, and yonder on the hill loomed Falcon's Lair, residence of the late Rudolph Valentino.

One's first glimpse of the interior, entering the front door, is promising. The floor is of deep red tile covered with oriental rugs especially woven for Lloyd, but the striking first impression is created chiefly by the handsome cantilevered stairway sweeping to the second floor. Directly ahead, the central garden — the house is actually a series of squares built around it — can be glimpsed through windows. A sharp right turn leads to the most comfortable public room at Greenacres, a library with a collection of books about comedy, comic novels, plays, and the like. There is a baronial desk and a display of the awards Lloyd had

received — ranging from a special Academy Award (which lauds him as both a "master comedian" and a "good citizen") to some bowling trophies. (This was the one game Mildred Lloyd forbade him to provide for in their home, so he simply opened some commercial lanes, which were not only profitable but ever-available to him.) The other particularly attractive room on the main floor is a breakfast room, cheerfully done in the French manner and overlooking Mildred's rose garden. As the years went by the Lloyds took more and more of their meals here, eschewing the heavy formal dining room just across the hall, which was capable of accommodating twenty-four at dinner, but rarely did. At one side at the end of the long main hall is a pleasant music room that Mildred fancied as a sitting room. Beyond that is the giant sunken living room, equipped with a pipe organ and piano (both of which — how typical of Lloyd — could be played mechanically), 35 mm projection equipment, and, in his last years, the booming 36-speaker stereo system which Lloyd rigged before such equipment was commercially marketed and which he sometimes played so loudly that its vibrations dislodged gold leaf from the coffered ceiling. To the left of the balcony which overlooks this grandiloquent room is the sun room or garden room, where his famous Christmas tree stood year round, five thousand ornaments permanently wired into place, while packing cases in the basement contained perhaps another fifteen thousand — yet another of Lloyd's hobbies was collecting these objects.

From the windows of the sun room one can gaze across a vast expanse of lawn toward a formal garden and the gazebo that served as a bandstand for the marathon housewarming the Lloyds held in 1929. A dance floor was laid on the lawn and relays of bands played four-hour stints from Friday night until early Monday. There were apparently more gate crashers than invitees, and in the middle of the week couples were still to be found wandering dazedly about the estate. Lloyd never threw a bash anything like that again, though there were some notably large affairs when he was running for Imperial Potentate of the Shrine in the late forties, and his wife once gave a luncheon for seven hundred wives of Shriners in Los Angeles for a convention. In the thirties the Lloyds often held handball tournaments and informal celebrity tennis tournaments (Doug Fairbanks, Ronald Colman, Robert Taylor, Loretta Young, were among the participants), and golfers like Bobby Jones, Joe Kirkwood, and Tommy Armour played the golf course, usually with movieland celebrities making up the foursomes. By and large, however, even in the decade or so when the house was a social center the Lloyds tended to keep their gatherings rather small and to do most of their entertaining around the swimming pool or in its huge pavilion.

If the gathering were smaller still, there was a unique basement playroom and cocktail den to which all could repair. One reached it by passing down a corridor hollowed out of solid rock; its walls were lined with hundreds of autographed photos of luminaries from every area of public life (C. B. De Mille's

inscription, the most amusing, expresses the hope that his spectacles will never draw as many laughs as Lloyd's). The room itself, done in art deco style, contains a variety of board and card games. Like the passageway, it is hollowed out of the stone of Lloyd's hilltop, and since it sits at the very edge of his bluff, it commands a striking view, even if the dankness of a cave has never quite been banished from it.

Those who have penetrated the second floor of the house, with its suites of private rooms for the Lloyds, their children and guests, report it cozy and sunswept, but neglected during the last lonely and rather sad years of the house's life as a family residence. Actually, one must wonder if a true family was ever a possibility in this pile. The Lloyds, after all, were not to the manor or the manner born. When they moved in, the three members of the family were severely outnumbered by the staff, which included between seven and twelve men to do the outside work, a personal maid for Mildred, a valet for Harold, a nanny for little Gloria (later there were two, as more children came along), plus a butler and a kitchen staff. The house could not have been a comfortable fit for the Lloyds, and they had scarcely settled in before the market crashed and the kind of social life that might have filled their echoing pile started to fade. The more one contemplates the place, the more it seems to be one of Lloyd's playthings that didn't work out — though plaything is admittedly an odd word to apply to any work on such a scale.

For nearly every feature of Greenacres exists to accommodate some interest of Lloyd's. Aside from collecting Dresden china and doing needlework, his wife appears to have had no hobbies and small interest in social life. Certainly she did nothing that required the space she was required to fill here. As for Gloria, the home appears to have isolated her — obviously there were no neighbor's kids to play with and doubtless the huge home inhibited such school friends as she may have invited home. In fact, there is some reason to believe — though this is tricky ground — that Lloyd adopted a daughter, Marjorie Elizabeth (Peggy), in part because he wanted to provide a playmate for his own child. This, at any rate, is Peggy's belief now.

As she told her story in a recent interview, her original name was also Gloria (Freeman), and she was a foundling taken in by a Mrs. Louise Sullivan, a Chicagoan who had comfortably retired to Pasadena, hoping to use her wealth to provide a foster home for a number of orphaned and abandoned children. The crash reduced her means considerably and she was forced to put her charges up for adoption. After a month's trial stay with the Lloyds, Gloria was legally adopted by them, though since they could not have two children with the same name, they required the five-year-old stranger to take the name she now bears. This, she has said, made for a traumatic introduction to the household. She claims that she would make quiet phone calls to Mrs. Sullivan begging to be taken back, though she does not deny that the Lloyds were completely generous with her,

111

that in the matters of toys, clothes, travel, schooling, she was in no way discriminated against. She also claims that she became good friends with her new sister as well as with the Lloyds' son, Harold, Jr., who was born in January, 1931.

The birth was celebrated, we are told, by a day-long ringing of the bell, a gift of the king of Spain, which surmounted the high tower that rose out of the courtyard. It was also the occasion for terrible anxiety. Not only was the child born prematurely — weighing a little less than three pounds — but his life was immediately threatened by a ransom note informing Lloyd the baby would be taken from his incubator at Good Samaritan and that Lloyd would find him dead in a shoe box if he did not pay a large sum of money, details to be arranged. Such threats were not taken idly at the time — the Lindbergh kidnapping being much on the minds of wealthy and famous people — and Lloyd immediately hired guards for the hospital and for the estate. Nothing came of the threat, but the guards stayed on at Greenacres, supported by an elaborate electrical warning system. Peggy would recall that she and her sister went under guard to school and were even accompanied wherever they went within the confines of the estate. This constant surveillance took its toll on her and, she implies, on the other Lloyd children as well.

Manifestly, she was a child with a greater need for love than most, and though she never lacked for attention or material objects, love she did not find. As we shall see, the Lloyd's natural children suffered the same deprivation, and proved as adults to be, if anything, more scarred than the adopted child. Somehow, rattling around in the great house, none of them could get in touch, in real touch, with an increasingly preoccupied father, an increasingly withdrawn mother.

Some of the former's preoccupation was explicable. Here, at last, was the great solidly rooted house, its earthquake-proof, steel-reinforced foundations anchored deep in the tough rock of his hill, that he had longed for since he was a wandering child. But, ironically, he had finished the house just as the source of the wealth that had made it possible was jeopardized by the final establishment of sound films as the only acceptable movie medium, and just months before the stock market crash had substantially reduced Lloyd's fortune. In the circumstances, he had a right to be self-concerned.

In any case, it seems doubtful that Lloyd was temperamentally suited for fatherhood. There was simply too much of the child in him to fulfill the role on more than an intermittent basis. His intense, serial interest in games and hobbies is evidence enough of that. It is the familiar pattern of the small boy, filling his fancy with one overwhelming concern after another, spending all his allowance on it, then suddenly abandoning it for the next thing. The house would become a museum of these interests, one layered atop another.

Lloyd's many superstitions were further proof of his childish nature. He

The handball star on the court
he built at the General Services Studio,
where he moved production
headquarters after the coming of
sound.

At play: Harold pauses to pose with his
children — adopted daughter Peggy is
on his shoulders, Gloria and the new
baby, Harold, Jr., ride his lap, in this
1931 snapshot.

The family, circa 1935.
Gloria wears the long curls.

always insisted on leaving a building by the same path that he had entered it. (He was once four hours in traffic trying to get away from a Rose Bowl game by his precise route of arrival.) He also believed it was bad luck for an auto to go completely around a driveway circle — which was particularly inconvenient for his chauffeur, since the main approach to the Lloyd home ended in a circle around the fountain in the courtyard; the fellow was always required to back out the way he came. He believed as well that it was bad luck to use the last check in the book, and since that superstition extended to travelers checks, he died with thousands of dollars worth of them uncashed. On the other hand, he believed that the recovery of forgotten money was extraordinarily lucky, and whenever he found change in coat pocket or drawer he immediately deposited it in the safe in his home, where thousands of dollars worth of coins and bills piled up, untouched. Along the same lines, he could never bring himself to part with any possession, which is why he had so many cars, many of them — like his 1924 and 1925 Rolls-Royces — turning into antiques as they stood in his garage (the 1924 Rolls was the car Audrey Hepburn's father chauffeured in *Sabrina* in 1952), and why his real estate all over California was never sold, even though he rarely used it. (Director King Vidor, who has a ranch near Pasa Robles, once asked Lloyd about a sign near his own spread announcing the Harold Lloyd Ranch. The comedian sheepishly admitted that besides never bothering to improve the acreage, he had never even visited it.)

There was a good side to the conservative instincts which informed so many of these superstitions. The real estate, like the Rollses, appreciated in value, further increasing Lloyd's wealth. His instructions to his gardeners never to exterminate bird and animal pests on his property — an instruction they sometimes had to quietly violate — doubtless had a happy effect on the woodland creatures of his domain. His reluctance even to cut down a tree or a shrub was no more than a harmless foible. And his inability to fire any employee created great loyalty among many of them, despite the fact that he was parsimonious about salaries, and despite the fact that when cutting staff became essential, the responsibility was shuffled off on overseers, who thus protected his benign image.

Still, it must be said that however endearing some of Lloyd's child-like qualities were, they had their dangerous aspects. The sad reminiscences of his adopted daughter demonstrate that, and the later lives of his own two children, as well as that of his wife, show it still more starkly.

11) The imaginations of some children are filled with fantasies of
disaster. Others serenely lack the ability to picture anything but a
sunny future, untouched by hints even of distress, let alone mortality. Even if we
knew nothing about Harold Lloyd but what we could deduce from his screen
character, we would know that he was a child-man of the latter persuasion. It is
what on screen led him to *Welcome Danger,* to borrow the title of the picture he
completed just about the time he moved into Greenacres. All the evidence leads
one to believe that he accepted the coming of sound without panic, with no fear
for his future. He had, in fact, planned *Welcome Danger* as a silent film,
completed and even previewed it as such, apparently certain that his popularity
was so great that he need have no truck with dialogue and all the other problems
attendant on making "talkies," as people were beginning to call them.

Then one day, as he liked to tell the story, he was strolling in downtown Los
Angeles and heard gales of laughter rolling out of a theater. He bought a ticket
and went in to find the audience laughing at simple sound effects — eggs frying
in a pan, the clink of ice in a glass. It was the laughter of recognition, an
expression of delight in a level of realism previously unavailable to the movies.
Later he would remember saying to himself, "Here we're working our heads off,
trying to get funny, humorous ideas and [they're] getting them on these sound
effects." He determined, on the spot it would seem, virtually to remake
Welcome Danger, scrapping about half his footage, adding dialogue sequences,
and dubbing sound effects into the action sequences, which otherwise remained
pretty much unchanged. His associates were aghast as costs came closer to a
million dollars than any other Lloyd feature ever had, and the press reported that
in its first previews the revised print ran close to three hours. Lloyd, however,
followed his customary practice of patient trimming based on audience response
(though he came to feel later that he should have excised another reel from the
picture). Ironically, since it is distinctly one of his lesser films, it made more
money than any of his other vehicles. Because he was the first major comedian
to break the sound barrier (Chaplin did not do a true dialogue picture until 1940;
Keaton, though he appeared briefly in an MGM all-star revue in 1929, did not
essay a starring feature in sound until the following year), the public was very
curious about how he would do.

It was probably disappointed. Attempting a new wrinkle on his basic
character, he appears as an extremely pedantic Boston botany student named
Harold Bledsoe, not so much a coward as a youth who had never been exposed

to danger in his scholarly little life, though his father had been chief of police in San Francisco. Summoned there to help stamp out a crime wave because the present captain thinks he may be a chip off the old block, Lloyd makes his way west awkwardly, prey to sundry not-very-exciting misadventures. Established on the force, where everyone thinks he's a blockhead, his scholar's mind becomes obsessed with the Bertillion fingerprinting system when he finds prints are like leaves — no two alike — and present glorious opportunities for cataloging and cross-cataloging. He makes a nuisance of himself insisting that everyone, including such above-suspicion characters as the police commissioner and a high-minded civic reformer, submit to fingerprinting. The latter's prints turn out to match that of The Dragon, mysterious overlord of the underworld, and Lloyd finally pursues him to a lair deep in Chinatown where, in an endless, stumbling rally (mostly in the dark) Lloyd finally brings him to justice.

There are some funny moments in the film: Lloyd's befuddlement when he enters a do-it-yourself photo booth, poses, and the machine delivers a picture of Barbara Kent, its previous occupant — with whom he will fall in love; an insanely inappropriate lecture on the glories of the petunia delivered in a fingerprint lab; a sublime moment when Lloyd, in hot pursuit of the reformer's fingerprints simply snips out the corner of a straw hat brim he has observed the man handling. On the whole, however, the film was regressive, for there again is the familiar structural defect — in this case no real connection between the film's first part (Lloyd making his way cross-country and its second (the crime story) — and the whole picture had, as *The New York Times*'s Mordaunt Hall reported, a "cumbersome" air about it.

Perhaps Lloyd was more insecure about sound than he admitted to himself, for especially in the climactic sequence he used quantities of material instead of a judicious selection, carefully paced. Moreover, those dialogue sequences which contain cross-talk are slow paced and for the most part unfunny. Finally, and this perhaps had more significance for his future than anything else, he had a vocal problem.

He did not recognize it. He had reported to a voice coach before going to work on the dialogue scenes because he recognized that it had been close on two decades since he had used his voice professionally. The fellow worked with him a few days, told him he was producing his tones too much from his throat, gave him some exercises designed to correct the defect, and discharged him. Lloyd, it seems, was perfectly content with this diagnosis and treatment, though he would later tell a friend, "I was born to be a comedian, not an actor," indicating that he understood the limits his voice put upon him. It was inescapably colorless and flat — prissy would be the best way to describe it. It was all right in the sense that it more or less matched the image he had been projecting for some years. It was not as if he were a leading man trying to mouth romantic lines in a falsetto. But it did restrict the range of roles he might hope to

116

essay, and it was ill-suited to his old go-getting type. It should also be remembered that Lloyd turned forty in 1933, and though he continued to look younger than his years all his life, the youthful timbre of his voice prevented him from permitting his character to age, allowing him to experiment — had he dared to — with character roles. Finally, as the decade moved on, a new comedy style established itself, the fast, cross-talk comedy, the screwball farce, mastered by Howard Hawks (*Twentieth Century, Bringing Up Baby, His Girl Friday*), entertainingly broadened by the likes of Leo McCary, Gregory La Cava, W. S. Van Dyke (who did the first Thin Man picture) and others. Lloyd, as we shall see, tried such a picture, but his thinnish voice tended to get lost in the verbal uproar. Gradually, his production pace slowed and, worse, his central position in the comic ranks eroded, and, finally, he fell silent.

Still, as of 1930, with *Welcome Danger* coining money at an unprecedented rate, he had reason to think that perhaps he was among the very few silent picture stars who had made the transition to sound with exemplary ease. He forthwith plunged into a new production, *Feet First*. His thinking was obvious — he would rekindle the beloved memory of his earlier stunting atop tall buildings. It is quite clear that the film began, as *Safety Last* had, with an idea for a spectacular thrill sequence, plot to be supplied later.

That proved to be his undoing. He is introduced as a meek and incompetent shoe clerk in Honolulu, earnestly studying Dale Carnegie-like courses on how to get ahead, but not getting anywhere. Opportunity knocks when he is called upon to wait on a lady whose husband owns the chain of stores for which Harold works. He also falls in love with a girl (Barbara Kent again) who turns out to be the tycoon's secretary. In pursuit of her he becomes a stowaway on the ship taking them all back to the United States mainland, and there is some mild fun to be found in his attempts to keep himself fed, to get a night's sleep, and to avoid arousing the suspicions of the ship's crew. There is also an unfortunate reliance on comic clichés here — exploding cigars, slippery banana peels, that sort of thing. Finally, the shoe magnate requires that an important contract be delivered to Los Angeles, and Lloyd, trying to ingratiate himself with the boss, the secretary, and the wife (who is beginning to remember him as the young man who made her last shoe fitting so uncomfortable), volunteers to take it to the ship's mailroom, whither it is to be transferred to a seaplane which will whisk the mail back to the States. Unfortunately, the ship's officer who is most suspicious of Lloyd enters the mailroom just as he does and Lloyd hides from him in a mail sack. He is still in it when crewmen bundle it up and deposit it in the airplane. It is the beginning of Lloyd's last great — perhaps greatest — thrill sequence, one so dangerous to shoot that brother Gaylord, watching from the sidelines, was actually nauseated by anxiety.

Harold rides all the way to Los Angeles in the sack, which is transferred to a delivery truck and dumped with several other sacks on a street corner. The sack

containing Lloyd, however, lands on a painter's scaffold which is resting briefly on the walk, then raised gently up, up, up the side of the building where the painters are working. In mid-air the sack begins to bounce alarmingly about on the narrow and rickety platform as Lloyd, ignorant of his location, begins trying to get out of the sack. It, meantime, catches on the metal support for an awning at just the moment Harold is using a pocket knife to cut himself free of his sack, the audience imagining he will step out of it into thin air. Just as that is about to happen, however, the scaffold reappears to provide footing, but cold comfort for the comedian, who makes a grab for a window sill — only to have the window come down on his hands as he loses his foothold on the scaffold. When it reappears, alas, it pushes down on the top of his head and only a desperate grab for the bottom of the scaffold saves him.

By this time he has acquired an ally, a black janitor of marvelous calm, a man constitutionally incapable of hurrying for help. He grabs hold of Harold's feet, attempting to pull him into a window, just as a cigar, left burning on the scaffold, rolls onto Harold's hand and down his collar. His agonized thrashings cause a bucket of paint to fall off the rig onto the upturned face of the janitor and the stock broker he has summoned to try to help Harold out of his predicament. The latter, by this time, has taken refuge on the top of an awning which first unfurls, then begins to split, finally threatens to tear entirely away from its moorings, Lloyd hanging from the slowly rending metal supports first by his knees, then his toes. He disembarks just in time, grabbing hold of another window — which turns out to be barred. His black friend's attempts to squeeze him through the bars by main force are unavailing, so he clambers up a story to an open window — out of which, at just the wrong moment, painters shove another scaffold. He grabs it, and it starts to slide diagonally out the window, depositing an empty paint bucket on his head, blinding him, though he manages to grab a dangling rope. The maniacally managed scaffold, inexplicably being hauled up and down by the oblivious roof-top workers, knocks into him again just as he has managed to gain a purchase on another window sill. He makes a flailing grab for anything he can find and gets hold of a fire hose which now unreels at an alarming rate. Just then, the janitor reappears and for some reason takes it into his head to turn on the water, causing the hose to gyrate wildly. "Cut it off!" Harold cries, and the janitor takes him literally, applying fire axe to hose — and sending Lloyd, still clutching the nozzle, into free fall, from which he is rescued by the timely reappearance of the scaffold. He should be safe now, except that it pauses briefly outside a taxidermist's window, where Lloyd spots a gorilla and in his addled state assumes it to be alive. He scuttles quickly up the scaffold's rope and pulls himself to the edge of the rooftop. The painters have left an open bottle of ether near the point where Lloyd is catching his breath. It puts him to sleep, he rolls back off the roof onto the scaffold, which begins to descend again. His head beginning to clear, he climbs woozily back up its rope, only to be

118

knocked out — and off the roof again as one of the painters gesticulates to make a point in an argument he is having with his partner. Lloyd's foot, however, is tangled in a rope which breaks this final fall (during which he faints). He wakes up screaming for help hanging from another window, just inches off the ground — to the bewilderment of passers-by.

Needless to say, his efforts turn out to be extremely valuable to the shoe tycoon, Lloyd gets the girl, and all's well that ends well. Amazingly, some critics found this great sequence "a trifle prolonged," and instead of treating it as a classic restatement of Lloyd's one unquestioned contribution to the vocabulary of screen comedy, implied self-plagiarism. To do so while applauding the weakish situation comedy of the film's opening reels — material that makes the wait for the skyscraper sequence well-nigh unbearable and, indeed, destroys the validity of the film as a total entity, is a startling example of critical misapprehension. But feeble reviews plus a feeble overall structure contributed to making the movie the closest a Lloyd feature had ever come to being an outright flop. Even if it had something more to depend on than one glorious sequence to carry it with the public, it probably would have failed, for Lloyd's ambitious young man, exemplar of the success ethic, was not in keeping with the spirit of the times in this first full year of the Depression. He actively reminded people of what now seemed to be extremely false values in a way, for example, that the anarchical Marx Brothers, visible now in *The Cocoanuts* and *Animal Crackers,* did not. In an unreasonable time, there was something a little too reasonable about Lloyd.

So, reasonably enough, Lloyd decided to take a little time off to think over his future course. He puttered about the estate, announced plans for another college picture, then apparently thought better of it, and finally went to work on what was to turn out to be the most satisfying of his sound films, *Movie Crazy.*

It opens with a splendid sight gag — Harold (Hall was his surname in this film) seeming to ride serenely along a street in a luxurious touring car, while "The Voice of Hollywood" is heard on the sound track, discussing the luxurious life of the stars. Then the car speeds up — and Harold is revealed to be simply peddling along on a bicycle on the far side of the car.* It is an energetic and imaginative shot, and gets one off happily, quite convinced that the tired and faltering qualities of *Feet First* will not be present here. And they are not. As so often happens when Hollywood turns to a subject it really knows, namely Hollywood, there is an infectious joy to the picture, an almost childish delight in putting itself on, that gives the movie a smartness, a knowledgeability, a confidence, that are very comforting. Throughout, one has a sense not of strain but of conservation, a

---

* The sequence ranks with the other great opening sight gag in the Lloyd filmography, the first shot of *Safety Last.* That is a somber tableau — a man in what appears to be ministerial garb praying, a uniformed guard, a mother and a lover weeping, Lloyd's head bowed in what appears to be sorrowful contrition, the shadow of what looks like a gallows on the rear wall, the whole photographed through bars. As the camera pulls back, what seemed to be some prison's death row is revealed as a perfectly ordinary railway station where family and girl friend have gathered to say farewell to the city-bound, fortune-seeking Lloyd — a perfect visual pun.

feeling that the film-makers have more material at hand than they can possibly use, are giving us only the top of a strong line.

Harold is once again an ambitious dreamer, desiring fame and fortune but not entirely certain how to obtain it. He has mailed an 8 x 10 glossy of himself to a studio's talent department, but unknown to him, his father has substituted a picture of a much handsomer man. Now a letter arrives, asking Harold to come to the West Coast for a screen test, for which he sets off hopeful to the point of overconfidence, ignoring his father's attempts to calm his hopes without revealing his own subterfuge.

Harold's train pulls into the Los Angeles Union Station, where a movie company is shooting on location. This is the film's first large island of comedy: the over-eager Harold is recruited instantly for extra work and in his eagerness spoils shot after shot — his suitcase opens in the middle of a simple walk-through shot, he knocks over a very large number of metal milk containers during a quiet scene — and he also goes quite rooky (to use Lloyd's word) over the Latin leading lady.

This first direct encounter with the motion picture industry at work sets the tone for all Harold's subsequent entanglements with it — in an interview with a studio casting director (he reduces the man's office to a shambles); in a screen test (miscast as a sophisticated man of the world, he answers the prop telephone before it has rung); most famously at a great Hollywood party, where he and a magician accidentally exchange coats in the men's room, and as he dances with the wife of the studio president, rabbits, a baby chick, and white mice appear at awkward moments, while his comic boutonniere keeps squirting her in the eye. This last routine is one of Lloyd's most delightful, doubtless the product of his lifelong interest in magic. The party-wrecking havoc he finally creates is reminiscent of what the Marx Brothers did to Mrs. Rittenhouse's weekend party in *Animal Crackers*.

Perhaps the most unusual feature of the film is the series of strange interludes that constitute its love story, the most enigmatic and the most lengthily developed of all the romances in Lloyd's movies. Following his interview with the casting director, Harold literally stumbles into a pretty young thing who is struggling, outside the studio gate, to put up the roof of her convertible in a rainstorm. He gallantly lends a hand, his general ineptitude leading first to general hilarity, then to a minor accident. Since he is, as ever, such an eager and amiable chap, she finally takes pity on him and invites him into her home to be dried out and patched up. What is so curious is that this ordinary, pretty young woman, called Mary Sears (and nicely played by Constance Cummings, an American actress whose career was mostly spent in England), is also the exotic, temperamental actress in the Spanish costume with whom Lloyd fell into first-sight love at the train station. What is even more curious is that for most of the picture's length she does not admit, and he does not discover, her double

identity. And what is most curious of all, Mary uses this misapprehension to toy with Harold, alternately encouraging his advances when she is in costume, discouraging them when she appears in her other role. It is really quite cruel, and though we are encouraged to think of this deception as a test of his affections, such a test is hardly necessary, given his puppy-like devotion to the girl in both her incarnations. In the denouement, which occurs after Lloyd has turned an expensive action sequence into a farce so funny the head of the studio offers him a comedian's contract, he cheerfully accepts her inexplicable behavior. The ultimate implication of the film is that he is completely willing to marry without question a near schizophrenic. Since the pace of the film is so fizzy, and we are so used to Lloyd's routine acceptance of extremely odd situations, we easily suspend disbelief in his weird passion and its weird conclusion, which has the air of a conventionally happy one. It is only later that questions begin to arise, that we begin to wish the movie-makers had at least acknowledged that she was behaving rather strangely, offering some plausible explanation for her cruelty, if not for Lloyd's blithe blindness to it. Instead, the whole business was treated as just another odd situation in an odd screen career — something like finding oneself hanging from a clock's hands far above the street, improbable but not totally impossible. It is further evidence that Harold Lloyd really never knew anything about people, tending to mix himself up with mechanical problems because they were explicable to him. On the other hand, there is something attractively absurdist about this relationship to a modern viewer. It gives the movie an enigmatic flavor of a sort generally missing from Lloyd's films, though at the time none of the critics paid it the slightest heed.

Mordaunt Hall, *The New York Times* reviewer whose incomparable imperceptiveness is one of the wayward delights of working in film history, was for once correct in his judgment and gave the movie a handsome notice, calling it "a relief" after the cycle of gangster pictures that had lately preoccupied movie-makers. In fact *Movie Crazy* was apparently the most commercially successful of Lloyd's films in this decade; it was also the last time he fully and successfully incorporated his basic silent screen characterization into a sound film.

One might expect that *Movie Crazy* would have been the film that consolidated Lloyd's position in talkies — it was so well made, so enjoyable in its kinky little way. Perhaps he had absorbed the lessons of his first, unsatisfying efforts in the new medium; perhaps he could now regain the consistency he had attained in the last years of the silent era.

This was not to be, though he certainly tried hard enough and long enough — two years — on his next film. For the first time he bought a story from an established non-movie writer, from Clarence Buddington Kelland, the very popular creator of comical fiction for the *Saturday Evening Post,* and he spent freely on the production. He recruited his old colleague, Sam Taylor, to direct and hired an

expert supporting cast (including Una Merkle as his leading lady and his director from prehistoric days, J. Farrell MacDonald, in a small role).

But *The Cat's Paw* was a disaster, undoubtedly the worst feature he had ever made. The story is of a missionary's son who returns to the United States and is asked by corrupt politicians to run for mayor on a reform ticket because they expect him to lose. He surprises them by winning and taking his reformer's creed seriously. It is a sturdy enough plot at first glance, but its development is routine. Lloyd indulges in almost no physical comedy in the course of the picture, and such verbal wit as the script offers is feeble.

Before the film premiered, Lloyd was trying to rationalize its lack of humor, claiming he planned it that way. He told an interviewer he had been dissatisfied with his previous sound pictures. "I felt I was standing still," he said. "These were just other Lloyd comedies, nothing new, nothing really different. And when you stand still, you go back." After he had bought Kelland's story, he said, his gag writers had gone to work on it "and some of their ideas were great, too. But every time we tried to put in a gag we found it spoiled the story. It was a tough decision, but we had to make up our minds what came first — the gags or the story. We fought the problem out for four or five months and decided, finally, to go all the way; the story was first."

Maybe so, but Lloyd's own story is distinctly fishy. He had successfully balanced in several of his best pictures the demands of story line against the imperative for gags, and some of these stories were no less complicated than the story of *The Cat's Paw*. They stood up very well against the intrusions of the gagmen. Nor could one say that Lloyd's characterization here was more subtly nuanced than before. His prissy and innocent missionary's son was essentially the same character he had played in *Welcome Danger* (which, like *Cat's Paw*, ends with Lloyd rather messily solving a crime wave by tracing its roots to Chinatown). What one can't help thinking is that Lloyd was attempting, in this film, to make a transition from comedian to straight actor, sensing correctly that his vogue as a comic had nearly passed.

He did not make it. Without gags to fall back upon, he was simply too colorless to carry a picture. And the film, despite surprisingly respectable reviews, didn't make it either. Nor does the passage of time impart any patina to it. As for Lloyd's claim that he was trying to break new ground, to satisfy the sound film's demand for greater realism, that was just whistling in the dark. What he needed, and what his old team of gagwriters could not provide him, was the verbal lunacy that made the Marx Brothers and W. C. Fields the class of his field in this decade, and that made the screwball farces such undying fun.

This much Lloyd apparently learned from *The Cat's Paw,* for two years later he appeared, for the first time since he had left Roach, in a picture he did not produce himself. He signed with Paramount, his distributor, to star in a film entirely of the studio's concoction. *The Milky Way,* based on a Broadway

comedy, was directed by the estimable Leo McCarey and included in its cast such worthies as Adolphe Menjou, William Gargan, Lionel Stander, and, as a wisecracking blonde in the Jean Harlow mold, Verree Teasdale. They all played members of the fight mob, and Lloyd becomes involved with them when, quite erroneously, he is credited with knocking out the middleweight champion of the world (Gargan). What actually happened was that Lloyd, a milquetoast milkman who stopped by a nightclub where his sister works as a hat-check girl, attempted to intervene as the champ and his pal (Stander) tried to force their attentions on the girl and ducked at precisely the moment the champ and his friend threw punches at him, putting each other out. Lloyd, we soon learn, became an expert ducker during the course of a cowardly childhood, and though he attempts to tell the truth about what happened, it is Lloyd that an excited crowd discovers standing over the fallen champ, and Lloyd the champ's manager (Menjou) decides to build up, through a series of fixed fights, into a challenger for his pug. One final mix-up — knock-out drops are placed in the champion's water — makes Lloyd's improbable challenge successful.

The picture received perhaps the best reviews Lloyd ever got in a talkie. It was, said Frank S. Nugent, who had replaced Hall at *The Times,* "a well-balanced picture, drawing as much merriment from its dialogue as from its slapstick and dividing attention equally between Mr. Lloyd and the other members of its excellent cast. We expected a one-man show; *The Milky Way* is nearer a three-ring circus." Otis Ferguson, the fine critic who had recently signed on with *The New Republic,* thought the ending of the picture a bit of a letdown but felt it was "by and large very near the top for screen comedy." Four years later, writing a retrospective piece on comedy in the thirties, he still felt it to be as "fine and crazy" as anything done in that decade. Overseas, Graham Greene, doing time as a reviewer before his suspense novels caught on, thought it "the best 'Harold Lloyd' to date."

Lloyd had some good gags in the picture. For example, unable to learn even the rudiments of boxing from Lionel Stander, he allows Miss Teasdale to teach him something like the proper rhythms by having him throw punches in time to a waltz record. He also does a pleasant routine at a society party, where he gives his dignified hostess a lesson in the fine art of ducking. There is also an excellent sequence in which he is required to smuggle a new-born colt — the beloved horse who draws his milk truck turns out to have been pregnant — in a taxicab.

Yet it was the balance Nugent spoke of that was the most important factor in the film's success. The tough, fast, cross-talk of the fight mob, led by the tricky-minded Menjou, stands in brisk contrast to Lloyd's star turns, providing him with something no previous supporting cast ever had, genuine support, a relief from trying to carry the film all by himself. Greene thought Menjou — "ranting, raving, wheedling, double-crossing" — stole the picture. Though that is perhaps something of an exaggeration, it does seem proper to pay brief homage to this

At the playhouse, circa 1936–37.

Lloyd strikes a suitably masterful pose with his favorite Great Dane. For a time he ran a kennel as a hobby.

delightful actor, whose reputation has been clouded by his avid support of Hollywood's witch-hunters in the McCarthy period. He had, as Greene said, "toughness and energy" and was, indeed, "unbeatable" when he could bring those qualities — in such odd contrast to his suave mannerisms and impeccable tailoring — to a role (cf. his managing editor in *The Front Page*).

The Milky Way was released within weeks of Chaplin's long-awaited second sound film, *Modern Times*, and it is interesting to note that not all the comparisons were in Chaplin's favor. Ferguson, for example, paid the ritual tribute to Chaplin's genius — undeniably evident in some sequences of his movie, but hardly in all — but then went on to say that he was not "a first-class picture maker. He may personally surmount his period, but as director-producer he can't carry his whole show with him, and I'll take bets that if he keeps on refusing to learn any more than he learned when the movies themselves were just learning, each successive picture he makes will seem, on release, to fall short of what went before." In all of film criticism there is no more accurate prediction, and a couple of weeks later, when he came to the Lloyd film, Ferguson was pleased to note that it was not "a one-man show," that it was "up-to-the-minute in construction," and "the work of many hands all laid on expertly." *Time's* anonymous critic also contrasted Chaplin's "egotism" in defying sound to Lloyd's conscientious attempt to adapt himself to it — an effort, the reviewer felt, crowned by *The Milky Way.* If the notion that Lloyd, whatever his defects, could be funnier than Chaplin needs proof, the critical response to these two films offers it. *The Milky Way* lacks any single sequence as brilliant as Chaplin's bout with the machines in the factory, and lacks the carefully controlled (for once) sentiment of Chaplin's relationship with Paulette Goddard's waif. On the other hand, if one were to lift *The Milky Way* out of its customary context, as a Lloyd vehicle, and put it where it belongs, among the "hard" comedies of the era, it would rank with the best of them. In any case, it is vastly superior to its soft, musicalized, over-mounted remake, *The Kid From Brooklyn,* which Danny Kaye made for Samuel Goldwyn a decade or so later.

For the moment, Lloyd seemed to be inspired by the picture, seemed to indicate he had learned something from it. In New York to promote it, he promised an interviewer a "New Deal" in production. "This one picture a year business is out," he said, conveniently forgetting that his pace was now one picture every two years. "From now on I'm going to make two a year, or at least three every two years." He promised that while he was in town he was going to look over the new novels and plays, or perhaps even recruit a prominent author to run up something especially for him.

Unfortunately, he did not follow through on this scheme. Instead, another two years went by, and though he recruited a promising young stage director, Elliot Nugent, to handle *Professor Beware,* and hired a good supporting cast, he did not employ them with anything like the skill of a McCarey. (The cast included

Raymond Walburn, William Frawley, Lionel Stander again, Sterling Holloway, Montague Love, and even the young Ward Bond, playing, as he often did in those days, a cop.) Again, he started out with five writers, and not until they had written themselves into deep trouble did he bring in Delmar Daves, who had had good luck bringing order out of the chaos of some Dick Powell-Ruby Keeler musicals, to shape the thing into some sort of coherence.

Essentially, the picture is one long chase. Lloyd, back in his mild-mannered professor's role, plays an Egyptologist convinced that an ancient curse will be laid on him should he marry a young woman he meets in circumstances very similar to those described on the fragment of an ancient tablet he has discovered. So Lloyd takes off, cross-country, trying to escape the forces his girl's wealthy father has unleashed to apprehend him. There are lovely bits in the picture, notably a scene in which Lloyd, riding the top of a freight train, sees a very low tunnel approaching and to avoid being brushed off his perch tries to run to the rear of the train. The train, of course, acts like a treadmill, its speed approximating Lloyd's, so that he appears to be running in place (for the shot, Lloyd ran on a real treadmill placed behind the train). There is also an excellent car chase, in which at one point Lloyd's vehicle, disguised under a tent, mysteriously crawls away from his pursuers — an old gag, but still a pretty good one, unlike some of the other material he recycled here.

Daves would remember Lloyd as an easygoing worker, even under the pressure of a faltering career, indulging his writers with plenty of time to concoct their inventions, ever-willing to stop work on the set and try to improve his material — as he always had — through improvisation, still shrewd about what he could and could not effectively do on screen. Yet the film did not work, and for the first time a Lloyd movie was treated brusquely by reviewers. *Time* put it down in one sentence, calling it "an overstocked museum of silent comedy technique." Frank Nugent, in *The Times,* was kinder. "Even a fair Lloyd, of course, is better than no Lloyd at all." But he too recognized that most of the material on view here had been seen before and to better advantage. He concluded: "Probably we should have been more enthusiastic about it had this been 1928. Or maybe we were younger then."

It was amazing how easily most comedy — always excepting Frank Capra's — had avoided the great issues of the 1930s, or had merely glanced at them. It was amazing how patient people had been with Lloyd in his attempts to adapt not only to new techniques but to imperceptibly changing taste in film comedy, a taste which had swung from the visual to the verbal and — especially during the war years — from the timeless to the topical. As much as anything, radio was responsible for this shift. It had recruited its leading comics from theater and from vaudeville of a slightly later era than the one in which the great silent comics had served their apprenticeships. Perhaps precisely because the pantomimic comedians were so readily available in the movie houses, these men

had fashioned a new comic style — basically a rapid-fire, ethnically neutral blend of wisecracks and insults — against which, manifestly, a silent screen could not compete. When radio grew into a great national institution this style proved perfectly adapted to it, and as the movies stressed their new-found ability to talk, these comics were able to move, with varying degrees of success into them. By the time *Professor Beware* had completed its disappointing run, Bob Hope and Bing Crosby had made their first highly successful *Road* pictures, and a whole new crop of comedians was either well established or on the way up. Burns and Allen and Fibber McGee and Molly had pioneered husband-and-wife situation comedies; Jack Benny had established his great characterization of an egomaniacal tightwad; Fred Allen was beginning to be recognized for the brilliant, dour satirist he was; Edgar Bergen was patiently absorbing the insults of his wooden alter-ego, Charlie McCarthy. In this fast company, Harold Lloyd seemed slow, out-of-date. And it was too soon for nostalgia to soften this harsh view of his gifts, or to nudge the public toward rediscovery. And he was wise enough to see that the struggle was an unequal one.

He never announced a formal retirement. He occasionally discussed plans for future films with friends and visiting journalists, but more and more he filled his days with other projects, other hopes. He never appeared bitter about it, in public or among friends, accepting it with that curious objectivity that had marked his demeanor from the start. And, as it turned out, he would have one more brief shot at a return to public favor.

12 Harold Lloyd frequently told interviewers that the only place he really felt at home was in front of the camera, on a set. Elsewhere he always had the odd feeling that he was doing an imitation of himself. The implication was that he couldn't feel at home in his own home — which may be why Greenacres feels less like a place to live than a stage set, a place to play out a fantasy of home life. Moreover, as late as 1938, when *Professor Beware* came out, a visiting journalist reported that Lloyd had "given little thought to what he will do when his natural ability lessens, or his popularity wanes, if it ever does." And, in fact, when it became impossible — or at least pointless — for him to go on starring in films, he literally had nothing to do. Which was irony indeed, considering the pleasure dome he had created, the delights a credulous public could imagine him enjoying in retirement.

The trouble was that like so many of the success-oriented young men who saw so much of themselves in the character he had created, he had never asked himself why he was working so hard, what his goals were. And now, only

127

forty-five, he was quite unprepared to face the fact that there was no pressing reason to get up in the morning anymore, that there was nothing that had to be done today that could not be put off until tomorrow.

He put a fairly brave — or at least stoical — face on his situation. "Resignation described his attitude better than anything else," Delmer Daves, the screenwriter (and later director), would put it later. A journalist interviewing Lloyd in the early forties would detect "an occasional undertone of sadness" in his tone as he talked about his descent from former heights. "Fame is fickle," he told the reporter, "and it's sometimes easy to believe your own press notices. You're up, you're down, and you'll only be on top a certain length of time no matter what you do. In Europe an actor who has acted well commands a certain amount of respect throughout his life. Here it's usually confined to who's putting out at the moment."

All of that *sounded* reasonably mature, and if Lloyd's fortune had been cut in half by the Depression, and if much of what he had left was frozen in real estate, if some of the Greenacres staff had to be let go, he could afford to be philosophical — after all, he could still lay out something like $100,000 a year to cover his running expenses. And he was not yet entirely out of the business. He had a contract with RKO, perhaps the least prosperous of the major studios, to produce features for them independently. He made two. *A Girl, A Guy, and a Gob* (it starred Lucille Ball and George Murphy) and *My Favorite Spy* were released in 1941 and 1942 respectively, with no particular success, critical or commercial. There was a somehow touching incident during the production of the first of these pictures. Edmund O'Brien, just beginning his movie career, had been given a little piece of business to do. A flirtatious girl was to drop a handkerchief in his path and he was to pick it up on the tip of his shoe, drop it in her lap, and pass on. They tried it several times, then reported to Lloyd that it just didn't seem to be working. "It just isn't funny," they said. "Shall we throw it away?"

Lloyd insisted that it was funny. Or at least it had been when he had done the same routine in *Welcome Danger.* So he reported to the set to see what was wrong. The problem, he thought, was clumsiness.

"No — you have to do it on the beat. You walk forward and you mustn't pause," he said. Then he demonstrated what he meant, got a big laugh from the assembled cast and crew, O'Brien imitated him perfectly, and the bit stayed in the finished picture.

It seems likely that Lloyd's greatest weakness as a comedian — his lack of a strong story sense — served him ill in a time of very plotty comedies. And then, of course, he never did develop much of a taste for humorous dialogue, which his competitors competently created in job lots. On the other hand, as the incident with O'Brien demonstrates, his mastery of the sight gag, and his ability to link series of them into a long comedy sequence, was entirely unimpaired.

And it was precisely these skills that American comedy has lacked for the last thirty or forty years. Lloyd knew it. He told Kevin Brownlow, "They don't build up the comedy, they don't condition the audience to expect a certain gag, and when the [gag happens] they don't work on it enough. They don't cap it with another one to bring an even louder laugh." He admitted that modern movie comedies get laughs, but insisted, quite rightly, that bigger ones could be drawn. They missed the most obvious way of getting them, he said. For example, many of the best gags of the silent screen resulted from the careful planting of expectation in the audience. If you let them see a hazard before the comedian did, then each time he postponed what they understood to be an inevitable confrontation, he would get a laugh. If, when he finally tangled with it, it somehow could catapult him into an even worse difficulty, you could get a still bigger laugh. And so on.

It all seems so simple and obvious, and it is a puzzlement that techniques based on such simple laws should become "lost." Indeed, in some realms of film art they are not lost at all. The basic requirements of physical comedy are exactly the same as those governing the creation of suspense and Alfred Hitchcock has been entirely open about how he employs them in interview after interview — though, come to think of it, he is almost alone in his regular use of them, and for that matter, of the comic variants on them.

Be that as it may, it seems blind and foolish of Hollywood to have relegated Lloyd so quickly to the status of has-been. He could have been employed, either formally or informally, as a comedian consultant, as a sort of super gagman, for another three decades, and his life as well as the life of the American screen would have been greatly the richer for it. That, however, was not to be.

As far as one can tell, the only major figure in screen comedy who paid the slightest heed to Lloyd during the 1940s was Preston Sturges, and it was, to say the least, an odd marriage. Sturges was the only truly original comic mind to emerge in American film in the late thirties and early forties, a deep-died eccentric who made some of the oddest, and (in their erratic way) funniest movies of the period. As Manny Farber and William S. Poster said in their definitive article about him, America is too fast-moving a society to be a suitable target for satire as it is customarily defined. A stable set of class lines and powerful traditions are the satirist's requisites. What Sturges recognized was what Lloyd and Keaton had instinctively acknowledged in the early days: in a fast-paced world, speed itself becomes the only logical target for the satirist. As Farber and Poster point out, "Some of the great early comic films . . . were scarcely comic at all, but pure and very bitter satires, exhausting in endless combinations all possible tortures produced as a consequence of the *naif* belief in speed." Keaton, perhaps, recognized the pain in all this more clearly than Lloyd, but because of his personal problems he was unavailable to Sturges, while the healthy, youthful-seeming Lloyd was perfectly capable of carrying a picture. Then,

129

too, Sturges, for all his contradictions and ambiguities, shared Lloyd's — and Lloyd's characters' — instinctive belief in the success ethic. No matter what contortions they went through, Sturges's people, like Lloyd's persona, always ended up handsomely rewarded for their troubles — often with money, certainly with psychological satisfactions. It should also be noted that Sturges nursed an abiding bitterness about an uprooted youth in which at his mother's insistence he endlessly toured the cultural capitals of Europe, effectively cut off from the common life in his own country. He therefore revered the heroes of the old popular culture and was apparently delighted to be in touch with Lloyd, at first vaguely, then determinedly, planning a comeback film for him. Among other things, Sturges, who was extremely restive under studio contract (Paramount), admired Lloyd's carefully preserved independence as his own producer.

But as they might have recognized earlier, there were substantial differences in their sensibilities. Lloyd was a pure product of small-town America. It had never occurred to him to question its values. Nor did he nurse any grudges against the economic system, which after all had handsomely rewarded him. Sturges was much more ambiguous about both points. Some of his mother's cultural conditioning had taken root in him, and he was acutely conscious of the narrowness, provincialism, and cupidity of the residents of Morgan's Creek, for example, and he couldn't resist treating them as grotesques. As for the rich, he treated them as addled wastrels (cf. *The Palm Beach Story* and *The Lady Eve*) or, if they were still engaged in commerce, not merely spending their earnings from it, he showed them as ignorant and actively malevolent (cf. the movie producers in *Sullivan's Travels*, the corrupt businessmen and politicians of *The Great McGinty*). Lloyd, to be sure, had introduced a few such characters in *Welcome Danger, The Cat's Paw,* and *Professor Beware,* but his heart had never been in cutting them up. At most he saw them as sports of nature, not as the inevitable products of a dangerous system.

Still, the two got along well enough. Though Lloyd, who had joined the Masons with his father in 1926, was by now deeply enmeshed in the activities of the Shrine (he became potentate of a Los Angeles temple in 1936, was now on the Imperial Divan — the national governing board — and heading for Imperial Potentate), he still had time to trade ideas with Sturges. He also had reason to be grateful to him for bringing him back into public activity in 1944. It seems he was sitting in Sturges's office one day when a call came from an ad agency offering Sturges a job as host of the Old Gold Comedy Hour, a program modeled after the Lux Radio Theater, which offered radio adaptations of current films. They wanted Sturges to do for Old Gold what another producer-director, C. B. De Mille, had done for Lux — front the show, give the impression that he was responsible for creating it. Sturges turned down the offer but said he happened to be sitting with just the man for the job. Lloyd took it — and for a season or so earned an estimated $5,000 a week for his untaxing duties.

The Man of Affairs: Sam Goldwyn digs right in at ground-breaking for his new studio. Other heavies on the scene: Ben Lyon, far left, and Howard Hughes, far right. Below, four-fifths of the board of directors of Los Angeles radio station KMPC — Bing Crosby, Freeman (Amos) Gosden, Lloyd, and Charles ("Andy") Correll. Paul Whiteman was AWOL that day in 1940 when the photographer came around.

Meantime, Sturges had become an increasingly obstreperous studio employee. It was his habit to write all night, sleep all morning, and turn up on the set afternoons, an eccentric schedule that had worked in the past because he was a fast director, but was now becoming expensive since he was slowing the pace of his directorial work. Worse, Paramount had two of his best films (*The Miracle at Morgan's Creek* and *Hail the Conquering Hero*) on the shelf, dubious about their commercial potential, so there was mutual relief when it was decided that Sturges would not renew his contract with Paramount.

Instead, he hooked up with a backer infinitely more eccentric than any of his fictional millionaires, Howard Hughes. They decided that the first project of their new company, California Pictures, would be *The Sin of Harold Diddlebock,* starring Harold Lloyd. It was a very promising project. The film opened with the last reel of *The Freshman,* showing the hero making the winning touchdown for Tate, then cuts to a locker room where a prominent alumnus (Raymond Walburn) offers Lloyd a job in his ad agency after graduation. It turns out to be a humble spot in bookkeeping, from which he is never promoted. During two decades in this job he has fallen in love with, and found himself unable to propose to, no less than seven sisters who have successively held the same job. Now Mr. Waggleberry, his one-time benefactor, turns against him ("You have not only ceased to go forward, you have gone backward .... You not only make the same mistakes year after year, you don't even change your apologies") and fires Diddlebock. There is a fine, sad sequence in which Lloyd quite impressively acts a small man watching his small dreams shatter — sadly removing his uplifting slogans from the wall above his desk, saying farewell to the last of the seven sisters he has loved. On the street, he falls in with Wormy, a down-at-the-heels horseplayer (Jimmy Conlin), who in the course of touching him for a loan, inveigles him into taking the first drink of his life. Their debate on this matter — a rapid fire exchange of asinine clichés of the sort Sturges loved to play with — is the movie's comic high point. Wormy speaks first: "You're never too old to learn." "You can't teach an old dog new tricks." "Every dog is entitled to one bite." "Let sleeping dogs lie." "A barking dog never bites." "He who sleepeth with dogs riseth with fleas," and so on. At last Lloyd is persuaded, and they repair to a bar where Edgar Kennedy presides. He is inspired by the challenge of mixing a drink for a forty-year-old man who has never touched a drop. "You arouse the artist in me," he cries and mixes a concoction that loosens four decades of inhibitions. And also blanks the next twenty-four hours out of Diddlebock's memory.

Unfortunately, from this point onward, Sturges seems to blank out. The first third of the film is a kind of elegy to the screen character Lloyd created in the old days and to the values that had sustained him. Here Sturges seems to be saying that they may have been naive and superficial values, values which made it easy for the system to rip off their adherents. Nonetheless, Sturges found nothing in

the brave new world of the forties that struck him as an improvement on them. Quite the opposite. In any event, had he been able to sustain the mood of his film's opening, he might have created a remarkable film, one of those rare movies (on different levels, *Ride the High Country* and *Last Tango in Paris* are such pictures) that is not only a gratifying fiction in itself, but an aesthetically satisfying ending to the larger drama of a star's career, answering our half-formed question about what became of all the characters he played in his younger days, the characters out of which we create the image which is his immortality.

Alas, it turns out that if Harold Diddlebock sinned, he did so in a highly conventional way during his lost day (the *Mad Wednesday* of the title under which it was finally released). There is wine, women, and song — and he buys a loud suit and a circus. He spends the remainder of the picture trying to peddle this last, mostly by invading Wall Street banks with a lion on a leash, trying to terrorize their officers into buying the show and running it as a free entertainment for children (Ringling Brothers finally tops all offers, since it wants no competing free circuses). Sturges worked a thrill sequence into this section when the lion leads Lloyd onto a high ledge, but it is so obviously a process sequence that it only reminds one of how much better Lloyd used to do things of this kind.

The business of making the film, which took most of 1945 and some of 1946, reminded Lloyd of how much happier things had been for him in the old days. Almost immediately he began quarreling with Sturges on the set, until, according to one report, almost every scene was being shot two ways — "the idiot way," as Lloyd called Sturges's method, and "the milquetoast way," as Sturges called Lloyd's techniques. Finally, according to a friend of Lloyd's, the comedian gave in, convinced that there was nothing he could do to save the picture.

He was probably right, but their backer, Hughes, also decided to get into the act. When the picture was finished and a limited release of Sturges's version drew poor reviews and business, Hughes undertook to re-edit it himself, with — as usual when he intervened in the creative processes of film-making — disastrous results.* Hughes finally released the re-edited and re-titled film in 1950, by which time considerable interest had built up in the long-delayed film. Moreover, other events which should have been helpful to it had occurred. The year before, Agee's famous article, "Comedy's Greatest Era," had appeared in *Life,* drawing unprecedented reader response and generally stirring new interest in the old art and its great practitioners. In the same year Lloyd was elected Imperial Potentate of the Shrine, which became the occasion of a *Time* cover story as well as an excuse for him to travel to almost every state in the union on behalf of the organization. As the first celebrity head he naturally attracted

---

* The writer has seen both versions, but the film discussed critically here is the Sturges cut, which exists in the archives at UCLA.

considerable attention from news media wherever he appeared. Finally, when the film appeared, *Life* printed an unprecedented editorial, calling the picture — with more enthusiasm than common sense — "the stuff that daddy used to laugh at — refined, rebottled and fitted with a sound track, but of the vintage nevertheless." None of this, however, did any good, for most of the important reviews were, at best, mixed, and the picture, which had turned into an extremely expensive proposition, lost money.

Lloyd's final evaluation of the film was as accurate as anyone's. He said, "There was far too much talk in the picture and not enough action. . . . My stuff has to rely on fast action to be any good and as soon as it's slowed down by a lot of talk it loses its humor." He had done well, of course, in a picture with lots of talk — *The Milky Way* — but Leo McCarey had been careful to provide him with long arias of action, and more important, the talk in between these sequences was genuinely funny and well played. Only in the beginning did Sturges attain that level of wit. Worse, as often happened in his pictures, he required his players to oversell weak writing, as if by shouting it they could compel us to laugh at it.

That, finally, was the end for Lloyd. And though his comments about the film's failure are mild enough, he did have one regret. He had turned down the lead in Mary Chase's huge Broadway success, *Harvey,* in order to make the picture — the part going to Frank Fay, for whom it provided a very satisfactory comeback indeed. Lloyd told people that though he had liked the play when he read it, he objected to sharing the stage with a huge rabbit, as the original script required. The rabbit, of course, disappeared from view — much of the play's humor depended on the fact that no one but the drunken hero could see him — but all Lloyd had to show for his brief flirtation with the project was further proof that his comic sense, his keen ability to spot the key flaws in other people's ideas, was still in excellent working order.

Still, it was small consolation for him, for with the failure of the Sturges film he must have realized that this time, approaching sixty, there would be no realistic hope of making another comeback.* Indeed, by the end of 1950, his year's duty as national leader of the Shrine, so pleasantly time-consuming, so gratifying to the ego in the warm receptions accorded him wherever he went, would finish, and though he would remain active in the organization, devoting particular attention to the hospitals it supported, it could no longer be counted on to fill his time. And yet he was still extremely vigorous. He had another couple of decades to live, a lot of time to fill.

He devised an astonishing number of ways to fill that time. Some time in the

* If he didn't know it in 1950, he did in 1952, when the Academy of Motion Picture Arts and Sciences presented him with his honorary Oscar, a sure sign that the industry considers a veteran washed up. In this case, too, it was a backhanded slap at his old rival, Chaplin, who had gone into exile rather than face questions from immigration authorities about politics, taxes, and his private life. Not only would there be no Oscar for Charlie, but Lloyd's would specifically commend his good citizenship, just in case Chaplin missed the point.

late thirties he had brought home from a business trip to Chicago a toy for his kids called a Hoot-Nanny, apparently a primitive version of the contemporary Spirograph. He and Mildred got to playing with it, and pretty soon they were holding contests among their friends to see who could make the prettiest designs with the thing. When they switched to color, Lloyd found himself fascinated by color theory, began reading and consulting experts, buying — literally — every artist's hue manufactured in or imported to the United States. First in a cold basement room, then in a little closet off the landing of his home's main staircase, then in a closet off the children's nursery, he daubed away at file cards, trying to systematize color, achieving subtle blends and neutralizations. At some point various scientific instruments were introduced into the study, at which he could spend as many as nine hours a day. Finally, he graduated to making small abstractions — "imaginettes" he called them — then to larger canvases, which in 1953 were exhibited at a Los Angeles gallery, where they gathered respectable notices. Along with his scientific interest in color he also practiced microscopy, spending hours mounting bits of natural objects so he could study their abstract beauty through his expensive microscope.

He had long been interested in photography as well, and around the time he started painting he attended a meeting of the Photographic Society of America, where he fell in with a group of stereophoto enthusiasts. Among the pleasures of his particular group, which in time took to calling itself "The Happy Seven," was arranging elaborate exhibitions of their joint work. (Generally they would all tackle a single place or theme, select the best pictures for the show.) Sometimes they would meet five nights running — usually at Lloyd's house — sometimes weeks would go by between meetings. But as the richest of the lot, Lloyd always had the most stereo slides to project, and there was a general agreement among them that he was the most gifted of their membership, perhaps because he had the time and the money to practice extensively. By the time he died he had a collection of 600,000 slides, each one of which cost three dollars in raw stock, lab, and mounting fees. In other words, he spent, in two decades, close to two million dollars on this obsession alone. It extended, in later years, to nude studies, which he frequently showed male friends, even the odd journalist passing through. They were the basis for a late-in-life renewal of friendship with Hal Roach ("I used to go up there to look at his dirty pictures"), but a possibly more objective viewer, a film historian, found "nothing even vaguely pornographic" in his studies of the waitresses and aspiring actresses recruited from the Sunset Strip to pose against "canyon views." On the face of it, this aspect of his hobby seems to run counter to his chaste public image, but his antiseptic treatment of his subjects was a manifestation of the look-but-don't-touch sexuality of the Middle West (soon to reach its finest flowering in the pages of *Playboy*), though it is said that in those late years he had some inconsequential affairs as well.

135

The family strides the lawn, circa 1945.

The Squire of Greenacres and consort get together with the Mistress of Pickfair and consort: Mildred and Harold Lloyd, Mary Pickford and third husband Charles ("Buddy") Rogers.

In short, he filled the days — and nights — but not his mind. As one friend put it, "he had hobbies, but he was not intellectually interested in anything." One gets the impression that he was never deeply satisfied by or profoundly committed to any of his activities, however lavishly he spent his time and money on them. And gradually his friends dropped away, until there were just a few retainers, a few cronies from the old days around him. Younger men, like Delmer Daves, felt slightly uncomfortable when they went up to Greenacres for dinner, for gatherings too small, too lacking in brilliance, for the setting Lloyd had created. Sometimes Daves would join the comedian to watch an old Lloyd movie, and, in a scene not entirely without parallel to some in *Sunset Boulevard,* observe Lloyd laughing delightedly at his own antics, almost as if they were new to him, almost as if the figure on the screen were a stranger to him. "He giggled a lot anyway," Daves recalled, often, it seemed, inappropriately, like a child not knowing quite how to respond to adult conversation. Others would say that he had a temper like a child, that he was perfectly capable of sitting down in the middle of a room and banging his head against the floor in frustration, then sulkily refusing for weeks to speak to whoever had offended him. A teetotaler and a non-smoker, Lloyd's one gustatory passion was also childish — ice cream.

Always, in Daves word, "remote" from his children — and with the girls both strict and suspicious about their dating — his relationships with all of them deteriorated drastically, tragically, in the last decades of his life. There is some reason to believe that Mildred bore a measure of responsibility for this. "They were both like kids, you know," Daves said recently. "If Harold never lost his boyhood, she never lost her girlhood. She had a kind of coy, young quality until she died. She was still living in the past. She dressed like a pretty little girl in aprons and flounces, as if she wanted to preserve for him the girl he had married."

This illusion naturally became increasingly difficult to maintain, particularly as the children grew into adulthood and she didn't know how to handle the advancing years — except by irrational intervention in their lives. According to her adopted daughter, who married in a fashionable ceremony in 1948, she was not welcome at Greenacres thereafter, though she says Lloyd and the children used to sneak out and visit her without Mildred's knowledge. This marriage and a second one ended in divorce, and she spent a good deal of time, later on, trying to find her natural mother, whose identity and whereabouts, she has charged, the Lloyds deliberately kept from her. She received the income from one-seventh of the estate after Lloyd's death (as opposed to the two-sevenths left to each of Lloyd's natural children), has worked at a variety of jobs (including stand-in work for Lee Remick, Julie Harris, and Nina Foch) and says she intends to write a book about her unhappy life.

It was not, as it turned out, more miserable than those of the natural children. Not long after Peggy's marriage, Gloria became the bride of William

Guasti, heir to a California wine fortune. Apparently Mrs. Lloyd did everything she could to break up the marriage, inviting Gloria to spend long periods at the estate without her husband, even taking her on a lengthy European tour in order to separate them. Whether or not Mildred's interference caused the break-up is not known, but Gloria Lloyd did eventually divorce Guasti, and almost immediately suffered a nervous collapse. For some years she has been in and out of a Swiss sanitarium, and more than one witness has declared that alcoholism is one of her problems. In later years Richard Simonton, president of Muzak and an organ buff, became friends with Lloyd after a mutual acquaintance arranged for Simonton to play the organ at Greenacres, and he eventually became a trustee of the Harold Lloyd Foundation, which is charged with the preservation of Greenacres.* He once accompanied Lloyd to Europe on an expedition to visit Chaplin in his retirement and to see Gloria at the sanitarium. Lloyd hoped he might find her well enough to obtain her release. "That bothered him terribly about her being there," he recalled. It appears that Lloyd was successful in bringing her home for a short time, but life at the Lloyd house was not suited to a woman as unstable as Gloria, and she soon left again. The Lloyds meantime had taken in her daughter, Sue, and they raised her more as a daughter than a granddaughter.

Finally, there was Harold Lloyd, Jr., known as "Duke." He had been, by all accounts, an extremely handsome youth, had attended Harvard Military Academy in Los Angeles, served some years in the Air Force, and harbored hopes of a singing career, which he pursued with modest success until the middle 1960s. But he, too, was an alcoholic, and he was also a homosexual, by all accounts a classic case of a sensitive young man who could never escape the shadow of a famous father. Lloyd supported him by giving him odd jobs — cataloging the photo collection, working as "story consultant" on the storyless compilation films. (He made these, *Harold Lloyd's World of Comedy* and *The Funny Side of Life,* in 1962 and 1963: the first, promoted heavily, did reasonable business in the United States, much better business abroad; the second compilation was released almost exclusively in Europe.) Young Lloyd, according to Simonton, pulled himself together for a little while after his father died, saying, "Now I'm the head of the family." But three months to the day after Harold, Sr., died, his son died, of alcoholism.

Drink was, in fact, the curse of the family. Mildred (or "Mid," or "Molly," as Lloyd called her) had been an alcoholic from some time in the forties, when it is said she wanted desperately to divorce Lloyd. In her late years a full-time nurse was employed mainly to see that her perfume bottles did not mysteriously get filled with booze, that her habit of drinking Listerine did not get out of hand. In a pathetic family — "a disaster," as even Lloyd's kindly friend Simonton put it —

* Since Lloyd died, the Foundation has been engaged in a lively dispute with the city of Beverly Hills, which fears hordes of sightseers disturbing its tranquility. At this writing the estate is closed, though some income is derived from renting it out as a location for movies and TV programs. Daves was the first to use it — in *Kings Go Forth* (1958) — and recently it was prominently used in *Westworld.*

The famous Christmas tree and its owner, 1966. Estimates of Lloyd's ornament collection range up to 20,000, of which 5,000 adorned the tree. It eventually remained standing year round.

she was perhaps the most pathetic member. One thinks of her — never a very mature, forthcoming, or stimulating person — wandering the halls of the great house, her husband either absent or preoccupied by one of his interests, her children all gone, and none of them bearing her any very kind feelings, caring mainly for her two companionable poodles and her booze, and one sees the end results of the flaws that, almost from the first, people had detected in Lloyd's art — its abstractness, its mechanical quality, its lack of real warmth. It is all dreadfully sad.

Still, ever the good and admiring friend, Simonton cannot believe Lloyd was entirely the author of his family's misery. He thinks the children were at least partly to blame for their own problems. They refused Lloyd's friendship, especially in the later years when he needed it most. "He'd hold his head in his hands and ask: 'What's wrong with my family? All they wanted is money — not companionship. They fought me; they never met me halfway.' " He thinks Lloyd spoiled them, did not require of them the discipline he had exercised over his own career. As a parallel he cites Lloyd's own deteriorating financial condition in these years, the result, Simonton says, of Lloyd's indulgently permitting old friends who could not move with the times to continue managing his affairs. (That situation improved considerably when Simonton introduced him to his own lawyer, who was able quite quickly to double the income on Lloyd's holdings.) Simonton also believes that from a mixture of good and bad motives (a desire to spare them concern, mixed with his own desire always to appear the all-providing *pater familias*), he kept from his children the knowledge and the responsibilities that would have helped them mature.

It is, of course, the classic double-bind of middle-class family life — both generations needing more love, greater mutual support, the long history of remoteness, of mutual silence and distrust, preventing either side from making the first moves. In this instance the problem was greatly complicated by the father's childishness, his profound desire to ignore the problem, to escape into the more manageable world of his hobbies and interests, where the human factor was not allowed to enter. Finally, we see, he slipped entirely away from the problem by skipping over involvement with his children's generation, focusing his concern on his granddaughter and her contemporaries, whom she introduced him to. Among them were Richard Correll, son of Charles Correll, "Andy" of the Amos n' Andy comedy team. Correll volunteered, with a friend, to sort and catalog Lloyd's film library and stills collection, which had been pretty badly disarranged when Lloyd made his compilation films, and after Lloyd's death he became an assistant manager of the estate. Lloyd treated him with enormous warmth, indulging him and his friends if they wanted to play football or some other game on the great lawn, even to the point of bringing down refreshments and constituting himself a one-man cheering section. He often asked Correll to accompany him when he made appearances at colleges, showing one or more of

his films, answering student's questions, visibly warming to the fact that his films still appealed to younger people. Correll has a particularly vivid memory of an appearance by Lloyd at the Cannes Film Festival one year. One of his pictures was shown as a homage, and the audience, knowing he was in the house, gave it and him a standing ovation. Lloyd did not content himself with taking a bow from his seat. Instead, he leapt to the railing of the balcony, grabbed an upright support with one hand and leaned out over the audience in rough approximation of one of his old, beloved thrill sequence stunts.

One would like to leave him so, an old man back for a moment in an element he loved, the mounting sadness of the years momentarily forgotten. But there was more to bear. In January, 1969, Mildred suffered a stroke from which she seemed to make a good recovery. Then, on August 10 of the same year, she was stricken by a heart attack and went into a coma from which she never recovered. She died on the 18th, and Lloyd kept repeating over and over, "I lost my bride, I lost my bride."

Now he became more dependent than ever on Sue and her friends, and one of them in particular, a school friend named Linda Hoppe, who had been trained as a medical assistant. She moved into Greenacres to become Lloyd's companion, often giving up dates in order to play games with him, keep him company when he watched television. Correll, of course, was often on hand, and Simonton and his sons dropped by frequently. But a year or so after his wife died, doctors told Lloyd he had cancer, and in December, 1970, they informed him it was incurable. Still, like his old character, he refused to admit defeat. On Halloween that fall he and Simonton decided to put on a show in the little theater the latter had built on his estate — and where Lloyd often went to screen his own and other old movies because it was equipped with an organ, proper accompaniment for silent movies. They worked up a tramp routine, costuming themselves elsewhere in order to surprise Simonton's family and guests. Simonton's own security men did not recognize them and briefly detained them. That pleased both men. "He was still the actor, even then," Simonton said.

Lloyd made one last appearance at Simonton's, in January, 1971, to see a slide show put on by The Happy Seven, but thereafter he was confined to Greenacres, during the last few weeks to his bed. Even so, when an earthquake shook Los Angeles, he insisted on getting out of bed and making an inspection to see how the house had withstood the shock — admirably, as it turned out. Even now, weakened by the cobalt treatments he was receiving, "Harold Lloyd would not face up to the eventuality of his own death," Simonton said. "To him, it could not happen."

But, of course, it did — just six days after he was finally persuaded to sign a will. One would have to say that the manner of his going was of a piece with the manner of his living, which was in turn of a piece with his work — unconscious of mortality, heedless of uncomfortable reality, motivated by a desperate desire

to avoid pain and gloom. The child was father to . . . a child. But one who had —
and still has — a unique ability to delight the child who resides in all of us. It is
not a great gift, not the stuff of great art. Perhaps one must squarely face
mortality — consider Chaplin's public contemplation of his own death in that
supreme act of egotism, *Limelight* — if one is to create immortal art. Yet it is no
small gift that Lloyd presented us, and one worth re-examining from time to
time, just for the pleasure of it. Not every work need be a masterpiece in order
to afford us delight. Indeed, Auden argued that masterpieces should be reserved
for the "high holidays of the spirit," too many of which are not good for us.
Moreover, we must admit that if there is a shortage of great work, there is an
equal shortage of stuff capable of unpretentiously pleasing us, of offering us
genuine and innocent escape from the cares of the day. Preston Sturges once
had one of his characters say, "There is nothing like a deep-dish movie to drive
you out in the open," and there was much wisdom, much of it forgotten by
modern movie-makers, in the remark. We can be glad the temptation never
arose in Harold Lloyd's mind, glad that through the simplicity of its style and
motives, his work remains capable of arousing a brief answering simplicity
among people trying to exist under that ancient curse that wishes on one's
enemies life in "interesting times."

The
Films

Lonesome Luke

1915-17

Things Fall Apart." At comedy factories like Mack Sennett's and Hal Roach's, the poet's weary observation was elevated to a guiding principle — really the only one — of comedy construction. Not that anyone read poetry at the comedy studios; they were all too busy scrambling for a thin buck along the precipice of bankruptcy in those early days. In fact, Mack Sennett sometimes made the possession of literature on studio property a firing offense. "No jokes in books," he would moodily snap. There was also no subtlety in those one-reelers. Chaplin said all he needed to make a comedy in those days was a cop, a park, and a pretty girl — the basic elements required to get a chase started. Failing to find that combination, producers like Roach might simply find an inexpensive location — a restaurant kitchen, a piano studio, a hotel lobby — and set the star of his first successful series, Harold Lloyd, to wreck it before a reel of film was cranked through the camera. As Lonesome Luke, Lloyd did this over fifty times — and in the process created an audience for himself that would grow and grow with the passing years.

Harold Lloyd as Lonesome Luke. Opposite left: Snub
Pollard, Lloyd's Australian second banana, is the man
behind the Kaiser Wilhelm moustache. Center: Gus
Leonard is the outraged professor of piano, and Bebe
Daniels, Lloyd's first, and most delightful, leading lady, is
at far right. Below: Hal Roach, director. He never really
liked the work, and gradually retreated to the front office
as his fortunes improved.

The Early Glasses Character
1917-21

With a little help from his friends, Harold Lloyd invented what the comedian liked to call "The Glasses Character" in 1917. For its moment, this mild young man represented a daring break with convention, for he was the first leading figure in a comedy series to abandon the conceits of grotesque costume and makeup, to try to get laughs while appearing to be just a normal, ordinary sort of chap. Only his horn-rimmed glasses made him stand out from the crowd. A "marketing strategy" (as we would now, alas, call it) required Lloyd to turn out a picture a week for a couple of years, relentlessly exposing him to the movie-going public, allowing them no escape from the earnest, ingratiating, eager young man whose personality was almost indistinguishable from that of the determined young comedian who had conceived the character.

Lloyd's staff was an extremely loyal one. The man behind the camera (opposite), filming *Spring Fever* (1919) is Walter Lundin, and he stayed with him to the end of his career. Below, in a rare topical film, *A Sammy in Siberia* (1919), Lloyd resolves the Russian Revolution.

Production on this film, the two-reel *Haunted Spooks,* was interrupted when Lloyd nearly lost his life — and did lose two fingers on his right hand — when a comedy bomb he was holding turned out to be charged with live powder. This sequence, completed before the accident, is one of the best in the entire body of Lloyd's early works. A lovelorn Harold tries to commit suicide but (a) the trolley car switches tracks at the last minute; (b) his lover's leap is into a stream that's only ankle deep; and (c) his pistol contains only water. A good thing, too — for in the end he got the girl.

A Sailor-Made Man

1921

A Sailor-Made Man was Lloyd's first feature, but that was an accident. It started out to be no more than two or three reels in length, but producer Roach thought Lloyd had so much good material to work with that he urged him to use it up, no matter how long it ran. The result — less than an hour long — just barely qualified as a feature, but the public cheerfully accepted it as such. In it, Lloyd plays a wealthy lounge lizard whom the U.S. Navy converts into a man of action, capable of saving his girl friend from a fate worse than death when a lustful Turk abducts her for his harem.

Opposite: A still reveals the unprecedented production values Roach lavished on the film. Below: Mildred Davis, later Mrs. Harold Lloyd, intercedes on Harold's behalf with her captor (Dick Sutherland).

Grandma's Boy

1922

Grandma's Boy was Harold Lloyd's favorite movie. Besides being funny, he thought it was a revealing study of cowardice and the way it was conquered by the character he played. When it was first previewed, its sobriety puzzled audiences and outraged Roach, who insisted his star "sort" more gags through the film. He did so without, in his view, spoiling its psychological acuity, and it proved to be a huge success with critics and audiences, establishing beyond question Lloyd's ability to carry a feature-length film. Actually, he would go on to make better pictures.

A meek Harold Lloyd (below left) encounters a tramp
(Dick Sutherland) who has been terrifying the
neighborhood. Grandma is played by Anna Townsend.
Lloyd (below right), after his transformation, leads a posse
to the villain's hide-out. The kitten is an extra.

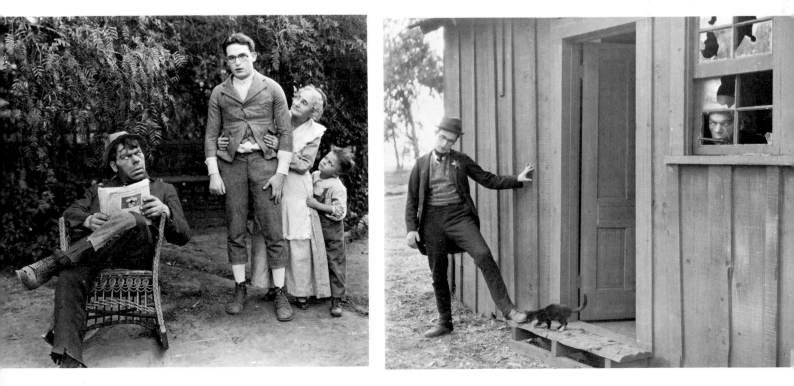

His own Grandpa: Lloyd plays a cowardly ancestor transformed — so the story goes — by a magical talisman. Below: The results of his heroism — a Union command post captured, secret plans revealed by the brave little spy.

Dr. Jack

1922

Of Lloyd's many optimistic heroes, Dr. Jack was perhaps the most positive-thinking of them all — a country sawbones who peddled more psychology than pills in the course of his rounds, a kind of public (mental) health officer. The film's best sequences are the ones concerning his life as a minor miracle worker in a bucolic setting. After he leaves for the big city to undertake the rehabilitation of the "sick little well girl," the story becomes at first unbelievable, then downright frantic, in its search for a comic conclusion.

The doctor is in: Lloyd convincing a potential truant (below left) that his place is in school, and (right) responding to an emergency call in aid of a broken dolly. Opposite, Lloyd consults on the case of an heiress (Mildred Davis) who has fallen under the quackish care of Dr. Ludwig Von Soulsberg, who looks on suspiciously.

Safety Last
1923

Safety Last was not Lloyd's first "thrill picture" (as he called the genre he invented). He had clung funnily and scarily to high, precarious perches in such early shorts as *Look Out Below, High and Dizzy,* and *Never Weaken.* But the spectacular building climb that climaxed this film established him forever as the comedian who would go to any lengths to get a laugh. It was also his most extended study of ambition and its perils. The reason he finds himself clinging for dear life to the hands of time (overleaf) is simply because he wants to make good in his job and make enough money to marry the girl he left behind when he came to the big city to make his fortune. Of course, he succeeded.

A perfect visual pun. What looks like a final farewell on
death row (opposite) is revealed in a pull back to be a
simple good-bye in a railroad station. Below, Harold
makes bad in his first job, undermanning a yard goods
counter at the height of a bargain sale. His sword is a
yardstick and it does not comfort him.

Lloyd's most famous single sequence was shot twelve stories above ground. No trick photography was used, but there was a safety platform out of camera range.

Why Worry?
1923

Harold the hypochondriac. Seeking a cure from imaginary maladies, he heads for a resort that turns out to be in the throes of revolution. He justifies the film's blithe title by strolling entirely self-absorbed through the final phases of the tumult. Opposite — the tumult — and a typical example of Harold's response to it. Nobody knew the term in those days, but *Why Worry?* is an absurdist film, a serene exercise in primitive surrealism and perhaps the most consistently lunatic feature Lloyd ever made, never pausing — as the comedian generally liked to do — to establish some extra dimension to his characterization or establish some reasonable explanation for what he was doing. It may be his most underrated movie and the one that modern audiences, trained by the Marx Brothers, would most appreciate.

YOUNG MILLIONAIRE SEEKS HEALTH IN QUIET SECLUSION OF TROPICS

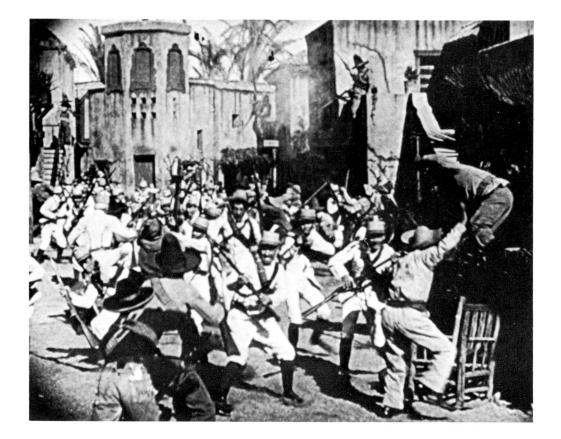

In order: Harold asks the revolutionary leader for directions to the hotel and is mistaken for a counter-revolutionary. In turn, he mistakes the soldiers, who are conducting him to prison, for an honor guard, and the jailor for a rather odd hotel's desk clerk. (What he thinks is the guest register — and cheerfully signs — is actually a list of those scheduled to be shot at dawn.) His cell-mate, the giant Colosse (played by Johan Aasen), of course turns out to be his salvation.

Before they can constitute themselves a two-man counter-revolutionary army, Lloyd must cure his large friend's giant-sized toothache. Obviously that's easier said than done, and after the initial failures recorded on this page, Lloyd finally throws the rope over a tree limb, ties the other end around his waist, and making himself a living counterweight, flings himself off a balcony to yank the offending molar. Giant Aasen was not a professional actor and was hastily recruited for this role when a circus giant died suddenly just as production was about to begin. He proved himself to be one of Lloyd's best foils, a benign presence whom Lloyd recalled as having an ironically high-pitched voice.

Girl Shy
1924

In *Girl Shy,* Lloyd cast himself as a country bumpkin nursing dreams of glory —
and realizing them in a spectacular fashion. Too shy to ask a girl for a date, let
alone try to kiss her, he nevertheless hopes to make his fortune by writing a
how-to book on lovemaking. This was Lloyd's first film after he obtained his
independence from Hal Roach, and if the basic plot was a little thin, he
compensated for that defect by creating the greatest of his chase sequences for
the movie's climax. All shyness banished, he rides desperately to the rescue of
his true love, who is about to marry the caddish Ronald Devore, a fortune-hunter
willing to commit bigamy in pursuit of wealth. After Lloyd married Mildred Davis

in 1923, Jobyna Ralston, who had started in Roach one-reelers, became his leading lady, working with him in six of his most important films.

Strangers on a Train. Lloyd uneasily meets the girl he's shy of (below left). He is carrying the manuscript of his book to a publisher in the city. Her dog is illegally riding among the train's human passengers, resulting in problems Lloyd helps to solve. Below, the newspaper article that starts Lloyd out on the wildest ride of his screen career.

BUCKINGHAM - DEVORE WEDDING TODAY

Society to Gather at Famous Buckingham Estate for Gala Ceremony

The wild rumpus begins. The only thing Lloyd doesn't miss is a boat. He does, however, miss cars, busses, and trains in his maximum effort to prevent Miss Buckingham from marrying a bigamist. The chase's high point is the purloined streetcar, which loses power when its trolley is disconnected from the power line. Lloyd's attempt to solve the problem leaves him groping desperately for solid footing.

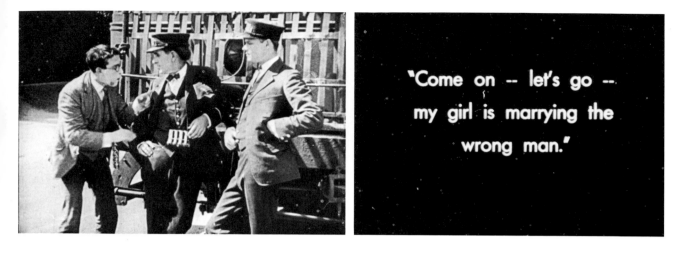

"Come on -- let's go --
my girl is marrying the
wrong man."

The motorcycle is a big help when the trolley fails Harold. But the bird, obviously, is not. Meantime, opposite, the bride is almost ready to walk the aisle — and Lloyd has to change his plans again.

Crosscutting to a climax. "With this ring . . ." "Giddyup Horsie . . ." Harold enters the Buckingham estate as the daughter of the house approaches the altar.

Overleaf, Harold loses the stammer that has afflicted him all picture long, managing to speak now and thus avoid having to forever hold his peace. The ending will remind viewers of the conclusion to *The Graduate*.

Hot Water

1924

Hot Water has scarcely more plot than a revue. It simply shows a harassed Harold trying to get through a typical day in the life of a typical young middle-class husband — picking up some groceries, taking a trial spin in his new car, entertaining his awful in-laws, and trying to maintain decorum. Among the groceries is a lively and extremely irritable turkey, and his attempt to take it home on a crowded streetcar is one of the finest little farce sequences he ever did. As for the car, see following pages. The film's third section is a sputtery mess, in which Lloyd tries and fails to top the hilarity that went before. *Hot Water* is one

of Lloyd's most carelessly structured movies, but this sequence and the one involving the turkey and the trolley car are among the greatest of his gag sequences — little epics of unsurpassed embarrassment.

The shopping expedition (left) begins in disaster and ends in embarrassment (center), as Harold and his outrageous bird are ejected from the trolley. Right, Harold and bride admire their short-lived status symbol.

177

"——and just think, dear, fifty-nine more payments and it's ours! Let's take it out for a trial spin — just you and I!"

"It's a pity I couldn't enjoy this ride without having to take charge!"

The proud new owner of a "Butterfly Six" takes his new car, his bride, and his in-laws out for a trial spin. Frame enlargements (and subtitles from the movie itself) tell the sad story. It should be clearly understood, however, that Josephine Crowell's performance as the Mother-in-Law is definitive, the living embodiment of a thousand jokes.

The Freshman
1925

The Freshman is Harold Lloyd's best remembered, most often revived movie —
and with good reason. The story of Harold ("Speedy") Lamb's desperate desire
to be the most popular man on campus at Tate College is his most brilliant
combination of the hilarious and the pathetic. It is at once a sharp satire on the
1920s craze for college humor and heroics and a biting commentary on the
empty values that lay beneath that craze (Harold's dress and manners are all
seen to be derived from the movies and popular magazines). The eagerness with
which the student body gangs up on the innocent Harold, cruelly leading him on
only to put him down, is a classic study in mob psychology.

In his room at home, *The Freshman* dreams of college
glory (below). On the train to Tate he meets the girl of
those dreams (above right), and finally, learns how he can
make them a reality — become a football hero.

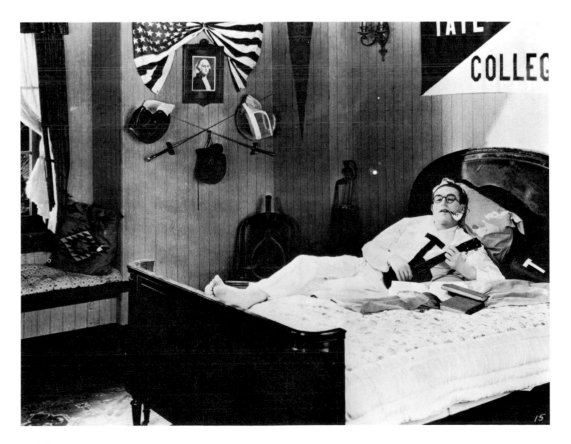

182

The height of the social season, a tuxedo that's only been basted, not sewn, a tailor too drunk to thread a needle, let alone make major repairs in a hurry — these are the basic ingredients of one of *The Freshman's* most memorable sequences, and one of the most original ideas for a comedy sequence in all movie history. The film was co-directed by Fred Newmeyer and Sam Taylor, both veterans of the Lloyd gag room.

"Speedy, old pal, can you let me have ten dollars?"

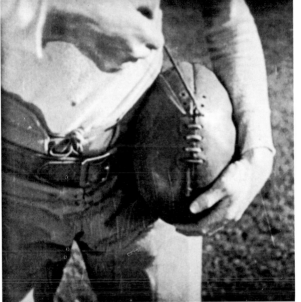

186

"Speedy" finally gets into the big game. Up to this play, he's been at the bottom of every pile up, but now, fielding a punt he has a chance to apply one of the most original minds in football history to the problem of surviving — and prevailing. An unlaced ball, a casual saunter, a wild dash — and failure when he stops for an unofficial whistle blown in the stands. Second chance coming up.

The last white line is crossed. And Harold Lamb is finally Mr. Touchdown, the hero he's dreamed of being. Did the crowd's cheers erase the memory of being used as a living tackling dummy in an earlier sequence? Did Harold Lloyd himself understand that *The Freshman* satirized the values he — as well as his standard screen character — lived by? It doesn't seem likely. But the picture remains his masterpiece, the one feature in which story, character, and unforgettable gag sequences were perfectly balanced and perfectly orchestrated, the one film that is indisputably the equal of the great long films of his great rivals, Chaplin and Keaton. For Lloyd it represented the culmination of a career-long desire to play the college boy he had never been.

187

For Heaven's Sake
1926

This was perhaps the weakest of Lloyd's silent features, the story of a wealthy idler reformed by love for a mission girl. His new mission in life is helping to save the church where she and her father minister to the denizens of skid row. Despite rather patchy construction, it does have its moments. Below, a get-me-to-the-church-on-time sequence in which Lloyd is rushed to his wedding on a wildly rocking runaway bus, commandeered by some of the congregation's tipsier members. Opposite, the film's great opening gag — in which Lloyd wrecks two brand new cars in a matter of minutes. Note undamaged cigar in top photo, undamaged crank handle in bottom one, unruffled "Harold Manners" in both.

The Kid Brother
1927

He is Harold Hickory in *The Kid Brother,* much put upon by his older, stronger siblings, and a great disappointment to his father, who is also sheriff of the backwoods county where the story is laid. But, as ever, Harold is dead game, and as quick of wit as he is quick of foot in avoiding the strenuous lessons they are always trying to teach him. It turns out to be good practice for more melodramatic problem solving when the need arises. The fact that the stick he picks up to defend Miss Ralston's honor comes equipped with a snake helps. But he has only his brains, and a monkey, to help him when he traces the same heavy (Constantine Romanoff) to the hulk of a ship where the villain took the money he stole from Harold's fellow townsmen. The monkey who exposes Harold here is about to don shoes and become his stand-in in one of the film's funniest gags.

Speedy
1928

Speedy was Lloyd's last silent film, and one of his finest. It is the only picture he shot on location in New York, and it is one of the three fictional films in which Babe Ruth appeared. Below, Ruth is seen as the unlucky rider in a cab driven by Harold with his customary disregard for both the speed laws and Newton's laws. Mostly, however, the movie is about Harold's efforts to save the last horse-drawn streetcar line in New York from extinction at the hands of some malevolent traction magnates. Its owner (and sole employee) is the father of the

girl Harold loves, and the film may contain more honest sentiment, more genuine warmth of feeling, than any other Lloyd effort. The director, Ted Wilde, received an Academy Award nomination for his work on it, but Lloyd always said that as star and producer he was senior officer present on all his sets and that much of the credit for direction properly belonged to him. Doubtless this is true, but there is no denying the difference in tone between *Speedy* and the rest of his work. Of course, as the still below proves, there were plenty of gags.

Welcome Danger
1929

Lloyd shot — and even previewed — *Welcome Danger* as a silent film before deciding it really ought to be a talkie. It is the story of a mild-mannered botany professor whose father used to be a tough police captain in San Francisco. His father's colleagues hope Harold may be a chip off the old block and help them solve a particularly unpleasant crime wave. As these pictures show, he does, but not before his prissy manner and scholarly ways drive everyone to distraction. Though it was by no means representative of his best work, the public was so curious to hear Lloyd speak that they made *Welcome Danger* his most profitable picture.

A Chinatown climax. Lloyd takes care of some pressing business (opposite), proves himself a proper cut-up (below left), then enjoys a well-earned culinary treat. The puzzled policeman was played by Noah Young, who started working in Lloyd's informal stock company in 1916 and is to be glimpsed in almost all the star's films.

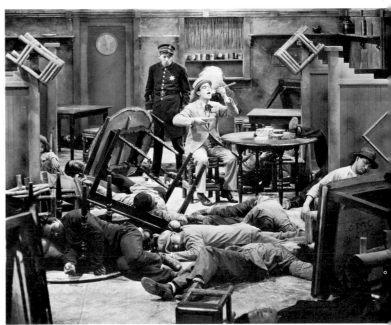

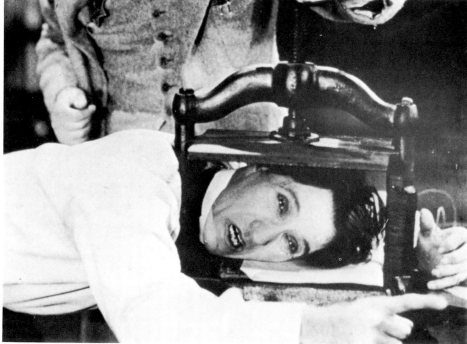

Feet First
1930

It was among the weakest films Harold Lloyd ever made, but ironically, *Feet First,* about a hopelessly inept shoe clerk who stows away on a boat and gets shipped home in a mail sack, contains Lloyd's greatest thrill sequence. Below, he gets the bird. Above right, he gets the sack. Below right, the sack (and Lloyd), having been mailed to Los Angeles via sea plane and misdelivered without Lloyd's knowing it, rolls onto a painter's scaffold and is lifted into mid-air, where it catches on a hook. It is at this point, naturally, that Lloyd decides it is time to cut his way out of his predicament. . . .

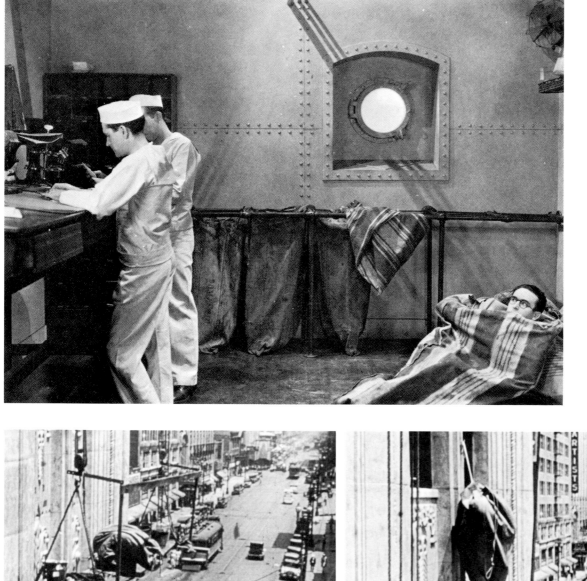

Sequences within the great sequence — Top: the offending scaffold reappears just when Lloyd doesn't need it. Center: One thing after another — a desperately grabbed plank proves no help at all. Bottom: an awning provides a soft landing, but no permanent perch. Soon, even its metal supports will tear away.

Firehose, spare that lunatic. And for a moment it does. Then a janitor, trying to be helpful, turns it on. . . .

"Cut it off," Lloyd cries. And as
we see below, the man follows Lloyd's
instructions all too literally.

Topping the topper. Lloyd finally gains the roof, only to fall exhausted next to an open bottle of ether. Down the rope he goes. Up the rope he woozily returns — only to be caught in the middle of an argument. Lloyd finally faints, but his foot is caught in a rope which breaks his fall. He wakes up, clinging to another window, screaming for help, not knowing he's just inches from the ground — the perfect end to a perfect comedic day.

Movie Crazy

1932

For the last time in his career, Lloyd plays the eager bumpkin off to seek fame and fortune in the great city — this time under the impression that he's been offered a screen test by a major movie studio. It takes more than a father's dubious expression to discourage Harold Hall (below), but the whole thing is a terrible mistake, as the director of his screen test (Sidney Jarvis) clearly indicates (opposite). But if Lloyd is hopeless trying to impersonate a suave lover, the eager pluckiness which carried him through so many cinematic *contretemps* would prove to be intact and — like the real-life Lloyd — he would gain success as a

comedian, not as a straight dramatic actor. The romance in *Movie Crazy* was a succession of strange interludes (co-starring the admirable Constance Cummings), but the film as a whole was the most successful approximation of his silent film style that Lloyd made after the coming of sound, and it continues to rank among the best movies about movies — comedy subdivision — that Hollywood ever turned out. The director was another long-time Lloyd gagman, Clyde Bruckner, vastly improving on his work on *Feet First*.

The great coat gag. In the men's room, Lloyd has accidentally exchanged jackets with a magician, a fact that is hilariously revealed to him as he dances with dignified Louise Closser Hale, playing the wife of his studio's president. The drunk who didn't order *hasenpfeffer* is played by Arthur Housman, and the whole sequence is reminiscent of the fall-away tuxedo gag in *The Freshman,* but no less funny for its distinguished precedent.

The Cat's Paw
1934

The Cat's Paw was a dog, the worst feature Lloyd ever made, a virtually gagless tale about a missionary's son who is hornswoggled into running as a reform candidate in a mayoralty election, surprises everyone by winning — and by taking his mandate to throw the rascals out seriously. As in *Welcome Danger,* there is a crime wave, and once again Lloyd arranges a mass round-up of the criminal element in Chinatown. There he stages a few fake beheadings to persuade the other crooks to confess (see stills below), but the sequence is neither funny nor

suspenseful. So despite a story by Clarence Buddington Kelland, the popular *Saturday Evening Post* writer, and the aid of Lloyd's favorite directorial graduate of his gag room, Sam Taylor, the picture failed. Lloyd told journalists it was an experiment — an attempt at straight drama — but that was just whistling in the dark. Times had changed and he and his loyal team just weren't suited to changing tastes in movie comedy.

The Milky Way
1936

Leo McCarey was one of the directors responsible for the new and dominant style in movie comedy in the 1930s, a style generally referred to now as "screwball." It was essentially a verbal, not a physical, style, featuring wisecracking dames, shady types from the fringes of the criminal world, and often some representatives of high society forced by the Depression to deal with the real world for a change. The crosstalk was so fast and furious that they frequently stepped on each other's lines, and it was always infinitely more cynical than anything the silent comedians of the previous decade would have dared. Indeed, it is greatly to Lloyd's credit that he agreed to work for McCarey in *The Milky Way,* which was pure screwball — the story of a meek milkman who is erroneously believed to have knocked out the middleweight champion of the world in a street brawl and is given a series of fixed fights in order to build him up as a legitimate contender for the crown — which he wins. It was the first film Lloyd made for a company he did not control since leaving Roach, and though he certainly played the central role, the success of the picture derived from the

ensemble playing of an expert supporting cast, headed by Adolphe Menjou, brilliantly flinging verbal firecrackers at each other. Still, Lloyd gathered his best set of notices in this decade for *The Milky Way,* and he might have extended his career had he essayed more films of this type.

The Milkman's dream of settling down with pretty Polly Pringle (Dorothy Wilson) (opposite), is realized by hard and accidentally watery work in training camp (below).

Professor Beware
1938

Professor Beware was Lloyd's last independent production. Directed by Elliott Nugent, most of whose previous experience was on the stage (with James Thurber he wrote *The Male Animal*), this tale of a timorous academic afraid that he may have fallen under an ancient Egyptian curse was contemptuously received by critics, who told Lloyd flatly that his imitation of himself had become a bore, and was indifferently received by audiences. Lloyd got the message, and quietly dropped out as a performer. Though he produced a couple of comedies in the early forties, he devoted himself mainly to private interests until 1945, when he made an unhappy attempt at a comeback.

Theft of Services turns out to be hard work for Lloyd, Raymond Walburn, and Lionel Stander. A low bridge is rapidly approaching in the final still in this series.

213

Mad Wednesday
(The Sin of Harold Diddlebock) 1947

Preston Sturges, a great and erratic director, recruited Lloyd for this film, but their mutual admiration society broke up on the set. Then Sturges's other professional romance, with producer Howard Hughes, fell apart during the post-production phase. As a result, *Diddlebock* went unreleased for five years, and when it came out in 1950, under the title *Mad Wednesday,* ineptly re-edited by Hughes, it flopped. The first third is a brilliant and touching examination of what might have happened to Lloyd's football hero from *The Freshman* after he entered the adult world. The rest of the movie, however, substitutes loud frenzy for real wit and is a dismal farewell to Lloyd's screen character.

Lloyd and friend (Jimmy Conlon) take a lion along as they beard Wall Street's bulls and bears, trying to unload a circus they've acquired. Opposite: The Lion is loose on a ledge, and his leash is a lifeline for Lloyd and Conlon in one last thrill sequence.

215

Filmography by Eileen Bowser

Note: As this book went to press, Eileen Bowser of the Department of Film of the Museum of Modern Art was completing work on a revised Harold Lloyd filmography and graciously consented to its being printed here. It supersedes all previous filmographies because, by consulting back issues of *Moving Picture World,* she has been able to identify the uncopyrighted, and mostly lost, films Lloyd appeared in — mainly as Lonesome Luke — in the period prior to 1917; it seems that there were at most fifty-three of these — not sixty-four, as previous filmographies have stated. She also discovered that a number of later one-reelers credited to Lloyd actually starred other comedians employed at Hal Roach's studio. In the list that follows a few 1915 titles that are probably, but not positively, the work of Harold Lloyd have been starred, and titles are listed in order of their release — also an improvement over previous filmographies. As to directors, Hal Roach must be credited with most of Lloyd's movies prior to 1917 though a few other craftsmen occasionally tried their hands at this work. From 1917 to 1919 he alternated mostly with Alf Goulding, though in the spring of 1918 a man named G. W. Pratt began handling some of the Lloyd films. Lloyd himself also entered a claim as director of some of his early pictures. All 1915 and 1916 releases are one reel in length. The longer films of 1917–1920 are identified as such below. Finally, it should be noted that in addition to straightening out the vexing matter of just exactly what Lloyd did in the early portion of his career, Ms. Bowser prepared brief plot summaries of those films based on early trade reviews, which space does not permit us to reprint here.

The early films are one reel, unless indicated as (2) or (3). The asterisks indicate films that are probably, but not positively, the work of Lloyd.

1915

Just Nuts
Lonesome Luke
Once Every Ten Minute*
Spit-Ball Sadie*
Soaking the Clothes*
Pressing His Suit*
Terribly Stuck Up*
A Mixup for Masie
Some Baby
Fresh from the Farm*
Giving Them Fits
Bughouse Bellhops
Tinkering with Trouble*
Great While It Lasted
Ragtime Snap Shots
A Foozle at the Tea Party
Ruses, Rhymes and Roughnecks
Peculiar Patients' Pranks
Lonesome Luke, Social Gangster

1916

Lonesome Luke Leans to the Literary
Luke Lugs Luggage
Lonesome Luke Lolls in Luxury
Luke, the Candy Cut-Up
Luke Foils the Villain
Luke and the Rural Roughnecks
Luke Pipes the Pippens
Lonesome Luke, Circus King
Luke's Double
Them Was the Happy Days
Luke and the Bomb Throwers
Luke's Late Lunchers
Luke Laughs Last
Luke's Fatal Flivver
Luke's Society Mixup
Luke's Washful Waiting
Luke Rides Rough-Shod
Luke, Crystal Gazer
Luke's Lost Lamb
Luke Does the Midway
Luke Joins the Navy
Luke and the Mermaids
Luke's Speedy Club Life
Luke and the Bangtails
Luke the Chauffeur

Luke's Preparedness Preparations
Luke the Gladiator
Luke, Patient Provider
Luke's Newsie Knockout
Luke's Movie Muddle
Luke, Rank Impersonator
Luke's Fireworks Fizzle
Luke Locates the Loot
Luke's Shattered Sleep

1917

Luke's Lost Liberty
Luke's Busy Day
Luke's Trolley Troubles
Lonesome Luke, Lawyer
Luke Wins Ye Ladye Fair
Lonesome Luke's Lively Life (This was the
    first two-reel Luke film; all subsequent
    Luke releases are of this length.)
Lonesome Luke on Tin Can Alley
Lonesome Luke's Honeymoon
Lonesome Luke, Plumber
Stop! Luke! Listen!
Lonesome Luke, Messenger
Lonesome Luke, Mechanic
Lonesome Luke's Wild Women
Over the Fence (Lloyd's first appearance as
    "The Glasses Character." For the rest
    of this year two-reel Lonesome Lukes
    alternated in release with one-reel
    Glasses Character films. Hereafter, the
    remaining Luke releases will be
    identified by the numeral 2, indicating
    number of reels.)
Lonesome Luke Loses Patients (2)
Pinched
By the Sad Sea Waves
Birds of a Feather (2)
Bliss
Lonesome Luke in From London to Laramie (2)
Rainbow Island
Lonesome Luke in Love, Laughs and Lather
The Flirt
Clubs are Trump (2)
All Aboard
We Never Sleep (2) (The last Luke)
Move On
Bashful

1918

The Tip
The Big Idea
The Lamb
Hit Him Again
Beat It
A Gasoline Wedding
Look Pleasant, Please
Here Come the Girls
Let's Go
On the Jump
Follow the Crowd
Pipe the Whiskers
It's a Wild Life
Hey There
Kicked Out
The Non-Stop Kid
Two-Gun Gussie
Fireman, Save My Child
The City Slicker
Sic 'Em Towser
Somewhere in Turkey
Are Crooks Dishonest?
An Ozark Romance
Kicking the Germ Out of Germany
That's Him
Bride and Gloom
Two Scrambled
Bees in His Bonnet
Swing Your Partners
Why Pick on Me?
Nothing but Trouble
Hear 'Em Rave
Take a Chance
She Loves Me Not

1919

Wanted — $5,000
Going! Going! Gone
Ask Father
On the Fire
I'm On My Way
Look Out Below!
The Dutiful Dub
Next Aisle Over
A Sammy in Siberia
Just Dropped In
Crack Your Heels

Ring Up the Curtain
Count Your Change
A Jazzed Honeymoon
Never Touched Me
At the Old Stage Door
Just Neighbors
Billy Blazes, Esq.
Spring Fever
Off the Trolley
Swat the Crook
Pistols for Breakfast
Back to the Woods
The Marathon
Before Breakfast
Si Senor
Young Mr. Jazz

Chop Suey & Co.
Heap Big Chief
Don't Shove
Be My Wife
The Rajah
He Leads, Others Follow
Soft Money
Count the Votes
Pay Your Dues
His Only Father
Bumping into Broadway (Lloyd's first two-reeler. Henceforth, no Lloyd film would be shorter.)
Captain Kidd's Kids (2)
From Hand to Mouth (2) (Mildred Davis replaces Bebe Daniels as leading lady.)

1920

His Royal Slyness (2)
Haunted Spooks (2) (The film interrupted by Lloyd's injury.)
An Eastern Westerner (2)
High and Dizzy (2)
Get Out and Get Under (2)
Number Please (2)

1921

Now or Never (3)
Among Those Present (3)
I Do (2)
Never Weaken (3)

THE FEATURE FILMS

The dates are release dates. Directors' names are italicized; the names following are those of featured players. The number of reels is indicated in parentheses.

1. 1921 A SAILOR-MADE MAN. Hal Roach–Associated Exhibitors–Pathé. *Fred Newmeyer.* Mildred Davis, Noah Young. (4)

2. 1922 GRANDMA'S BOY. Associated Exhibitors. *Fred Newmeyer.* Anna Townsend, Mildred Davis, Charles Stevenson. (5)

3. 1922 DR. JACK. Pathé. *Fred Newmeyer.* Mildred Davis, John T. Prince, Eric Mayne, C. Norman Hammond. (6)

4. 1923 SAFETY LAST. Hal Roach–Pathé. *Fred Newmeyer and Sam Taylor.* Mildred Davis, Bill Strothers, Noah Young, Westcott Clarke, Mickey Daniels. (6)

5. 1923 WHY WORRY? Hal Roach–Pathé. *Fred Newmeyer and Sam Taylor.* Jobyna Ralston, Johan Aasen. (6)

6. 1924 GIRL SHY. Harold Lloyd Corp.–Pathé. *Fred Newmeyer and Sam Taylor.* Jobyna Ralston, Richard Daniels, Carlton Griffin. (8)

7. 1924 HOT WATER. Pathé. *Fred Newmeyer and Sam Taylor.* Jobyna Ralston, Josephine Crowell. (5)

8. 1925 THE FRESHMAN. Pathé. *Fred Newmeyer and Sam Taylor.* Jobyna Ralston, Brooks Benedict, James Anderson, Pat Harmon, Joe Harrington. (7)

9. 1926 FOR HEAVEN'S SAKE. Paramount. *Sam Taylor.* Jobyna Ralston, Noah Young. (6)

10. 1927 THE KID BROTHER. Paramount. *Ted Wilde.* Jobyna Ralston, Walter James, Leo Willis, Olin Francis, Eddie Boland, Constantine Romanoff. (8)

11. 1928 SPEEDY. Paramount. *Ted Wilde.* Burt Woodruff, Babe Ruth, Ann Christy, Brooks Benedict. (8)

12. 1929 WELCOME DANGER. Paramount. *Clyde Bruckman.* Barbara Kent, Noah Young, Charles Middleton, William Walling. Lloyd's first talkie. (12)

13. 1930 FEET FIRST. Paramount. *Clyde Bruckman.* Barbara Kent, Robert McWade, Lillian Leighton, Alec Francis, Noah Young. (9)

14. 1932 MOVIE CRAZY. Paramount. *Clyde Bruckman.* Constance Cummings, Kenneth Thomson, Sidney Jarvis, Eddie Fetherstone, Robert McWade. (8)

15. 1934 THE CAT'S PAW. Fox. *Sam Taylor.* George Barbier, Una Merkel, Grant Mitchell, Nat Pendleton. (12)

16. 1936 THE MILKY WAY. Paramount. *Leo McCarey.* Adolphe Menjou, Verree Teasdale, Helen Mack, William Gargan, Dorothy Wilson, George Barbier, Lionel Stander. (8)

17. 1938 PROFESSOR BEWARE. Paramount. *Elliott Nugent.* Phyliss Welch, Raymond Walburn, Lionel Stander, Cora Witherspoon, Etienne Girardot, William Frawley. (8)

18. 1947 MAD WEDNESDAY (THE SIN OF HAROLD DIDDLEBOCK). United Artists. *Preston Sturges.* Frances Ramsden, Jimmy Conlin, Edgar Kennedy, Rudy Vallee, Arline Judge, Franklin Pangborn, Lionel Stander. (8)

19. 1962 HAROLD LLOYD'S WORLD OF COMEDY. Continental Distributing. Produced and edited by Lloyd. An anthology of comedy sequences, mostly from *Safety Last, The Freshman, Hot Water, Why Worry?, Girl Shy, Professor Beware, Movie Crazy,* and *Feet First.* (9)

20. 1963 THE FUNNY SIDE OF LIFE. Another compilation film, produced and edited by Lloyd. Not generally distributed in the U.S.

Acknowledgments

When Time-Life Films, which will be re-releasing most of Lloyd's films over the next few years, invited me to attempt this critical-biographical sketch of the comedian, it had already commissioned a veteran correspondent of the Time-Life News Service, Martin O'Neill, to interview as many friends, relatives, and co-workers of Lloyd's as he could find. His remarkably thorough dispatches were placed at my disposal for this book, and it is a pleasure to acknowledge my indebtedness to Mr. O'Neill. I am sure he would like me to express gratitude to those who provided him information. I was able later to extend his list of interviewees somewhat. Therefore our mutual thanks go to Richard Correll, Delmer Daves, Walter Dymond, Merle S. Ewell, Mrs. Marjorie Elizabeth Patten, Hal Roach, Richard Simonton, and Sam Taylor, Jr. I owe a special debt to Robert Hoag, producer of the Lloyd re-releases, and to Rich Correll, who is associated with him in this task, for arranging screenings of Lloyd's films. As he has in the past, George Pratt of George Eastman House has been helpful in pointing me toward some rare printed material on Lloyd, and I was particularly blessed on this project to have access to Time-Life's editorial reference library, which among other invaluable items contains the late Alfred Wright's reportage for the *Time*'s cover story on Lloyd in 1949. Eugene Stavis of the City Center Cinematheque in New York and the UCLA film archives arranged for me to view the Preston Sturges cut of *The Sin of Harold Diddlebock*, for which they deserve a salute. Finally, I am more grateful than I can say to Eileen Bowser of the Museum of Modern Art for making available for this book her new and authoritative Harold Lloyd filmography, which is an invaluable contribution to film scholarship. Of course, the basic printed source on Harold Lloyd's early life is *An American Comedy,* which he wrote with the assistance of Wesley W. Stout, which was reprinted in paperback in 1971 by Dover Publications, Inc., portions of which are quoted, all of which informs the earlier portions of this book. Other printed sources that I found especially useful are all, I hope, cited in the text. To Myrna Greenfield, who typed this manuscript with speed and accuracy, to Betty Childs, who saw it through the press the same way, special thanks. And to Jill and the kids, who were so nice about my preoccupation with Lloyd during a summer that really belonged to them, special, special thanks.

Richard Schickel
New York City
August 12, 1974

Photograph Credits

The author and publishers are grateful to Dave Nowell and Rich Correll for their expert researches into the rich archive of film stills at Greenacres. Almost all the illustrations in the book are from these files or are frames from the films. The illustrations on pages 62, 180, 181, 211, and 212 are from the Museum of Modern Art Film Stills Archive; the one on page 215 is from Culver Pictures.

Library of Congress Cataloging in Publication Data

Kampf, Avram.
   Jewish experience in the art of the 20th century.

   Bibliography: p. 220
   Includes index.
   1. Art, Jewish. 2. Art, Modern—20th century.
I. Title.
N7417.6.K35   1984   704'.03924'0904   83-11884

ISBN 0-89789-039-6

First Published in 1984 by
Bergin & Garvey Publishers, Inc.
670 Amherst Road
South Hadley, Massachusetts 01075

Printed and bound in Hong Kong by Mandarin Offset

Contents

Preface 6

Introduction 7

CHAPTER ONE The Quest for a Jewish Style
in the Era of the Russian Revolution 14

CHAPTER TWO The Encounter with the West 48

CHAPTER THREE Paris 88

CHAPTER FOUR The Holocaust 112

CHAPTER FIVE The Search for Roots in Israel 144

CHAPTER SIX The Evocation of the Religious Tradition 176

CHAPTER SEVEN Reaching for the Absolute 190

Notes 203

Artists' Biographies 212

Select Bibliography 220

Chronology 223

Illustrations 233

Index 235

Preface

This study evolved from my association with the Jewish Museum of New York City in 1967–8 and in 1972–6. It seemed to me then that the Museum in order to discover and to affirm actively its identity in the world of today had to base its work in the modern field on the awareness of its own historic roots and concerns. It had to gather and bring into relief certain scattered and submerged aspects of the modern art movement and relate them to the historic context of Jewish life experience in all its variety, complexity and ambiguity.

The catalogue of the Museum's large exhibition (16 October 1975–25 January 1976), 'Jewish Experience in the Art of the 20th Century', of which I was the curator, formed the basis for the present book, which aims to bring into sharper focus some of the themes and motifs which the exhibition explored.

I would like to thank Montclair State College Development Fund for giving me a grant which enabled me to carry out this study. I wish to thank also the many artists and collectors who assisted me in gathering the material. Acknowledgement is due to the Jewish Museum of New York City for putting at my disposal its photographic file; to the librarians of the Archives of American Art, the Whitney Museum of American Art, and YIVO (the Yiddish Scientific Institute), all in New York City; and to the librarians of the Hebrew University in Jerusalem and of Haifa University for their untiring assistance. I am grateful to Professor Moshe Barasch of the Hebrew University, with whom I had the opportunity to discuss several possible approaches to the subject of the book.

I am deeply indebted also to frequent discussions with Professor Jonathan Silver of Montclair State College, who helped to clarify many issues. Both he and Dr Harriet Senie read the manuscript and made valuable suggestions. I would also like to thank Ms Irith Miller for her assistance in bibliographical, biographical and photographic research, Ms Paulette Jellinek for helping to organize the photographic files, and Ms Rose Yager for her help in editing the manuscript. Many thanks also to Mr Bernard Dod for his most helpful editorial work.

Avram Kampf
University of Haifa

Introduction

The work of art does not fit into any of the conceptual categories which the rational mind constructs. It explodes them. It cannot be tamed into a social or personal document without impairing its essential character—integrating impulse, feeling, and thought. It acts as a nodal point of formalized energy, shaping personal, historical and cultural motifs into an autonomous, self-sustaining world. On the other hand, the work of art can never be completely grasped without sensing and bringing to consciousness the multitude of personal elements, cultural aspects, and historical relations that it contains.

There is a need to affirm that the tendency in the visual arts to regard works as autonomous aesthetic objects only denies these essential truths. By disregarding their intricate historical context and seeing only formal qualities we diminish them. The art object is the vortex of individual and cultural experience. It is of its own time and transcends it. It is form and content, illusion and reality, affirmation and deception, conviction and play, sensual and spiritual.

One could choose a large number of works produced by Jewish artists and create an aesthetically impressive book by showing what they have done in the twentieth century. One could even claim that whatever filters through a Jewish mind can be termed 'Jewish experience'. To define the book in this way would have made an extremely complicated issue simple, perhaps far too simple to be true.

Such an approach would at best demonstrate the wide participation and activity of Jewish artists in all the art movements of the twentieth century, but it would have been sectarian without interpreting and clarifying the major and unique experiences which have marked the life of Jewish individuals and communities in this century. Experience is a continuous process of the living organism interacting with aspects of the world in which it lives. Experience means observing, encountering, and undergoing. It is feeling, sensing, thinking, and remembering. It means enduring situations and conditions, and it means changing. When many encounter or undergo similar conditions we may talk about shared or collective experiences, even though each person reacts in his own way to a common situation. As one scans the twentieth-century landscape of art one discerns salient features of the Jewish collective experience, which are only too familiar to those who have been alive in this century.

There have been the large migrations from east to west, from close-knit communities to a strange atomized world. There was a meeting with the culture, ideas, and art of the West. There are the problems arising out of the struggle to survive. There is a need to strike roots in a new environment, to adapt, assimilate, and yet to preserve one's identity. There are tensions between tradition and innovation, the options which life offers, and the decisions it forces on us. There are roads which part, cross and meet again. There are new beginnings, new landscapes, new cities, new planting, new work. There is a reconstruction and an affirmation, a losing and finding, which is echoed in the work of artists, whether born in America or Lithuania, whether setting up their easels in São Paulo or London, whether coming as immigrants to Israel or settling in Paris or New York, whether open or closed to religious thought and feeling, or merely indifferent.

That this century has been one of continuous upheaval is known best by those who lived through it as observers, participants, victims, or survivors. There were the trials of the First World War, the Russian Revolution, the period between the wars, the catastrophe designated as the Holocaust with its trains and the death camps of the Second World War, the survivors wandering across Europe, sailing the seas, endlessly seeking new homes. There has been the continuous struggle for Israel, its building and defence, the encounter with the Biblical landscape, and the rebirth of an ancient language. That interaction between man and the world, which we call experience, produces friction and fissures in the individual and the collective, stirs emotions and ideas, and leaves the traces which we attempt to discover in twentieth-century works of art.

This study defines itself by focusing on the Jewish background, concerns, or motifs which feed into the creation of works of art. There has been a strong claim that modern art is largely built on the narrow aesthetic precedents of other works of art, and that its formal problems grow out of older formal problems. This emphasis on formal invention and innovation has diminished the value of content. Not only has there been a tendency to devalue or deny the narrative, the pre-artistic, the experiential sources which continuously nourish art; but we have also thereby been induced to overlook the relations, loyalties, and tensions between the artist, his background, his culture, sources and concerns. This study rests squarely on life experiences collectively shared, intensified, interpreted and transformed by the artist. It is not meant to illustrate or document Jewish history in the twentieth century, nor is it a study only of Jewish artists. Our aim is not to tell a story or demonstrate the existence of Jewish art. It is Jewish experience in the art of the twentieth century that concerns us. This study reflects, however faintly, the Jewish experience by considering in a communal context works that are scattered in different places. It thereby re-establishes the social matrix to which they were originally related, and out of which they emerged.

I hope that this thematic approach, which determines the selection of artists and the works discussed, can give us an insight into twentieth-century art which could not be obtained by analysis of periods, styles and schools. If adhering to this approach allows only marginal treatment of such important artists as Modigliani, Pascin and others, it is not for lack of appreciation of their significance as artists. Literally thousands of Jewish artists are at work in all parts of the world today. My choice was determined by the necessity of documenting major themes, and should not be interpreted as diminishing the merit of the work of artists who were not included in this study.

Works of art, however, do not fall neatly into any preconceived categories. Sometimes they only touch or hint at the experience which was their source; often they refer to it more directly. Occasionally the work has transformed experience so that it seems to extend beyond the boundaries of this study. Our

2. Ben Shahn, *Identity*, 1968. Mixed media on paper, 40 × 27½ in (101.5 × 69.8 cm). New York, Kennedy Galleries, Inc.

categories and comments should be seen as limited interpretations, having a bearing on particular historical data, not as restricting or confining the meaning or significance of the work of art. The classifications and groupings are intended to be ontological or metaphysical in nature, binding artists' reaction to events which may have occurred far apart in time and place. Thus, immigration or new

planting may refer to the different waves of immigration and new beginnings in England or the United States, or in Israel, at the turn of the century, in the 1940s, or currently. Our themes should be seen as points on an axis along which we group twentieth-century works of art.

This study makes no claim to completeness, either in the categories it proposes, or in the works of art or the artists singled out for discussion.

The failure to recognize the expression of a specific Jewish experience in twentieth-century art stems largely from a prejudice of modern historiography which studies history in terms of nation states and often ignores the strength of the culture in Europe whose history is not bounded by political geography. The culture of the Jews of Eastern Europe transcended political borders, so that Jews of Poland, Lithuania, Romania, the Ukraine, and other nation states shared a pervasive identity and language and had more in common with one another than they did with the ethnic majorities of the countries in which they lived. From the late nineteenth century the culture of the Jews of Eastern Europe spread across Western Europe, South Africa, North and South America, and Australia, and they sustained their ties through their common ways of thinking and feeling, their language, their religious traditions, their publishing houses, and their unique historical consciousness.

This study intends to shed light on the submerged context which thus far has been largely ignored by contemporary art historians and critics. It intends to explore some of the unexamined relationships in twentieth-century art by considering art and artists in the context of an ancient, potent and resilient culture, which is still undergoing vital transformation.

3. Samuel Hirszenberg, *Funeral of the Zadik*, 1905.
Oil on canvas, 30 × 81 in
(76.2 × 205.7 cm).
New York, Jewish Museum.

The study *Jewish Experience in the Art of the Twentieth Century* comprises roughly the timespan between the painting of Samuel Hirszenberg's *Funeral of the Zadik* and Ben Shahn's *Identity* (figs. 2, 3). Hirszenberg's dark and starkly dramatic picture, painted about 1905 in Lodz, Poland, gives us the sense of a compact, cohesive community carrying its leader to rest. Like a bark tossed upon the waves of a restless sea, the coffin is carried on the shoulders, the hands, the intense emotions of the mourners. The artist, whether participant or observer, represents death as an intensely felt loss, as a traumatic event. The long horizontal composition, the overcast sky, the black coffin and the mass of darkly-clad mourners pressing forward, straining and stretching their arms in their effort to touch the coffin, convey an intensely communal and religious sentiment. In Ben Shahn's work *Identity*, hands stretch, tortured and grasping at nothing as if searching for purpose, for selfhood or identity, as the title implies. It can be seen as a picture of the modern post-emancipation era, conveying a desperate quest for belonging and community. Hillel's saying, inscribed in Hebrew on the top of the canvas, 'If I am not for myself, who is, and if I am only for myself, who am I, and if not now, when?' impressed the artist to a point where he seems to offer it as a piece of ancient wisdom, a golden mean between self-reliance and community orientation, and as a healthy posture for contemporary man.

During the period between these two works the old Eastern European Jewish community underwent a total transformation. It gave birth to the various Jewish national movements and at the same time was eroded by various social and historical processes: Enlightenment, modernity, and assimilation, which acted as solvents; and by the enormous destruction of the Second World War. The process of enlightenment was an important element in the dissolution of the traditional faith of the Jewish community, whether doubt was stirred through contact with the world of learning from the outside or whether it arose from inner sources.

The Enlightenment period which generally marks the end of the Middle Ages came late for the Jewish community in Eastern Europe. It gathered force in the latter part of the nineteenth century, and its conflicts became manifest in social and religious life, leaving their imprint on the art and literature of the early twentieth century.

Marc Chagall's picture *Calvary* illuminates in its composition, in its manifest and latent content, in its iconography and its symbolic gestures, much of the tension and conflict which the Enlightenment and the processes behind it brought into the Jewish community (Plate II). It points to the gap between the generations which the Enlightenment created and which drove artists and intellectuals beyond the Pale. In *Calvary* we face the ethereal figure of the pale blue child mounted on a pole as if he were being crucified, against the dark expanse of green colour. Curved lines appear, disappear and reappear in the canvas as they converge on the child. The child is bemoaned by a tall bearded man with a torn sleeve, and a small woman in a green dress decorated with little flowers. Both are firmly grounded in the red soil. A colourful river separates the red soil in the lower part of the picture from its vast green background. Palms and cactuses are on the other side of the river. A boy passes by in a winged boat with a sail which is the colour of the blue sky, and an old man on the far right carries a ladder.

The appearance of the crucified child as early as 1912 is worth noting. It is a result of Chagall's migration to the West and the re-evaluation by Jewish artists and men of letters of their altitude towards the figure of Christ. Like many of the younger generation around the turn of the century, Chagall was powerfully attracted by the light which shone from the West. Its science, technology, and art were a magnet. These young Jews strove to cross the river or climb the fence which physically or symbolically encircled many of the Jewish towns and separated them from the rest of the world. They strove to break out of the confines of the ghetto and explore the world beyond the river, which might have meant Moscow or St. Petersburg, but more often Berlin, Munich, London, New York, or Paris. To some it meant the Holy Land. In any case, the Pale of cold, dark, oppressive Russia was to be left for a brighter, sunnier climate. Parents saw in this process a threat to community stability and continuity. They saw their children leaving the traditional faith and mourned the loss. The children saw the process as a move upward and outward into a new and hopeful realm. Some Yiddish and Hebrew poems of this period express this yearning. They portray Christ, venerated by the outside world, as a brother, a fellow artist, a performer of miracles. For Chagall he will become the symbol of Jewish martyrdom.[1]

At the beginning of the century the figure of Christ became an object of sympathetic contemplation as a new relationship emerged, conditioned by historical insight and Enlightenment; artists dealt in a secular way with ideas hitherto repressed or forbidden. Christ is addressed by the newly emancipated Hebrew poet as a brother who will in the future return to his people, wrapped in the traditional prayer shawl. The Yiddish and Hebrew poet Uri Zvi Greenberg writes:

> . . . What happened to Jesus our
> brother crucified
> on several poles exiled in the world?
> Is it true that thousands of bells
>   from thousands of towers ring
>   for him?
> Has he sheaves on his head
> and does he expose his
>   nakedness to the wind
> to the rain
> to the heat
> to the lips of the people so
>   that they can kiss him?
>
> . . . He hangs there
> on poles by day,
> on stones by night
> and no one saves him . . .
>
> . . . He hangs in the middle of the world

and looks out to the end of all times.
Deep is his longing.
He will return with a prayer shawl
around his shoulder
on the day of redemption
at the end of time
and the crown, which was removed,
on his holy head. . . .[2]

But it was the Hebrew poet Saul Tchernichovski who broke sharply with tradition when he expressed the attraction which Enlightenment generated for art. Writing in Odessa in 1899 he exhibited a totally new attitude toward the West and its art. In a poem, he addresses Apollo:

. . . I come to thee and bow before thine image,
Thine image-symbol of the light in life:
I prostrate myself to the exalted and the good,
To things of high estate upon the earth,
To all majestic in creation's bounds,
To all the highest mysteries of art. . . .[3]

4. Mitchell Siporin, *Endless Voyage*, 1946. Oil on canvas, $34\frac{1}{2} \times 39\frac{3}{8}$ in (87.6 × 99.5 cm). Iowa City, University of Iowa Museum of Art.

CHAPTER ONE

The Quest for a Jewish Style in the Era of the Russian Revolution

The term 'Jewish art', although in use for about 100 years, has been, up to now, only vaguely defined and inexpediently used. One defined Jewish art in terms of content, in terms of iconography, in terms of the specific use to which objects were put, or the fact that the artist happened to have been of Jewish birth. As an appellation, 'Jewish art' remained vague and elusive, at best a working tool which helped scholars organize their material, but which often generated confusion because of its contradictory uses and because it was felt that the term was applied either too narrowly or too broadly.[1]

In the West the notion of Jewish art arose largely from the need of the Jewish minority to affirm a distinct cultural identity, and it was given currency by the presence of a large number of newly emancipated Jewish artists.[2] Martin Buber, who had studied art history with Alois Riegel and Franz Wickhoff,[3] categorically denied the existence of Jewish art, 'because a national art needs a soil from which to spring and a sky toward which to rise . . . a national style needs a homogeneous society from which it grows and for whom it exists.'[4] Although there was no Jewish art which met Buber's criteria, there was a vital and significant attempt to create a modern Jewish art in Russia, where the concept seemed at one point to have a stronger foundation than in Western Europe.

Five million Jews lived in Russia before World War I. They were spread throughout the Pale of Settlement in a wide belt which stretched from the Baltic to the Black Sea. They lived in hundreds of little towns and hamlets and formed sizcable majorities in the urban population of several provinces. They possessed their own religion, their own juridical institutions and educational system, and preserved their national identity to the extent that 97 per cent of them spoke Yiddish at the time of the Russian Revolution. For many of the artists the quest for a Jewish secular art was inseparable from the quest for political emancipation and cultural autonomy.

In Russia, the concept of Jewish art was first noted positively in the nineteenth century by Vladimir Stassof, then the most influential Russian art critic, who frequently wrote about Jewish art. He encouraged the development of various national styles. Spiritually close to the *Peredvizhniki* ('Wanderers'—a group of artists who, in the 1860s, rejected the dominant Neoclassical tradition centred in the art academy of St. Petersburg), and a personal friend of the sculptor Mark Antokolski, Stassof was concerned with the realist presentation of subject-matter. Being aware of the early work of the Palestine Exploration Fund[5] in archaeological research in the Holy Land, and the Strauss Judaica Collection at the Paris World Exhibition of 1878, and following the aesthetic credo of Nikolai Chernichevsky in regard to the relation between art and reality,[6] Stassof uncritically assumed the existence of a Jewish art. He urged

5. Marc Chagall, *The Praying Jew*, 1914. Oil on canvas, 46 × 35 in (116 × 88 cm). Chicago, The Art Institute of Chicago, the Joseph Winterbotham Collection.

15

Antokolski and other artists to find their artistic salvation in the subject-matter of their own culture, 'because the highest achievement in art derives from the depth of a people's soul. What the artist is born with, the impressions and images that surround him, among which he grew to manhood, to which his eye and soul were riveted, only that can be rendered with deep expression, with truth and genuine force' (1878).[7] A realistic representation was for him a condition of national authenticity.

However, the generation of Jewish artists born in Russia between the 1880s and the 1890s, who came to maturity between the Russian Revolutions of 1905 and 1917 and who felt the need and possibility of a national Jewish art, could no longer accept Stassof's aesthetic programme. Not only had the process of secularization and enlightenment among Jews proceeded relentlessly, but by the time the generation of artists that included Marc Chagall, Nathan Altman, Boris Aronson, Robert Falk, El Lissitzky, Issachar Ryback and Joseph Tchaikov had matured, the wave of the realist 'Wanderers' had receded and given way to Impressionist and Post-Impressionist tendencies, marked by the *Mir Iskutswa* ('World of Art') movement, which had discovered its own Russian Byzantine tradition. Russian art had become a vigorous part of the international art scene. Subsequent artist groups and their magazines embraced primitivism, folk art, Rayonism and the abstract tendencies of Suprematism and Constructivism—all schools which upgraded the formal aspects of art at the expense of the literal features of the content of art. The Jewish artists who shared in the new aesthetic directions participated actively in the exhibitions of these groups, but often drew from their own traditions. We find them searching for aesthetic folk sources in the Jewish *lubok* (popular print), Jewish illuminated manuscripts, gravestone carvings, religious objects from the home, and in the art and architecture of painted synagogues, all of which they considered folk art.

6. Jewish *lubok*, popular print for Simhat Torah, from Boris Aronson's *Contemporary Hebrew Graphics* (Berlin, 1924).

7. Anonymous working drawing
for a gravestone.
Collection of Boris Aronson,
Grandview, New York.

With all their devotion to Jewish nationalism, these artists found themselves having to re-evaluate and, at times, reject the realist works of nineteenth-century Jewish artists such as Mark Antokolski, Samuel Hirszenberg, Isidore Kaufman, Leopold Pilichovsky, Mauricy Minkovsky, Ephraim Moses Lilien, and Mauricy Gottlieb, work which seemed to them to be dated, belonging to the world of literature or photography rather than to painting. The question for the young generation was not whether this was Jewish art. For them the question was—is it art? This generation had consciously divorced itself from the religious heritage it had absorbed in one form or another—the religious messianic ideal which had been a keynote of Jewish religion—and transformed it into a secularized messianic yearning for the redemption of mankind. It found some anchorage in Jewish folk conceptions which had emerged in the early part of the twentieth century. Their leanings, although mainly aesthetic and cultural rather than political, were strengthened by the dominant revolutionary and nationalist mood, the rise of a militant Jewish labour movement committed to cultural autonomy and freedom from Tsarist oppression, and the emergence of an active Hebrew and Yiddish literature and theatre.

The Discovery of Jewish Folk Art

The folk conception was further advanced by the research in Jewish ethnography emanating from St. Petersburg, where S. Ansky, the one-time *narodnik* (populist) and playwright,[8] organized in 1912 the first Jewish Ethnographic Expedition[9] into the towns and villages of Wholinia and Podolia. The expedition collected photographs, folk legends, songs, melodies, customs, games, rituals, proverbs, charms, superstitions, historical documents and manuscripts, and bought about 700 objects for the collection of a Jewish museum planned by the Ethnographic Society.[10] The expedition had a photographer and a musicologist, and one of its members was the painter and graphic artist Shlomo Yudo'win. On the whole the expedition was largely composed of students from the Jewish Academy at the University of St. Petersburg, who worked with the help of a carefully composed questionnaire covering all aspects of life from childhood to death and containing over 2,600 questions. The expedition was supported by Baron Horace Ginzburg, who was a banker, owner of railroads and silver mines, philanthropist, Maecenas, a leader of the Russian Jewish community and a supporter of the Jewish Academy. The Jewish Academy was officially known as 'Courses in Oriental Studies', and was headed by his son, David, the scholar and financier.[11]

David Ginzburg, together with Vladimir Stassof, had published in 1905 *L'Ornement hébraïque*, a collection of illuminated pages from medieval manuscripts taken for the most part from the Imperial Library of St. Petersburg.[12] These illuminated pages were largely of eastern origin. In this extraordinary, visually striking publication, the authors maintained that there had existed an art of ornamentation which could be called specifically Jewish, and that the motifs underlying this Jewish art could be traced clearly, through various modifications, in the ornamented Hebrew manuscripts coming from different countries of the Diaspora. *L'Ornement hébraïque* was severely criticized and fully refuted on scholarly grounds[13] but was, nevertheless, widely admired in the circles of the Jewish Ethnographic Society and in circles close to the nationalist cultural renaissance. The publication may also have influenced the bold use of Jewish calligraphy which we find several years later in the illustrations of Altman and Lissitzky. The fact that the calligraphy in the portfolio of *L'Ornement hébraïque* had an Oriental and Slavic character, and that Stassof and Ginzburg were carried away by their enthusiasm for their discoveries, must have been of no concern whatsoever to the artists nor even to some scholars. The wish was father to the thought. There was to be a Jewish art because it was wanted—because it was needed.[14]

Concurrently, the interest in the findings of the expedition of the Jewish Ethnographic Society, which were purely ethnographic in character, also stimulated interest in the aesthetic side of folk art. The Society also financed the expeditions of the artists Issachar Ryback and El Lissitzky, who, in 1916, started exploring the art and architecture of the wooden synagogues along the Dnieper River. Ryback, 19 years old, and Lissitzky, 26, went from village to village, from building to building, measuring, copying, taking notes. Lissitzky, who had recently returned from four years of architectural and engineering studies in Darmstadt, Germany (he had been refused admission to the Art Academy of St. Petersburg because he was Jewish), was particularly qualified to study these buildings.[15] Folk art was the focus of widespread interest at this time, as this kind of art was closely related to the populist tendencies which surged among the Jewish masses from the turn of the century. The term 'folk' was charged with strong emotions and had a mystique of its own. It was a

8. *Lion*, from a wall painting in the Mohilev synagogue. Copy by El Lissitzky, *c.*1916. Watercolour and charcoal, $9 \times 9\frac{1}{2}$ in (22.8 × 24.1 cm). Collection of Boris Aronson, Grandview, New York.

wellspring of the most significant values. It was a spiritual matrix of social, political, national and cultural movements, and a powerful component of the prevailing *Zeitgeist*. And the idea of folk art, like primitive art or children's art, was an important component of modern art.

Ryback and Lissitzky, in search of personal and collective roots, drew plans, made coloured drawings and gathered inscriptions from about 200 wooden synagogues, among them the famous synagogue of Mohilev. The murals of this synagogue have since then been widely published, but they came to the attention of scholars for the first time only in 1914.[16] Lissitzky himself has left us with a remarkable essay of reminiscences of his expedition and the days which preceded it. It includes expressions of feelings and ideas which shed significant light on this enigmatic figure whose shadow looms ever larger over contemporary art. Lissitzky's recollections, written in 1922, six apocalyptic years after the event, still convey something of the anticipations fulfilled after a long pilgrimage, and the experience of the numinous as he stood in the doorway of the wooden synagogue of Mohilev after having searched for it an entire day.

> It was quite a different feeling from the one I had when I first entered a Roman basilica, a Gothic chapel, a Baroque mosque in Germany, France or Italy. I felt like a child enveloped by a screen, opening his eyes upon awakening and being startled by the sunflies and butterflies glittering in the rays of the sun. The walls are built of timber laid horizontally. There are beams and oak planks which make a sound when you touch them. Above the wall, there is a ceiling also of timber. Here, there is no camouflage. No make-believe. The work of the carpenter is open, plain for the eye to see. But the whole structure organized by the painter is full of a few simple colours giving the impression of a world alive and blooming, filling the whole space.[17]

The interior of the synagogue was painted with primitive, rustic freshness, love of detail, and great decorative and compositional skill. The main hall, square at floor level, turns by means of cove and pendentives into a tent-like structure supporting an octagonal cupola. Light breaks through the high-arched twin windows, revealing by the hour different sections of the rough timber walls, sparkling and scintillating with colour. The walls were painted from the height of the benches to the very top of the cupola: the city of Worms and the Tree of Life; Jerusalem and the Tree of Knowledge; the leviathan, the ox, the elephant and the fawn; water, land, sky, twinkling stars turning into flowers; fish hunted by birds; the fox carrying a bird in his mouth; birds carrying snakes in their beaks (fig. 10); a bear climbing the tree in search of honey; and all intertwined with acanthus plants that bloom and move on the walls of the wooden synagogue. 'Behind the masks of four-legged animals and winged birds there are the eyes of human beings. This is the most characteristic aspect of Jewish folk art. And is that face of a lion in the drawings of the zodiac in the synagogue of Mohilev not the face of a rabbi?' (figs. 8, 9).[18]

Without question, a major work of folk art was revealed to Ryback and Lissitzky. There was also no doubt as to the identity of the artist or his status in the community. Among the many Hebrew inscriptions there was one conspicuously framed and held by two lions: 'By the artisan who is engaged in sacred

9. *Lion*, from a wall painting in the Mohilev synagogue. Copy by El Lissitzky, *Rimon*, 3 (Berlin, 1923). Photo: Geoffrey Clements.

craft, Haim the son of Isaac Segal from Sluzk' (fig. 11). The story has it that the artist painted three synagogues in three different towns, and when he finished he fell from the ladder and died. People of the three towns all claim that he died in their synagogue.[19]

Obviously, Ryback's and Lissitzky's experience was most notable. They stood, as it were, at the source. Even the sophisticated Lissitzky seemed overwhelmed. In his account, written years after he had ceased to use folk art as a basis for his own art, and after he had set out in a totally different direction, one still senses a tide of a strong emotion.

Ryback's painting, *The Old Synagogue* (May 1917), is of the synagogue of Dobrovna (a town near Mohilev), and probably the result of impressions gathered at the time of the expedition with Lissitzky (fig. 12); the painting of *The Synagogue of Chiklov* (August 1917) seems to derive from the same source. *The Old Synagogue* is a celebration of folk art by someone familiar with Cubist procedures, but far too strongly attached to the object to dismantle and reassemble it. Rather than adopting simultaneously different points of view and exploring the building from inside and outside, he geometricizes, distorts and abstracts to achieve expressive and dramatic effects. Ryback turns the old synagogue into an architectural monument which stretches and lifts itself like a mythical giant. It is a pointed arrow stabbing into the sky, imposing on it and on the surrounding landscape its own forms, compressing the space and the grey atmosphere into dense, wedge-like, luminous forms echoing the shape of the building. Cubist-influenced but not cubistic, it glorifies folk art by presenting both a mystical and an apocalyptic vision of the 'people's house' shaking and trembling in the first days of the Russian Revolution. *The Synagogue of Chiklov* (fig. 13), in reality a dilapidated wooden structure in a village baroque style, rises powerfully, gleaming in the setting sun. Here, strong expressionistic tendencies dominate and colour plays a far greater role than in the former painting.

The Old Jew (October 1917) is closely related to Ryback's synagogue paintings by its formal severity and restrained use of colour. Rachel Wischnitzer gives an interesting description of this painting (fig. 14):

10. (LEFT) *Birds of Paradise*, from the Mohilev synagogue. Wall painting by Haim B. Isaac Segal of Slutzk, 18th century. Copy by El Lissitzky, *Rimon*, 3 (Berlin, 1923).

11. (RIGHT) Artist's inscription, from the ceiling of the Mohilev synagogue. Copy by El Lissitzky, *Rimon*, 3 (Berlin, 1923).

12. (OPPOSITE TOP) Issachar Ryback, *The Old Synagogue* [of Dobrovna], 1917. Oil on canvas, $57\frac{1}{2} \times 38\frac{1}{8}$ in (146×97 cm). Tel Aviv Museum of Art.

13. (OPPOSITE BOTTOM) Issachar Ryback, *The Synagogue of Chiklov*, 1917. Oil on canvas, $28\frac{3}{4} \times 21\frac{1}{4}$ in (73×54 cm). Tel Aviv Museum of Art.

Here comes Ryback and paints an old Jew. He has been painted repeatedly by many artists in many forms; we all know him and have loved him since the days when we were young. But the Jew of Ryback is different. He does not need the mercy of the observer. He stands there, as if cast in bronze, eternal, self-assuming, angry, a whole world. His clothes are worn out, his surroundings tiny, like the clock in the background. Who has not seen such a clock in a room or corridors of Jewish homes in the Pale? The man in the canvas, we do not like him, nor do we hate him—he is simply there—and we know that he is present and exists. Ryback creates this impression by the scale of the man and the cubist construction. The heavy forms with which he builds his composition strike us as a still and mute thought, as lasting as a building made of stone. Through the cubic construction he removed that which is insignificant and incidental.[20]

That the forms of Jewish folk art deserved close scrutiny for their artistic possibilities had already occurred to Nathan Altman in 1913 when he went to Gritzew, a small Jewish town in southern Russia. He had spent the years 1910–11 in Paris, Munich and Vienna, absorbing influences of contemporary Western art, and had then returned to St. Petersburg. Coming from major capital cities to the small remote town of Gritzew was like going back in time to a slow-paced, simple, primitive way of life reflecting the organic cultural wholeness and the steady rhythm of traditional communities. Among the places he searched was the Jewish cemetery at Shepetovka near Gritzew.[21] In this old cemetery, along with the sense of pervasive unity expressed through the equal and common features of all Jewish gravestones, Altman found, in the specific artfulness of each one, the genuine interest and the critical judgement of the gravestone carver. While being tied to tradition, the carver had made an effort to render the form and content of each stone in an original way. Altman gathered his impressions from the stele-like, flat, gabled or arched gravestones, decorated

14. Issachar Ryback, *The Old Jew*, 1917. Reproduced from *Rimon*, 1 (Berlin, 1923). Present whereabouts unknown.

15. Issachar Ryback, *Portrait of a Jew*, c.1917. Sepia chalk on tar-paper, 24 × 17¼ in (60 × 44 cm). Collection of S. Bak.

with slender, intricately intertwined plant and linear motifs. Ribbon-plaited and wickerwork ornaments framed the engraved or raised text memorializing the dead. There were many carvings of the seven-branched candelabra, Sabbath candles, the Torah crown, the dying candle, the broken branch, the blessing hands of the priest, the hand holding a jar, columns, flowers, leaves, the Tree of Life, the lion, bear, bird, serpents and fish. These carvings evoked in Altman echoes of ancient Assyrian sculptures.[22] He may have encountered these gravestones coloured in red, blue, gold or silver, as it was often customary in south-eastern Europe to paint gravestones. Illuminated by the morning sun and seen against the background of green meadows or the white snow, these coloured gravestones emanated a primitive magic, creating that utter otherness which evokes the atmosphere of a holy place.[23]

The Idea of a Modern Jewish Art

16. (LEFT) Nathan Altman, *Eve*, illustration from *Jüdische Graphik* (Berlin, 1923).

17. (RIGHT) Nathan Altman, *Two Birds Flanking a Vase*, illustration from *Jüdische Graphik* (Berlin, 1923).

Max Osborn, the noted German art critic, claimed that in the close-knit communities of south-eastern Europe Jews not only were a distinct religious group (as was the case in Western Europe), but were felt to be a unique nation within a state. They stubbornly stuck to the tradition of their fathers, and in spite of the fact that they absorbed many aspects of Russian civilization, Slavic culture could not penetrate the walls of synagogues, and forms there kept their original ancient Jewish imprint.[24] Altman, Osborn perceptively stated, did not copy these forms but embedded them in the modern art vocabulary, thereby attempting to create a modern Jewish art style, based on traditional

Jewish forms, yet highly personal and contemporary. Thus Altman created a series of motifs based on Jewish folk art: lions, pigeons and plants found in *haggadot* (Passover stories), and synagogue ornaments and gravestones. He rendered these forms graphically by means of symmetrically balanced compositions, decorative distribution of black and white, alternately rapid and slow transition from dark to light, deliberate deformation and adoption of an anti-naturalistic archaizing form, cubist-inspired intersection, and soft, mysterious, transparent overlapping of planes. The abundance of forms provided by the objects of Jewish communal life he directed into his modern graphic art. These compositions were drawn with black Italian chalk and mounted on pale gold surfaces which were treated with transparent lacquer (figs. 16, 17).

Like Altman, Lissitzky also, in his numerous illustrations for Yiddish books, strove to combine the sources of Jewish folk art and Western European modern art and to create a Jewish style (figs. 36–9). In his best-known work, the *Chad Gadya* series of 1917 (fig. 18), simplification, abstraction and stylization dominate—flowing lines for emphasis on movement, independent linear patterns both sharp and crisp, active surface play, careful arrangement of light and dark patterns of composition, accent on flatness and on mere suggestion by

18. El Lissitzky, study for the cover of *Chad Gadya*, 1917. Brush, gouache, pen and ink with traces of pencil on paper, 11 × 9 in (27.5 × 22.5 cm). New York, Museum of Modern Art.

19. Boris Aronson, untitled, 1920.
Woodcut on fabric, $5\frac{1}{4} \times 6\frac{1}{2}$ in
(13.3×16.6 cm).
Collection of the artist,
Grandview, New York.

shading, depth, overlapping and intersecting of planes—and in all cases departure from natural appearance.

Towering over artists at that time was Marc Chagall, who had the capacity to combine and draw on icon and Jewish folk art. He fictitiously adopted the eighteenth-century Jewish painter of the synagogue of Mohilev, Haim the son of Isaac Segal, as his grandfather.[25] At that moment he presented the most organic and convincing synthesis between East and West, between Jewish life experience, Jewish and Russian folk art and contemporary Western art. His apprenticeship in St. Petersburg with Leon Bakst and the years 1910–14 in Paris gave him the necessary tools and a direction to his art, enabling him to fuse his individuality with Hassidic pantheism and to make that unlikely union flourish.

One is struck by the fact that Chagall's work seems almost a natural product of this union. There is no desire to create a synthesis—there simply is one. Without consciously wanting to, even without seemingly thinking about the problem, and without the explicit study of and immersion in folk art subjects, Chagall absorbed the living attitudes of the people who surrounded him. He absorbed their speech, their proverbs, their gestures, their dealings with each

other, their dressing, walking, praying, courting and loving. Intuitively he grasped the style and attitudes of the folk and rendered them in pictorial form. How they fiddled and danced, how they argued and smoked, how one spread one's finger or stuck out one's hand. There seems to be something airy, unreal about the figures he painted. They are homely and grotesque and funny with their chickens, their goats, their cows, their clocks, their fish and their Torah scrolls. They are also awkward and coarse, though not vulgar. In Chagall's world, they are colourful and unpredictable, endowed with that spontaneous vitality of oppressed people who feel that they are princes disguised as beggars and believe that in the world to come they will be kings and sit at the table of the Almighty God (figs. 20–21). With Chagall there disappears from Jewish painting that note of sorrow and gloom which hovered over the works of Jewish painters from the East at the turn of the century. Instead, there is a sheer delight in the sensuous aspects of colour and form, and frivolity, humour and wit gleaned from keen observation and intimate knowledge.[26]

There is in Chagall's work a deep understanding of Jewish folk ways and wit,

20. Marc Chagall, *Over Vitebsk*, 1914. Oil on paper mounted on canvas, $27\frac{1}{2} \times 35\frac{1}{4}$ in (69.8 × 89.5 cm). Toronto, Art Gallery of Ontario, gift of Sam and Ayala Zacks, 1970.

21. (OPPOSITE) Marc Chagall, *Green Violinist*, 1923–4. Oil on canvas, $78 \times 42\frac{3}{4}$ in (198.1 × 108.5 cm). New York, Solomon R. Guggenheim Museum.

27

a keen penetration into the psychological attitudes of the people and an intimate knowledge of the artistic conceptions by which modern Hebrew and Yiddish writers and poets like Mendele, Sholom Aleichem, Peretz, Ansky, Bialik and der Nister approached the people. Like them, he presents the modern Jewish artist still fully planted in the culture of his people, while freely absorbing the many trends of modern art. He stands culturally rooted in traditional Biblical lore as transmitted by the Cheder, yet already open to the whole world and capable of assimilating fully the icons of St. Petersburg, French, Italian, Russian and Spanish folk art, Gogol and Lermontov, aspects of Cubism and modern French poetry. He moves freely in those domains but remains most deeply attached to his own culture. It was not only the shock of Paris, its artistic climate and hospitality, that liberated the artist who came from the Ghetto, but the unique condition of that generation of Eastern European Jewish artists, for whom going into the world was simultaneously an act of escape, separation and self-emancipation. They were ready to make the big stride and accomplish in their own lifetime, each one on his own, what it takes the collective effort of generations to accomplish.

Yet it is precisely that sharp break Chagall and other artists of his generation had made which also left them stranded when they left the Pale. By suddenly transporting themselves to the West, they had sacrificed their protective habitat. They may have made friends among the artists and even formed a loose social group of their own, but they were outsiders and strangers in Western European countries. Paris, Munich or Vienna were not home or a substitute for their old community, but fields of adventure. When some of them returned home just before World War I, to a language and landscape deeply inbred, to folk ways and customs intimately felt and secure as the palm of their hand, they longed to immerse themselves among their kind where they could perceive with a single glance the intricacies of any situation and could meet it with that liberating aesthetic detachment essential for the creation of an authentic social and national art. They could devote themselves fully to a worthwhile and stimulating task. This unique situation would never repeat itself.

Many of those who concerned themselves theoretically with the development of a specific Jewish national art as part of a secular Jewish culture saw in Jewish folk art and primitive art (the terms were used interchangeably) a true basis for the fine arts. Folk art was the folklore, the deepest level of the fine arts, their true origin and ancestor. On the basis of folk art a true national style could be built. Seen from this point of view and from the aesthetic standpoint of modern art which the painter generation of the revolution had absorbed, the older, turn-of-the-century generation of Jewish painters were found to be lacking.

In an important article published in 1919,[27] Issachar Ryback and Boris Aronson argued that just as the Russian *Peredvizhniki* were mistaken when they undertook the realistic representation of Russian subject-matter and ignored Russian icon painting, so too the Jewish nineteenth-century artists were mistaken when they took to Jewish subject-matter but ignored Jewish folk art. 'From a national point of view,' they reasoned, 'they contributed nothing . . . they were pseudo-artists and only showed us how not to paint.'[28] Thus the sculptor Antokolski, who had followed the realist Russian tendencies and who had been seen by Stassof and large sections of the Jewish intelligentsia as the embodiment of Jewish art, was seen now 'as a sickness which has to be overcome', and his 'merit' was that 'he was the first sculptor among the Jews who strode the first great stride in the wrong direction and thereby misled Jewish sculpture . . . he was a Jew according to his life conceptions but not according to his plastic conceptions.'[29] Antokolski is depicted as a rootless product of the Russian and Jewish intelligentsia, sharp-minded, formalistic and dogmatic, looking for symbols through which to embody his ideas. Antokolski's art needed an ethical justification, it could not just be; it existed in the service of ideas and as a means for their propagation.

Most of the nineteenth-century Jewish artists were given short shrift by Ryback and Aronson. They were compared to the writers of the Enlightenment movement, who were seen as assimilationist. Ephraim Lilien, for instance, who had been strongly influenced in his work by Aubrey Beardsley and artists of the Munich-based *Jugendstil* movement, and who celebrated in his numerous illustrations the sentiments of the incipient nationalist Zionist movement, was dealt with severely. He was seen as a graphic artist who was attracted by the Jewish character and who endeavoured to create a Jewish ornament and a Jewish book. But he did not draw from what they considered to be the wellsprings of Jewish art; they thought that he did more harm than good and that he actually 'destroyed' the Jewish book. A deep socialist-Bundist bias can be felt when he is said to be influenced by a 'nationalistically-tinged ethnographic clericalism' and to be an 'outsider who was remote from Jewish organic art, failed to grasp the rhythm of the Jewish ornament and was ignorant of the Jewish letter . . . It is not without reason that he was so closely associated with the Bezalel Art School in Jerusalem,[30] that he rejected the spirit of the people and embraced the Biblical, Zionist sentiment with all its superficialities and pseudo-romanticism—the palm tree from Goldfaden's theatre and the *Menorah* from the poems of Frug.'[31]

A similar view of the importance and significance of Jewish folk art was held by Yekhezkel Dobrushin, playwright, essayist, literary critic and teacher who had lived in France before he settled in Kiev in 1910. He was one of the important members and founders of the *Kulturlige* in Kiev. This was a secular Yiddish cultural organization, founded in 1918, which represented a broad spectrum of Jewish nationalist and socialist tendencies. It was committed to Yiddish as the national language and developed significant activities in the fields of education, teacher training, regular university courses, and publications. It intensively cultivated theatre, music and the plastic arts. The quest for cultural autonomy inherent in the programme of the *Kulturlige*, which was encouraged in the initial stages of the Revolution, was a driving force behind its widespread activities.

In one of his articles, Dobrushin makes a thorough, detailed inventory of Jewish folk art as it was found to exist in thousands of cities and hamlets, and carefully describes its characteristic features.[32] Ansky, several years before in his study of Jewish folklore, had made the acute observation that the hero of the Jewish folk tale is not distinguished by his physical prowess but by his spiritual power.[33] Dobrushin finds similar features in Jewish folk art:

The Jewish *lubok* has an abstract spiritual quality. The Jewish lion, leopard or ox do not distinguish themselves by their pronounced physical structure, their naturalistic appearance or physical material characteristics. In the main they are spiritual, symbolic and abstract creatures. They do not derive from the woods or fields but from legends and Jewish cabbalistic folklore. These are the sacred animals of the *Cabbalah*, the legendary lions and eagles of King Solomon's throne. They are the creatures and doves of the heavenly spheres.[34]

The anti-naturalistic, abstract tendency and the lack of a fixed, binding tradition created for the Jewish folk artist opportunities for a large variety of original configurations, whereas his Russian counterpart produced in the Russian *lubok* a fixed, stereotyped image.

Dobrushin, like Ryback and Aronson, found in Jewish folk art, whether painted or carved, a marked formal preference for two-dimensionality and avoidance of depth. 'In all Jewish painted, carved, drawn or etched figures, form is flat and two-dimensional. Three-dimensionality does not exist.'[35] Even in gravestone carvings, which have a bas-relief quality and in which certain coloured sections stand out from the surrounding area, even in such essentially

22. (LEFT) Nathan Altman, calligraphy page, 1922. From Boris Aronson's *Contemporary Hebrew Graphics* (Berlin, 1924).

23. (RIGHT) Nathan Altman, *Head of a Young Jew* (self-portrait), 1916. Bronze, 18½ in high (47 cm). Moscow, Tretiakov Gallery.

sculptural works, the Jewish folk artist employs special means to achieve a two-dimensional effect. As to the general layout of Jewish ornament, linear and floral decorative motifs do not stand in contrast to a central motif; rather, they are fully integrated into a harmonious, overall ornamental design.

Another important element in Jewish folk art, noted especially by Ryback and Aronson, is the Hebrew letter, which often is also its sole content. The cultivation of the Hebrew script has been an unbroken tradition through the continuous writing of Torah scrolls. The geometric character of the Hebrew letter is preserved, there is emphasis on its two-dimensionality and a recognition of the importance of voids. The letter is distinguished by the great variability of its vertical and horizontal components. They can be expanded or shortened, thinned or thickened according to the will of the artist. The distinguishing quality of the Hebrew letter is in its simplicity, reserve and completeness. A page of a Hebrew book in which the letter has an important, autonomous function is like an ornamental carpet. A page of the traditional Hebrew book is a picture in itself with a distinct physiognomy of its own created by the different types of letters of the various traditional commentaries which surround the main text with their uniquely distinguishing script.[36]

24. Boris Aronson, untitled,
no date.
Woodcut on paper, 14 × 11 in
(35.5 × 28 cm). Collection of
the artist, Grandview, New Yor

As to colour, both Dobrushin and Ryback and Aronson mention the fact that Jews seem to prefer deep, dark tones, grey and violet, in contrast to the Russian *lubok* which exhibits loud yellow and greens. Whenever colour is bright, the Jewish folk artist tones it down. 'It is the same as the Jewish woman who, before putting on her new brightly coloured dress, washes it, and the peasant woman, on the other hand, who likes her dress in its bright colours . . . The distinguishing Jewish colours are black velvet, violet, grey and a pale gold, like an echo of an often told legend.'[37] Not only are those the colours of the Jewish *lubok*, but Ryback and Aronson refer to those which possess 'an analytic, synthetic greyness and a deep dark polychrome palette which passes into half tones'. The proper colours for Jewish paintings, they maintain, are deeply saturated velvety tones, multi-layered, because Jews have a sacred attitude toward velvet, silk, satin and other textured materials which they prefer for their religious needs such as Torah mantles, prayer-shawls, phylacteries and Torah curtains.[38]

In the same article, whose title was 'Di Vegen fun der Yiddisher Malerei' ('The Paths of Jewish Painting'), Ryback and Aronson shed some light on their theoretical position. They open with a motto written in the style of the revolutionary prose of the time: 'Long live the abstract form which reveals the specific material—it is national.'[39] After giving thumbnail sketches of the most characteristic features of Egyptian, Greek, Japanese, Persian, German, Italian and French art, and after attacking Russian realism and Jewish realist artists, they state their maxims categorically:

> Form is the essential and necessary element of art and content is harmful. The composition of a picture is more important than its idea, and the richness of tone more significant than the realistic representation of an object . . . Art, the pure form, is always abstract . . . [The national element in art is expressed by] abstract painterly feelings, which are revealed through a specific material conception. Art which thus takes shape mirrors racial aspects and national forms . . . Only through the principle of abstract painting, which is free from any literary aspects, can one achieve the expression of one's own national form . . . thanks to the character of abstract painting which deals with the 'how'; many modern Jewish artists discovered their racial bent even if they had no intention of finding it or of stressing their national conception. However much the artist may strive to be international in his work, his painterly feelings, when expressed in the abstract, will be national because the spiritual character of the artist always grows from the accumulated feelings of his environment . . . Therefore, it is the emphasis on formal aspects of painting rather than the subject-matter which reveals the true racial identity of the artist . . . Abstraction, which is an autonomous form of painting, does not allow for any other form of painting than the pure painterly, and therefore stresses its pure essence which is manifest in the 'how', and thus, the artist reveals his painterly feelings.[40]

Pure objectification of the racial strain can only be achieved when painting is not hampered by academic restrictions or the external aspects of nature but derives from the intuitive subconscious and spontaneous reaction of the artist to form.

Among the artists discussed in Ryback's and Aronson's article as pioneers of Jewish art, much is said about Nathan Altman, Robert Falk and Marc Chagall. The latter is lionized because of his palette and his use of velvety black, violet, grey and deep blues which pass into bordeaux red. In general Chagall is seen as a product of Jewish culture 'who through painterly values mirrors the forms and life of his people and who in abstract form reveals both the painterly as well as the national aspects of the material'. Especially singled out for praise is *The Praying Jew* of 1914 (fig. 5), a painting which the authors considered a cornerstone for the newly revived Jewish art. They thought that in no other work had the culture of generations and the heritage of accumulated experience been given such sharp and palpable expression. The essence of the picture is seen in the plane on which the portrait and sheer painterly depth meet. The portrait is said to possess the monumentality of a fresco, especially where the architecture of the picture is concerned. The treatment of the texture and the picture plane are said to best express the national elements in Chagall. Further praise is given to the work because it handles the face in the picture in one way and the surrounding areas quite differently, something many artists believed could not be done. For these reasons and for its constructive painterly pathos, the authors thought that Chagall's *Praying Jew* should take first place in a Jewish museum. In their evaluation of this work one senses a purposeful evasion of the question of subject-matter. Is it accidental that the most Jewish painting is indeed that of a praying Jew? And does not the subject-matter largely determine the composition as well as the choice of colour? On the other hand, the authors are quick to point out that many of Chagall's works were literary and anecdotal, and they find that he cannot be excused for that.[41]

Nathan Altman comes under severe criticism from Ryback and Aronson. They see his canvases as coloured drawings rather than as paintings. Thus, his famous painting *Anna Achmatova* is found to be intellectual and cerebral. In addition, the naturalistic face is said to contrast with the cubist structure of the painting. They conclude that in Altman two elements meet—'the modern Jewish painter and the remnants of an older painterly tradition which blocks the revelation of the specific qualities deriving from his Semitic constructions'.[42]

Robert Falk comes very close to the ideal equipment the Jewish painter should possess. 'The national elements express themselves in Falk's synthesis of tone and in his palette. In many of his still-lifes and landscapes one feels the synthesis of rose, black or blue. Only a Jew can have such a conception. But Falk really had no intention of revealing his national elements. Who knows, if Falk had been educated in Jewish culture and developed a proper attitude toward it, his creations might have been even grander and more universal . . . the Jewish conception [about which he did not know] played a very great role with the artist Falk, for he possesses a genuinely painterly form and an understanding of abstract art.' They especially praised Falk's paintings from his Crimean period (1916–17), notably the portrait of a Tartar, for combining achievements of Cézanne and the Cubists.[43]

Issachar Ryback and Boris Aronson had made valiant efforts to create some kind of theoretical framework which would unite in harmony the radical artistic positions of Western Europe and Russia, and their own strong Jewish national loyalties. A formal basis had to be found which could unite folk art, national expression and formal treatment. The affinity of folk art to modern art, its frequent distortions of natural appearances, its conventions and abstractions made a synthesis possible. It is interesting to note that the Second Commandment, which prohibits the making of images, is never evoked as a supporting reason for the use of abstract form; rather it is the cerebral, analytic character of the Jews which is cited. One wonders about the avoidance of any reference to this Commandment, especially as one of the authors was the son of the Rabbi of Kiev and must have been aware of the analogy. Yet in 1920, when their article was published, the power and influence of the *Yevsektsiya*, the Jewish section of the Communist Party, was already felt in the Jewish street, and this perhaps precluded the use of an argument which might have given it a religious rather than a purely racial foundation.

This development may also have played a role in the position of the graphic artist and sculptor Joseph Tchaikov (fig. 25), who had returned to Kiev after having been in Paris between 1910 and 1914. He had lived and worked in La Ruche, a building containing many studios occupied by artists of different nationalities, among them a sizable number of Jewish artists. Tchaikov represents a direct link between artists in Russia and a group of Jewish painters at La Ruche who were concerned with Jewish art and called themselves *Machmadim*.[44] This group included Pinkus Kremegne, Itzhak Lichtenstein, Henry Epstein, Leo Koenig, Marek Schwarz and the sculptor Leon Indenbaum. They published in 1912 what must be the first Jewish art journal in the twentieth century, *Machmadim*, a textless art magazine 'without manifestos and without theories, because one should not talk publicly about art, but art one has to show'.[45] The very existence of this small, little-known group created important links with other Jewish artist groups whose members were connected by personal ties to a whole Yiddish avant-garde network who gathered in various European cities. These artists clustered around a series of artistic and literary magazines such as *Schriften, Yung Yiddish, Renaissance, Ringen, Chaliastra, Albatross, Rimon, Oifgang, Baginnen, Eigenes*,[46] creating ties between artists and writers all over the Jewish artistic world. Joseph Tchaikov designed the cover for *Machmadim* in Paris and also for *Baginnen* in Kiev.

25. Joseph Tchaikov, *Self-Portrait*, 1920. Lithograph from Boris Aronson's *Contemporary Hebrew Graphics* (Berlin, 1924).

Tchaikov's concern for Jewish art was also manifest in the graphic illustrations for the Song of Songs and for various children's books published by the *Kulturlige*. By 1921, when his book *Sculpture*[47] appeared with the motto, 'Pure plastic form is deeply national and the direct approach to art creates this form', he was in opposition to those young leftist artists who hoped to build a synthesis between folk art and the advanced tendencies in modern art, because it results in 'stylization, a false aestheticism, individualistic capriciousness and the cult of the beautiful'. Art, Tchaikov claims, will not be created by looking at the archives of past history or at primitive folk art. Since Jews are latecomers to the field of the plastic arts, and since the growth of their artistic consciousness occurs in the period of the invention of electricity, industrial technology and ferro-concrete, as well as in the period of psychoanalysis, therefore the Jewish artist is not bound by any historical tradition which has dominated artistic thinking. 'The specific material determines the form and the form determines the artist, and vice versa. Up to now the Jewish artist has not displayed any specific inclination in the field of modern plastic art, and now he will stride through the arts of all nations and create a synthesis through the prism of his specific material.'[48] National creations do not express themselves through ethnographic content, and the sculptors Antokolski, Ginzburg and Glitzenstein, Tchaikov thinks, did not create any Jewish sculpture. 'Art, in order to be alive, must be capable of invention and must be atuned to the Tomorrow. Thus the Jewish sculptor can realize himself.' Between 1919 and 1921, Tchaikov turned from representational to ever more abstract sculpture, giving many of his works Jewish titles (fig. 26). Stylistically he is close to Schlemmer's abstract sculpture from 1920. Tchaikov's essay on sculpture was also printed in 1922 in *Chaliastra*, and in 1922 his work was reproduced together with the work of Ryback, Louis Lozowick, Marek Schwarz and Henryk Berlevi in *Albatross* (the expressionistic Yiddish journal edited by Uri Zvi Greenberg in Warsaw and Berlin).

There is a great deal of sophistication and mental acrobatics in the arguments of the authors we have cited.[49] Russian avant-garde art was, in the years immediately preceding and following the 1917 Revolutions, the boldest and most adventurous European art. The essays written by Ryback and Aronson as well as those by Tchaikov can be seen as an attempt by artists committed to the idea of modern art and Jewish identity to save and affirm the idea of national Jewish art by bringing it into harmony with avant-garde tendencies current at the time. The tension between modern art and Jewish folk art could well be maintained before the Revolution, during the chaotic and hopeful days between February and October, and even in the early days thereafter when the Revolution defended itself and when the weak Soviet state sanctioned and encouraged the development of the national arts among the various nationalities of Russia. The message of the Revolution could be most effectively spread through the channels of the various national languages and cultures, and thereby reach the broad masses of the people. The February Revolution freed the long-repressed energies of the Jewish masses everywhere, but it was particularly in Kiev, the capital of the Ukraine, a major centre of Jewish life and institutions, that its effect was strongly manifested in the Jewish cultural, artistic and educational fields and that the idea of a Jewish national art could best be entertained.

The majority of Jews were concentrated in the Ukraine, and the Ukrainian national movement strongly supported Jewish national tendencies and cultural institutions in order to counter the process of Russification among Jews which the Russian schools reinforced. The founding of Hebrew elementary schools and gymnasiums, higher educational institutions and especially the founding of Yiddish secular schools, teacher seminaries and popular universities, all necessitated the creation of various educational organizations, and brought a large number of the Jewish intelligentsia into the orbit of Jewish national activities.

The concern with Jewish art grew on a wide social base as part of the general concern with a Jewish secular culture, and was especially cultivated by the *Kulturlige*.[50] This organization not only founded various art courses but also sponsored art exhibitions, published many children's books illustrated by well-known artists, and several literary publications which probed the aesthetic

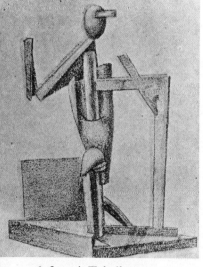

26. Joseph Tchaikov,
A Young Jew, 1921.
Drawing from Tchaikov's
Sculpture (Kiev, 1921).

problems posed by the creation of a Jewish national art. It even planned a 'Universal Jewish Museum'.[51] In addition to the artists mentioned above, writers such as David Bergelson, der Nister, David Hofstein and Joseph Lestschinsky, together with musicians, actors and journalists, developed an intense Jewish cultural life. Yet the years 1917–20 were years of great upheaval as Kiev was conquered and occupied in turn by the Red Army, the Germans, the White Russians, and finally reoccupied by the Red Army. After this the running of Jewish communal affairs was handed over to the *Yevsektsiya*, which, aiming at the Bolshevization of the Jewish masses, started the systematic destruction of traditional and nationalist Jewish aspirations.[52]

Jewish Artists and the Hebrew and Yiddish Theatre

Nationalist Jewish tendencies survived longer in the Yiddish and Hebrew theatre than in the plastic arts. The theatres were founded after the Revolution with the express intention of preserving and expanding Jewish national consciousness. The establishment of the Moscow Yiddish Kamerni State Theatre and the Hebrew Habimah Theatre found both striving for the achievement of a distinct Jewish national style. The theatres provided a meeting ground for the interaction of all avante-garde movements in drama, dance, music, literature and stage design.

The Yiddish Theatre was under the direction of Alexander Granovsky, who had studied in Germany with Max Reinhardt, and the Hebrew Habimah was under the leadership of Nachum Zemach, who was influenced by Stanislavsky and his pupil Vechtangov. The very collaboration of the different artists, dancers, musicians, actors and stage designers reinforced the search for a distinct national style. The cultivation of national elements was, of course, also manifest in the theatres' constant search for a proper repertoire. The theatres' national tendencies were protected by the spoken word, namely the very languages of Hebrew and Yiddish, and by the audience to whom they were addressed. The determination and immense resourcefulness of the theatres' leaders as well as the sheer artistic level which they achieved carried some weight among the literary, artistic and political élite of Moscow.[53]

But outside the theatres' walls the forces of change, the quest for speedy industrialization and the subsequent idolization of the machine, and the hope for a worldwide revolution dissipated the favourable climate of national art, especially in the plastic arts, for one which was international in character. The quest for a national art assumed provincial and limited proportions. The idea of folk art, easel painting or even of fine arts seemed now for many an artist irrelevant and anachronistic in the face of a society aiming to advance on the path of technology. Art was to be overcome; 'just as one overcomes religion one has to overcome art.'[54] 'The idea of "artistic work" must be abolished as a counter-revolutionary concept of what is creative, and work must be accepted as one of the functions of the living organism.'[55]

Comfuturists and Constructivists identified their art with the aims of the Revolution and drew parallels between its political aspects and their own artistic revolution. Both had broken the back of an old order. The flat, geometrical, precise forms of the Constructivists suggested to the artist a new order, objective and universal rather than individualistic; planned, economical, well organized and purposive, it erased inhibiting and restraining peculiarities. Inherent in its architectural forms was the promise of real buildings and cities, the design of furniture and of schools. Implied also was the rejection of all traditional art and the abandonment of the useless individualistic activity of easel painting. Art would be related to science and industry. It would not imitate, it would create. The artists would be an engineer and designer organizing and directing production; he would be fully integrated into the workaday world.

Jewish artists, who at the beginning of the Revolution still toiled for an art based on Jewish folk art, were suddenly full-fledged citizens. The same process which opened the way for a large number of the Jewish intelligentsia to enter government service, replacing those who were not willing to co-operate with the Revolution or who could not be trusted, catapulted some Jewish artists into positions of power and made them the spokesmen for their generation and active in the very centre of artistic and political art activities. Immense new horizons opened before them. Suddenly, not only were they free, but they had the power to direct the fate of art and art institutions. The whole art establishment had to be revamped. Museums and schools had to be reorganized, private collections nationalized, a far-flung programme of exhibitions and popular lectures initiated and public celebrations arranged. In addition, posters, stamps, money and publications had to be designed.

Anatoly Lunatcharsky, the new and influential Commissar of Education, once a guide to Russian visitors at the Louvre and sympathetic to modern art, appointed David Sterenberg (a painter and graphic artist who had returned to Russia from Paris where he had worked at La Ruche) to head the Division of Plastic Arts in his department. Sterenberg in turn persuaded Nathan Altman, who had been in Paris, to abandon his plans to emigrate to America. Altman was appointed professor at the Academy of Art in Petrograd and Director of Plastic Art of the People's Commissariat. He headed the art celebrations of the first anniversary of the Revolution at Uritzky Square. Once a pioneer of Jewish folk art, associated with the 'World of Art' and 'Knave of Diamonds' movements, he went through a Cubist and Constructivist period, became a leading figure of the left Comfuturist wing and thought now that art had either to be abandoned or turn to concrete materials such as coal, iron, wood and paper.

Altman threw himself into his new artistic task. He organized thousands of workers, soldiers, sailors and actors in the staging of an immense political mystery play which re-enacted the storming of the Winter Palace, utilizing for the occasion 20,000 yards of scarce canvas. He became the portraitist of Lenin, the 'Louis David of the Russian Revolution'.[56] At the same time Altman designed the stage and costumes for *Uriel Accosta* at Granovsky's Kamerni Theatre (fig. 27) and for the *Dybbuk* at the Habimah, the Hebrew theatre's most

27. Nathan Altman, stage design for *Uriel Accosta* in the Kamerni Yiddish Theatre in Moscow, 1922. *Rimon*, 3 (Berlin, 1923).

famous play. Ansky had based this Hassidic mystery play on legends that he and his associates had gathered on the Jewish Ethnographic Expedition to the villages of the Ukraine (see above, p. 17). The legends were about restless souls rising and falling, floating in mid-air and attaching themselves to other souls, about souls inhabiting the bodies of living human beings, and about the authority of miracle-performing Hassidic rabbis. Vechtangov, a distinguished pupil of Stanislavsky, who directed the play, desired to adapt it to the spirit of the times and gave it a distinct social meaning. By omitting certain sections of Ansky's text, by a careful elaboration of the choreography of the Beggars' Dance and by prolonging the time allotted to it he turned what was originally conceived as a secondary, background motif into the major theatrical focal point of the *Dybbuk*.[57]

Altman designed the sets used for the first act, which takes place in the synagogue (fig. 28). They incorporated a blend of Cubo-Futuristic elements and traditional Jewish folk art motifs—the carved and painted ark, the soft velvet curtain embroidered with precious ribbons, and the Hebrew cut-out letters suspended in mid-air, suggesting their mystical significance. But in subsequent acts Altman moved toward a more abstract conception and introduced

29–32. (ABOVE) Nathan Altman, four of the costume designs for beggars in the *Dybbuk*, by S. Ansky, Habimah Theatre, Moscow, 1920.
Sketches, pencil and gouache on paper, height 10½ in (27 cm). Courtesy Benjamin Zemach, Jerusalem.

28. (OPPOSITE) Nathan Altman, stage design for the *Dybbuk*, by S. Ansky, Habimah Theatre, Moscow, 1920.
Sketch, pencil, ink and gouache on paper. Courtesy Benjamin Zemach, Jerusalem.

solid architectural forms which lent an awesome monumentality to the Hassidic play and which in turn were animated by the spirit of folk legend and mystery. The set was constructed rather than painted, and the sharp geometric volumes which cut through space were not designed to represent anything in particular but to transmit a concept of the environment in which the actor performed; they were to add concentration and intensity to the drama.

The costumes of the actors were simplified, sharply angular and circular Cubo-Futuristic forms (figs. 29–32). Relying on the principles of disharmony, asymmetry and arhythmicality, Altman destroyed the central axis of the costumes and thereby intensified the deformity of the beggars, especially in the second act. He dramatized the wretchedness, the stammering yet threatening step of the crippled masses on the stage. Their miserable lives glow for the moment as they dance one by one with the bride Leah, the beautiful daughter of the wealthy merchant. (Stanislavsky's dictum is realized: if you want to show a miser, show how he gives; if you want to show someone wretched, show how he is happy.)

Doubtless influenced by the most advanced stage designers at that time, Altman's work meshes with that of Tatlin, Malevich, Yakulov, Stepanova, Popova, Vesnin, his former teacher Alexandra Exter and other avant-garde artists.[58] This is especially felt in his sets for *Uriel Accosta*, Carl Gutzkov's play written in Paris in 1846 and now brought to the stage by the Kamerni Theatre. Altman made dynamic use of immobile forms. Furniture was absent from the stage, the set reduced to different levels of height which made the stage but an instrument for the actor, who thus became the pivotal element of the theatre. The walls of the stage were covered with black cloth; and the stark set, built of wood, iron and glass, occupied the very centre of the stage. Conceived as space, volume, steps and arches, the set lent support to the action's tragic intensity.

In the early days of the Revolution, the cultivation of national culture and service to the Revolution were not considered contradictory or incompatible. The Revolution itself called all purposes into question and among them the place of art in the emerging new order. Art trends as well as art groups vied with each other for positions of power and influence. While the avant-garde felt its art to be the expression of the new social forces which stood for the Revolution, the government encouraged a variety of art expressions without endorsing any particular trend. In the prevailing social turmoil all cultural groupings and primordial loyalties were undermined, weakened or destroyed to the point at which one could actually come close to creating a Jewish art without believing in its essential existence, value, necessity or feasibility.

Shortly after the Revolution Marc Chagall was appointed Art Commissar for the government of Vitebsk. In this capacity he organized the celebrations for the first anniversary of the Revolution, for which he himself painted banners with green cows and horses flying through the sky—all very much to the amazement and chagrin of the political committee. After two and a half years he was removed from his post by his fellow artists for not being revolutionary enough in his art. He surfaced in 1920 in Moscow, which was seething with artistic and theatrical energies. The intense experience of the Revolution and his own involvement with the organization of the Vitebsk Art School did not weaken his tie with Jewish folk art.

At the beginning of 1920 we find Chagall working as costume and stage designer for the newly founded Kamerni Jewish State Theatre. Alexander Granovsky, the director, had returned from Germany after the beginning of the Revolution, and had moved with his young theatrical group from Leningrad to Moscow, where he invited Chagall to work on a new type of Jewish drama. Chagall was also given the task of decorating the auditorium of the small theatre (fig. 33).

For the large mural—actually a 12 × 36 foot oil painting on canvas mounted on the long wall of the auditorium—Chagall adopted a firm two-dimensional composition by resorting to geometrical forms used by many of the advanced Russian artists who worked in the constructivist manner. Into the geometrical structures he introduced supple, airy Sholom Aleichem-type figures, brightly coloured, crooked, spirited, forever running, limping, bouncing, trumpeting and fiddling. They are figures of the theatre—actors, dancers, musicians and somersaulting acrobats wearing phylacteries. Chagall himself, palette in hand, is being carried by the well-known drama critic Effross. There are references to the director of the theatre and the actor Michoels. And there are also charging animals, goats, and an upside-down cow being milked by a fellow with his feet in a basin. A painted frieze of fruit and dishes extends above this painting and throughout the whole theatre.

On the opposite wall, in the spaces between the windows, Chagall placed personifications of Music, Dance, Drama and Literature: the street musician sitting on the top of a roof and playing the fiddle, the dancer, the wedding jester and the scribe. They were all part of the Jewish folk tradition and also symbols of the new Jewish theatre and modern Jewish secular culture.

There is an air of riotous Dionysiac self-abandon about this *Introduction to the Yiddish Theatre*, as the paintings were called. 'They were aimed at a large public and have the significance of a Manifesto.'[59] They may have expressed the idea of the world theatre as Meyer suggests, but quite intuitively and fittingly the *Introduction to the Yiddish Theatre* had about it the air of a Purim Carnival. The modern Yiddish Theatre had its roots in the Purimspielers, a popular, informal and intimate group of amateur actors that included jesters, clowns, singers and acrobats who used to enact the Purim story. This was a popular form of entertainment which emerged in the sixteenth century among Ashkenazy Jews and appealed mainly to the lower, less educated classes. Similarly, the stories and characters of Sholom Aleichem to which Chagall alluded in these paintings were known to Russian Jews.

These and other stories by other Jewish writers depicted the impoverished inhabitants of the small Jewish towns, with biting satire and yet lovingly, as clowns living in complete misery, without economic roots, and jokingly ignoring the grim reality of their existence. The *Luftmensch* was the common symbol in literature for that character. He represents the man who literally walks on air, on roofs, everywhere except on firm ground. The *Luftmensch* shares with the acrobat the precariousness of his posture, the danger of his existence, the slim base of the ground on which he stands, although he is physically ill-equipped to match the latter's skills. The *Luftmensch* is a metaphor for people out of balance

33. Marc Chagall, *Introduction to the Yiddish Theatre* (detail), 1921.
Wall painting in the Kamerni Yiddish Theatre, Moscow.

in the economic, physical and social sense—people without capital or professions, deformed by life, limping, and blind, whose existence is ephemeral. Yet to stay alive they have to be resourceful like acrobats. The *Luftmensch* shares with the clown the exaggerated gesture and the capacity to mock his own shortcomings. He became a fertile source for the artistic imagination. About such people Sholom Aleichem wrote:

> They are never sad. They are born clowns, humorous, with sharp tongues and always joyous. You ask one: 'What are you making a living on?' He answers, 'What am I making a living on? Ha! Ha! Ha! You see I live.' They are always running. You ask one, 'Where are you running?' He answers, 'Where am I running? Ha! Ha! Ha! I am running!'

Chagall, who was thoroughly familiar with the Jewish writers of that time and who had illustrated many of their stories, carried their descriptions of the fantastic into his art. There is a circus air about his mural—shafts of bright colour and continuous movement, a jazz-like rhythm and gaudy, burlesque elements. This atmosphere also prevailed in the contemporary theatrical scene. It was a sign of the times. The theatre reached for the masses. Meyerhold advocated the biomechanical theory according to which the actor had to train his body to be as flexible as that of the acrobat. Yakulov, who at times turned the theatre into a circus, stressed the principle of perpetual motion and the kaleidoscope of form and colour as the basic ingredients of the theatre. Even elements of the cabaret and the music hall—buffoonery, farce and caricature— which would have been inconceivable in the pre-Revolutionary professional theatre, were introduced into the Russian and Ukrainian theatre after the Revolution.[60]

34. Nathan Altman, portrait of the Jewish actor Michoels. From M. Etkind, *Nathan Altman* (Moscow, 1971).

While Chagall painted the figures in the mural and designed the sets, costumes and make-up for the theatre, starving actors were enthusiastically rehearsing Sholom Aleichem's lines for their forthcoming performance of three one-act plays—*Mazel Tov*, *The Lie*, and *The Agents*—in the unheated auditorium. An intense collaboration developed between the painter, the composer, the musicians and the actors, especially Solomon Michoels, the most gifted actor of the Yiddish stage, and the director Alexander Granovsky. They all felt compelled to respond artistically to the immense changes the Revolution had brought about and in which their lives were enmeshed. They were determined to move away from the traditional Jewish theatre with its self-deprecating farcical type of acting.[61] A new interpretation of contemporary life was called for. Granovsky gave Chagall a free hand, and the painter more than anyone else shaped the anti-naturalistic, expressionist style of the Yiddish Theatre, even of the Habimah Theatre.[62] Michoels understood fully the unique character and energy of Chagall's line and colour and knew how to turn them into a new style of acting on the stage.

Michoels gives us an idea of the kind of collaboration taking place in the make-up room and of the expressionist tendencies of Chagall:

> On the day of the premiere, Chagall came to my dressing room, laid out his paints and started to work. He divided my face into halves. One part he coloured green, the other yellow (as one says yellow and green [i.e. expressing

revulsion]). He raised my right eyebrow two centimetres higher than the left one. He extended the creases around my nose and mouth over the whole face. These lines expressed the tragic character of Menachem Mendel.

I looked into the mirror and convinced myself that the make-up created the dynamism and expression of the character. The artist continued to work with great intensity. Suddenly his fingers stopped as if uncertain. Something disturbed him. He put his finger to my eye, removed it again, stepped back, looked at me with a sorrowful expression and said: 'Oh Solomon, Solomon, if only you didn't have a right eye, you could do such marvellous things.'[63]

There is more independent testimony to the remarkable influence of Chagall's painting on the Jewish theatre. O. Lubomirsky, in a book on Michoels, states:

His influence was visible not only in the stage sets, costumes and make-up techniques, but even in the gestures of the actors. . . . The actors found in the grotesque stylization of European gestures and the exaggeration of the Jewish, as well in folklore, what they needed to express their idea of the Jewish character. In many cases they came close to the conception expressed in Chagall's forms. Their efforts, together with the trend started by Chagall, gave rise to what was later considered the national form of that theatre.[64]

Thus we find a collective effort of artists in different fields aiming towards a Jewish national style. While the disintegration of the traditional Jewish community was accelerating and the future of the secularized Jewish community doubtful, Chagall, Granovsky and Michoels at the Yiddish Kamerni and Altman, Vechtangov Zemach and the musician Engel at the Habimah were reconstituting the community on the scale of the theatre. They kept alive a collective consciousness by remembering old folk legends, by examining past and contemporary writings and turning them into stylized dramatic stage forms. They moved towards the crystallization of a Jewish style.[65]

If there was a theatre, there had to be a community; and if there was a community there had to be a theatre. The existence of one was proof of the existence of the other. In the theatre there was a strong accent on collectivity rather than on individuality, which was an echo both of the spirit of Jewish tradition and of the Revolution, and gave the painter an extraordinary share in the staging and interpretation of the play.

The Fading of Hope for a Jewish Art

Yet a very short time after Chagall had completed his feverish activity at the Moscow Yiddish Theatre, he expressed certain doubts and a certain ambivalence about the possibility of a Jewish art as it apparently preoccupied the Jewish intelligentsia of Moscow. In the literary magazine *Der Shtrom*, whose cover he himself designed (fig. 35), he wrote:

Since the Renaissance national art has started to decline, boundaries have become blurred. There were artists, individuals subject to one or another state, born here or there (blessed be you Vitebsk!), and one needs a good registration system and a passport to nationalize all artists. And yet the thought springs to mind: If I were not a Jew (according to the meaning which I put into this word) then I would not be an artist, or I would be quite a different one.[66]

The statement is not very clear; it compounds the confusion about Chagall's ambivalence toward Jewish art, an ambivalence which remained with him for most of his life.[67] Did he who personified to his generation the very model of the new Jewish artist suddenly recognize that as soon as the creation of Jewish art becomes a conscious goal the whole problem becomes a burden to art and to the artist? Or was he suddenly aware of the unique position of art, which has its own condition and cannot be defined in terms of national categories? As a former Russian Commissar of Art, had he learned that the most essential qualities of an artist cannot be put into the service of communal institutions or even of the most exalted ideals, and that the very nature of modern art excludes identification with institutions however dear they may seem? That art mandates the acceptance of a spiritual independence? We shall never know.

In the spring of 1917, Eliezer Lissitzky, who the previous year had investigated the wooden synagogues along the Dnieper River (see p. 18 above), illustrated in Moscow the *Prager Legende* (Sichot Chulin), a story by the Yiddish poet Moshe Broderson. With strokes of his pen he drew arabesque-like floating figures reminiscent of the Art Nouveau style, and thereby created a richly ornamented margin which frames the traditional Hebrew script (fig. 36). The edition consisted of 110 copies, 20 of which Lissitzky coloured individually with watercolour. The copies were designed in the form of a scroll and fitted into an especially designed wooden case, like the Torah.

Lissitzky had first-hand knowledge of the architectonic and decorative possibilities of the Hebrew letter from studying the inscriptions on the walls of wooden synagogues. From medieval illuminated Hebrew manuscripts he knew the variety of compositional arrangements in which letters were used: they formed curves or vertical or diagonal lines across the page. Hebrew microscript letters were used for intricate ornaments. Lissitzky doubtless was also aware of the custom of using Masoretic diacritical marks beneath and above the lines of sacred Hebrew books to alert the reader to the proper timing, rhythm and volume while chanting the text.

These sources must have stimulated Lissitzky to experiment with new artistic forms for the Hebrew alphabet and with new compositions for the printed page. These ideas appear first in the illustrations for his children's books and lead later to his innovations in modern book design, innovations which he later carried into Russian and German typography.[68]

In the Yiddish books for children, he experimented with Expressionist and Cubo-Futurist illustrations, at first strongly influenced by Chagall, and with title-pages whose designs, with their diagonal lines, sharp angular construction and flat projections across the page, point toward the later Constructivist composition of his *prouns* and posters. Like the title-page for *Yingl Zingl Chwatt*

35. (TOP LEFT) Marc Chagall, cover of the Yiddish periodical *Shtrom* (Moscow, 1922).

36. (CENTRE LEFT) El Lissitzky, illustration for the *Prager Legende* (Sichat Chulin) by Moshe Broderson (Moscow, 1917).

37. (TOP RIGHT) El Lissitzky, design of title page for *Yingl Zingl Chwatt* by Mani Leib, 1918 (Kulturlige, Warsaw, 1922).

38. (BOTTOM LEFT) El Lissitzky, illustration for *Yingl Zingl Chwatt* by Mani Leib, 1918 (Kulturlige, Warsaw, 1922).

39. (BOTTOM RIGHT) El Lissitzky, illustration for *Der Ber* by Feter Ben Zion (Raskin), Kindergarten Series (Folks Varlag, Kiev–Petersburg, 1919).

בער ווען פון ווייטע וועגן
קומט דער ווינטער אָן מיט רעגן,
און קיין שניי איז נישט צוזען,
ווי קיין שניי וואָלט ניט געווען —

ווייזט זיך צינגל פייך פון בויגן,
פון דער נאַכט ארויסגעפלויגן,
ניט געזען און ניט געהערט,
אויפן פריצס גוטן פערד.

און ער טראָגט זיך גיכער, זיכער,
ווי דער ווילדער ווינט און ווילער,
מיטן רינגל דורכן מאַרק,
דורכן מאַרק און אויפן באַרג.

טפרו! דער פערד בלייבט שטיין, און
טוט אַ נעם דעם כישוף־רינגל,
טוט אים זיבן מאָל אַ דריי
און עס פאַלט ארויס אַ שניי.

איז דער בער אַוועקגעשפרונגען ווייטער,
שפרינגט ער און שפרינגט, שפרינגט און יאַמערט,
ביז ער האָט באַגעגנט אויפן וועג אַ הונט,
ווענדט זיך דער בער צו דעם הונט:

— הינטעלע הונט, פאַרניי מיר מיין פוס, פאַרשטעפ
מיר מיין פעל,
דער בייזער יון האָט מיר אָפגעהאַקט!
— אין ווייך ניט!

5

(Little Boy, Little Tongue, Tomboy), which he completed in 1918, the lines and letters float unsupported in space and thrust into every conceivable direction, doing away with traditional composition (fig. 37). The size, position and spacing of the letters are determined by architectural considerations, and type is seen as a form in space. The text, however, is illustrated in a Cubo-Futurist style since Lissitzky must have considered the children for whom the book was written. The illustrations merge with lines or letters of the poem and occupy the space of a verse, and human figures fuse with letters of the Hebrew alphabet.[69]

Between 1917 and 1920 Lissitzky served both the Revolution and the cause of Jewish nationalism without any seeming conflict between his loyalties. He designed the flag which was carried across the Red Square on May Day 1918 by the leaders of the Revolution. He also designed the famous speakers' rostrum (also known as the Lenin Podium). At the same time he continued to design children's books. Among the most famous are the ten lithographs he made for the poem *Chad Gadya* (A Goat Kid), sung on the first night of Passover (fig. 18). Here, while he responds to prevailing Jewish customs and sentiments, he also makes the text and its long tradition of illustrations refer metaphorically to the struggling Revolution. He created two sets of lithographs for the *Chad Gadya* poem, one in 1917 and the other in 1919. Alan C. Birnholz, who carefully studied Lissitzky's relation to the Jewish tradition, observes:

> The meaning of Chad Gadya also changes in direct correspondence to the Revolution and the ensuing counter-revolutionary upheavals. If we compare the final episode in the story, in 'And God Slays the Angel of Death', we see that in 1917 the Angel of Death is in the act of dying: in 1919 he is dead. Chad Gadya is a tale of retribution, of forces overpowering the vanquishing other forces, with the ultimate power of God victorious in the end over death and evil. The relevance of the story in the light of the final victory of the Bolsheviks over the Whites in 1919 is clear. In Chad Gadya, Lissitzky presented a parable of the final complete victory of the Revolution.[70]

Lissitzky's famous poster of 1919, 'Krasnim Klinom Bei Byelikh' (Beat the Whites with the Red Wedge), in which he uses forms related to the work of Tatlin and Malevich and to the symbols on military maps (which were adapted by Russian artists at that time for propaganda purposes), appeals for Jewish support for the Communist cause by a shrewd choice of words which Ilyah Ehrenburg suggested to him (fig. 40).[71] While Jews welcomed the downfall of the Tsar, many kept aloof from the Bolsheviks. The poster was designed to bring them closer to the aims of the party by reminding them of the pogroms that were accompanied by shouts of 'Bei Zhidow' (Beat the Jews). The words of the poster identify the Whites with the pogroms, by applying the dreaded word *bei* (beat) to the Whites and not to the Jews.[72]

In 1919 Lissitzky was invited by Chagall, then Art Commissar for the region of Vitebsk and head of the Art School in Vitebsk, to join the School's staff as Professor of Architecture and, in addition, to head the Department of Applied Arts. There Lissitzky's tendency toward an abstract art gained reinforcement through the influence of Malevich, who also joined the teaching staff. At that time Lissitzky created the *proun*, which he defined as 'the interchange station between painting and architecture'. He soon became a leading Constructivist.[73]

Meanwhile, the hopes for the development of a national Jewish culture were beginning to fade as the publication of Jewish books became restricted. Lissitzky's training as engineer and architect and the opportunities which presented themselves now that the Revolution emerged victorious largely determined the gradual transfer of his loyalties from Jewish nationalism to a messianic international socialism.[74]

By 1922 the idea of a Jewish national art had faded. The enormous political changes in Russia had undermined its social foundations. Although the Jewish theatre lingered on for several more years, the search had come to an end. The decline of Jewish culture as a unique national culture was part of a deeper process which affected all areas of Soviet life. It was in the interest of a weak Soviet State to encourage the development of national cultures in order to spread the message of the Revolution effectively through the channel of national languages. But with the consolidation of Soviet power the forces of industrialization and political integration adversely affected national tendencies.

By 1922 the enchanting and moving encounter with Jewish folk art and the attempt to use it as a base for a national art, which had occurred just several years before, seemed now ages away. It was an episode, a burst of energy, a flash of summer lightning. Artists had witnessed and participated in enormous events. In Lissitzky's essay on the Mohilev synagogue, written in Berlin in 1922, one senses in some of its passages a tone of disillusionment and alienation. He questions now the very originality of the national character of Jewish folk art and draws attention to the fact that the style of the paintings of the Mohilev synagogue bears an affinity to the style of painting of other people who lived in the area at the same time. The 32-year-old Lissitzky was now aware how art was being manipulated by state bureaucracy and commissars of culture. He was sceptical of the use and abuse of national art:

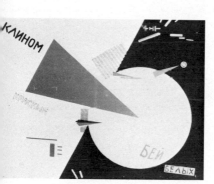

40. El Lissitzky, poster, *Beat the Whites with the Red Wedge*, 1919.

> In this hour when one judges the culture of a people by its national literature, its magazines, its theatre and its paintings—we have, as it were, all of these things: we are a cultured nation. We just do not possess a famous book of genealogy. But if for this reason we are pushing toward the past, and if this is our only reason for our interest in folk art, it is better that we give up the notion of culture altogether. That which we call art is always created in an absent-minded fashion. When one does not know that one creates art—that is the sign of culture.[75]

He ends with a paradoxical sentence which suggests that the true creators of art are those who fight against art. 'Art is created today by those who are strangers to it. We prefer the live dog to the dead lion. Because we know that when the dog dies he turns into a lion.'[76]

By 1922 the leading artists who once were concerned with the creation of a national Jewish style had, for one reason or another, gone to Berlin and created there a temporary enclave of Jewish immigrant artists. Here we find Aronson, Ryback, Chagall and others. Whether they were still clinging to their faith in Jewish art or whether they had a change of heart, they could all agree that it could not have taken place in Soviet Russia.

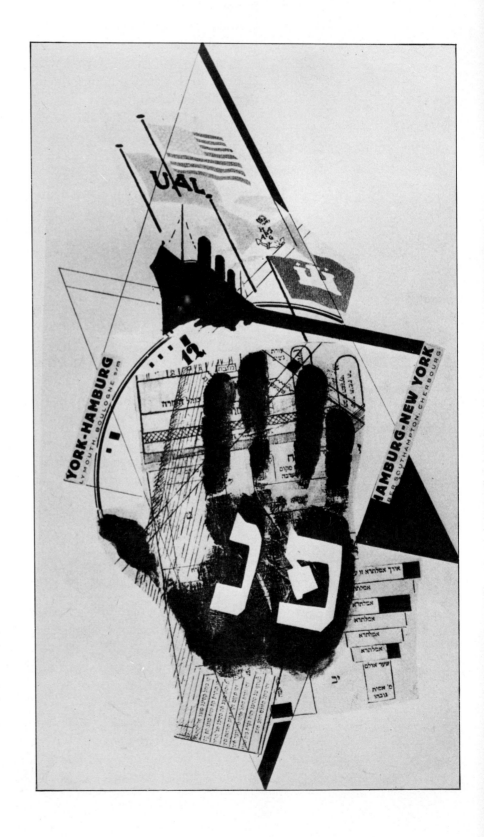

CHAPTER TWO

The Encounter with the West

The Russian episode was unique because of the clear national tendencies that enlivened it and preoccupied a considerable number of serious artists. There seemed to be, for a brief moment, a definite purpose and direction to their efforts to find painterly and plastic expressions that could define their Jewish identity and their unique relationship to the world. Yet at the beginning of the 1920s, the major figures of this movement either dispersed in all directions, driven by events far beyond their control, or adapted to the new political realities that had emerged in the Soviet Union.

As we look into centres of the West with large Jewish populations, or where Jewish artists gathered, we hardly ever encounter again this degree of serious preoccupation with 'Jewish Art'. There existed neither the will nor even the assumption that to create such an art was possible or even desirable. The realities that presented themselves to the Jewish artists or to Jewish communities in Western countries went far beyond the traditional concepts of Jewish life and their political experience in Russia.

In Eastern Europe nineteenth-century Enlightenment had produced a vibrant and authentic Jewish secular culture, in spite of marks of assimilation. In Western countries the Enlightenment, which had arrived there an entire century earlier, had been primarily responsible for assimilation and the gradual or even rapid disintegration of Jewish culture. El Lissitzky had already denied the possibility that a national art can be created in a conscious fashion, claiming that the emergence of any national art is the result of a natural process which cannot be engineered, and that national art is forged in an unconscious manner by artists who are not even aware that they are creating it (see above, p. 47).

In Western Europe and in the United States, Jewish themes and Jewish sentiments continue, of course, to appear in the work of many an artist. The discussion of Jewish art rises to the surface from time to time, but it is never as deeply informed or as solidly based on a coherent life style as in Eastern Europe. Neither is it as goal-directed or as fully motivated by the need for realization. The process of migration to the West, the change in countries, language, customs and occupations not only shook Jewish communal life, which was still reeling from the effects of the Enlightenment, but also threatened the identity of the individual and strained the ties that bound him to the Jewish community. Religion, once the mainstay of life, was discarded by many or relegated to certain ceremonial functions. That which was a way of life and a cultural unity was reduced in its dimension, its continuity broken, thus bringing into full relief the complexity and ambiguity inherent in Jewish cultural existence.

A Jewish secular culture could not maintain itself permanently against the dynamic force of modern Western civilization, in spite of many attempts to do so. Such institutions as the Educational Alliance in the United States and the

41. El Lissitzsky, 'A Journey to America', illustration from Ilya Ehrenburg's *Six Stories with light Endings* (Moscow, Berlin, 1922). The initial letters 'p' and 'n' stamped on the upraised hand stand for the Hebrew 'Here passed away . . .' often found on gravestone inscriptions.

49

Ben Uri Society in England were designed to offer the newly arrived immigrant help in his adjustment to the new country. The Educational Alliance offered the art student a vital programme of studies which was especially effective in the Americanization of the immigrant. Not only did it guide the young artist into American customs but it also gave him an opportunity to express his own cultural background and thereby smoothed the road of transition.

The various socialist ideas which swept with almost religious intensity across the East Side of New York City and the East End of London struck roots among the Jewish masses and won the passionate loyalty of many artists. This was due of course to their peculiar revolutionary experience in Eastern Europe and their continuing identification with the struggle of their kinsmen back in Russia. The misery of their immigrant status and the central place they occupied in the sweatshops of the New York garment trade and in the printing and building trades made them natural carriers of socialist ideas. Their Biblical tradition with its messianic appeal and their own yearning for redemption reinforced their role in the great strikes of the burgeoning labour movement and made them particularly prone to embrace socialism.

Many of the socialist tendencies carried strong secularist, cosmopolitan and anti-religious feelings, and the socialist belief that one stood on the threshold of Utopia foreshadowed the dissolution of the Jewish community. But even these processes were to take time; the liberation from the past occurred gradually.

New York and London: East Side and East End

In the meantime the Jewish East Side in New York City turned into a restless, vibrant, politically and intellectually active community. Gatherings, heated discussions, demonstrations and parades, often marred by conflict, were characterized by a zest and a peculiarly lively texture of Jewish folk culture which had a character of its own. Even simple people actively and ardently took part in the pursuit of ideas, the veneration of books, and the love of the theatre, music and art—all means by which the day of redemption could be brought closer. The attachment to Jewish tradition and even to the problems of Jewish existence diminished, and the Jewish folk culture which the people had brought with them increasingly dwindled and became absorbed into the stream of general immigrant culture. Nevertheless, Yiddish and Hebrew secular groups attempted to preserve the Jewish people as an ethnic, historical entity and to cultivate some aspects of their tradition—not because they venerated the past or considered it a norm, but because they were bound by a sense of its ultimate value, of its ethical, prophetic and humanitarian essence which had formed them, linked them together from ancient times and committed them for the future.

Traditional values do not easily perish—they are transformed. Deep and powerful tendencies searched for an outlet into other channels. Deep-seated loyalties rooted in Jewish culture were transferred into the fields of art, science, social work and political action, and in turn were shaped by those fields until their sources often became blurred or forgotten. Traditional learning, once a cornerstone of religious faith, became a secular, intellectual pursuit. Talmudic erudition, which had fostered attitudes of logic and rationality, was transmuted into the discipline of legal and scientific thought. Divine ordination and cabbalistic and messianic expectations became social action, revolution, the quest for the absolute, and artistic avant-gardism.

As part of this process, even in the United States the question of Jewish art surfaced among the Yiddish-speaking community which concentrated on the East Side of New York City during the first decades of this century.

In 1911, the weekly Yiddish magazine *Dos Neie Land*, edited by Abraham Reisen, published a proposal by its art and theatre critic Saul Raskin for exhibitions of Jewish artists, together with practical suggestions on how to go about it.[1] Interestingly, the suggestion for the exhibitions was opposed in a letter to the editor a week later; the writer felt that many good artists would refuse to exhibit their work and that mostly amateurs would bring their paintings. He felt that it would be better to prepare the ground for art appreciation in the Jewish community first by exhibiting reproductions of good works of art in certain public places.[2]

In another article in 1911 in *Dos Neie Land*, Raskin explores 'The Future of Jewish Art' and in vain attempts to find a specific common characteristic Jewish trait in the works of Israels, Antokolski, Pasternak, Leviathan, Liebermann, Bendemann and Pissarro.

> It is difficult, very difficult [Raskin writes], to find a common core and to predict the main road which Jewish Art will take. They are too diverse in their technique, in the forms they create, in the manner in which they absorb sensations and in the expression of their artistic ego. . . . It seems that to answer our question we have first not to look at the 'how' [they paint] but at the 'what', to the themes which they paint, and, even better, to the themes they avoid.[3]

In spite of the fact that the work of the artists he names does not support his ideas, Raskin concludes that Jewish artists are indifferent to still-life, and have little inclination for landscape paintings or even for portraits. Their real preference is for genre and historical paintings. Their choice does not derive from a lack of sympathy for landscapes, still-life, or animals but depends on spiritual force rather than on aesthetic development. Thoughtful artists deal with material best suited to express thought, he feels:

> Doubtless, the fate of man is the most thoughtful theme, and this is the reason why Jewish artists are indifferent to still-life and animals and are not particularly attracted to landscapes or even portraits, because the Jewish spirit is focused mostly on the moral quest and deals in the main with the relation between man and man.[4]

Raskin longs for the pathos of Tintoretto, Giotto and Michelangelo and believes that the unique trials of the Jewish people would require such an art.

It is likely that Raskin did not know the work of Soutine or Chagall at that time, but clearly he was familiar with the landscape paintings of Leviathan and Pissarro whom he mentioned at the beginning of his article. He could not find a common formal denominator for a Jewish art, but thought he had found it on a thematic basis. However, even on this ground he encountered difficulties. He may also have been influenced by an early essay of Martin Buber, *Jewish Artists*, in which Buber claimed that the accent in the work of the Jewish artist is on relations rather than on the unique, differentiated substance.[5]

Theories aside, the life of the immigrants attracted the attention of artists who grew up among them, knew them intimately and felt at home there. Other artists were also drawn to this life by the picturesqueness of the Jewish neighbourhoods of the Lower East Side, with their special character. Artists could find there an abundance of material in the streets full of peddlers, traders, day workers, vendors, and children. There was the clamour of arguing, bargaining, shouting voices. In the dense Jewish neighbourhoods there existed a web of relationships which gave this area a distinct flavour and authentic old-world appearance. Yiddish was spoken and Yiddish books and newspapers were read. Art thrived on colour, movement, energy, vitality, and the struggle of people to find a place for themselves in the new country. Throughout the first decades of the twentieth century, even into the 1980s, in the Lower East Side and similar centres in Boston, Baltimore and the East End in London, artists have drawn on the immigrant experience and the experience of their children.

One of the artists who drew on this wealth of material, Jacob Epstein, born on the Lower East Side of New York City, decided not to join his parents when they moved out from their crowded tenement into a more respectable but duller area—the Upper West Side. He rented a room on Hester Street, in a ramshackle wooden building, in the very centre of the Lower East Side, and turned it into a studio. From his window he looked out on the most densely populated street of the Lower East Side, an open-air market, lined from one end to the other with pushcarts and peddlers, and filled with slow-moving crowds that packed the sidewalks. Among this crush of humanity children played and screamed by the hundreds.

42. Jacob Epstein,
East Side People, 1900–1.
Chalk on paper, $26\frac{1}{4} \times 23\frac{1}{4}$ in
(67.3×59 cm). New York, Jewish Museum, gift of Karl Nathan.

> I could look down upon the moving mass below and watch them making purchases, bartering and gossiping. Outside stood carpenters, washerwomen, and day workers, gathered with their tools in readiness to be hired. Every type could be found there, and for the purpose of drawing I would follow a character until his appearance was sufficiently impressed upon my mind for me to make a drawing.[6]

The black crayon sketch of the massive figure of a man stepping out for a moment from the crowd surely came about in this manner (fig. 42). His round bowler hat, firm like a helmet, sets the tone for the other rounded shapes that echo throughout the sketch. His beard frames and partially masks his lined, beaten face. His curved, drooping shoulders support the rope he presses to his body with a strong, indifferent hand as if it were a sign of rank. Posture and attire express his patient, dignified endurance of untold burdens. He is a silent,

dumb figure, a trader of old trinkets or a hand for hire, a Bonze Schweig cast upon the New York Lower East Side like thousands of others like him to fend for his daily bread. He is drawn against a mass of other silent figures, bent, silent, weary, dressed in heavy, coarse garments, shuffling their feet as if they carry the burden of the world. The sketch is animated by swiftly moving, linear patterns, a vigorous chiaroscuro of spontaneous outlines. Indeed, the young Epstein's bent for sculpture can be detected in the massive forms of the drawing and in the sweeping, energetic lines breaking at points into sharp angles.

Although he was enrolled in classes at the Art Students League and the Educational Alliance, where he drew from models and painted, Epstein felt that his main studies remained in the streets where he grew up. 'I was known in the market, and whenever I took up a position to draw I was looked upon sympathetically and had no difficulty in finding models. Jewish people look upon the work of an artist as something miraculous, and love watching him, even though they may be extremely critical.'[7] When Hutchins Hapgood commissioned him to prepare drawings for his book *The Spirit of the Ghetto*,[8] Epstein drew a great variety of Lower East Side types and institutions—students, journalists, peddlers, rabbis, writers, poets, actors, socialists, anarchists, freethinkers, Yiddish newspaper offices, coffee houses and theatre audiences.

Looking back later on these formative years, Epstein recalled that throbbing place full of vital intellectual energy and ever-changing sights: 'I sometimes think I should have remained in New York, the material was so abundant. Wherever one looked there was something interesting, a novel composition, wonderful effects of lighting at night, and picturesque and handsome people. Rembrandt would have delighted in the East Side.'[9] He also thought that his own feeling for expressing a human point of view in his work rather than following the abstract implications of modern sculpture derived from his intense contacts and involvement with the people of the East Side. 'I saw so much that called for expression that I can draw upon it now if I wish to.'[10]

William Gropper also grew up on the Lower East Side. His first job was to carry bundles of cloth home for his mother, who was a seamstress, to sew at night. Gropper himself soon also became a bushel boy in a sweatshop of the garment industry and got to know the meaning of piece work. While working he studied at night with Robert Henry and George Bellow. He early developed into a well-known cartoonist whose work expresses a keen social consciousness. Yet his paintings lose none of the directness and rebellious spirit for which his cartoons were known. Whether Gropper paints simple folk—weary tailors bending over their work, cigar makers in their shop, pretzel vendors on the street corner—or bloated senators waving their arms and thrashing the air, his paintings render more than the eye perceives. He describes relations and conditions under which people toil. His tailor figure squats cross-legged on a heap of cloths locked in by the sewing machine and the large scissors, sewing down a hem (fig. 43). The characterization of his subject—the painfully contorted pose and fatigued facial expression—as well as the technique with which it is rendered, the dynamic composition, the resolute speedy line, and the richly toned but subdued colour, bring the painting in close relation to the tradition of Goya and Daumier.

Abraham Walkowitz arrived as a young boy with his mother from the plains of Siberia in 1886 and is largely a product of the Lower East Side, where he spent most of his youth. His adopted home offered him a continuous source of rich impressions before his European tour of 1906 and again after his return. Observers of his work have noted the deep sympathy he expresses for the toiling and struggling humanity among whom he lived—crowds, men and women, standing, sitting and talking to each other; vendors, saleswomen, lovers,

43. William Gropper, *Tailor*, 1940. Oil on canvas, $21\frac{1}{4} \times 26\frac{1}{4}$ in (53.9 × 66.6 cm). Washington D.C., Hirshhorn Museum and Sculpture Garden, Smithsonian Institute.

scholars, men lifting the Torah or studying in the synagogue and men engaged in hard physical labour.

Remarkably, in much of his work Walkowitz finds also a pastoral side to city life. People play in the open, and dance and relax on the grass in city parks. There are outings and picnics at the seaside, a holiday atmosphere among colourful East Side crowds, and there is always joy in the presentation of the body.

In *East Side Crowd* (fig. 44), the black and white composition, representing an informal crowd at the theatre, is built on two parallel planes in a manner stylistically related to Matisse. People seem to be as much interested in each other as in the play. Their attention and animation, as expressed by their poses, intensity of gesture and rather formal dress, are poetic evocations of a deeply engaged theatre crowd. The composition is built on the firm structure of parallel planes by means of swift, intense lines and deft, fluid, delicate brush-work applied in broad areas, with little modelling or gradation of tone and without lingering over picturesque details; in this way he realizes a sense of vivaciousness, ease and informality. Intensely intuitive, the composition seems

44. Abraham Walkowitz, *East Side Crowd*, 1903. Ink on paper, 10 × 7 in (25.4 × 17.7 cm). Private collection.

almost unplanned, yet its pronounced two-dimensionality, its inner rhythmic vitality and the distribution of the white and dark areas must be the result of a highly conscious method of design.

It was David Ignatoff, a Yiddish writer and poet, who saw a certain Jewish aspect in the work of Walkowitz. Purposely ignoring the various Jewish themes and ghetto motifs which abound in the artist's work and which, of course, point to some Jewish concern, Ignatoff refers to a specific familial element and to a spiritual human dimension:

Walkowitz possesses a pure Jewish attachment and love for the sentiments of the family. This sentiment shines forth with primeval purity not only in works representing the family but even in his first picture in his book *A Hundred Drawings of Abraham Walkowitz*, published in 1925 by Huebsch. In 'The Kiss', a man and woman stand before you nude. Everything there is permeated by a pure primitive earthy sentiment. You see a basic healthy sexual drive, but purified not Hellenic. Earthly, really earthly, but not quite so. There is a feeling of Jewish family relatedness. There hovers over the pair that eternally trembling, faithful feeling of 'you are sacred to me.'[11]

Benjamin Kopman has a different view of Walkowitz's Jewishness. He grounds it in his life and temperament rather than in his work.

Walkowitz is of a nervous temperament. This nervousness is a Jewish characteristic, and it makes him, I like to think, a Jewish artist even more than the family sentiment which he displays. This characteristic of nervousness, although it enters all his work, is easier to recognize in life than in his work. Perhaps he freed himself of it in his work because he wanted to approach his work like a European, like an aesthete, like an artist who thinks first in terms of art problems. When he has achieved that and calmed his unrest, it becomes again difficult for him to deal with purely aesthetic problems. After he has derived pleasure from his work, restlessness again takes hold of him: why did he please himself? A Jew has to know why and wherefore. It is difficult for him just to enjoy himself.[12]

The Yiddish theatre alluded to in Walkowitz's *East Side Crowd* reminds us that in the East End of London in the first decade of the twentieth century a teeming Jewish immigrant section had come into being similar to that of New York, and here also the Jewish theatre played an important role. The community had been swollen by an influx of thousands of Eastern European Jewish refugees, many of whom aimed to continue their journey further to the United States, but having exhausted their means settled in London's East End. They soon developed an intense cultural life. Yiddish was spoken, literature, theatre and social issues were debated vigorously, and as in New York, new ideas were eagerly discussed. Although most of the immigrants adhered to religious custom, anarchist, socialist-bundist and Zionist groups soon flourished among them.[13] By 1911 several of the children of these immigrants were students at the Slade School of Fine Art. Among them were David Bomberg, Jacob Kramer, Mark Gertler and the poet-painter Isaac Rosenberg.

Mark Gertler, in the patriarchal family of immigrants gathered around the old man (fig. 46), gives us in simplified, solid forms an image of inner strength, endurance, and quiet and patient dignity. The drawing *Jewish Theatre* by David Bomberg was done while he was still a student at the Slade. Bomberg in this drawing searches for clearly defined interlocking forms in the various postures and attitudes of individually engaged spectators, as well as for 'the formal possibilities of the audience as a block and patterned shape' (fig. 45).[14]

The fifth child of an immigrant leather worker from Poland, David Bomberg grew up in Whitechapel and from an early age practised drawing at the Victoria and Albert and the British Museum. He was encouraged to intensify his study when John Singer Sargent observed him in the museum copying a bust of

Michelangelo. From 1908 till 1910 we find the youngster taking evening classes in design for book production and lithography at the Central School of Arts and Crafts with W. R. Lethaby, one of the leading figures in the English Arts and Crafts movement, and on alternate evenings studying drawing and painting from life under Walter Richard Sickert at the Westminster Technical Institute. The Slade School of Fine Art, to which he was admitted on the recommendation of Solomon J. Solomon, a member of the Royal Academy of Art, and with the help of a grant from the Jewish Educational Aid Society, was undoubtedly the most advanced art school in England at that time. It stood in opposition to the taste of the Royal Academy, especially in its awareness of modern art, and Roger Fry in his lectures articulated his theories on Cézanne, and his views about the implications of his work.

When Bomberg graduated in the summer of 1913, aged 22, he already was boldly experimenting with abstract forms, following ideas of modern design to their logical conclusion in such works as *Ezekiel's Vision*, *Reading from the Torah*, *The Mud Bath*, and *In the Hold*, which put him then in the forefront of English avant-garde art.[15] A trip to Paris with Jacob Einstein in 1914 in order to organize a Jewish section for Whitechapel's 'Twentieth Century Art' exhibition, which opened in May that year, only reinforced his independence from conventional ideas about representation.

45. David Bomberg, *Jewish Theatre*, 1913. Black chalk drawing on paper, $21\frac{3}{4} \times 23\frac{3}{4}$ in (54.6×60.3 cm). Leeds City Art Galleries.

46. (OPPOSITE) Mark Gertler, *Jewish Family*, 1913. Oil on canvas, 26×20 in (65.5×51 cm). London, Tate Gallery.

I appeal to a Sense of Form. In some of the work . . . I completely abandon Naturalism and Tradition. I am searching for an intenser expression. In other work . . . where I use Naturalistic Form, I have stripped it of all irrelevant matter.

I look upon nature, while I live in a steel city. Where decoration happens, it is accidental. My object is the construction of Pure Form. I reject everything in painting that is not Pure Form. I hate the colours of the East, the Modern Mediaevalist, and the Fat Man of the Renaissance.[16]

47. (TOP LEFT) David Bomberg, *Vision of Ezekiel*, 1912. Oil on canvas, 45 × 54 in (114.4 × 137.2 cm). London, Tate Gallery.

48. (TOP RIGHT) David Bomberg, *The Mud Bath*, 1914. Oil on canvas, 60 × 88¼ in (152.5 × 224.3 cm). London, Tate Gallery.

49. (BOTTOM) David Bomberg, *Ghetto Theatre*, 1920. Oil on canvas, 30 × 25 in (76.2 × 63.5 cm). London, Ben Uri Art Gallery.

Finding little official or private encouragement in England in his search for pure form he returned to representation, but representation stripped of anecdote and focused on essentials. The painting *Ghetto Theatre* (fig. 49) of 1920 is based on a clearly defined geometrical design both in drawing and colour. The artist is primarily concerned with conveying the tactile sensation of mass and weight. The interior architecture of the building, the balcony, the wooden floor, the thin iron railing are felt through being seen. One senses in the work the presence of physical form, a spirit of mass and weight. The architecture of the building merges with the body architecture of the theatre-goers into one tight composition. The massive figures, plainly dressed, serious and deeply engrossed in the action on the stage, point to the popular character of the life of the theatre. This is not an illustration or a painting of a genteel, refined theatre audience. Arms, legs, heads are 'building blocks' in a carefully calculated composition. The painting has force and vitality. The artist has created a work which is a homage to the active spiritual engagement of toiling men and women with the world of ideas and with continuous self-education and growth.

The theatre provided education, entertainment, and food for the soul. The spirit of the Yiddish theatre included the audience, which was an active and interested participant in the drama. This is evident also from the drawing *Jewish Theatre* as well as from the painting *Ghetto Theatre*. Both works are probably based on Bomberg's frequent visits to the Pavilion Theatre at Whitechapel, where *Hamlet* was performed in Yiddish. It was the only place in London where the plays of Gogol, Chekhov, Strindberg and Tolstoy were performed. They could only be understood by Yiddish-speaking people.[17] The theatre audiences probably comprised the very same assertive East European Jews who founded in 1915 the Ben Uri Society for the advancement of art among the Jewish masses and published later the Yiddish magazine *Renaissance*, in which Bomberg published poetry and drawings.[18] We find similar developments as we turn again to New York.

Developments in New York

Stunned by the sounds and sights of the New World, Yiddish poets and writers influenced by modern trends in poetry gathered together in New York City under the name 'Di Junge'. They were determined to celebrate the fresh, the new and the original in their songs, but without particular emphasis on their Jewish origin. In 1912, one of their leaders, the novelist, poet and painter David Ignatoff, who had come to the United States in 1906 from Kiev, established the avant-garde Yiddish journal *Schriften* as a literary organ for their ideas. In this journal original works of art were reproduced, especially in the issues of the early 1920s. Several well-known painters gravitated toward *Schriften*, among them the Yiddish poets and painters Max Weber, Benjamin Kopman, and Jennings Tofel, all of whom published drawings, woodcuts, reproductions of their paintings, poems, stories, illustrations and essays. Also among the painters whose works were reproduced were Abbo Ostrowsky, Abraham Harriton, Boris Anisfeld, Ben Ben, Chaim Gross, Louis Ryback and Abraham Walkowitz. Other contributors to *Schriften* were Boris Aronson, who had emigrated to the United States in 1923 after publishing a book on Jewish graphics in Berlin, and Louis Lozowick, who returned in 1924 from his extensive journey to Paris, Berlin and Moscow, where he had met Ryback, Lissitzky, Chagall and Altman. Lozowick had also participated in modern art exhibitions in Germany while acting as art correspondent for *Broom*.[19]

The editors of *Schriften*, to underline their independence from the classic Yiddish writers Sholom Aleichem, Mendele and Peretz, also published original translations into Yiddish of the Finnish epic *Kalavalla* and passages from the writings of Homer, Sappho, Anacreon, Catullus, Walt Whitman, Tagore, Knut Hamsun, Hugo von Hofmannsthal and Hermann Hesse. They also published Yiddish translations of poems from the Japanese, Chinese and the American Indians—all in addition to the poems and writings of contemporary Yiddish writers such as Sishe Landau, Mani Leib, J. Opatasho, Peretz Hirschbein and Leiwick.

From the very beginning, the chief editor, David Ignatoff, attempted to complement in his journal the secular worldwide concerns of modern Yiddish literature with the most modern tendencies in the plastic arts. He consequently published *Schriften* in an artistically striking form. The group around Ignatoff often gathered in his Brooklyn home for discussions, song and music. His home was covered with paintings from floor to ceiling. Even the lamp shades were painted with scenes from folk tales.[20] Among the frequent visitors were Weber and Walkowitz, who already by 1906 had experienced the impact of the budding modern art movement in Europe. The imprint of the works of Matisse, Rousseau, Cézanne and Picasso and of Negro art was clearly apparent in their paintings.

Some members of the Ignatoff circle were among the founders of The People's Art Guild, which had a strong socialist impulse and emerged from the Friday evening gatherings at the home of John Weichsel. An invitation, printed in Yiddish and English, was mailed to a number of artists:

> In view of the now prevailing art conditions in our Ghetto, a number of Jewish painters and sculptors have decided to meet at the home of John Weichsel, 918 Cauldwell Ave., Bronx, on Saturday, January 9th, 1915 at 8:30 p.m. for the purpose of organizing themselves into an association. Your presence will be welcome if you are in sympathy with the cause.[21]

50. Chaim Gross, *East Side Girl*, 1948. Lignum vitae, 48½ in high (123.1 cm). New York, Forum Gallery.

Despite the two languages of the initial announcement, the Guild never again identified itself as a specifically Jewish organization. Included at one time or other was every member of the Eight, the Ashcan School and most of the artists who showed with Stieglitz at his 291 Gallery. Yet while the Guild depended for its activity on the community and not on Jewish artists per se, it directed its activity strongly toward the Jewish immigrant community of the Lower East Side, printed its constitution in both Yiddish and English, and had its 26th—its most ambitious—exhibition of art in the building of the *Jewish Daily Forward* in 1915, when 89 of its artist members displayed 286 works of art. The Guild was defined as an association of artists and art lovers of diverse art trends whose purpose it was to 'reclaim the people's life for self-expression in art and to make it an hospitable ground for our artists' work'.[22]

In order to bring art to the people, the Guild, in the three years of its existence, between 1915 and 1918, arranged about 60 exhibitions in neighbourhood playhouses, coffee houses, restaurants, community centres, settlement houses, parish houses, public and vocational schools, workers' clubs and various public libraries. The movement was largely directed against commercial art dealers, and was motivated by a strong missionary impulse to restore social significance to art and to carry art to those people who were deprived of the benefits of aesthetic surroundings. The Guild also opened art classes, study groups, sales and work groups in schools, settlement houses and artists' studios. The Guild thereby hoped to diminish the artist's dependence on a small class of wealthy patrons and to widen popular support for the arts.

John Weichsel, who headed the Department of Mechanics and Drafting at the Hebrew Technical Institute in New York City, was a mechanical engineer trained in Germany, at the University of Zurich and eventually at New York University, where he pursued his interest in aesthetics and psychology. He had published several interesting articles in Stieglitz's *Camera Work*. Although he recognized the significant ground work done by Jewish poets, playwrights and novelists in kindling enthusiasm for the life of the mind and the creative imagination of the people, he nevertheless felt that a local sentiment for art and sculpture did not exist:

> Meanwhile these pioneers of a literary Renaissance are suffering from an immersion in an art-bereft atmosphere and they fear for the future of the masses that breathe devitalized art. . . . Meanwhile an art proletariat is fast evolving, of the Jewish artists who are disowned by their kin, and unaccepted by others. Meanwhile East Side perspicacity leads untutored art-despising enterprise to fatal power. Through that a veritable flood of hideousness finds an inlet into markets and homes, into senses and souls. The violation of the art instinct is becoming proverbial. In building, in manufacture, in professions, in publications and crafts cruel abuse of finer feelings is ruthlessly practised, to the stunting of the living as well of the coming generations.[23]

By means of his exhibitions, Weichsel hoped to convince people that the ugliness of the East Side was an urgent problem. He proposed to organize classes for the advancement and regulation of local arts. He proposed an East

Side art centre, to be built 'as a token of reverence to the tradition of the district, a local museum as well as a local art school, galleries, studios and work places so that creativity might flower and find a home'.[24]

While the Guild obviously emanated from Jewish initiative, Weichsel shunned the idea of a parochial or segregated art or even ethnic art, although he was aware that the diverse ethnic backgrounds of the people who lived on the East Side had to be considered. Yet when he devised in 1917 a plan for a Jewish museum in New York City, he did so with rare intelligence as to the requirements and implications of such a plan.[25]

There must have been a felt need for a special gallery among the many Jewish artists and among certain sections of the public who did not feel welcome in the uptown galleries. Raphael Soyer, in his memoirs, speaks about an association of Jewish artists he was invited to join.[26] During the 1920s, a rather obscure club of writers and artists, called 'The Jewish Art Center', came into existence, largely under the influence of David Ignatoff. Among its founders were Abraham Walkowitz, Benjamin Kopmann, and Jennings Tofel, who had all contributed to *Schriften*.

The Art Center was dedicated to the Jew and to the worker. Members also included Yiddish poets, intellectuals, writers and actors. Its purpose was to encourage the creation of a distinct secular Jewish culture within a pluralistic society. The founders felt a strong cultural affinity with one another and had the need to assert and identify themselves as Jews. They foresaw the possibility of creating a Jewish artistic movement as an element of a viable subculture, but seemed to have failed to take into account the dynamic nature of American society and of twentieth-century art.

Jennings Tofel offers us a clue to the thinking of the founders of The Jewish Art Center in the Yiddish journal *Der Hammer*.[27] He felt that in the 1920s, a 'new dignity was bestowed on the concept of nationality'. He saw the pioneering work of Ignatoff as bestowing upon several artists a sense of Jewish cultural affinity and a lessening of the felt need to assimilate. 'An older generation of Jewish artists in America rejected its Jewishness as something disturbing and detrimental,' but there had arisen now a new type of artist, 'who is an independent human being', 'who does not deny his identity', 'who stands on firm ground', 'who does not pretend that he is a Russian, a German or an American, [who] is self-conscious and knows that he is standing on the ground of Jewish culture.' The price of assimilation seemed too high; there was a deep desire to go back to one's people, to the source of one's being.

The Center started out on 11th Street in Manhattan and arranged five exhibitions in the first year of its existence. In 1927, it moved to larger quarters in an apartment on 51 East Tenth Street and continued its programme of alternating large group exhibitions with shows of two or three artists. Among the artists participating in its shows were William Zorach, Benjamin Kopman, Moses Soyer, David Ignatoff, Samuel Halpert, Boris Aronson, Minna Harkavi, William Gropper, Louis Lozowick, Louis Ryback, Maurice Stern, Abraham Harriton, Saul Raskin, Ben Shahn and Abraham Manievich. One three-man show in 1927 is of special interest because of the emergence of Ben Shahn. Showing with him were Louis Ryback and Betty Engel.

Jennings Tofel, writing about the Center in *Der Hammer*, asks, 'Can one see there Jewish Art?' He continues,

> I will be frank and say that I still do not know what the marks of Jewish art are. When it does come into existence I am sure I will know. But I do not want definitely to assert that Jewish motives cannot be a valuable source of Jewish art. They can be such, and I firmly believe that if people and artists will come close to one another, then the art of the Jewish artist will of itself assume a more mature, wholesome and unique expression. The artist will sense the clarity of his source and that will enable him to traverse the whole world of appearances and be his own, an authentic genuine human being. . . . But how does one get close to the people? There is only one road, one has to bring art to the people even if they have always stubbornly refused to cultivate the sense of sight. And in order to learn to understand art, one has to see it. . . . Pictures themselves are the most efficient teachers of art. The love of art guarantees freedom. . . . Through art, through the holiday, through the free spirit—toward freedom.[28]

Indeed during the 1920s the number of Jewish artists increased greatly in New York City. Art provided them an avenue for self-emancipation and freedom. They were now visible in all the currents of modern art and participated in current exhibitions.

All sources we have point to the fact that the emergence of the Jewish artist in the United States happened without any substantial nourishment from the Jewish community. What Moses Rischin writes about the literary and theatrical preference of New York Jews in the first decade of this century, and the poor regard in which the visual arts were held, continues to apply during the 1920s.

> Art was a stranger. Tradition and the context of East European life combined to restrict artistic statement to the conventionalized techniques of printing, engraving, and calligraphy, sanctified by their immediacy to the word. . . . Jacob Epstein's sketches for *The Spirit of the Ghetto* and Abraham Walkowitz's drawings, like George Luks's oil painting *Hester Street*, failed to arouse a Jewish audience. For a people whose aesthetic joys sprang from the Hebrew word, who detected the flavour of Isaiah in ordinary family correspondence, plastic forms seemed irrelevant and unworthy.[29]

When Louis Lozowick returned to the United States in 1924 and reviewed the New York art season in the *Menorah Journal*, he was struck by 'the number and importance of the Jewish artists seen at individual and group exhibitions'.[30] He found them represented in all significant galleries and exhibitions in the city and active in all directions modern art was taking. The list of artists overlaps the one exhibiting at the Jewish Art Center but several other artists are also mentioned: Morris Kantor, Max Weber, Theresa Bernstein, William Meyerowitz, Boris Anisfeld and artists from abroad like Epstein, Lipchitz, Feder and Lissitzky. 'It is perhaps unprofitable but curious to consider', Lozowick wrote,

> how few of the men in this roster devote their interest to the expression of Jewish themes and the Jewish spirit. In one sense this is inevitable, for the more abstract tendencies in modern art offer the artist an almost perfect escape from the specific demands of both his personality and his racial and

social environment. It is likewise inevitable, when we recall that the Jewish community as such makes practically no claim upon the artist, offering him neither encouragement nor requirement. There can be Jewish artists but no Jewish art, unless there be a social need for it. Men like Max Weber who often mould their art out of Jewish material, because their soul is bound up with Jewish memories and interests, will remain exceptional.[31]

Indeed Max Weber in those days seemed to be an exception in his poetic response to Jewish tradition (figs. 157, 159; Plate V). Demands on the artist from the Jewish community arose only in the 1940s when that community reconstituted itself, when its self-consciousness was awakened by the Holocaust and by the struggle for Israel. At the same time there arose the contemporary American synagogue, which functioned also as communal center. The establishment of the Jewish Museum in New York City, followed by the rise of such museums in Chicago and Los Angeles, also marked the appearance of a new kind of Jewish collector.

But in the 1920s, isolationist policies, restrictions on immigration, the revival of the Ku Klux Klan and anti-labour agitation radicalized large sections of the artist community. This process was reinforced with the onset of the Depression in 1929 and with the rise of Fascism and Nazism in Europe.

Perception was now directed to the failings and injustices of society. The world was defined as a class struggle between capital and labour. Socialism was seen as the only viable alternative and art was seen as a weapon in this struggle. Many Jewish artists expressed now not only their immediate personal experience as immigrants but tapped the roots of their social values anchored in the prophetic tradition.

Louis Lozowick presents a significant link with the Jewish artists who had come to Berlin, after the Russian Revolution had disappointed their hopes. He provides us with significant information and interpretation of their views in spite of his obvious disagreement with them.[32] His work was reproduced in *Albatross*, the Yiddish art and literary magazine appearing at that time in Berlin, and he himself exhibited also with the November group and acted as European correspondent for *The Broom*.

In the coloured drawing entitled *Autobiographic* (fig. 52). Lozowick provides a synthetic view of some highlights in his life. The literal dividing line is 1906, before and after his arrival in the United States. In the center of the lower section there is a portrait of himself as a child. One half of the head shows him as a pupil in a religious Hebrew school, and in the other half he is dressed in the uniform of a student of the Kiev Art School, in which his brother enrolled him in 1904. The large sunflower in the lower section was the most common flower in his native village of Ludvinovka and was used for decorative purposes. On the left, there is the one-room peasant shack and his father's windmill, where the youngster spent many hours watching the peasants grind the grain. To the right of the lower part, there is a scuffle between a demonstrator and a soldier, a common sight around 1905 in the Ukraine. In the upper part, the artist appears as a grown man, an artist sketching a machine, repairing telephone wires, and, in the background, the Eiffel Tower and a semi-abstract skyscraper—symbols of his travels abroad. 'To tell the full story woven around these few symbols and

51. Jack Levine, *The Passing Scene*, 1941.
Oil on composition board,
48 × 29¾ in (121.9 × 75.5 cm).
New York, Museum of Modern Art.

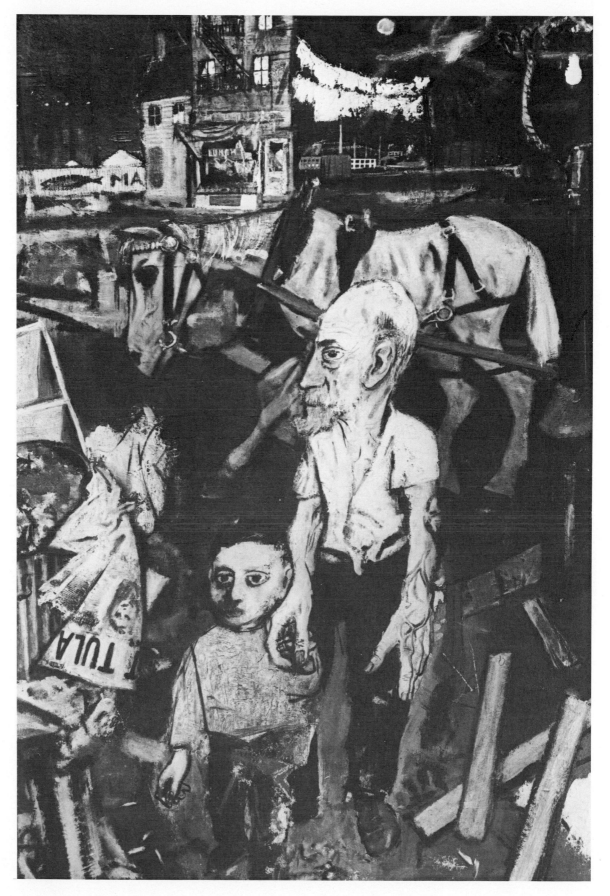

realities would take a good-sized volume,' commented Lozowick on his own drawing. Indeed, his sketch does not reveal enough of the wide-ranging activities and commitments of this unusual man.

Louis Lozowick came to New York in 1906 at the age of 14. Here he had to fend for himself while he studied for three years at the National Academy of Design in New York City and then at Ohio State University. During World War I he volunteered for the U.S. Army The drawing sheds no light on his wide-ranging activities as artist, print-maker, stage designer, theorist, writer, lecturer, editor and correspondent who was deeply involved in the issues which stirred the art community in the 1920s and 1930s.

While he was still at college a conception of art matured in him which brought him remarkably close to the strong anti-aesthetic position of revolutionary Russian artists, and which undoubtedly had its source in his youthful experience in Russia and perhaps was reinforced by Russian literary sources. One single factory seemed to him a greater force in the establishment of social harmony than all stories, novels and dramas. It seemed to him then that science was more nourishing to the imagination than novels. Art was useless and bound to perish. Art had performed important useful functions in earlier times and among primitive people. But, in the modern era, this young Marxist argued, reason proves to be more powerful and efficient and replaces emotion as a leading force. Art now lives by inertia only, a superfluous remnant and luxury which will be eliminated by science and by life itself.[33] Good minds are capable of great errors.

When he came to Berlin in 1922 Lozowick felt immediately attracted not only to the work of El Lissitzky but also to the works of Antoine Pevsner, Naum Gabo (figs. 53, 54), Moholy Nagy and Theo Van Doesburg, whose art can also appear as dominated by science and reason rather than by emotion. But while for many of the Russian artists Constructivist geometry and planning pointed to technical goals that still had to be realized, for Lozowick these goals were not merely visions of the future. In his American experience he had seen and experienced at close quarters the concrete images of a new industrial civilization. Lozowick had travelled across the entire United States before he went abroad, and during his student days he had supported himself by working in industrial plants where he had gained first-hand contact with American technology, tools and work processes. The socialist orientation he developed told him that a new social order could be erected only on a fully developed industry and upon a proper material foundation. The promises inherent in industry—the liberation from want and the building of a just social order—constitute the moral aspects of his work. He was fascinated by American technology and its implications, and created a series of ornamental drawings based on the machine which were designed to replace the traditional ornaments based on plant motifs. He painted and made prints of rising skyscrapers, steel bridges, grain elevators, shipyards, steel mills, copper mines and lumber yards. He was fascinated with the flawless performance of cranes, pneumatic drills, blast furnaces and concrete mixers, by the precise adjustment of structure to function, and by 'the spirit of objectivity excluding all emotional aberration', embodied in these machines.

Indeed his ambiance was not the East Side. Not for him were its peddlers and

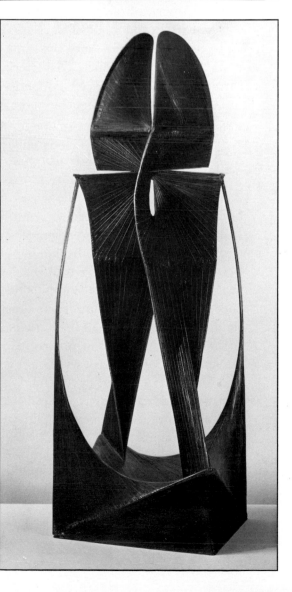

52. (ABOVE) Louis Lozowick,
Autobiographic, 1967.
Coloured ink drawing, 24 × 12 in
(61 × 30.5 cm). Collection of
Mrs Adele Lozowick, Milburn,
New Jersey.

53. (TOP RIGHT) Naum Gabo,
Column, 1923.
Plastic, wood, metal,
41½ × 29 × 29 in
(104 × 73 × 73 cm).
New York, Solomon R.
Guggenheim Museum.

54. (BOTTOM RIGHT) Antoine
Pevsner, *Twinned Column*, 1947.
Bronze, 40½ × 14 × 14 in
(102.8 × 35.5 × 35.5 cm).
New York, Solomon R.
Guggenheim Museum.

pushcarts, its noises and dirt, its pushing and shoving, its accents on emotion and human idiosyncrasies. In the work he exhibited in 1927 at the Machine Age exhibition, in New York City,[34] he portrayed American industry idealized, abstracted from the problems of private ownership and without any reference to its social implications. American industry appears as a gigantic system, flawless, smooth and predictable, as his own scientific Marxist theories seemed to him. In it he saw a precise adjustment of structure to function. 'The dominant trend in America today,' he wrote, 'beneath all the apparent chaos and confusion, is toward order and organization which find their outward signs and symbols in the rigid geometry of the American city.'[35] Nevertheless, while in his early work he abstracted American industry from its social implications for aesthetic reasons and dealt with its cubic and cylindrical shapes only, by the end of the 1920s his deep social commitment becomes visible in the introduction into his compositions of the worker as a heroic figure (figs. 55, 56).

Lozowick's concern for an equitable social order was shared by other artists who grew out of a similar cultural environment and who identified themselves with the oppressed. William Gropper, Ben Shahn, Mitchell Siporin, Jack Levine, the brothers Raphael, Moses and Isaac Soyer, Mark Rothko, Seymour Lipton, Mervin Jules, William Zorach, Leonard Baskin, George Segal and others were all brought to America as children by their immigrant parents or born in America from immigrant parents.

Their styles and mode of work are different, their subject-matter is different, and yet they seem to share the same moral cosmos, partaking in a profound moral earnestness which characterizes the Jewish tradition. There shines through their work a deep sympathy for the disadvantaged and exploited, a quest for meaning, an appeal to moral conscience and an active commitment to social justice.

All of them refuse to be mere entertainers or engage in art for art's sake. No image is satisfying unless it also condenses knowledge and expands awareness. To be truly relevant art must provoke thought about social issues, stimulate feeling rather than delight the senses only. They frame universal issues in terms of a morally intense heritage, and variously describe themselves as social realists, moral realists, and personal realists. By responding to the social turmoil of the 1920s and 1930s, by joining government-sponsored art projects, they became linked with the central concerns of a large segment of American life at that time and merged into the mainstream of American art. The Depression speeded their Americanization. They became an active, vocal force in the political aspects of art in the various art organizations. In time some of them became leading figures in American art of the twentieth century.

Yet with the easing of the Depression, the pact between Stalin and Hitler, and the emergence after World War II of power bloc politics, it became apparent that art and artists were being exploited, that ideologies, ideas and the life of the mind were being politicized. In response the artists planted their socialist convictions on the ancient ground of their religious heritage or withdrew in their art to a personal sphere of abstract art, into a highly personal, inward-looking realm.

When after World War II the scale of the Holocaust became apparent, when

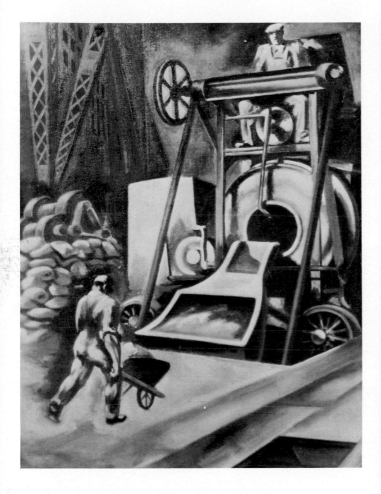

55. (ABOVE) Louis Lozowick, *The Concrete Mixer*, 1939.
Oil on canvas, 24 × 18 in (60.9 × 45.7 cm).
Collection of Mrs Adele Lozowick, Milburn, New Jersey.

56. (RIGHT) Louis Lozowick, *Minneapolis*, 1926–7.
Oil on canvas, 30 × 22¼ in (76 × 56.5 cm). Washington D.C.,
Hirshhorn Museum and Sculpture Garden, Smithsonian Institute.

the survivors streamed across Europe southward and crowded the boats moving toward the blocked shores of the promised land, the mind and perception of many of the artists turned toward them and toward the battle to survive and build a home. Each one of them responded in his own way, compelled by events that touched the existence of the Jewish community and the core of his own identity.

Ben Shahn was not interested in the religious experience as such, nor in devotional prayer, but in the poetical heritage and the ethical tenets of the Hebrew tradition. He found therein, as well as in the poetry and the teachings of other great religions, the secure ground for his strong ethical and social commitments. In the teaching of Hillel, who argued for self-reliance paired with social responsibility, in the Passover Haggadah, in Ecclesiastes and the Psalms and the prophets he found a basis for the convictions he acted on and painted for all his life. From the series on the Dreyfus affair in 1930 through the Passion of Sacco and Vanzetti in 1931, the Tom Mooney affair in 1932, his work for the

Works Progress Administration and the Farm Security Administration in 1935 and for the Congress of Industrial Organizations in 1943, we find him supporting the struggle for social equality. As the struggle became politicized in the late 1940s, he retreated and planted his own convictions on religious ground.

Ram's Horn and Menorah, East Side Soap Box, and *Identity* (figs. 2, 58) point to the social and Jewish sources which concerned Ben Shahn. *Ram's Horn and Menorah* (Plate VI) enables us to see the artist's attempts to combine symbols of the Hebraic tradition and contemporary ideas concerning the equality of man and man's hope for redemption. In this sensitive and forceful statement Shahn has synthesized images born from the struggle of the working class with the iconography of religious motifs, pointing to their common ground in the words of the prophet (Malachi 2:10): 'Have we not one father? Has not one God created us? Why do we deal treacherously every man against his brother to profane the covenant of our fathers?' The quotation in Hebrew calligraphy, which Shahn knew well and which he used in many other works, runs across the entire length of the painting. These lines appealed to an artist who had executed murals for the WPA and posters for the CIO. He painted the

57. Ben Shahn, *New York*, 1947. Oil on canvas, 36 × 48 in (91 × 121 cm). Collection of David L. Shapiro, Cambridge, Massachusetts.

58. (OPPOSITE) Ben Shahn, *East Side Soap Box*, 1936. Gouache, $17\frac{1}{2} \times 11\frac{1}{4}$ in (44.4 × 28.3 cm). Private Collection.

די נאטור האט יעדען
געגעבן אן אפעטיט
אבער אנזערע באסעס
האבען צוגעגאנועט די
שליסעל פין אונז

work in preparation for a mosaic mural on the vestibule of Temple Oheb Shalom in Nashville. Certain imagery in the painting had appeared in Ben Shahn's earlier work. Dominating the paintings is the blue hand which emerges from the red flame and symbolizes the presence of God. The hand refers to God's creative power and intervention in the affairs of man. The figure on the right sounding the Shofar, the ram's horn, is wrapped in what seems to be the traditional prayer shawl. The pale figure is spiritualized by the severe distortions of his features. He has a haunting ghost-like quality due to the ash grey overtones of his skin, and the enormous square-pupiled eyes which stare at the spectator. The tension lines that surround the eyes are echoed in the many lines of the prayer shawl that envelops his head, and in the detached, tense ceremonial position of the fingers which barely grasp the Shofar.

The intricate black and white pattern within the Shofar contrasts with the exaggerated extension of its own silhouette, drawing the viewer across the canvas toward the Menorah. The tremendous Menorah is in full bloom and richly adorned with gold. It rises from a base which is at once both a metallic stand and an earthen hill. The men beneath the Shofar are differentiated in race, and are contrasted in their mundane individuality with the otherworldly character of the figure that blows the Shofar. They are patiently waiting for the blast of the ram's horn. Waiting, as one of the conditions of human existence, is a theme which fascinated Shahn, and one that has consciously been accepted by generations of Jews who have elaborated it into a cultural force in their history. The powerful hand which emerges from the red flames of the Shekhinah pleads, demands, even threatens. It is at once the hand of compassion that 'uplifts those who fall', and a warning against those who deal treacherously with their brothers.

The image of a disembodied hand had precedents in ancient Jewish art. It appears in the scenes of Abraham's sacrifice in the ancient synagogues of Dura Europos and Beth Alpha. Ben Shahn's hand, however, is a worker's hand taken from the vocabulary of twentieth-century social realism. We have already noted that Shahn, especially in his later periods, grounded his socialist ideas in myth and religious thought. His own art he called personal realism. He constantly enriched it through a combination of actuality and allegory. *Ram's Horn and Menorah* alludes to the racial conflicts which embroiled the Southern States in the 1950s; the words of the Hebrew prophet and the traditional attitudes of Judaism are enlisted in the battle for equality.

The work of print-maker and sculptor Leonard Baskin also has its roots in the moral concern of Hebraic traditions. Baskin refers to himself as a moral realist, and like many artists before him has adopted the print as a medium with which to reach as wide an audience as possible. In the woodcut *Four Mystics* he alludes with his bold Hebrew calligraphy to the Talmudic passage describing an early second-century encounter between ancient Judaism and the mystical, syncretic tendencies of the Greco-Roman world. In the story the Rabbis Ben Azzai, Ben Zoma, Elisha Ben Avuyah and Akiba entered the Pardess, the garden of esoteric knowledge. Ben Azzai cast a look and died, Ben Zoma lost his mind, and Elisha Ben Avuyah, who was also called Acher (the different one), left the fold. Only Rabbi Akiba came out of the garden with his faith intact (fig. 59).[36]

59. Leonard Baskin, *The Four Mystics*, 1952. Woodcut, 19½ × 12 in (69.2 × 30.5 cm). New York, Galerie Sumers.

The trials of the Rabbis who ventured into the garden are shown by the birds and beasts who prey on them, in effect flaying them, revealing beneath the skin a complex web of nerves, arteries and sinews whose tangle echoes the state of confusion, conflict and bewilderment of the Rabbis attacked by doubts and birds of prey. Only the figure left of the Hebrew inscription is left unscathed. It is of special interest that he is clean-shaven and his powerful hands are visible, and that he resembles the artist. No doubt the artist symbolizes his own situation by identifying himself with those who have left the fold.

Baskin, who is especially intellectual and articulate among contemporary artists, is a Rabbi's son who between the ages of seven and fourteen attended an orthodox Yeshivah, which marked him with its rigorous scholastic discipline and sharp logic. It instilled in him an intense love of books in general and a profound knowledge of Jewish tradition in particular, and perhaps above all a sense of otherness.

> The pride of books was early installed in me. And thus I was forever soured on the ubiquitous American good-time Charlie. The cracked world around me impinged at every open sluice, and my very air is charged with waves and echoes and rays from a society and civilization in which I feel like a mixture of outlaw, leper and pariah.[37]

Resolving at the age of fourteen to become a sculptor, he in effect discontinued his course of study, broke the Second Commandment and rebelled against the

60. Larry Rivers, *Bar Mitzvah Photograph Portrait*, 1961. Oil on canvas, 72 × 60 in (182.8 × 152.4 cm). Private collection. (Photo Eric Pollitzer.)

faith of his father. Like the Four Mystics, Baskin left the field of traditional Jewish studies and immersed himself in William Blake, John Donne, Homer, Shakespeare, and the wide field of secular culture. He came out enriched, a different person, of wider concerns and perspectives, yet detached from his personal tradition. This road many Jews of his generation have travelled. For Baskin the Talmudic story has quite a different meaning from the traditional one, for it seems to me that he identifies with 'the different', the outcast, Rabbi Elisha Ben Avuyah. Nevertheless, Baskin draws many of his themes from the Bible.[38]

The generation gap and the rejection of the tradition and values of one's parents are clearly revealed in Larry Rivers's *Bar Mitzvah Photograph Portrait* (fig. 60). The painting is a parody on the Bar Mitzvah ceremony as widely practised in America. It is often a diluted ritual, social rather than religious, imposed by a tradition which has lost meaning, and conspicuous for waste and pretence. Negation, contempt and self-mockery are expressed in the boldly stencilled 'rejected' superimposed on the rapid pencil marks, the smears and murky colour and overall whimsiness of the group portrait. The painting is an ironic variation of Abstract Expressionism in its combination of spontaneous technique with the banal commercial elements of photography and stencilling.

Joe Lasker's *Scissor Grinder* (fig. 61) treats the same conflict in a manner which invites interpretation from a psychoanalytic point of view since it is charged with images which symbolize the threat of castration. The large Yiddish inscription (Scissor Grinder) threatens the child as much as the scissors that are pointed at him. The repressive authority implicit in his Jewish background is the dominant motif. Even the sign of the clasped hands, symbol of the International Ladies' Garment Workers' Union, calling for unity and solidarity among workers, which first appears to contradict ironically the parting of the ways of young and old, in fact underlines it by the impossible way in which the hands are clasped. In another Lasker painting, *Memo* (fig. 62), the issue is still clearer. There is a fragment of a portrait of a Greek philosopher on the right against an American flag symbolizing aspects of an alien Western culture; an arm bound with phylacteries on the left symbolizes the confining tradition of the Jewish world to which the child submits. Again the threatening scissors are pointed in the direction of the child, who, standing near the large Menorah, seems to experience an uneasy awareness of conflicting signals. Lines from a poem by Karl Shapiro come to mind:

61. Joe Lasker,
Scissor Grinder, 1954.
Oil on board, 26 × 38 in
(66 × 96.5 cm). Collection of
Charles H. Renthal, New York.

Are you looking for us? We are here.
Have you been gathering flowers, Elohim?
We are Your flowers, we have always been.
When will You leave us alone?
We are in America.
We have been here three hundred years.
And what new altar will you deck us with?

. . . Immigrant God, You follow me;
You go with me, You are a distant tree;
You are the beast that lows in my heart gates;
You are the dog that follows at my heel;
You are the table on which I lean;
You are the plate from which I eat. . . .[39]

62. Joe Lasker, *Memo*, 1954.
Oil on masonite, 20 × 33¾ in
(50.8 × 85.7 cm).
New York, Kraushaar Galleries.

Indeed, the ancient Hebrew God follows them wherever they go. The values and sense of reality of George Segal were not shaped by a strict adherence to Jewish tradition or by the normal tension between the immigrant parents and the American-born son. They were shaped in the home culture of working people whose socialism and humanism were largely influenced by Jewish religious tradition and could be as demanding as that tradition. It is a socialism not derived from intellectual abstractions and world-encompassing political programmes, but from a pragmatic attitude towards the issues which concern them in their immediate situation, and from a sense of nobility which they attribute to work and toil.[40] These values did not permit Segal to escape into the pure self-referential realm of art, which by the late 1950s, when Segal ended his formal art studies, already dominated the art departments of universities and the art world. His work is an affirmation of the daily effort of common people to maintain themselves and the world in which they live and act. The bus driver, the passengers, the gas station attendants, farm workers, men on scaffolds, or women combing their hair or drinking coffee, people going about their everyday tasks; these are the subjects of his sculpture.

63. (OPPOSITE LEFT) George Segal, *Abraham and Isaac*, 1978. In Memory of May 4th, 1970. Plaster, wood, rope and metal, 84 × 120 × 50 in (212 × 305 × 127 cm). Princeton University Art Gallery.

64. Morris Kantor, *Farewell to Union Square*, 1931. Oil on canvas, 36 × 27 in (91.4 × 68.6 cm). The Newark Museum, New Jersey.

Like other postwar artists, Segal reacted to the abstract academy of his own time and, like them, he searched his surroundings and probed the thin line where art and reality meet. He rebelled against the mystification and unintelligibility which isolated art from the daily concerns of life and which made it the prerogative of the affluent. There is a sense of seriousness about his work and his preoccupation with man which sets him apart from other Pop-artists of his generation. He developed an art which concerned itself with the common man and thereby echoed in the affluent 'sixties and 'seventies the concern of the Social Realists of the 'thirties. The harsh problems of the decade of economic crises seemed remote in the 1960s and 1970s, pushed into the background and muted like the calcified figures which Segal sculpts. However, in contrast to Social Realist art, Segal's models are intimately known to him.

Not unlike Ben Shahn and the generation of artists who matured in the 1930s, Segal, who came to the fore as a significant force in the 1960s, expresses in *Abraham and Isaac* (fig. 63) his social convictions in the language of Jewish religious tradition. The sculpture, which was commissioned in 1978 by Kent

State University, echoes the tradition of Social Realism. Primarily a vertical composition, it is in commemoration of the events at Kent State University in May 1970 in which four students were cut down by State troopers. Differing from the Tel Aviv Akedah which Segal made in 1973 (fig. 154), Isaac is begging for mercy and the father is not a Patriarch but in a position of power. The artist interpreted the events as a violent conflict between generations; the son tall, college age, old enough to rebel, bound and kneeling before his father whose intentions seem clear. As in the Tel Aviv version, Segal brings the Biblical story down to everyday reality, but here he turns it into a social, psychological and political act.[41]

In Jack Levine's *The Passing Scene* (fig. 51), one senses that it might not be just an ordinary street that Levine paints, but that the father and son move tentatively across a dangerous no-man's land. Above all the painting expresses the insecurity of the immigrant in a new and untried environment, communicated through touch, glance and step to the son. The overworked, emaciated white horse, which often appears in the canvases of Levine, is a metaphor for the fate of man. It is Don Quixote's Rosenante, or the white Klatcke of Mendele's story who has wandered into the twentieth-century slums of Boston. The father's head is closely juxtaposed to that of the horse and they are further identified by similarities of expression and bearing.

Jack Levine's *Tombstone Cutter* (fig. 65) was painted under the impact of the

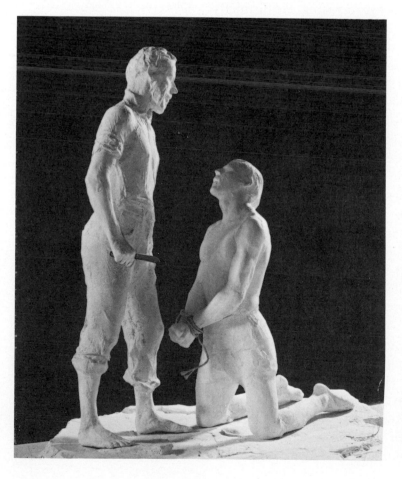

Holocaust in Europe. The old man assumes the character of the stone as if the chisel had cut deep furrows into his own face and body and covered them with marble dust. The artisan is at rest. There is a deep identity between him and his work, between the anatomy of his flayed body and the intricate carving of the tombstone, with its Star of David, lion, palm tree and bits of Hebrew calligraphy. The artisan has migrated with his craft and with the ancient symbols of his Eastern European community to New York's Lower East Side. His fragile body, the tombstone and the hanging lamp evoke a contemplative mood, the sense of passing time and thoughts about both loss and continuity.

In the painting *Planning Solomon's Temple* (fig. 66), the artist went back far into his Jewish heritage. In actuality the painting relates to the death of the artist's father, who was called by his friends Reb Shlomoh Hachacham (Rabbi Solomon the Wise). It is also an unconscious reaction to the collapse of the WorksProgress Administration, which had at one time employed the artist, helped him through the Depression and provided him with a sense of community. When his father died in 1939 and family and friends gathered at the Boston cemetery, Levine suddenly saw his father, who had been in life a poor shoemaker, as head of the clan and king of all Israel, now robed royally in a white prayer shawl, before being lowered into the ground. In the painting, one of a series dealing with his father, King Solomon, crowned and in royal attire, unrolls the ground plan of the Temple, while King Hiram stands near him holding a trowel, compass and angle iron tucked under his arm. King Hiram with his workmanlike dress looks more like a builder than a King. He distinctly resembles the painter Levine. By a subtle process of transformation, displacement and condensation the artist's wish is fulfilled in the painting: the painter Levine, out of work, after the collapse of the WorksProgress Administration, isolated and mourning the death of his father, sees him now as the king, risen from death, and preparing a large programme for reconstruction, and himself employed again as painter, enjoying the prestige of the king's patronage.

Planning Solomon's Temple belongs to a series of small paintings of kings from the Bible and scholars of Jewish history which occupied the artist over many years: Saul, David, Asa, the Scribe, Hillel and Maimonides. These small paintings, echoing in their colours and distortions El Greco and Soutine, are unusually intimate for the artist. Generally the artist's work is sardonically witty, and satirical about contemporary heroes and institutions. These small paintings do not deride or mock their subject but express a strong personal connection with them. They are intimate and self-accepting, as if the artist had retreated into a ground immune from the issues of the day on which much of his work is based.

Raphael Soyer's *Artist's Parents* (fig. 67) gives us some clues about the artist's father. He was a teacher of Hebrew literature and history in Russia, a *maskil* ('enlightened one') rooted in the Hebrew tradition and open to ideas of enlightenment and liberalism. He wrote tales for children and short stories and novelettes for adults in the style of Chekhov. A lover of art and music, he taught his sons to draw while still in Russia, where he decorated the cold and dreary walls of his home with postcard reproductions of Russian art in a fan-shaped design and spoke to his sons about Raphael, Rembrandt, and Michelangelo. His

65. (TOP LEFT) Jack Levine, *Tombstone Cutter*, 1947. Oil on canvas, 30 × 36 in (76.2 × 90 cm). Collection of Mr and Mrs Jacob Schulman, Gloversville, New York.

66. (TOP RIGHT) Jack Levine, *Planning Solomon's Temple*, 1940. Oil on masonite, 10 × 8 in (25.2 × 20.2 cm). Jerusalem, Israel Museum, gift of Mrs Rebecca Schulman.

67. (BOTTOM) Raphael Soyer, *Artist's Parents*, 1932. Oil on canvas, 28 × 30 in (71.1 × 76.2 cm). Collection of the artist, New York.

library included books by Tolstoy, Turgenev, Twain, and Dickens, which the children read in Russian. In the painting, the father has a powerfully developed head and a face lined with fine, sharp features and charged with intellectual energy. The man seems somewhat disoriented and worried; he supports his head with his hand. His thoughts are far away. In contrast, his mother places both hands on the table; she is centred on the here and now. The composition is reminiscent of *The Absinthe Drinkers* by Edgar Degas, an artist whom Soyer greatly admired. *Dancing Lesson* (fig. 69) is set in the typical middle-class Bronx apartment into which the family moved following their arrival from Russia. Raphael Soyer describes the picture:

> It was a 20 × 40 canvas, which I called the *Dancing Lesson*, depicting our sister Debbie teaching Moses to dance to the harmonica music of our youngest brother Israel, who was pictured sitting on the sofa with Avrohom and our grandmother. Near them, on a heavy rocker, sat Beyla with a Yiddish newspaper in her lap. On the floor was a flower-bordered rug. The blue wall was embellished by an enlarged framed photograph, popular in those days, of our grandparents. Beyla's rubber plant was in the corner.[42]

In their social awareness and their democratic impulses, Soyer's themes

68. Raphael Soyer,
The Bridge, 1926–7.
Oil on canvas, 22 × 30 in
(55.5 × 76 cm).
Collection of the artist.

70. Moses Soyer, *Old Man in Skull Cap*, after 1913. Oil on canvas, $20\frac{3}{4} \times 21\frac{1}{2}$ in (75.5 × 54.6 cm). New York, Jewish Museum, gift of Mr Henry Margoshes.

69. Raphael Soyer, *Dancing Lesson*, 1926. Oil on canvas, 24 × 20 in (60.9 × 50.8 cm). Collection of Mr and Mrs Chaim Gross, New York.

continue the tradition of the Ashcan School. The influence of John Sloan is particularly evident in the sympathetic portrayal of people in his cityscapes. *The Bridge* (fig. 68) is remarkable for its bold composition and its holiday atmosphere. People are at leisure, lounging on benches, strolling, playing, scattered randomly on the roadway of the bridge leading away from the squalor of the city up to the iron tower of the bridge, looming in the distance like a gateway to heaven. In its spaciousness and its festive mood the painting contrasts sharply with the drab work-day atmosphere of *East Side Street*, where dilapidated buildings line the narrow street as far as the eye can see.

Soyer's canvases are peopled with transients, derelicts, laundresses, dancers, poets, dressmakers and office girls. He is committed to an art which communicates. His representational art is marked by a search for individuality in the city dweller. In him he finds a pervasive inwardness and melancholy.

His painter brothers share similar artistic commitments. Isaac Soyer's sympathies are especially with the unemployed. Moses Soyer, who also wrote art criticism for the New York *Jewish Morning Journal*, painted portraits like *Lover of Books* and *Old Man in Scull Cap* (fig. 70), among other subjects. These works are distinguished by their quiet dignity.

Scholars, books, discussions were common in Jewish life. This is a tradition which has rarely been interrupted although the subjects of scholarship and debate may have changed. Jennings Tofel shows in *Family Reunion* a scholar quietly reading at his table, in the very same room in which his whole family lives (fig. 71). Joseph Herman, who works in London, has two young men engaged in a heated debate in which the swaying lamp, the furniture and other members of the family seem to participate (fig. 72).

The characteristic Jewish preoccupation with the book takes shape in other ways very remote from the straightforward narratives of Jewish life we have just been discussing. Seymour Lipton's sculptures of scrolls, codices and manuscripts, which superficially seem unsuited to be sculptural objects, also derive from that deep attachment to and veneration of the book and written word in the Jewish home (fig. 75). After explaining his concern with formal matters like his need 'to find an image of three-dimensional planal tensions', Lipton states,

71. Jennings Tofel, *Family Reunion*, 1928. Oil on canvas, $18\frac{1}{8} \times 21\frac{3}{4}$ in (40.2×55.2 cm). Washington D.C., Hirshhorn Museum and Sculpture Garden, Smithsonian Institute.

72. Joseph Herman,
The Discussion, 1940–1. Tempera
on board, 25 × 27 in
(63.5 × 68.5 cm). Collection of
the artist, London.

my concern with leaf-like forms in nature, unfolding sheets of growth and
life, a feeling for broad cosmic and historic sweeps as metaphors in terms of
books, pages, etc., I believe influenced me here. Also such things as the
Dead Sea scrolls, all had a cumulative effect in bringing out a broad
preoccupation with planal parallel forms in spatial tensions. But these
tensions occur to me always as moods of suggestions about the forces of
nature, man, and the world.[43]

The sculpture spreads like a slightly opened book. It is not an architectural
sculpture or space-divider. The large flat areas contrast sharply with irregular
plant-like forms which seem to bind the slightly open pages of the manuscript.

In the sculpture of Seymour Lipton form and content stand in reciprocal
relation to each other. His sculptures are poems constructed in sheet metal by
cutting, welding, soldering and brazing. The result is rich textural surfaces and
subtle chromatic variations. While his art is abstract, it strongly suggests
biological and mechanical forces, which function in his composition as metaphors for states of feeling, ideas, and also as allusions to historical events. Like
other artists, he had the opportunity to work on synagogue commissions
without compromising his position. Menorah sculptures, an eternal light sculpture for the ark at Temple Israel in Tulsa, Oklahoma, and Menorah sculptures
for the interior and exterior for Temple Beth El in Gary, Indiana, permit him to
merge his botanical themes with ancient Hebrew motifs.

The fertile branch on top of the ark at Temple Israel is a horizontal sculpture
which recalls the tenacious struggle of plant life. Intertwining long-drawn-out

forms spread in both directions toward the extreme points of the ark. Their alternating attenuation and swelling, twist and tension, are expressed in the continuous metamorphosis of a branch which becomes a leaf, a leaf which becomes a swelling fruit, a fruit which in turn brings forth the branch again.

Lipton's *Eternal Light* is a sculptural metaphor for shelter (fig. 73). Branches or wings spread and fold to form a protective enclosure for the flame. The image evokes the words of the Psalmist: 'Hide me in the shadow of Thy wings' (Psalms 17:8).

In his various Menorah sculptures Lipton reverted to the myth of the Tree of Life, whence the Menorah originated (fig. 74). In all his Menorah sculptures he splits the trunk of the 'tree' and explores several formal and symbolic possibilities. In Temple Beth El in Gary, the Menorah is robust and massive. A tree split and damaged by age is still capable of asserting itself and growing, whereas other Menorahs express energy bursting which cannot any more be contained, like the coming of spring. Branches unfold in a rhythmic ringing movement, on both sides of the stem.

73. Seymour Lipton, *Eternal Light*, 1953. Nickel-silver and steel, 38 × 40 in (96 × 101 cm). Temple Israel, Tulsa, Oklahoma.

After World War II, the American synagogue suddenly appeared on the scene as a significant patron of the arts. The rise of a second and third generation of American Jews, many of whom had moved to the suburbs, necessitated new means of preserving collective intimacy against the threat of assimilation. The Holocaust and the continuing struggle for Israel brought with them a heightened Jewish consciousness which demanded a modernization of Jewish education to meet the requirements of Jewish life. The synagogue also became a community centre to which Jews gravitated for the purpose of identification with their group, even if their religious beliefs had been weakened. In order to respond to new demands coming from its members and in order to evoke the spirit of the sacred, the synagogue had to call on the architect and the artist. Frank Lloyd Wright, Erich Mendelsohn, Pietro Belluschi, Walter Gropius, Louis Kahn, Philip Johnson, Fritz Nathan, Percival Goodman, Minoru Yamasaki and many other architects planned the building of synagogues in the postwar era. Among the architects it was especially Percival Goodman who in his attempt to underline the religious and cultural character of the synagogue called in the modern artist and thereby put into motion a trend which brought paintings, sculpture, mosaic, stained glass windows and weaving into the synagogue, on a scale hitherto unheard of. Some of the foremost artists were actively engaged in this work, among them Adolph Gottlieb, Seymour Lipton, Boris Aronson, Ben Shahn, Mitchell Siporin, Ibram Lassaw, Robert Motherwell, Luise Kaish, Anni Albers, Gyorgy Kepes, Ludwig Wolpert, Bernard Rosenthal, Milton Horn, George Aarons, Ilyah Shor and many others.[44]

The work of these modern artists gave new form to traditional Biblical motifs, imaginatively introduced new themes into the synagogue, and created a sympathetic climate for the expression of Jewish motifs.

The large publication of etchings of the Bible by Marc Chagall, the Saul and David lithographs by Oscar Kokoschka, and the Haggadas of Ben Shahn and Leonard Baskin,[45] while themselves significant artistic events, point to an ever-growing interest in Jewish circles in an art linked to their own tradition.

74. (LEFT) Seymour Lipton,
Menorah, 1953.
Nickel-silver and steel,
54 in high (136 cm).
Temple Israel, Tulsa, Oklahoma.

75. (RIGHT) Seymour Lipton,
Manuscript, 1961.
Brazed bronze on monel metal,
$63\frac{3}{8} \times 84\frac{1}{8} \times 37\frac{1}{8}$ in
($161 \times 213.8 \times 94.4$ cm).
New York, Museum of Modern
Art.

The expression of Jewish experience in twentieth-century art comes mainly from artists who were immigrants or children of immigrants, who struck roots in their new environment and brought with them the vivid memories and values of a tradition which perceived the world in an intensely moral way. In spite of the great changes which this tradition underwent in the West, its values persisted and subtly imbued the artists' perception with a critical attitude which evaluates sense data according to their moral significance. Whether their art represents a dialogue between the artist and the world or expresses a social commitment, they found, in the West, a tradition of art concerned with social values with which they could easily interact. Drawn into the major art trends, many of them have remained conscious of their own cultural sources, which seep through and are refracted in their work, in their choice of subject-matter, their attitude toward art and their personal loyalties.

A unique feature of this cultural tradition is that the artist conceives the Biblical source as metaphor for contemporary events; he is often compelled to take certain positions, he senses subtle tensions within his surroundings, which he feels part of, and yet seeks to maintain a historical consciousness that is essentially one of defiance and intransigence.

CHAPTER THREE

Paris

From the second decade of the twentieth century to the time of the conquest of France by Germany in 1940, Paris became the home of a great number of Jewish artists, painters and sculptors, who came mainly from Eastern Europe and spent the best years of their creative lives there. Among the artists who arrived early in this period were Marc Chagall, Jiri Kars, Jules Pascin, Moshe Kiesling, Michael Kikoïne, Pinkus Kremegne, Jacques Lipchitz, Leopold Gottlieb, Mané-Katz, Amedeo Modigliani, Hanna Orlof, and Chaim Soutine. In the 1920s Max Band, Sigmund Menkes, Abraham Mintchine, Reuven Rubin and others went to Paris. Most of these artists were in their early 20s, all of them were unmarried, and none had independent means.

Those who arrived from the East, and they were the great majority, felt the transition to be an especially sharp one. Writers speak about the shock of Paris. There was the experience of being free, of being able to sit on a bench without the policeman chasing you away.[1] There was the sheer physical beauty of the city and the spirit of friendship, acceptance and equality in the artistic community. There were the museums which represented the art of all ages, and there was the vigour of contemporary French painting. When the Jewish painters arrived, the Fauvist wave was receding and Cubism was re-evaluating the foundations on which Western painting had based itself since Giotto. In this atmosphere those who had studied in the East quickly discarded what they had been taught and re-examined their ideas about art in the light of the new aesthetic emerging in the studios and in free discussions which artists engaged in wherever they met.

It has been noted by George Waldemar that the stereotyped view of the Jewish artist, who comes from a small, backward but sympathetic village or ghetto to Paris to make his mark there, has to be discarded. While some of the artists came from the most squalid, ignorant and unloving circumstances, others came from large modern cities, from well-to-do and assimilated families. But the intensity of artistic activity in Paris and the conditions of modern art, the stress on originality, individuality and invention made it possible for each artist to find his own road to fulfilment. Whatever his perception, whatever his temperament, whether mystical or rational, expressionist or romantic, he could expect a sympathetic hearing within the artistic community; and the value of his activity would be enhanced by the activities of others.[2]

Doubtless, the fact that there was no classical tradition behind them, that they were strangers and wanderers made it easier for them to join the movement of modern art and commit themselves to various avant-garde positions. Jewish artists, because of their common language and common background, tended to meet frequently. Some historians speak about an enclave of Jewish artists, others about a Jewish School of Paris. The gathering of a relatively large

76. Amedeo Modigliani, *Portrait of Jacques Lipchitz and his Wife*, 1916–17.
Oil on canvas, 31½ × 21 in (80 × 53 cm). Chicago, The Art Institute of Chicago, Helen Birch Bartlett Memorial Collection.

number of Jewish artists in Paris is a fact of twentieth-century art and of Jewish social and cultural history.

Chagall, who came to Paris in 1910, has been identified largely by the way in which he combined Jewish Hassidic and folkloristic motifs with elements of twentieth-century French painting. We have already touched on his work in Russia after his return there in 1914. In retrospect, it was not Chagall, but rather Soutine who became the leading figure among the Jewish artists in Paris. The distinctness of Soutine's vision, his absolute modernity, the echo he evoked

77. Leopold Gottlieb,
Plasterers, 1928.
Oil on cardboard, $38\frac{5}{8} \times 27\frac{1}{4}$ in
(98×69 cm).
Ein Harod Art Museum, Israel.

in others, and the very wide influence he exerted on the modern art movement made him a formidable figure.

Soutine seems to have had a greater impact than any other artist on the Jewish painters of his generation. His personality and style are reflected in the thinking, the feeling and mode of living of less well-known painters like Michael Kikoïne, Pinkus Kremegne, Jacques Chapiro, David Seifert and others. While Chagall's mysticism is that of the Hassidim, the mystical element in Soutine's work is of an intimate, personal nature, it is experience itself, the dread of existence. Chagall cast a nostalgic look and produced his work out of reverence and love for the past: a vision so personal and lyrical could not be shared by others.

There is not a single painting by Soutine which we can identify as being Jewish in subject-matter, there is no iconographical symbol which is even remotely related to Jewish historical memory, no painting which is a tribute to his past, his family, or his childhood. The absence of any artistic reference to the Hebraic tradition or the events of his own early life is certainly striking. Other artists found in both areas rich sources and natural avenues for artistic expression. Soutine is silent on this point, and from what we know of him we may assume that repression plays a large role. Nevertheless, he is seen by many of his critics and fellow artists as a very Jewish, un-French, painter.

78. (LEFT) Abraham Mintchine, *Self-Portrait*, 1926. Oil on canvas, $31\frac{7}{8} \times 21$ in (81×53.5 cm). Jerusalem, Israel Museum.

79. (RIGHT) Jules Pascin, *Young Girl Sitting*, 1921–2. Pastel drawing, $24 \times 18\frac{1}{2}$ in (60.5×47 cm). Los Angeles County Museum of Art, Mr and Mrs William Preston Harrison Collection.

The work of Soutine seems wild, unpremeditated, lacking logic, construction or plan. Chaos and turmoil emanate from his canvases. In his landscapes, houses seem to slide down the hill, trees turn and twist as if caught by the whirlwind; children flee from the tempest. His still-lifes consist of dead fowl, slaughtered oxen, and flowers which glow and curl as they grow twisted and tortured out of the vase. The colours, sensual, visceral, with finely nuanced brush strokes, combine to form fleshy patches, and quiver as if they will never come to rest. There is a clear preoccupation with the materiality of physical substance, with primordial and decaying matter. The portraits are deformed and their faces prematurely old, awry and painfully distorted, their hands clasped, their bodies stiff or leaning from their chairs in an attitude of discomfort, self-containment, or despair. He paints cooks, porters, page-boys, men and women without name or status (Plate I).

Here is no fairyland of Chagall, none of the latter's humour or childhood dreams. Soutine's canvases are a wild storm, a tempest whipped by fear and fury, by the nervousness and the anxiety of the hunted and persecuted. They are extremely sensuous, yet imbued with a deep spiritual and metaphysical quality. Colours are resonant, played fiercely against each other, sombre reds against blacks and fathomless blues, contrasts are sharp, values masterfully controlled. His work contains the poetry and violence of the victim, the stranger, the outcast, the creature lost in a world he has not made. It is the work of an artist who yearns for relief and redemption in the very act and process of painting, in the immediate impulsive and spontaneous response to what he sees and feels, who finds refuge in creating agitated textures, in spreading pigment with fingers and brushes over old shabby canvases. His work emanates from a life

80. (OPPOSITE) Chaim Soutine, *Hanging Turkey*, 1926. Oil on canvas, $36 \times 28\frac{1}{2}$ in (91.5×72.5 cm). Collection of Mr Richard S. Zeisler, New York.

81. (RIGHT) Chaim Soutine, *Fish and Tomatoes*, 1925. Oil on canvas, $25\frac{1}{4} \times 33\frac{1}{2}$ in (64.1×85 cm). Collection of Dr and Mrs E. Kafka, New York.

experience which did not know of planning, of stability, of harmony or of a confident look into the future.

Soutine is representative of the artists who came from the ghetto to Paris. Eli Faure, who knew him, was among the first to call attention to the artist's ethnic background, in which he saw the key to an understanding of his painting. He seemed not to be quite sure if he was an Asian, a Tartar, or a Jew:

> This face of an Asian whose forehead is covered by his hair, who is driven by the force which compels the magician to look for the stars. He is less a Jew than a Tartar if you look only at his physical type, but if you know his habits he is a Tartar just like a Jew. He goes after an ever-changing horizon, and his nightly escapes are an escape from himself and his quest to find at some crossroad stability, some point of rest which does not exist. . . . From where does he have the ability to paint, so seldom seen in the East and almost unknown with Jews? . . . Perhaps the suddenness of the freedom gave birth to this desire, I don't know. We can only say all or partly a Jew, a great painter who came from the Ghetto of Minsk.[3]

To French art critics, Soutine's work seemed utterly perplexing. Maurice Raynal, writing in 1928, reacted to it with a mixture of admiration and scorn; Soutine's art seemed to him: '. . . an expression of a kind of Jewish mysticism through appallingly violent detonations of colour. His work is a pictorial cataclysm, comparable, in its exasperated vision, to the reckless frenzies of martyrs and heroes.'[4] And speaking about Soutine's landscapes and figures he considered them: '. . . an ebullition of an elementary Jewish rigorous Talmud, [which] has kicked over the Tables of the Law, liberating an unbridled temperament and indulging at last in an orgy of criticism, destruction and reconstruction of nature—cursing the while, and cursing very copiously, its Creator.'[5]

George Waldemar refers to Soutine's background: 'The curse which rests on the painter rests on his race, it decided the whole psychic life of the artist. It leads his hand and his brush. . . . Formal art has nothing to do with this kind of creation, which is all release and elevation . . . Soutine does not revolt against Raphael or Academic art. He does not know it. He is free, desperately free, totally free. . . . The most emphatic expression of the Jewish genius is his mobility . . .'[6] Maurice Tuchman suggests that Soutine's preoccupation with animals and food was a symbolic violation of Jewish law, and his stress on the importance of concretely conceived objects a reaction to the visual prohibitions of Jewish doctrine deeply honoured in the 'Shtetl'.[7]

While the intrinsic Jewishness of Soutine's work will remain a matter of controversy and opinion, it is perhaps interesting to note that Israeli art critics, feeling a sense of kinship and identification with the mood of Soutine's canvases, have responded to him as one in whose pictures 'all the terrible events of our generation' were felt.[8]

Soutine was the eleventh son of a poor mender in Smilovitchi. His father was not a skilled craftsman, 'but only put patches on clothes, he never made a suit.'[9] Soutine exhibited an unacceptable penchant for art at a very early age. His older brothers wanted desperately 'to drive out the Dybbuk of painting'[10] from

Soutine. They treated him so badly that he would run away from home for days at a time.

These and other well-documented, turbulent events in Soutine's childhood would go far to explain some persistent features of his work: his relationship to his home, to people and the world. Yet we know too little about the laws of genius and how it fulfils its function with energies of desperation, to indulge in psychoanalytic speculation. We know very little about his student days in Vilna, except that he was actively interested in the theatre, and displayed great ability as an actor. While he had very little contact in Paris except with the Russian Jews, he befriended Seroya, a man versed in Spinoza and the Cabbala, and Hanna Orlof and her son, who was a biologist. Soutine generalized from his own experience to include all men and the whole world. His energies mobilized the spirit of rebellion toward the past, the ghetto; he insisted on the primacy of self, of his own total experience, which was to him the highest form of sensation.

82. Chaim Soutine, *The Old Mill*, c.1922–3. Oil on canvas, 26⅛ × 32¼ in (66.4 × 82 cm). New York, Museum of Modern Art, Vladimir Horowitz and Bernard Davis Funds.

Thus Soutine emerges as an artist-hero, the forger of a new style and a new vision, toward which many other Jewish artists in Paris gravitated. Soutine, who had torn himself from his surroundings and his past, created an art which was filled with nervousness, anxiety and fear—the life experience of others who were less articulate in the medium. His work was believed to mirror the situation in which they and all European Jewry found themselves in the period between the two World Wars. It was later seen to prefigure the Holocaust.

83. (LEFT) Chaim Soutine, *Portrait of Moise Kisling*, c. 1925. Oil on canvas, $39 \times 27\frac{1}{4}$ in (98×69 cm). Philadelphia Museum of Art, given by Arthur Wiesenberger.

84. (RIGHT) Chaim Soutine, *Self-portrait*, 1917. Oil on canvas, $18 \times 21\frac{1}{2}$ in (45.7×54.6 cm). Collection of Henry Pearlman, New York.

Plate I. Chaim Soutine, *Woman in Profile*, 1937. Oil on canvas, $18\frac{1}{2} \times 11$ in (46.9×27.9 cm).
Washington D.C., Phillips Collection.

Plate II. Marc Chagall, *Calvary*, 1912. Oil on canvas, 68¾ × 75¾ in (173 × 191 cm).
New York, Museum of Modern Art, acquired through the Lillie P. Bliss Bequest.

Plate III. Marc Chagall, *Time Is a River without Banks*, 1930–9. Oil on canvas, $39\frac{3}{8} \times 32$ in (99.5 × 81.2 cm).
New York, Museum of Modern Art.

Plate IV. Hyman Bloom, *The Synagogue*, 1940. Oil on canvas, $65\frac{1}{4} \times 46\frac{3}{4}$ in (165.7×118.1 cm).
New York, Museum of Modern Art, acquired through the Lillie P. Bliss Bequest.

Plate V. Max Weber, *Adoration of the Moon*, 1944. Oil on canvas, 48 × 32 in (121.9 × 81.2 cm).
New York, Whitney Museum of American Art.

Plate VI. Ben Shahn, *Ram's Horn and Menorah*, 1958. Tempera, $16 \times 27\frac{1}{4}$ in (40.6 × 69.2 cm).
Collection of Mr and Mrs Jacob Schulman, Gloversville, New York.

Plate VII. Jankel Adler, *Two Rabbis*, 1942. Oil on canvas, $33\frac{7}{8} \times 44\frac{1}{8}$ in (85.5 × 112 cm).
New York, Museum of Modern Art, gift of Sam Salz, 1949.

Plate VIII. Fritz Hundertwasser, *Blood Garden—House with Yellow Smoke*, 1962–3. Mixed media on paper, $31\frac{7}{8} \times 25\frac{5}{8}$ in (81.3×64.8 cm).
Collection of Joachim Jean Aberbach, New York.

Plate IX. Max Beckmann, *The Synagogue*, 1919. Oil on canvas, $35\frac{1}{2} \times 55$ in (90 × 140 cm).
Frankfurt, Städelsches Kunstinstitut und Städtische Galerie, acquired in 1972 by gifts from citizens and city of Frankfurt.

Plate X. Samuel Bak, *Thou Shalt Not*, 1977 (from Landscapes of Jewish History). Oil on canvas, 32 × 32 in (81 × 81 cm).
Collection of the artist.

Plate XI. Menashe Kadishman, *Trees in the Ocean*, 1975–7 (model). Eight steel plates, each $39\frac{1}{4} \times 20$ in (100×50 cm).
Tel Aviv, ocean front.

Plate XII. Yosl Bergner, *Excursion to the Kinnereth*, 1980 (from the series 'The Pioneers'). Oil on canvas, $36\frac{1}{4} \times 28\frac{3}{4}$ in (92 × 73 cm). Collection of the artist.

Plate XIII. Mark Rothko, *Green and Maroon*, 1953. Oil on canvas, $90\frac{3}{4} \times 54\frac{1}{2}$ in (229×137.3 cm).
Washington D.C., Phillips Collection.

Plate XIV. Mordecai Ardon, *In the Beginning*, 1970. Oil on canvas, $51\frac{1}{4} \times 51\frac{1}{4}$ in (130.2 × 130.2 cm).
Collection of Mr and Mrs Jacob Schulman, Gloversville, New York.

Plate XV. Yehoshua Kovarsky, *Temple Above the Moon*, 1958. Oil on canvas, 40 × 50 in (100.8 × 126 cm).
Collection of Mr and Mrs Jack L. Stein, Los Angeles.

CHAPTER FOUR

Plate XVI. Maryan S. Maryan, untitled, 1973. Acrylic on canvas, 38.5 × 58 in (97 × 145 cm). Paris, Galerie de France.

The Holocaust

There was hardly an artist in Europe who was not affected by World War II. Jewish artists became refugees and went into hiding. Many were sent to the concentration camps, and more than 200 artists died there.[1]

The Holocaust did not come about all of a sudden. Political anti-Semitism was already emerging in the 1870s, and came into the open in the arts when, on 20 July, 1879, Prince Luitpold of Bavaria, on the opening day of the official Munich Exhibition, removed Max Liebermann's *Christ in the Temple* from the central position determined by the Jury, to a small side room. The German press and art critics unleashed a barrage of hateful invectives against the artist, the painting and the Jury, and the speakers of the Bavarian Landtag, in the 15 January 1880 session, followed suit on this issue.[2] The seeds of hatred finally bore fruit when the Nazis came to power. Although Liebermann was recognized as one of the most important German artists of his generation and was one of the founders and President of the Berlin Secession, and during the Weimer Republic was the President of the German Academy of Art, he was forced to resign, forbidden to paint and his work was removed from all official collections.

In spite of Liebermann's experience, his work gives us no clue of what was to come, unlike the work of the Expressionist Ludwig Meidner, who in 1912 experienced a dramatic return to Jewish sources and whose canvases were increasingly filled with apocalyptic visions of cities being razed, and groups of wandering prophets receiving and transmitting divine messages. These figures are intensely listening and pleading, striding and kneeling in vast, empty landscapes as if they are animated by strange forebodings.[3]

Max Beckmann's well-known picture of 1919, *The Synagogue*, is distinguished by its complex and tense composition, and its sinister and foreboding mood. The fact that the building was burned down with the other synagogues of Frankfurt in the Kristallnacht Nazi pogroms of 9 November 1938 makes us see it now as charged with prophecy (Plate IX).

The time is dawn. The pale sickle of the moon is still visible in the sky. The windows of the neighbouring buildings are mostly dark. Three roads recede from the foreground of the painting with the result that the shapes by the synagogue and the fence are thrust wedge-like to the frontal plane, threatening the viewer with their forceful projection. The thrusting forms are further strengthened by lines marking the pavement, the fence in the centre, and the steep foreshortening of the synagogue front. The short left wall of the synagogue and the building on the far right further increase the tension by narrowing the picture. Tall oblique lamp posts standing on round bases block the interlocking diagonal movement and countermovement. A large cat sits quietly on a protruding plank.

The synagogue is marked by its red violet colour, the flickering light behind its large arched windows, and the large, green, onion-shaped dome in the rear crowning the building. The green dome, itself resembling a celestial body, counters the sharp angularity of the composition, and blocks the flickering orange of the rising sun, thereby adding a complementary contrast of colours to one of the focal points of the work. Toward the green dome converge the vertical and horizontal lines of force which constitute the scaffolding and architecture of the composition. Photographs of the synagogue before its destruction show it to have been a monumental structure, reassuring in its solidity. The artist has transformed the building and its environment to create the opposite effect. That which ought to convey a sense of restfulness and stability exudes a sense of danger. The sudden narrowing and widening of spaces, the compression and straining of forms, the stiff gothic linearity, the angular, sharply pointed, projecting cornices, the extended mouldings and pointed gables and the three small figures moving up the empty street further add to the oppressive air of the scene. The inscription 'Not' ('distress') on the advertising column within the fenced-in area gives us the meaning of the picture.

As has been pointed out, the painting bears a formal and thematic relationship to the cityscapes of Meidner and Kirchner and has a significant source in Van Gogh.[4] In 1919, the date of the painting, one year after Germany's defeat in World War I, we find religious impulses among German architects who longed for a sacred building which would redeem man and the community.[5] But it was also the year when anti-Semitism again raised its head after it had abated during the war years, and several militant anti-Semitic organizations took shape. In that year also some of the prominent leaders of the German revolution who were Jewish, Rosa Luxemburg, Kurt Eisner and Gustav Landauer, were murdered.

In the same year, 1919, during the civil war in the Ukraine, Abraham Manievich painted *The Destruction of the Ghetto*. While the painting has its source in one of the frequent pogroms of that time, in which the artist lost his son, it becomes symbolic of the events which were to unfold with the rise of the Nazis.

The painting, fully informed with the principles of modern design, is held in

85. (LEFT) Abraham Manievich, *The Destruction of the Ghetto, Kiev*, 1919.
Oil on canvas, 78 × 74 in (196.5 × 186.5 cm).
Private collection, New York.

86. (RIGHT) Marc Chagall, *Solitude*, 1933.
Oil on canvas, 45.5 × 67 in (102 × 169 cm). Tel Aviv Museum of Art.

87. Marc Chagall,
White Crucifixion, 1938.
Oil on canvas, 61 × 55 in
(154.9 × 139.7 cm). Chicago, The
Art Institute of Chicago, gift
of Alfred S. Alschuler.

colours of grey and black lit with spots of red. It is a homage to the ghetto. The buildings are still intact, crowding around the double-roofed synagogue in the centre. But the ghetto is empty. What was once a lively habitat is still. Only a lonely black goat, an animal cultivated by many of its former inhabitants, stands in the lower right corner.

Chagall's work *Solitude* of 1933 (fig. 86), in which a Jew with Torah and calf sits forlorn on the roadside, suggests the dire events to come. He may have felt the approaching catastrophe as early as the 1920s when he started working on *The Falling Angel*, a work which he continued during the 1930s and only completed in 1947. *White Crucifixion* of 1938 (fig. 87) was the first of a series in which the artist reacted to the mounting crisis in Europe. The figure of Christ is central and accentuated by the shaft of light cutting diagonally across the picture. Franz Meyer has commented that this is by no means a Christian representation.[5] The artist reminds us of Christ's Jewishness by integrating him into contemporary Jewish history. Christ's loincloth with two black stripes resembles the traditional Jewish prayer shawl. Nor is he portrayed as God's Son, who by taking upon himself the suffering of the world redeems it. Meyer writes:

> Here instead, though all the suffering of the world is mirrored in the crucifixion, suffering remains man's lasting fate and is not abolished by Christ's death. So Chagall's Christ figure lacks the Christian concept of salvation. For all his holiness he is by no means divine.[6]

The world around the central figure is in a state of upheaval. Everything is in motion and tilted, except for the Menorah at the foot of the cross, which is the only solidly vertical object in the composition. Its opalescent circle of light is balanced by the halo around the head of Christ. A Jew in the lower left grasps the Torah and turns his head back to the synagogue, which is on fire. Chairs are overturned in the lower right, and a Torah scroll thrown on the ground is burning. The flames spread to the bottom of the ladder, which leans against the cross. A Jew escapes with a sack on his shoulder. In the left corner a man weeps and another carries a sign that once read in German, 'I am a Jew.' In the upper left an armed mob invades the village, houses tumble, and people escape in a boat. Nearby, instead of the traditional angelic mourners, common Jewish figures grieve.

Through these and other paintings, Chagall expressed, by means of symbols deeply embedded in the art of the Christian West, the tragic events of the Holocaust and some aspects of its profound religious and historical dimensions.

Jankel Adler's fate as a Jewish painter in Germany was sealed when the Nazis came to power. He had established himself as a significant force in German painting of the 1920s, and participated in every important Expressionist show. Many of his works were lost or destroyed, and after he was forced to flee Germany in 1933, he wandered restlessly through many lands—France, Poland, Russia, the Balkans, Spain—until he joined the Free Polish Army. After he was discharged, he settled in Glasgow, where he exerted a major influence on postwar British painting.

In Adler's painting *Two Rabbis* (Plate VII), the heavy-set figures confront us with monumental seriousness as they plead for mercy for their people. The urgency of their plea is concealed behind their silent appearance—the tight lips, the small penetrating eyes, the carefully combed beard and hair create a tense, enigmatic image which tends toward abstraction. In their pleading, one senses the denial of the plea, the deafness and lack of response. The rabbis become icon-like representations of wisdom, rationality and human dignity. All formal elements—composition, colour, and texture—serve as the projection of an idea, rather than merely providing visual representation. The word 'Misercor [dia]' ('pity'), written on the tiny scroll the rabbis carry, seems to be addressed to no one in particular. It is an essential part of their own humanity.

Adler differed from most Eastern European Jewish artists in that he did not go to Paris, but made his home in Düsseldorf. There he experienced the strong influence of German Expressionism. His persistent interest in the technique of painting—exploration of new textures—derives largely from his studies with Gustav Wiethuechter, at the School of Arts and Crafts in Barmen. He also was influenced by Klee and Picasso. With Klee he had close personal contact, for in 1931 they both taught at the Düsseldorf Staatliche Kunstakademie and had adjoining studios.

Some critics have remarked upon the affinity between the grave seriousness of Jankel Adler's figures, his firmly constructed compositions, the deep resonant colours of his paintings, and the strength and severity of the Jewish orthodox religion in which he was raised. Some see in Adler's paintings a blending of the mathematical clarity of the Talmud with the mysticism of the Cabbala. Many of the portraits he painted are of members of his family, and often he used traditional Jewish themes or introduced Hebrew letters into his work.[7]

A powerful sense of identification with the Jewish people emanates from many of Adler's canvases, a point to which Else Lasker Schüler refers in a poem she dedicated to him:

> Weiht er doch jedes Bildnis das er malte,
> Mit dichterischer, grosser Harfen-schrift
> Seinem jungen Gotte Zebaoth.[8]
> [He dedicates every one of the pictures that he paints with a large poetic harp-like inscription to his young God, Zebaoth.]

Concerning Adler's *Two Orphans* (fig. 88), his friend, the painter Josef Herman, relates:

> In 1942, the Red Cross transmitted to me a message that my whole family in Poland had perished. I was terribly distressed. One day, Jankel Adler appeared at my studio and brought me this picture he had painted as a gift. There are two orphans in the picture; after a while I understood that one was me and the other he himself.'[9]

88. Jankel Adler,
Two Orphans, 1942.
Oil on canvas, 32 × 42 in
(81 × 106.5 cm). Collection of
Joseph Herman, London.

There is a generation of painters whose childhood was suddenly shattered when the Holocaust struck, dominating their early perceptions and thus determining all their future perceptions. Artists born in the 1920s became the youths victimized by the Nazi terror. Some were inmates of concentration camps; some went into hiding; others were troubled by what they knew and feared.

Yosl Bergner was born in the shadow of the Holocaust. An apocalyptic mood permeates the objects that haunt him (fig. 89). Various household articles appear in his canvases—graters, pots and pans, spice boxes, tea kettles, chairs, doors, and closets. They fly through the air, over the sea, like birds and leaves; they are carried by draughts of air to a distant shore, walk on the desert sand, lie prostrate on the seashore, their destination unknown. The postures of these objects remind us of human beings: like them they bend, stretch or recline. The graters especially assume human features. They are nailed to poles, wrapped in loincloths, or pried apart by powerful tools. Blue and silver-grey, they have been torn from their surroundings, are homeless and displaced. They are dented and broken, battered from use, tinny and hard. They are personal and collective objects, secular and sacred, invested with a particular warmth, smell, touch, and quality of home. They bring back memories of childhood, of place, of play, and of family.

The symbols of a destroyed community, of twisted life, of escaping, wandering, and searching dominate Bergner's paintings. Born in Vienna, he spent his youth in Australia and came to Israel via Canada, America, England and France. Distant, ever-shifting and criss-crossing frames of reference have made the irrational commonplace. The experience of the strange and the surreal in the existence of man and community became the norm of the artist's vision at an early stage.

Born in 1929, Erich Brauer was sent at the age of 13 to a Nazi labour camp. There he saw more than his share of pain and degradation, but in a wondrous way he overcame those difficult years, and balanced their bitter memories with early childhood experience, which plays an important role in his work. When, in 1945, the Russian tanks crossed the Danube Canal, he fled from the labour camp. 'My garden was the burning city of Vienna,' he wrote later.[10] He enrolled in the Vienna Academy of Fine Arts while the building was still smoking.

Brauer was very much the product of Vienna. As an adult he draws strength from childhood memories. There were colourful beggars, cripples, strange men and women and street gangs. There was his father, the cobbler, who used to hum Yiddish and Hassidic songs while repairing shoes. All these turned his childhood into an enchanting memory.

Brauer's work is strongly influenced by the Viennese school of Fantastic Realism, which established itself after the Second World War as a distinct movement on the continent, and of which he is a leading figure. He sees himself as an heir of the Viennese Secession tradition, and has extended its concept of total art into his own life, which he has transformed into a 'work of art'. Brauer turns his canvases into a paradise where childhood fantasies dwell side by side with the daydreams of adults (fig. 90). Human figures, plants, and insects are metamorphosed into a colourful, transparent, legendary world, bathed in light,

89. Yosl Bergner,
Flying Spice Box, 1966.
Oil on canvas, 32 × 39⅜ in
(81 × 100 cm).
Ein Harod Art Museum, Israel.

with groups of people interlaced boisterously in a Bruegel-like atmosphere. This holds true even for his series of seven paintings of 'Persecution of the Jewish People', which deal with mythical and historical disasters: *Slaves were we in Egypt*, *Destruction of the Temple*, *Masada*, *The Martyr*, *The Kishinev Pogrom*, *Israel Besieged*.

Many of Fritz Hundertwasser's paintings derive from childhood experience. In *House with Yellow Smoke* (Plate VIII), green houses are surrounded by pointed, bright yellow-green fences, placed in an intensely brilliant red area. There is a mark of a footstep in the red. Yellow, red-streaked smoke issues from the chimneys. It is similar to another painting, *Jew's House in Austria*, where the houses too seem to drown in a sea of blood.

Hundertwasser, the son of a Jewish mother and a German father who died shortly after his birth, found himself in a most precarious legal situation. Eleven years old when the Nazis marched into Vienna, he became the protector of his

Jewish mother, grandmother, and aunt who had enrolled him in the Hitler Youth Organization for his safety. When the boy came home from his activities, he would enter the door of his apartment on which a yellow star was fastened by law. When at midnight the SS made their usual inspections, the boy was prepared to fend off the SS officers for the sake of his family. As the knocks at the door were heard, he would quickly slip into his brown Hitler uniform and meet the SS men at the door, wearing the several medals that his father, a German officer, had won in the First World War. He thus 'proved' to them his pure Aryan descent. This device was successful on a number of occasions, but once it failed. In spite of his well-rehearsed act, one night they took his aunt and grandmother, and he never saw them again.[11] In 1943, Hundertwasser made his first conscious crayon drawing from nature. In the same year, 69 of his Jewish maternal relatives were deported to Eastern Europe, and killed. Hundertwasser remembers hiding with his mother in a trench in 1945 during the last days before Vienna was conquered by the Russians. He was terrified that he would be denounced as a Jew to the SS and be killed.

While the spiral labyrinth and the decorative aspect of Hundertwasser's work can be related to a tradition stemming from Gustav Klimt, Egon Schiele, and the Viennese Secession, they cannot be seen as strictly formal motifs. His spirals are quite different from those of Klimt. Less regular, they often change form, thin and swell, become square and change colours. It would be rash to relate the appearance of this motif exclusively to the traumatic events of the war. The artist's war experience must have been a contributing factor in the selection of this preferred form, but it clearly also satisfied deep psychological needs. He himself thought of the spiral 'as a fortress that I have constructed for myself in an unknown territory . . . a bulwark for myself against my environment'.[12] Indeed, in the theory of military defence, the connection between fortress and spiral is still very much alive. The purposeful irregularities of labyrinthine structure, and the long narrow winding paths are designed to confuse the attacker and thus create a certain advantage for the defender. The artistic form of the spiral-like labyrinth was always the carrier of important symbolic values. The one-way direction of the path that leads from the outside toward the centre creates for the eye a beautiful pattern that is easy to comprehend, but hard to follow; it symbolizes man's capacity to progress toward his goal, without doubting or turning back. There is a compelling force about the obsessive repetitiousness of a spiral pattern. It is a sensuous expression of the inescapability of fate and necessity, an archetypal image that follows sinuous lines to a centre, where Theseus fights the fateful battle with the Minotaur to gain his freedom. The centre is the end of a perilous journey; it is a sacred place where salvation lies. Once we start a spiral, we abandon the possibility of returning for a fresh start. Its form is a perfect metaphor for an infinite journey.

Today, Hundertwasser and Brauer continue to paint a paradise of dream-enchanted memories. Their art is beautiful to behold, decorative and life-enhancing. Form and colour have transformed their experiences. Brauer lives in Vienna, from which he frequently escapes to the Orient. Hundertwasser built himself a boat—a new country—to escape from the problems of men, a floating island where he rules supreme.

90. Erich Brauer,
The Rainmaker of Carmel, 1964.
Oil on canvas, $48\frac{1}{2} \times 58\frac{1}{2}$ in
(123×149 cm).
Private collection, Paris.

Maryan S. Maryan spent his childhood in Auschwitz, the most infamous of
the Nazi death camps. As a result of a serious injury one of his legs had to be
amputated. After liberation, he spent the rest of his youth in German camps for
displaced persons, working as a stage designer for the Jewish drama groups that
were organized by inmates. He had lost his family; there was nothing to return
to. He migrated to Israel in 1948, but could not find a home. From there he
went to Paris and then on to New York, always carrying the Holocaust with
him. The Holocaust is manifest in all his paintings: inmates of camps, prisoners
with striped uniforms, inquisitors, victims, jailers, sharp-clawed cats, horned
lions, slaughtered lambs with a predatory look as if they were both hunters and
hunted. He paints priests who raise their arms in a gesture of benediction, but
their faces are merciless. Strange human beings with donkeys' ears stick out
their tongues in defiance and dejection (fig. 93), colourful banderilleros pierce
the necks of dying bulls; there are medieval knights in shining armour, open-

mouthed and eyeless. His paintings are filled with butterflies that have dog heads, with interlacing worms, with monsters and eyeless machines which resemble human beings. He paints condemned people with pointed hats, men with wheels screwed to their hands, legs and chests, imprisoned in narrow cells.

Maryan's work is by no means literary; he makes use of the values of abstract design. Although he generalizes from what he has experienced, we know only too well the sources of his images. That he could give them form testifies to his strength as a person and as an artist.

In spite of the several distinct styles which mark the work of Maryan, one is struck by the amazing unity which pervades his work. From the days he took instruction at Bezalel in 1949 and expressed with sharp distortions, albeit untutored directness, his anguish by painting a black cat flexing its claws and arching its back ready to jump or retreat, to his last works of 1977, his paintings are suffused with fear and terror, with the raw energy and vibrant tension of a tightly drawn spring. Heavily contoured, pointed and spiked forms, mysterious signs, anxiously scribbled knotted marks, scratches and smudges, impulsive splashes hurled at the canvas sting our visual senses and directly assault our nerve ends. Indeed it seems that many of those paintings aim to strip from men and women the veneer of culture and civilization and present them as shame-faced, spitting, vomiting, posturing freaks. Half-dressed bipeds with donkeys' ears have disengaged themselves from the cycle of nature and mask their creatureliness by posturing in stiffly ornamented collars and grandiose Napoleonic headgear with dangling genitals and tails.

Maryan in his painting does not differentiate between the foolish and the wise, between the guilty and innocent, between the prison warder and the prisoner, between the victim and executioner. The hunter and the hunted are one. He does not denounce evil, nor plead the case of the weak. He is not concerned with order, morality, guilt or victimization.

One could easily label Maryan an inspired but deranged madman if his life experience did not vouch for the authenticity of his vision. A comprehensive view of his paintings points to an inner logic in his development and to the significant relation his work bears to the problems of contemporary art.

Maryan was 21 years old when he came to Israel. He was born in Nowy Sacz, a small town in Poland, and was taken to Auschwitz when he was 12. After the loss of his family there, he himself was selected for execution. In his one-page-long autobiography, Maryan writes:

In 1943 it was very cold outside. Some fellows from the Gestapo arrived. One was in uniform and his name was Ester, and another was in civilian clothes—Gavron. They chose 22 out of 44, and I was among the 22. They took us to a square called Poniatowski Square. They put us in a line and I was the last one to be executed, and was forced to look at what was happening in front of me. Since the two Germans were drunk as hell, they always aimed at the neck, which they missed, and everybody screamed and went on moving and was shot again somewhere else. My turn came and I felt nothing any more. They shot at my neck and of course missed. As you know, I am still alive. Of course after having been through such a 'circus', it isn't surprising I carry guilt feelings all my life.[13]

91. Page from the 'Autobiography' by Maryan S. Maryan, 'I Declare Formally, my Paintings are Paintings of Truth', 1976. Paris, Galerie Ariel.

From then on it was him against the world. No society could have made good the personal losses and the damage, and it is doubtful if any social group could have tempered his violence and hatred and suspicion and disgust. Israel in 1948, in the midst of the War of Independence, was not equipped to handle Maryan, or to 'absorb' him, the official term used for helping the thousands of survivors who inundated the country at that time. Maryan felt that the punishment inflicted upon him by fate or by being a Jew was more than enough advance payment for any act he could ever commit. Therefore he considered himself morally absolved from responsibility and felt free to do anything. In Israel he associated with other survivors of concentration camps who had formed a group of outcasts, a special enclave largely segregated from Israeli society, depending on each other for support and human closeness and hating each other at the same time. Among this group were several gifted artists.

In 1950 Maryan left Israel abruptly for Paris. Henceforth, his home would be the place in which he worked best, be it the attic or the cellar of Montparnasse or the Chelsea Hotel in New York City. The break was abrupt and decisive. In Paris he encountered a seething avant-garde, pregnant with innovations with which he could interact, which could release potentialities in him and allow him to develop in directions best suited to his needs. It was in the late 1940s and early 1950s that European painting, which again was centring in Paris, reacted to the events of World War II. Largely under the impact of Sartre's Existentialist philosophy, several artistic trends emerged which reacted strongly against the still dominant Post-Cubist Abstraction. There emerged Art Informel, Art Brut, Art Autre, Lyrical Abstraction, Tachism, in addition to other trends which stressed the centrality of signs, symbols and calligraphy as archetypes of magical origin, mysteriously giving evidence of man's existence.

92. (LEFT) Maryan S. Maryan, *Figure with Upraised Arms*, 1963. Oil on canvas, 29 × 24 in (73.6 × 60.9 cm). New York, Jewish Museum, gift of Mrs Rose Cohoron.

93. (RIGHT) Maryan S. Maryan, *Personage, Man with Donkey Ears*, 1962. Oil on canvas, 50 × 50 in (127 × 127 cm). New York, Allan Frumkin Gallery.

Evil was real and could not be overcome. Uncertainty, defeat, and disappointment were now recognized as inescapable aspects of man's existence and became the dominant forces in the art of the early 1950s. Paris of 1950 also became the home of the Cobra Group. Maryan interacted with all these trends.

These groups explored the gesture, the mark, the scratch and the expressiveness of the single patch of colour. They investigated the accidental, the slip, the chance, and the splash—aspects of art not transmissible and therefore not teachable. They glorified in unplanned, uninhibited expressions of vitality and distinct individuality. They despised Culture and held in contempt the aesthetic notions which had failed mankind, and they embraced instead the art of the psychopath, of children and of primitives. These groups waged an artistic attack on art, against its assigned function of providing the beautiful and sublime, of presenting something 'higher' or 'deeper'. And thereby they attempted to reflect the inner world of man and the world itself—unpredictable, irrational and brutal, the world of which man is part.

These were artistic trends that Maryan could relate to, for they helped release his own emotional energy and gave him the elements out of which he could construct his artistic language. While many of the innovations happened in what we would consider the abstract field, artists who returned to or never had left the human figure incorporated all the new formal and technical discoveries into their work. Although Maryan never joined any of these groups and guarded his individuality and independence, he nevertheless became part of this environment. Especially during the 1950s, we can detect in his work several influences of the avant-garde of the École de Paris. There appear in his painting the dark, masked, totem-like figures pointing to his interest in the art of the Aztecs, an interest probably stimulated by Maryan's growing friendship with the Algerian Jewish painter Jean-Michel Atlan, who had also been a student of philosophy at the Sorbonne. Some of Maryan's dark canvases of that time are reminiscent of the Surrealist Expressionist painting of Wilfredo Lam, of Robert Echaurrent Matta and Victor Brauner. Others of Maryan's canvases show influences of Pierre Soulages, of Henri Michaux, one of the creators of Tachism, the French version of Abstract Expressionism, and of Jean Dubuffet, Karel Appel, Asger John and Pierre Alechinsky.

Maryan synthesized the most diverse aspects of contemporary trends in Paris and later on in New York City, and emerged with a unique personal style. He himself admitted only to two influences—those of Léger and Soutine. In Soutine, he found a model of personal identification. Both had a strong sense of drama, and both had some theatrical experience, Soutine as art student in Vilna and Maryan as stage designer for plays in the European displaced persons' camps. Yet while there are similarities, there are also important differences. Soutine's apocalyptic vision may have foreshadowed the Holocaust, but Maryan experienced it. There is much anguish and empathy in Soutine's work. In Maryan there is only anguish. Maryan's works, especially in the 1950s, abound in Jewish motifs. Jewish types look over the edge of an empty grave and laugh scornfully as if they had outwitted fate or had found God a liar. Icon-like figures raise their hands in benediction, and others are boxed in and bound by black phylacteries, like punitive idols of the African jungle. They are boxed in

94. Maryan S. Maryan,
untitled, 1961.
Oil on canvas, 51.5 × 38.5 in
(130 × 97 cm).
Paris, Galerie de France.

by their laws. They sit on a box, step out of a box, and return to a box. Others are wheeled from place to place—a private symbol whose source is perhaps his childhood memory of a bicycle. In certain images, the wheels have turned into shooting targets drawn on the dress or the pointed hat of condemned figures reminiscent of Goya's paintings and the presentation of Jews in medieval manuscripts.

Maryan's diverse types fit into a general image which he had of man. The prisoner and the prison warder are the same. So are the judge and the criminal, the priest, the museum guard, the torreador, the card-player and the henchman, the cannibal and the robot. They are all victims of the Janus-like nature of man. By presenting them half-dressed, he juxtaposes the mask of civilization and man's 'creatureliness'. He devalues the social roles people play. His mask-like faces of the 1960s and 1970s seem as if they belong to creatures who have regressed to a state of idiocy, to a protoplasmic stage of breathing and defecating. As a mature painter, Maryan did not paint the world of the concentration camps. He did not want to be known as a painter of the Holocaust. He saw himself as the painter of truth (fig. 91).

The theme of the Holocaust is central in Samuel Bak's work. Like Brauer, Hundertwasser and Maryan, he too is a child of the Holocaust. He spent his early years under German occupation in the Vilna Ghetto. His father was shot a few days before he and his mother escaped the burning quarter. He was one of only 150 survivors among 80,000 Jews of that city famous for its Jewish learning and academic tradition. Yet, even while wandering through the occupation zone from camp to camp toward Palestine, his mother saw to it that he had instruction in drawing, as well as the materials needed to develop the talent that he had displayed very early. Later he wrote, 'I grew up without a permanent address, without a father and without God.' Bak does not hide in a maze, nor does he take flight in dreams, nor does he rage against God. He knew all too early that meanings and relationships were at best provisional and vulnerable and could not be trusted. The objects in Bak's paintings are but metaphors for the human drama as he experienced it.

Even as a child he felt the utter absurdity of finding logic in the events surrounding him. Samuel Bak became a painter-philosopher. His impressions were so dreadful that they could not be told as they were, so he fell back on symbolic language. In the painting, *The Family* (Fig. 96), he pays homage to the people, dead or alive, to whom he feels related—from his great-grandfather, the

95. Samuel Bak,
Father and Son, 1972–3.
Black crayon and sanguine,
21 × 16 in (49 × 41 cm).
Collection of the artist.

dignified inventor whose features remind us of Leonardo da Vinci, to his soldier friends still in battle dress with whom he had fought in Israel's wars. The picture is an assembly of faces and figures like an old-fashioned group portrait. The figures are set against a sky darkened by smoke and glowing with the reflections of distant fires. These are the people he remembers with various degrees of intensity by showing them alive, embalmed, silhouetted in relief, petrified, or as incomplete monuments. They had little idea of the fate that awaited them.

Having matured as an abstract painter, Bak turned suddenly, under the influence of a protracted stay in Italy, to the tradition of the Renaissance. He also felt sympathy for the rising trend of Pop Art when it appeared in the late 1950s. Pop Art displayed detachment and cool objectivity. It took stock of the tangible environment. It downgraded the significance of the creative process itself in favour of the final outcome. Bak reacted positively to these changes but could not quite be part of them, since the Pop artist grew out of the world of

96. Samuel Bak, *The Family*, 1974.
Oil on canvas, 65 × 90 in (160 × 200 cm). Collection of Joachim Jean Aberbach, New York.

advertisement and the comic strip, an ambiance alien to Bak's upbringing. Yet in some way Pop Art cleared the ground for his return to representational art.

Today Bak blends his own experiences with images drawn from specific art-historical sources. He thereby implies a criticism of the 'achievements' of the twentieth century—its technology and its art. *Father and Son* (fig. 95) could be called 'The Sacrifice of Isaac', although there are hints of the story of Daedalus and Icarus, a sacrifice for the sake of mechanical invention and progress. In several of his paintings, man seems trapped by technology. Metal wings, wires, and mechanical paraphernalia are attached to man and angel, making their attempt to reach the sky absurd and ridiculous.

The impact of Pop Art ideas can still be felt in a series of paintings called *Landscapes of Jewish History* (Plate X), which Bak painted in the 1970s. The Tables of the Law, a common, one could say popular, emblem of the Jewish visual tradition, are central to this series. They appear hewn out of rock, standing on top of mountains, oversized, dilapidated, hovering in the air, perforated by bullets, carved with Hebrew letters and Roman numerals, resting heavily on the rooftops of broken houses of the ghetto, sometimes clamped together by nuts and bolts. Bak's Tables of the Law are obviously worn by time. They loom large, they are a heavy yoke, they are gravestones which mark the outline of future graves. For better or worse, the fate of the people is tied up with the Tables of the Law.

Smoke (fig. 97) evokes the poetic imagery of Nelly Sachs's poem 'Oh the Chimneys'[14] and Paul Celan's lines from 'Fugue of Death':[15]

> Black milk of daybreak we drink you at nightfall
> we drink it at noon in the morning we drink it at night
> drink it and drink it
> we are digging a grave in the sky it is ample to lie there.

Harold Paris, born in 1928, experienced the Holocaust when, as an American soldier—an illustrator for *Stars and Stripes*—he was among the first to enter the Buchenwald camp after the Allied Forces discovered it. The son of an actor of the Yiddish Art Theater, Paris has always been preoccupied with performance and ritual, death and immortality, the sacred and the numinous. He brings to his work a sense of drama, a mastery of new materials, new processes and their combination in multimedia art. Wonderment, blackness, and the occult are part of his private mythology, which is attuned to hidden combinations that he discovers in places, events, Hebrew letters, poetry, reminiscences, and ideas. The theme of life and death is never far from him. He has made a series of biomorphic bronze and plastic sculptures, which he calls *Chai (Life)*, and is known to have put one of them in a coffin and buried it in an elaborate ceremony. He has created ceramic walls called *Mems*, after the Hebrew letter Mem, because they are the initials for the Hebrew words, *malach hammawet*, the angel of death, Moloch (an ancient tyrannical Semitic deity), and Malach (angel), as well as the capital letters of the names of Majorca, Madrid, and Munich—three cities in which he stayed in 1950.

The Holocaust, ever on his mind, includes all that happened in Europe during the War, and all that happened in Vietnam and America during the

97. Samuel Bak, *Smoke*, 1977 (from Landscapes of Jewish History).
Oil on canvas, $23\frac{3}{4} \times 23\frac{3}{4}$ in (60×60 cm). Collection of the artist.

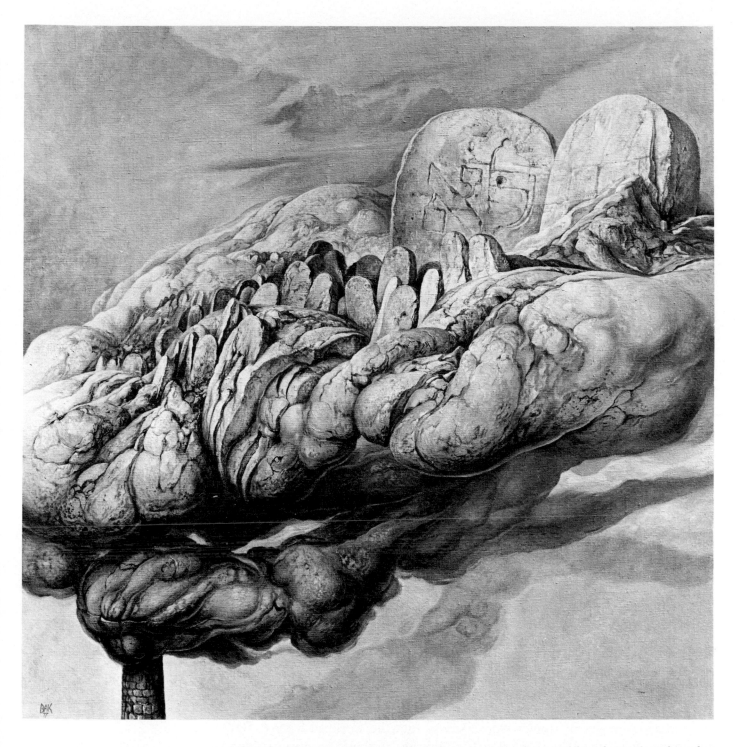

1960s. In his notes, Paris envisaged a room that he would make and seal so that no one could enter and see his dream—the sculpture he had placed inside. This room was a 'Kaddish', a 'Homage to the past, to wonderment and loneliness . . .

What does it look like?
Like the inside of a) my soul.
Who can see it?
Only the blind with two small
  children

> where does it come from—
>   the wail of the shofar
>   the 3,000 years
>   and a scream in Vietnam . . .'[16]

This was a

> Kaddish for all the 'lost' in my—your life, all that cannot be again. . . . This huge black room, this ineffable statement—black, black and inside is all the wonder I can evolve—all the love I project and summon forth. . . . What is it—this Kaddish—this refutation? It is a long voyage into my past—the war, my childhood, the constant searching and seeking. A black solemn box, solemn and brooding and with it all that I know (and do not know, but sense and feel). White, white forms with heat and cold imbedded—gutting these irresolute shapes. To make this huge chamber and to stand mute, unknowing, severed, torn, bleeding within. Before it a small mound to gaze and stare and ponder at these never to enter walls. No one may ever see this room to wonder at and to know. The blind can be witness to this—tell us—What do you see? All of the blood and pain of time sits within—truly for you it is sealed and a seal upon my life and mind. No door, no entrance and no one to enter . . .[17]

He pays homage to the souls of artists dead and alive, to whom he feels close, to the souls of events and objects that move him. The soul, that which endures, that which ascends and descends according to a Hebrew song that he must have heard in his father's house, he enshrines in a sensuous, intimate, luminous, translucent and dematerialized form.

The *Souls* are slabs of silicon gel, in which objects are embedded and into which delicate colours, organic, inorganic, and phosphorescent have been fused in the process of solidifying. They have the quivery resilience of human flesh and are analogous to the frailty and vulnerability of human life. *Moment in M.*, *All that Remains*, and *Torah Soul* are voyages into realms that move and concern the artist (fig. 99).

We have discussed the work of several artists whose childhood was destroyed by the Holocaust, who carried its memory with them and for whom painting was the only possibility of living with this memory. Through a world of symbols and metaphors which they created and through the formal means at their disposal they attempted to come to grips with the world they had experienced. We have seen the labyrinthine shapes of Hundertwasser designed to afford him refuge; the fantastic images of Brauer who takes us into the world of legend; Bak's probing philosophical approach which establishes aesthetic distance and lures us unwittingly into the domain of the incomprehensible; or Maryan who survived by raging on the canvas against God and man. These and other artists—all of whom spent their childhood under immediate threat of extinction—were compelled by an inner force to come to grips with their experiences.

There remains, however, a central moral and aesthetic question in depicting the Holocaust. How can one justify making the portrayal of the Holocaust a source of aesthetic experience, however broadly we may use that term? Is it at all possible to do justice to the theme?

98. (LEFT) Alfred Aberdam,
Deportation, 1941–2.
Oil on canvas, $47\frac{1}{4} \times 31\frac{7}{8}$ in
(120×81 cm).
Ein Harod Art Museum, Israel.

99. (RIGHT) Harold Paris, *Torah Soul*, 1975 (from Soul Series).
Cast silicone and colourants,
16×6 in (40.2×15 cm).
Collection of the artist,
Oakland, California.

The presentation of atrocity poses a nearly insurmountable artistic problem. While violence may maim or destroy, its causes are generally intelligible. Atrocity in contrast to violence is wholly bizarre and inexplicable because it exceeds human reason and comprehension. It is outside its domain. It may be within the artist's reach but most surely not within his grasp. However, artists have to respond to what touches them deeply, to events which are outside human understanding and therefore outside art. Beyond these considerations there is the collective demand to remember to which artists have to respond.

The events in Europe cut deep into the consciousness of artists everywhere. Alfred Aberdam, who was hiding in Paris during the German occupation, painted *Deportation* (fig. 98), a sombre picture of men, women and children, gathered silently in the street in an atmosphere charged with apprehension.[18] Mordechai Ardon, who had fled to Jerusalem, painted *Train of Numbers* (fig. 100), which, with its sharply etched lines and numbers slashed across the landscape and the sky, evokes the rhythm of freight trains speeding the tattooed victims to their death.

The physical torture and brutal degradation of inmates in the camps is evoked in the works of Edward Kienholz, Mauricio Lasansky, Rico Lebrun,

Olly Ritterband, and Lasar Segall. Pablo Picasso painted *Charnel House* (fig. 102)
after two of his lifelong friends, the poets Max Jacob and Robert Desnos, died in
the concentration camps of Drancy and Theresienstadt. The composition was
influenced by the photographs of atrocities which were published at the end of
the war. 'In the Charnel-house,' writes Alfred H. Baar, 'there are no symbols,
and perhaps, no prophecy. Its figures are facts—the famished, waxen cadavers
of Buchenwald, Dachau, and Belsen. The fury and shrieking violence which
make the agonies of Guernica tolerable are here reduced to silence.'[19]

Kurt Seligman, in *Sabbath Phantoms—Mythomania* (fig. 103), painted a
ghostly choreography of pelvis-like structures, reminiscent of the dance of
death. In 1943 Jacques Lipchitz sculpted *The Prayer* (fig. 101) directly in wax.
Years later the artist recalled details about its making:

> Technically, it was extremely difficult and caused me terrible suffering
> when I was forming it and when it was being cast. I made many modifi-
> cations in the wax and even, through weldings, in the bronze. . . . It was
> done in the most terrible moment of the war; it was a prayer, a Jewish prayer
> of expiation; you sacrifice the cock which has to take all your sins. In the
> left hand the man holds a book, in the right hand the cock; the man wears
> the Jewish prayer shawl. The cock is actually killed by a man who is trained
> to do this. This prayer takes place before the Day of Atonement. Actually
> the figure is not a rabbi; it is Everyman, every Jew who has to do this, who is
> asking for forgiveness. The figure is completely disembowelled; in the open
> stomach are heads of goats, and the innocent victim, a lamb. The entire
> subject is the Jewish people, whom I thought of as the innocent victims in
> this horrible war. I find this whole subject so difficult to explain because it
> emerged from so many different feelings. I was praying, I was crying when I
> made this work. . . . it meant so much to me. . . . It had something to do

100. (ABOVE) Mordecai Ardon,
Train of Numbers, 1963.
Oil on canvas, 29 × 57⅛ in
(73.5 × 145 cm).
Ein Harod Art Museum, Israel.

102. Pablo Picasso,
The Charnel House,
1944–5. Oil on canvas,
$75\frac{5}{8} \times 98\frac{1}{2}$ in
(190.5×248 cm).
New York,
Museum of
Modern Art.

103. Kurt Seligman,
*Sabbath Phantoms –
Mythomania*, no date.
Oil on canvas,
$37 \times 50\frac{1}{4}$ in
(93.9×127.6 cm).
Collection of
Harold Diamond,
New York.

101. (LEFT)
Jacques Lipchitz,
The Prayer, 1943.
Bronze, $42\frac{1}{2}$ in high
(107 cm).
Philadelphia
Museum of Art.
Given by R. Sturgis
and Mario B. F.
Ingersoll.

with the horror I felt about Auschwitz and the other Nazi concentration camps.[20]

Minna Harkavy sculpted the *Last Prayer* (fig. 104), the head of a Jew wearing the phylacteries, a portrait of inexpressible sorrow.

Abraham Rattner, in *Ezekiel's Valley of the Dried Bones* (fig. 108), painted a tangled, chaotic abstract canvas, influenced by photographs from concentration camps.

Jack Levine's *To an Unknown German* (fig. 106), based on a widely-known German photograph, depicts women and children with raised hands being marched through the streets of Warsaw.

Sigmund Menkes, who usually painted richly coloured canvases of the joy of life, turned to a sombre palette in his painting of the *Uprising of Ghetto Warsaw* (fig. 105). Luise Kaish went to Dachau after the war and faced the ovens. When she made the sculpture *Holocaust* (fig. 109) she did not emphasize interpretation, but made permanent its tangible reality by modelling and casting into bronze the front of the oven: monolithic architectural slabs pierced by a black void. 'Doors. Doors that could be opening, or closing. Flowers that could be dust, emerging from the void or circling beneath in an upsurge of vibrant growth.'[21]

Louise Nevelson, in *Homage to Six Million 1* (fig. 110), dedicated one of her wall sculptures to their memory. She envelops the spectator in a phantom-like black structure created from stacked boxes which are filled with familiar objects—legs of chairs and tables, abstract shapes resembling discs, violins, organ pipes, all vestiges of former dwellings.

An air of tragedy and doom hung over the decade of the 'forties. The war, the deportations, the resistance, the death camps, the Exodus and Israel struggling to emerge are inextricably linked and manifest themselves in art to this very day. Several artists, groping for expression, turned to traditional Jewish themes: the prayer, the sacrifice, the Akedah (the binding of Isaac), Jacob wrestling with the angel of the Lord, Daniel in the lion's den, the Exodus. As events became known and Jewish survival continued to be a salient issue, these themes are permeated by a haunting actuality.

The binding of Isaac occupies a central place in Jewish religious and social history. It is a trial of faith imposed on Abraham, the founding father of the Jewish religion. Abraham's willingness to heed God's request has traditionally been held as the highest model of fidelity. The struggle for survival has brought the reality of the ancient myth of the Akedah into the consciousness of contemporary Jews. William Zorach, Milton Horn, Naftali Bezem, Jacques Lipchitz, Mordechai Ardon, Shraga Weil, Leonard Baskin, Anna Wilansky, George Segal and others worked on this theme (figs. 63, 107, 154). Jacob wrestling with the angel (Genesis 32:25) tests the limits of human strength in the struggle for survival. By an act of will and faith, man transcends himself. Max Band, Elbert Weinberg, Nathan Rappoport, Leonard Baskin found that Biblical motifs gave shape and meaning to contemporary trials. By using those themes the artist attempts to integrate the incomprehensible into a continuous cultural pattern and into a Jewish artistic tradition going back at least to the third century AD. However, this pattern presupposes a context of some form of religious faith.

104. (ABOVE) Minna Harkavy, *The Last Prayer*, 1949. Bronze, 18 in high (45.7 cm). New York, Whitney Museum of American Art.

105. (OPPOSITE TOP LEFT) Siegmund Menkes, *Uprising of Ghetto Warsaw*, 1943. Oil on canvas, 41 × 25 in (101.1 × 63.5 cm). Collection of the Artist, Riverdale, New York.

106. (OPPOSITE TOP RIGHT) Jack Levine, *To an Unknown German*, 1969. Lithograph, 31¼ × 30 in (78.5 × 76 cm). New York, Kennedy Galleries, Inc.

107. (OPPOSITE BOTTOM LEFT) Naftali Bezem, *The Binding of Isaac*, 1968. Oil on canvas, 35⅜ × 51¼ in (90 × 130 cm). Collection of the artist.

108. (OPPOSITE BOTTOM RIGHT) Abraham Rattner, *Ezekiel's Valley of the Dried Bones*, 1963. Oil on canvas, 77½ × 51 in (196.8 × 129.5 cm). New York, Kennedy Galleries, Inc.

Art follows life like a shadow. History forces its themes on artists. Images of ships on high seas, packed with homeless persons with no friendly shore in sight emerge from experiences immediately following World War II. Mitchell Siporin, a Social Realist in the 1930s, an American soldier stationed in Europe in the 1940s, reacts in a moving work, *Endless Voyage* (fig. 4), which depicts the plight of the refugees who find no refuge but are determined to reach the land of Israel. 'It took a troop ship ride back from Italy to make me feel what a wooden tub headed for Israel in the night would feel.'[22]

Lasar Segall, who established himself as a painter in Brazil, draws on his own experience there, stemming from his first voyage in 1912. A mature painter from Vilna, he studied in Germany, and was intimately connected with German

Expressionism when he sailed from Hamburg. Spending four weeks on board ship between sea and sky, among the human cargo emigrating to Brazil, he stored impressions to which he returned in 1947, when he painted the large canvases which dealt with refugees floating aimlessly, unable to land (fig. 113). The canvases are painted in muted greys, and ochre-toned passengers crowd the deck. In *Exodus* (fig. 114), Segall spiritualizes the painting by erasing the boundary of the ship, but hints at it through the composition of the figures on deck.

Seymour Lipton, who during the 1930s had culled his themes from the social conflicts which stirred the New York art world, sculpted *Exodus* (fig. 115; at one time called *Panorama of Judea*), a heavy elongated lead sculpture conveying slow and painful movement. Albert Elsen describes the sculpture as suggesting 'a type of ancient calligraphy punctuated by mystical signs, as if the whole was a grim pictogram or morbid cartouche of a tortured terrain that has survived by indomitable toughness. The amputated fist–tree stump at the left, for example, is a defiant avowal of survival. Its quality of inelegance is exactly the strength of Exodus 1.'[23]

The quality of inelegance marks also William Zorach's *Moses*, the leader of the Biblical Exodus (fig. 112), and *Man of Judah* (fig. 111), carved in hard Maine granite. Elongated, compact and primitive, the sculptor has significantly departed from his classical norms and boldly simplified the expressive features.

109. (OPPOSITE) Luise Kaish, *Holocaust*, 1975. Bronze, 80 × 61 × 15 in (203.2 × 154.9 × 38.1 cm). Collection of the Albert A. List family, New York.

110. (BELOW) Louise Nevelson, *Homage to Six Million I*, 1964. Painted wood, 108 × 216 in (2.78 × 5.48 m). Brown University, Providence, Rhode Island, gift of the Albert A. List family.

The hard stone conveys the ruggedness of face. Determination rather than intellect, nobility of character rather than rank are strongly conveyed.

Jacques Lipchitz, whose art is rooted strongly in the Biblical and Jewish tradition, and who has been extremely sensitive to the mood of his time, created a Menorah Sculpture, *Exodus* (now lost), whose stem and arms formed the mast and sails of a ship from which people hung. Lipchitz escaped from Paris in 1940 after the German occupation and fled to Toulouse and from there in 1941 to the United States. Having witnessed the collapse of Europe and himself a refugee, he continued to express the fate and hope of millions of other refugees. As early as 1926 he had departed from Cubist sculpture because he could not express through it the ideas that stirred him. From 1930, he returned to his Jewish roots with the creation of the bird-like *Mother and Child* (fig. 117) and themes like The Prodigal Son and Jacob and the Angel, all based on highly personal experiences which refer to his origins. In 1933 he sculpted a *David and Goliath*, in which David strangles Goliath, on whose body the artist has carved a swastika. It was a sharp departure from the traditional presentation of the Biblical story. But for Lipchitz this story had a frightening actuality, and he had an artist's faith in the capacity of his work to affect events. The classical themes which followed are an

111. (LEFT) William Zorach, *Man of Judah*, c. 1957. Granite, 17 in high (43 cm). Washington D.C., National Gallery of Art.

112. (RIGHT) William Zorach, *Head of Moses*, 1956. Granite, 36 in high (91 cm). New York, Columbia University.

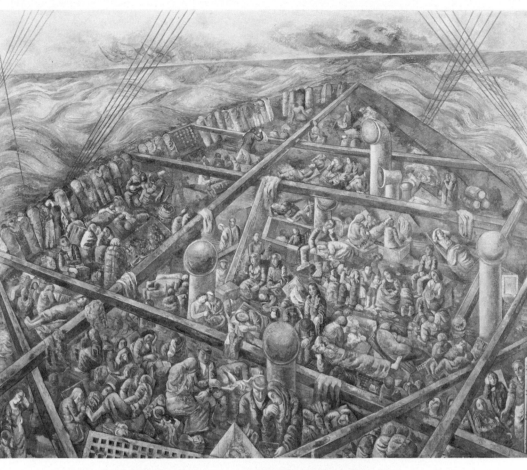

113. Lasar Segall,
Emigrant Ship, 1939–41.
Oil on canvas,
7 ft 6 in × 9 ft
(2.30 × 2.75 m). São Paulo,
Brazil, Museu Lasar
Segall.

114. Lasar Segall,
Exodus, c.1940.
Oil on canvas, 52 × 54 in
(132 × 137.1 cm). New
York, Jewish Museum,
gift of Messrs James N.
Rosenberg and George
Bocker in memory of
Felix M. Warburg.

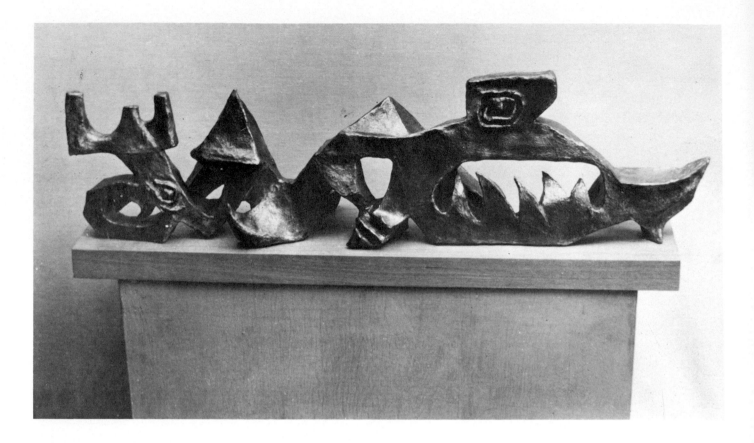

attempt to influence events further by gaining a larger audience than he felt would be accessible through exclusively Jewish themes. He sculpted in the following years *Prometheus Strangling the Vulture*, *The Rape of Europa*, and *Theseus and the Minotaur*, all the result of his being now a fully engaged artist.

After Lipchitz's arrival in the United States, themes of Rescue, Return, Sacrifice, Blessing and Miracle abound in his work and signal his continuous preoccupation with Jewish survival and redemption. He also returned to the Mother and Child motif which for him is bound up with ideas of personal rescue (fig. 116). The monumental sculpture portrays a massive woman cut off at the legs and wrists. She spreads her truncated arms to heaven in supplication. Her face is turned upward and a child clings to her back, weaving its arms around her neck. The feeling of great strength, despite her utter helplessness, is reinforced when we become aware that the whole figure also conceals the face of a bull.

In 1947, Jacques Lipchitz willed Israel's survival and rise in *Miracle*. Simultaneously, he responded to the plight of Arabs who had fled their homes, and he created a series of sculptures on the Biblical theme of Hagar in the Desert (fig. 119). The sculpture *Miracle II* (fig. 118) is drawn from the theme of Exodus and poetically evokes the Menorah's origin in the cosmic tree, and its transformation by Judaism. The miracle is in the ability of the ancient tree to bloom again. The Menorah has returned to its original source—a spreading tree—whose trunk has been opened to reveal the Tablets of the Law. A man kneels before it, simultaneously imploring, supporting, and protecting it. Lipchitz

115. (ABOVE) Seymour Lipton, *Exodus no.1*, 1947. Lead construction, 33 in long (83 cm). Collection of the artist, New York.

116. (OPPOSITE TOP LEFT) Jacques Lipchitz, *Mother and Child II*, 1941–5. Bronze, 50 in high (127 cm). New York, Mus. of Modern Art.

117. (OPPOSITE TOP RIGHT) Jacques Lipchitz, *Mother and Child*, 1930. Bronze, $51\frac{1}{4}$ in high (142 cm). Cleveland Museum of Art, the Norman O. and Ella A. Stone Memorial Fund with a contribution from Bernard J. Reis.

118. (OPPOSITE BOTTOM LEFT) Jacques Lipchitz, *Miracle II*, 1947. Bronze, $30\frac{1}{2} \times 14$ in (77.4×35.5 cm). New York, Jewish Museum.

119. (OPPOSITE BOTTOM RIGHT) Jacques Lipchitz, *Hagar*, 1971. Stone, 72 in high (183 cm). New York, Marlborough Gallery, Inc.

expressed this triple role by merging the man's legs with the roots of the tree. Man, Torah and Tree all derive sustenance from one another. The miracle does not occur by itself; it is man who produced it by his own effort. The sculpture offers a striking analogy to the ancient representation of the man in armour carrying the Menorah on his head in the catacomb of Beth Shearim in Israel. Lipchitz studied examples of ancient Jewish art that had been unearthed.

The associations evoked by *Miracle II* stem from its form and its organic unity. The arms of the Menorah rise in a V-like form on both sides of the Tablets of the Law. The branches are deeply cut, and a similar shape is shared by the buds and the man's arms and hands. The V-shape is repeated in horizontal form in the Tablets of the Law, which recede and meet at an angle. It is inverted in the man's feet and in the larger folds of his garment as they fall from his shoulders to his sides. The texture of the whole is rough, leaving the strong imprint of the artist's modelling.

In Kibbutz Mishmar Haemek the sculptor Ben Zwi created in 1947 a memorial to the children of the Holocaust (fig. 120). The Mother and Child

120. Ben Zwi, *Memorial to the Children of the Holocaust*, 1947. Stone, 13ft × 50 ft 8 in (3.90 × 15.50 m); area of memorial setting 263 sq.ft (83 sq.m). Kibbutz Mishmar Haemek, Israel.

121. (LEFT) Nathan Rappoport,
Scroll of Fire, 1971.
Bronze, 26ft high (7.9 m).
Kesalon, Israel.

122. (RIGHT) Nathan Rappoport,
Scroll of Fire (detail).

group is set into the back of a partial enclosure built into the slope of the hill and thereby integrated into the physical setting of the Kibbutz. It is placed right in its centre, surrounded by trees, schools and farmhouses but secluded and inviting meditation. The child clings to the mother, who shields it with her whole body and arm; but powerless to save, she turns her head from the pleading child.

Influenced by Cubist and Expressionist trends in Western sculpture, Ben Zwi carefully adapted his work to the social concerns of the Kibbutz and helped to articulate the deepest feelings of its members by setting aside amidst its bustling activities a space for remembrance.

Near the village of Kesalon, in the Judean hills, Nathan Rappoport erected in 1977 a public monument in which he combined the events of the Holocaust and the rise of Israel. Cast in bronze in the form of a huge scroll, he renders in sculptural language a continuous narrative made up of details of selected events from the uprising of the Warsaw Ghetto till the Six Day War (figs. 121, 122).

CHAPTER FIVE

The Search for Roots in Israel

The Coming of the Pioneers

When one's perception is bent by the promises of a promised land, when the eye is not riveted to immediate needs and one carries a blueprint of an earthly paradise in one's pocket, the strife-torn land of Israel looks as quiet and peaceful as it does in the canvases of Reuven Rubin. His landscapes are serene: villages merge into gently sloping hills, donkeys loaded with fruit travel on winding roads. His canvases are peopled with Hassidic Jews dancing in ecstasy, colourful Arab fishermen throwing out their nets or offering fish for sale. Skinny black goats eat from the trees. The landscapes with their ancient olive trees, whose silver-leaved feathery branches grow toward a hazy and filmy sky, seem legendary and Biblical (fig. 124). Young women with long black braids and almond-shaped eyes and healthy, well-built young men carry the first fruits of the season or Sabbath bread toward home (fig. 123). Boys carry flowers or play the flute. Window sills are filled with ripe pomegranates, and through the window a caravan of camels walks beside the sea.

Indeed, Rubin painted a promised land. His works are distinguished by a strong architectural sense and are filled with simplified forms, reminiscent of the innocence and naïveté of Henri Rousseau. Their bright colours reflect the artistic will of one who delights in forms appropriate to the simple pioneering society settling in Israel. The Biblical and Midrashic imagination rules the canvas. The romantic nationalism, with its oriental and exotic overtones, that emerged in Israel in the early 1920s—largely under the influence of Reuven Rubin—was the first attempt to create a native Israeli art and to celebrate the hopes and values that brought idealistic people to the new country.

Rubin went to Palestine in 1912 at the age of 18, with the intention of studying art at the Bezalel School of Arts and Crafts—a school established with the support of the Zionist movement in 1906, under the leadership of the conservative sculptor, Boris Shatz. Rubin's decision to go there had been made long before:

> From my early childhood I had dreamed of going to Palestine. It seems to me now that I always knew instinctively that there was the country where I would develop as a 'Jewish Artist'. By 'Jewish Artist' I don't mean a painter of Jewish subjects, but one whose roots are embedded in the soil of his own homeland, Zion—where the Bible lives naturally for him and where he feels in his rightful place and is spiritually at ease. I could not have been more than six years old when I began to feel and understand the call of the land of the Bible. [1]

123. Reuven Rubin, *First Fruits*, 1923. Oil on canvas, 71 × 82 in (188 × 202 cm). Tel Aviv, Rubin Museum Foundation.

124. Reuven Rubin, *Early Morning in Galilee*, 1937. Oil on canvas, 45 × 64 in (115 × 153 cm). Collection of David Lloyd Kreeger, Washington D.C.

Later he wrote:

> How can one ever forget being eighteen years old, and coming for the first time to Jerusalem on a beautiful spring day to fulfill a dream? In the little Turkish train that brought me from Jaffa, I had my eyes glued to the window, gazing at the landscape and breathing in the air of Eretz Israel. I could hardly believe that it was I, Rivile, from the little town of Falticeni in the Carpathian mountains of Romania, who was actually in Palestine, travelling toward the hills of Judea. I was amazed to note that everything looked familiar to me; it seemed as if I knew every rock, every tree, the desert hills. As the train came to Jerusalem, I felt I was coming home.[2]

In order to understand a passion one has to be part of it. The romantic and nationalist mood can also be found in the paintings of veteran Israeli painters such as Israel Paldi, Nahum Gutman, and Moshe Castel. They revolted against the academic teachers whom Boris Shatz had brought from Eastern Europe to the Bezalel School, and who had not come under the influence of the new modernism. Rubin spent a year at Bezalel, then left in disappointment over the poor instruction and the philosophy that guided the school. In the following seven years, he returned to Romania, studied in France, went to Italy and New

York, and absorbed various artistic influences. He was particularly impressed by Ferdinand Hodler's work; he returned to Israel in 1922 to settle. He continued painting in a serene and joyous mood. His works are marked by an archaic quality and an absence of conflict—they are a celebration of wholesomeness and fulfilment.

Under the impact of the School of Paris, Israeli painters like Josef Zaritsky, Avigdor Stematsky, Yehezkiel Streichman and their followers come close to creating pure abstract compositions. Their early sun-drenched landscapes and cityscapes dissolve in colourful compositions of expressive, sensitive, and dynamic brush strokes. Their styles, removed from any mystical or idealistic interpretation, disregard the world of appearances and move toward painting for painting's sake. Romantic idealism continued well into the 1930s, when more artists arrived in Israel, some of whom had studied in Germany and Austria. Palestine was then a land of hope and vision; people felt reborn and formed a new society.

Johanan Simon studied with Max Beckmann in Frankfurt and spent several years in France with a group of young artists who gathered around André Derain. In 1934, he worked with Diego Rivera in New York. Tired of decadent aspects of art and life in the West, he went to Israel in 1936 and joined a kibbutz in which he spent 17 years. He believed then in the possibility of being a

125. (LEFT) Reuven Rubin, *Portrait of Ahad Ha'am*, 1926. Oil on canvas, 64 × 50½ in (162 × 115 cm). Tel Aviv, Public Library, Ahad Ha'am Room.

126. (RIGHT) Reuven Rubin, *Meal of the Poor*, 1920. Oil on canvas, 14¼ × 15½ in (36 × 39 cm). Tel Aviv, Rosenfeld Art Gallery.

member of the collective society, a worker and an artist. Like other members of the kibbutz, he tended bees, worked as a carpenter, drove a tractor, and irrigated the orange groves. Soon he found himself decorating the dining room of the kibbutz for holidays, and later painting canvases that celebrated the self-governing young men and women workers who had created new social forms of living.

In Simon's paintings the composition, the strong architecture, the intuitive tendency towards verticality, monumentality and sculptural forms show traces of Léger, Beckmann, Derain, and Rivera. Simon's art is not lyrical, romantic, or exotic, nor does it succumb to a sterile classicism or the dogmas of Social Realism. There is a *Kunstwollen*, a will to art, which draws on the sources of Israeli experience and creates colours and forms that evoke the desert, heat, and the collective will. He renders the hard and resolute outlook of the heroic days of the kibbutz and reflects the values which this society placed on simplicity of living, hard physical labour, co-operation and mutual help, communal rather than private property, and new forms of leisure, child-rearing, education, and culture (figs. 127, 128).

The kibbutz was the most concrete manifestation of the change in attitude toward physical labour in twentieth-century Jewish history. There, labour was seen as an essential aspect of the rebirth of the individual and the community, healing the distortion of exile by turning the social, economic pyramid back on its base. Physical labour was given a quasi-religious status.

127. (RIGHT) Johanan Simon, *Sabbath in the Kibbutz*, no date. Oil on canvas, $25\frac{3}{4} \times 19\frac{3}{4}$ in (65.5×50 cm). Tel Aviv Museum of Art.

128. (LEFT) Johanan Simon, *In the Shower*, 1952. Oil on canvas, $37 \times 25\frac{1}{}$ in (94×64 cm). Tel Aviv Museum of Art.

129. (LEFT) Marcel Janco,
Maabaroth in Grey, c.1950.
Oil on canvas, 30¾ × 38½ in
(78.1 × 97.7 cm).
New York, Jewish Museum.

130. (RIGHT) Marcel Janco,
The Wounded Soldier, no date.
Oil on canvas, 27½ × 19¾ in
(69.8 × 50.1 cm). Tel Aviv,
Rosenfeld Art Gallery.

This attitude toward manual labour was not confined to the kibbutz. Contrary to accepted belief, many of the Jewish immigrants in America were artisans who swelled the needle and building trades. Louis Lozowick in *The Concrete Mixer*, David Levine in *The Pressers*, William Gropper in *Tailor*, Isaac Soyer in *Employment Agency*, and Raphael Soyer in *Seamstress* all respond to the world of manual labour (see figs. 43, 55). Leopold Gottlieb in France, and David Bomberg, who visited Palestine in the 1920s, as well as Shalom Seba and Abraham Naton who lived there, were stimulated by new kinds of work, and often present it as an ennobling experience (fig. 134).

The confident outlook of practical idealism and sheer optimism of Johanan Simon was not shared by Marcel Janco, who arrived in Israel in 1940 as a refugee from Romania. He was a member of the original Dada group in Zurich, which, under the impact of World War I, had rejected the forms and values of Western civilization. In Israel he attempted to integrate himself into the tasks and problems of the society of settlers and incoming refugees. There is no innocence in his paintings, no ideology, no naïve belief in the resurrection of the legendary Biblical land. Instead there is the harsh reality which an experienced person encounters: the transition camps, overcrowded tent cities which cover the hills in a relentless zigzag pattern. A painter of armed partisans, Maccabees fighting for their existence, wounded soldiers bending over their rifles, Janco does not glorify war (figs. 129, 130). Rather he sees it as part of the reality which surrounds him and which he cannot ignore.

The land was not a peaceful garden of ancient olive trees with silver-green leaves shining through the morning mists or a tranquil orange grove whose golden fruit sparkled in the sun. Nor was it a barren stretch of rocks to be cleared or a malaria-ridden swamp to be dried and reclaimed by the dream of socialist brotherhood alone. As Arab and British resistance to Jewish immigration and settlement increased in the mid-1930s and as the situation of European Jewry became daily more desperate, it became clear that, if need be, the land would have to be fought for, that it demanded an intimate knowledge of its terrain and its climate, full identification with its history and geology, and a submission to its moods and seasons.

Many of the artists who came to the fore in the 1940s had joined the various youth groups and underground movements of the time and roamed the country, exploring its most distant regions in hikes and strenuous marches, camping out in the desert, and spending time in the pioneering settlements of the Negev. All this sparked the imagination and turned this ancient region into a source of new values reflecting what they regarded as the culture of an ancient Hebrew society, values they now linked to their own emerging community.

The desert became the home of these emerging artists. Quite contrary to their predecessors, they were not tourists in the desert. They were exposed daily to the blinding light, the heat and the scorching winds of the desert. The primeval landscape became the arena for their dreams and loves, and the training ground for physical survival. The desert became a giant stage for elemental life forces. For some it also became the crucible in which their growing identification with the landscape and the ancient culture of the region blossomed into a conception of art linked on the one hand to the primitivizing tendencies of modern art and on the other to the ancient art of the region.

Many of these artists, among them Itzhak Danziger, Koso Elul, Achiam and Yechiel Shemi, shared a longing for community, for an organic tie between man and his surroundings—the tent, the tree, the sheep, the well, the stone. There is a longing for a simplified life-style, for a social frame that is anti-urban, intimate, protective, uncomplicated and footloose. By fashioning archetypal images, they condensed the basic experiences of life in general and of the region in particular into rich visual forms. Recurring motifs culled from the history of the land of Canaan appear in their work—the hero, the hunter, the shepherd, the ram, the sacrifice, the altar, the gift, Baal, Ashtoret, Anat, Nimrod, the desert, the bird, the messenger, and the magic sign incised on stone. There are romantic aspects in the escape of the artist from the shield which civilization provides and in his turning toward a simpler life where only the sky or the cave shelter him. In wedding himself to a primeval region, he embraces the forces which shaped it and finds shelter in the mystic and pantheistic atmosphere which rises from the stillness of the desert, from its barren hills, its corroding rocks, its bleached sand. This silent landscape guards the secrets of the Tohu Vabohu (the Biblical chaos) and the traces of creation when the earth trembled and brought forth cliffs and craters, piled rock upon rock, and penetrated them with red veins of copper and blue arteries of lead.

The scorching wind, the blinding light and the heat envelop the body and set the mountains aflame in red and violet. They melt the veil which culture puts between man and nature and erase the boundaries between the past and the present. This might account for the fact that these artists were attracted to sculpture, which appeals more to our tactile sense than does painting. Here, the partition between the Jew and nature, between the moral law and nature, and

131. Abraham Melnikov, *The Roaring Lion*, monument of Tel Khai, 1926.
Stone, 108 × 73 × 43 in (275 × 185 × 110 cm).
K'far Giladi, Israel.

between the Jewish ethos and nature disappears. In the work of these artists one also senses the element of rebellion against the complexities of Jewish existence which is inherent in that intimate relation to a primeval landscape where the ancient Hebrew tribes once wandered. Their work reflects a return to a simpler mode of existence free of Talmudic argumentation or the Sholom Aleichem-type way of life, which always questions, qualifies, contradicts and excuses. At the same time it also reflects an instinctive repression of the facts of the Holocaust which were beginning to emerge, and a quest to return to the ancient, more natural existence which had been suppressed so long, a quest we already find expressed in early modern Hebrew literature, especially in the writing of Joseph Micha Berdichevsky, Saul Tchernichovski and Chayim Hazaz. This trend also appears in contemporary Hebrew literature—in poetry, the novel and theatre—in music and in the world of social and political ideas.[3] In the visual arts we find a clear plastic expression of the process of secularization where the loss of traditional religious sentiments is compensated for by the feeling of reverence for the act of creation.

This tendency manifested itself strongly in the monument of the *Lion of Tel Khai* (fig. 13), carved in 1926 by the sculptor Abraham Melnikov, in memory of Trumpeldor and his comrades who died in the defence of Tel Khai in 1921. Carved of hard granite, the wounded lion, still majestically erect in his pain, roars toward the Galilean hills.

Melnikov consciously turned to the art of the ancient Near East. We are immediately reminded of the monumental ancient sculpture of the winged Assyrian bulls which guarded the gates of the citadel of King Sargon at Khorsabad, of the bas-relief sculptures of the dying lioness of Nineveh, and of Nimrud from the palace of Ashurbanipal, all of which he knew from the British Museum. The massive figure of the lion, the treatment of the mane, the tail and the legs show the influence clearly, although he considerably simplified the forms and incised patterns.

The monument of Tel Khai became an early communal symbol of strength and defiance for the embattled settlers because of its archetypal character and because the image of the lion had been adopted by Judaism since Biblical times. The symbol of the lion can still be found in the synagogues of today on top of the ark or embroidered on the curtain that covers it.

Itzhak Danziger's *Nimrod*, carved in 1939, pointed to a new direction in Israeli art and heralded a trend which was to gather force in the 1940s and 1950s, a trend characterized by the culling of motifs from the myths of the Bible and from the art of the ancient people who inhabited this region. This archaic art was characterized by elements of distortion, geometrization and abstraction. The artists of that period embodied in their work the collective experiences of their generation, looking for metaphors and parallels for contemporary events in ancient sources. These artists aimed to give expression to the upheavals which stirred their times in terms of archetypal images of the culture and myths of the ancient Near East.

The hunter Nimrod is a far cry from the Western version of the Biblical hero, from the urbanized Florentine conception of David as he appears in the sculptures of Verrocchio, Donatello and Michelangelo. Nimrod is a creature of

132. Itzhak Danziger, *Nimrod*, 1939. Nubian sandstone, 40 × 12 in (100 × 33 cm). Collection of Mrs S. Danziger, Haifa.

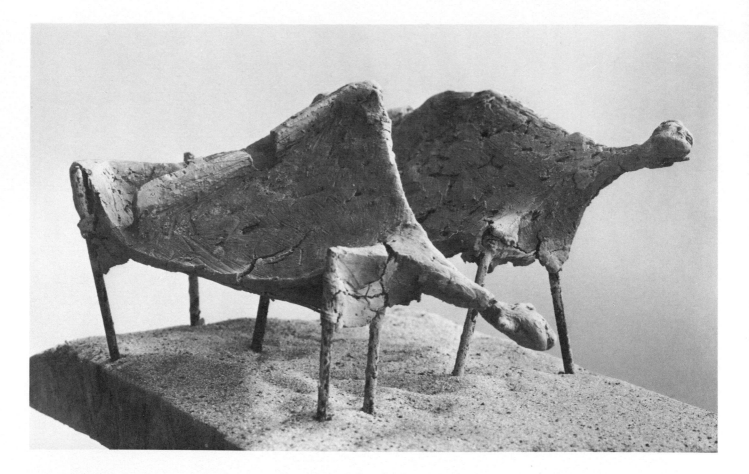

133. Itzhak Danziger, *Negev Sheep*, 1964. Bronze, 34 × 104½ × 91 in (85.6 × 263 × 204 cm). Washington D.C., Hirshhorn Museum and Sculpture Garden, Smithsonian Institute.

the desert. The hawk perched on his shoulder that frames his skull heightens the tense watchfulness and the sense of danger lurking behind the rock. Man-sized, lean, arms tightly pressed to his body, his back slightly curved like a stretched bow, low-browed, his face sharply pointed like a threatening arrow, he is every inch a hunter; his sword is his spine. He is carved in the grainy red Nabatean sandstone found near Petra. The sculpture evokes the specific colour, ring and atmosphere of the region of Petra, an ancient city carved out of rock and surrounded by hills of red sandstone from which the Nabateans, the ancient inhabitants of the city of Petra, carved their tombs and temples. The sculpture expresses physical and emotional unity between the hunter, the hawk, the sandstone, Petra and the Nabateans—a meeting of heroic myth and desert rock.

According to the legends of the Jews, Nimrod was the first of the leaders of corrupt men. He had come into possession of the clothes which God gave to Adam and Eve, and these garments gave him unheard-of strength. He was invincible in combat with beast and man and became ruler of the whole universe. 'Since the flood there has been no such sinner as Nimrod. He fashioned idols of wood and stone, and paid worship to them.'[4] He set himself up as God and men had to pay him divine honour. Rebelling against God, he also built the tower of Babel.

In mythology, Nimrod is God, ruler, builder of cities, hero and hunter, and the personification of courage. But Jewish tradition rejected him, the 'mighty hunter before the Lord'. It considered him an arch sinner, a worshipper of idols,

134. Shalom Seba,
Shearing of Sheep, 1947.
Oil on perspex, 18⅞ × 24¾ in
(48 × 63 cm).
Tel Aviv Museum of Art.

the builder of the Tower of Babel and the personification of evil. Danziger, in an act of defiance, resurrects Nimrod and thereby expresses not only the fateful encounter of pre-Biblical man with ancient Canaanite culture but also the transformation of values in his own generation. In *Nimrod* Danziger created a collective portrait, a self-image of his own generation which lived and trained in the desert and which fought the War of Independence. Danziger directs the impulses of a whole generation past the post-Biblical era of Judaism with its injunctions against graven images, past the teachings of the prophets, of Rabbis and scholars, past the Diaspora and its encounters with Western civilization, to its ancient tribal beginnings.

This meant also a conscious turning away from European culture, from the values of the Jewish Diaspora and from the major artistic trends which had emerged in Paris and had been a strong influence on artists in Palestine during the 1920s and up to the Second World War. 'The history and the archaeology of a place are part of the landscape,' noted Danziger. 'The landscape is reflected in trees, stones and soil—in all these and animals and people which inhabit them, in their faces and their surroundings. In *Nimrod* I first became aware of my inclination to create compositions combining all these features.'[5]

Danziger expresses this search for unity between the landscape and the object in several sculptures of sheep, which he considered the most typical animals of the region. In these sculptures he combines the animals with the slopes of the terrain, the wadis, the sheepfold, the trough and the conduit for carrying the water, the sloping canvas of the tent and the poles which support it.

> A flock of sheep resembles a carpet, something which glides down the hill and covers the ground, the slope of the valley. Sheep are also useful animals; they have a distinct relation to water. And in this region people once went from one waterhole to the other, and they continue to do so in the desert even to this very day. Sheep are symbols, models. Through the sheep I reach what interests me, the soil, light and shade. Sheep resemble the tent of the Bedouin. The legs of the sheep are the poles of the tent; sheep are moving sculpture. If we look at a photograph of a flock of sheep, they look like plants growing in the desert.[6]

We could add that the sheep is an archetypal symbol of weakness and a metaphor of innocence and of the need of anguished creatures for a shepherd. The founding fathers of the ancient Hebrews were shepherds. The sheep had already become an important element in the paintings of Reuven Rubin, together with his landscapes, self-portraits and portraits of his family. Shalom Seba, who had emigrated to Palestine in 1936, leaving behind him a successful artistic career, adapted the ancient theme of the shepherd and also the act of sheep-shearing which he had observed in one of the kibbutzim (fig. 134).

Like Danziger, most of the artists who turned to Biblical myths and the cultures of Mesopotamia, Canaan and Egypt grew up in Europe and came to Israel in their childhood. Many of them came from a culturally rich background. They had witnessed in their early youth the turmoil of events leading to World War II and to the Holocaust, had participated in the struggle against the British Mandate, the establishment of the State of Israel and the War of Independence. Their search for a new identity in an awareness of their ancient culture was spurred on by archaeological excavations which threw light on this ancient culture—the discovery of the cities of Hatzor and Megiddo, of the mosaic floor of the sixth-century synagogue of Beth Alpha, of the Ugaritic language and of the Dead Sea Scrolls. They also encountered the life-style of Arabs and Bedouin who dwelt in the desert and the old Jewish communities isolated from Western European influences such as the Yemenite Jews, whose ancient tradition was still intact.

Aharon Kahana came to Palestine with the wave of immigration in 1934 after the Nazis rose to power; he had studied in the art academies of Stuttgart and Berlin. Once in the new country he made a conscious effort to respond to the new landscape. *Dialogue at Night* (fig. 135) cloaks the tent, reclining figure, hill and narrow paths in a serence and restful stillness. A flat, two-dimensional composition, firmly constructed of predominantly horizontal ideograms, and subtly orchestrated colour evoke the sound and inscrutable spirit of the desert. A restrained lyricism prevails. Earth colours discreetly heightened by touches of ochre, green, blue, vermilion and white, bounded by terse lines, create an archaic Biblical mood.

Even in the works of artists such as Koso Elul, Shamai Haber and Achiam, who live outside Israel today, the impact of the desert and the Negev is strongly felt. These artists work in massive stone or wood; they set their figures carefully into the landscape and, with their archaic forms, express states of mind allied to Biblical myths. Sometimes one senses vaguely religious moods, responses to

135. Aharon Kahana,
Dialogue at Night, 1950.
Oil on canvas, $51\frac{1}{2} \times 77\frac{3}{4}$ in
(130×195 cm). Collection of
Mr S. Abraham, Milan.

the Tohu Vabohu that stretches before them in the desert—majestic, over-whelming and numinous.

Shamai Haber goes back to rough unhewn stone, gathered from the field or quarried from the mountain, and through it evokes the simplest human activities—the marking of a field, of a sacred spot, or the raising of an altar. For his sculpture *Altar*, he put stone upon stone and placed them in a precarious equilibrium (fig. 138). Achiam carves Canaanite idols and Biblical figures in hard basalt. His clearly defined forms are simplified and heavily distorted. Like the primitive artist's work, his deals with basic human drives. In *Adam and Eve* (fig. 136) and in *Pregnant Woman* (fig. 137) he celebrates sexual desire and fertility.

Koso Elul, when he was still in Israel, placed a rough-textured square block of stone on a ledge overlooking a deep Negev canyon south of Mitzpeh Ramon (fig. 140). The block has carved in its centre a mysterious shape suggesting an all-seeing eye, or perhaps a symbol of fertility, at any rate, the presence of man in the wilderness. 'It's the same urge', says Elul of his sculpture, 'that forced prehistoric man . . . to go and carve a form, a shape, which became an affirmation of his existence on this earth, his God, his touch with the unknown and his anchor on life—the life of his time.'[7] The symbol he creates is equally convincing and strong when considered as a special offer, gesture or sacrifice.

Hava Mehutan also tames a wild and desolate, unpredictable region with the

136. Achiam,
Adam and Eve, 1955.
Basalt, each figure $39\frac{1}{2}$ in high
(100 cm). Collection of the artist.

137. (LEFT) Achiam,
Pregnant Woman, 1952.
Basalt, $43\frac{5}{8}$ in high (110 cm).
Collection of the artist.

138. (RIGHT) Shamai Haber,
Altar, 1957.
Granite, 30 in high (75 cm).
Collection of Alix de Rothschild.

139. Hava Mehutan,
Offering, 1963.
Wood, $19\frac{3}{4} \times 47\frac{1}{2} \times 16$ in
($50 \times 120 \times 40$ cm).
Collection of the artist.

140. Koso Elul, *Horizon*, 1963. Stone, 5 ft 11 in × 7 ft 10½ in × 2 ft 5½ in (180 × 240 × 75 cm). Mitzpeh Ramon Canyon, Israel.

bold rhythm of her calligraphic signs hewn in marble. The signs echo the craggy outline of the hilltop and the shifting pattern the wind presses into the desert sand, as well as the undulating geological strata she has observed in the depth of mountains. Born and raised in Philadelphia, since the 1950s she has lived and worked in Beer Sheba, on the edge of the desert. Her work draws heavily on the physical features of a landscape charged with Biblical lore and myth, a landscape she explores during long and lonely roaming. Intersecting mountain ranges become wooden shapes that are firmly locked into one another, and the wide stretches of the yellow Negev desert are turned into finely grained wooden planes laminated layer upon layer, meeting and parting at a gentle incline.

Hava Mehutan's series of sculptures called *Offering* (fig. 139) are unique. The allusion is to the Biblical concept of Minchah, which has a broad range of meaning from gift to present to sacrifice. The sculptures are trunks of wood worked with axe or mallet, or gouged into truncated organic shapes that are reminiscent of cattle. They are stacked horizontally like fire wood, creating an interplay between mass and void, round and oval, concave and convex. They represent the offering and the wood that consumes it. They allude to the Biblical and ritual sacrifices performed in the land; they allude to the sacrifices Israelis know only too well. However, for the artist the Biblical concept of sacrifice is charged with personal and social meaning. 'It is the giving of mother to child, of woman to man, of son to parents, of man to his friend, people, country and God. It is giving the gift of love, of birth and life.'[8] The giving is accepted, glorified and praised in her sculpture as a condition of meaningful life.

Moshe Castel, since the mid-1940s, has alluded in his work to the geological formations and archaeological excavations of the Negev and Galilee. He brings to his work the unique characteristics of the Sephardic Jewish community, which developed within an oriental rather than Eastern European culture. Ancient Hebrew, Sumerian and Canaanite inscriptions play a major role in his work. Castel is the descendant of an old Spanish family from Castile who escaped to the land of Israel during the fifteenth-century Spanish Inquisition. Among his forebears were cabbalists, Rabbis, scribes and musicians, and his memories are filled with colourful Sephardic and Bucharan costumes and folk art. His background is therefore quite different from that of artists who immigrated from Eastern Europe or the West. He was born in Jerusalem. The visual surroundings in which he grew up were filled with specimens of Jewish

141. Moshe Castel, *Sephardic Wedding Feast*, 1942. Oil on canvas, $21\frac{1}{4} \times 28\frac{3}{4}$ in (54×73 cm). Tel Aviv Museum of Art.

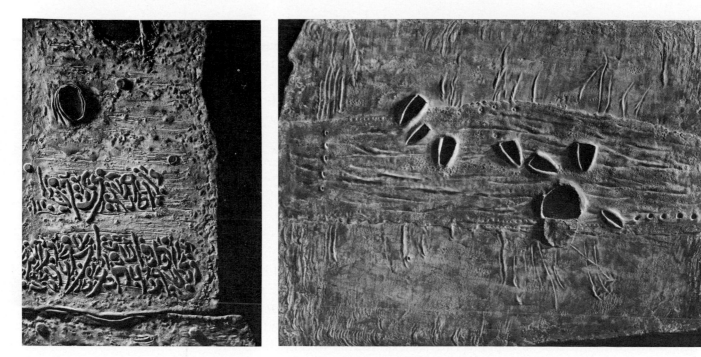

142. Moshe Castel,
Basalt of Galilee, 1964.
Basalt and mixed media,
58 × 45 in (146 × 114 cm).
Collection of Mr and Mrs
Recanati, New York.

143. Moshe Castel,
Basalt Relief, 1959.
Mixed media on canvas,
38½ × 51½ in (97 × 130 cm).
Collection of the artist.

ceremonial art of oriental origin and flavour—cameos, medallions, plates, parchments, manuscripts and scrolls, Turkish and Bucharan textiles and dresses, Torah crowns, Torah mantles and ark curtains and lamps, all with Eastern ornaments. Castel's father was a Rabbi, oriental scholar and calligrapher who wrote parchments and Torah scrolls and designed and executed ornamental silk Torah coverings and curtains for the ark.

It was this background Castel sought to reconcile first with his own mystic tendencies and then with the abstract tendencies of modern art. In 1927, he went to Paris and stayed there for 13 years. Upon his return he settled in Sefad, a picturesque city of old synagogues in the mountains of Galilee, a centre of cabbalistic learning and the Zohar. His early work often dealt with Jewish communal and religious customs—Passover meals, Sabbath meals conducted in spacious vaulted halls, Hebrew manuscript pages, prayer shawls or motifs from the synagogue—and was decidedly influenced by Rouault and Chagall. He later approached the style of the Spaniard, Tapies, after a chance encounter with the ruins of the ancient synagogue of Chorazin.

> The spring whence I draw my inspiration rises from ancient Hebrew sources, which link me close to the fundamentals of Oriental, Sumerian, Assyrian and Canaanite art. . . . One day I chanced to be in Chorazin, the ruins of an ancient Galilean synagogue, built entirely of basalt stone, black lava stones, carved with figures and ornamentation. I decided to take some of the basalt stone, grind it, knead it and restore it, creating out of it new forms of my own, in high relief texture, as did my ancestors.[9]

From then, Castel's interest in signs, letters and ancient calligraphy has dominated his work. He re-creates low-relief, rock-hard ancient stone tablets by means of a paste of basalt ground in oil, and raises the letters above the surface, or incises signs and patterns into the surface. He works in iridescent colours of blue, red and green to which the Western eye is hardly accustomed but which add a mysterious glow to the cryptic messages from the past. His roots are located in the ancient Near East; by evoking undecipherable ancient inscriptions on slabs and tablets and imbuing them with the patina of age he brings us closer to this world from which Israel emerged and where it became embedded.

The Return of the People

The romantic attitude toward the desert and toward the art of the region could not survive the harsh realities which presented themselves when World War II had come to an end and when the War of Independence was fought and the Jewish State established. The masses of immigrants arriving in the crowded ships from Europe and Africa, who had to be fed, clothed and housed in tent cities, changed the texture of a pioneering society. Reality overwhelmed the visions of the prophets of the Return. Artists, prodded by the 'New Horizon' group, looked toward the art centres in the West from which they had been isolated during World War II and during the War of Independence in 1948. Suddenly the country was flooded with new influences blurring its efforts and undoing the dream of returning to or creating an indigenous culture. Many things were suddenly forgotten and many things suddenly changed.

> The ships in which they brought us here to build
> the Pithom and Raamses[10] departed as they came
> and we are left on the shore with the giant mute buildings
> which could not tell us for which ruler and for which
>   purpose they were built
> soon the great night will descend, the night of the desert . . .
> we work at dusk, the bit of light was not ours
> but the light which was left from another generation.[11]

Artists and art students, eager to be in touch with new ideas, went to the large art centres for protracted stays and often settled there permanently. Paris, New York, London, Mexico City, Brazil and Florence were preferred places. In the major museums and galleries they were confronted with various trends of post-World War II art and with the works of art of ancient civilizations and primitive cultures. The influence of these cultures and of their rituals and myths, whose esoteric contents and forms had influenced the character of twentieth-century art from its very beginning, did not go unnoticed by Israeli artists. They found out that what their isolation had permitted them to regard for a time as a preoccupation with archaic themes peculiar to their own experience was in fact the common ground of modern art. This they had known all along but now they had to confront it directly. The pervasiveness of the underlying concern with archaic styles in modern art reinforced in some artists the search for roots in the ancient culture of Canaan, Assyria, Babylon and Egypt. Thus in spite of the changes in the cultural climate, the search for roots in the region of the Near East continued into the 1950s and beyond. It is a factor of some constancy and can also be observed today in the work of some of the younger artists for whom the landscape and ancient myth of Canaan continue to be a fertile source. Others were fascinated by technology and some assimilated the two interests in their work.

Menashe Kadishman, of the younger generation of Israeli artists, develops further Danziger's notion of a flock of sheep being a moving sculpture. Strongly influenced by the various avant-garde developments during the 1960s and 1970s such as happenings, earth works, art povera, work with natural processes and the use of elements of unchanged reality, he probes the boundaries which divide art from life and participates in the constant redefinition of art. In the 1978 Venice Biennale he built a sheepfold and introduced grass, hay and 18 live sheep, the backs of which he coloured with blue markings. As the sheep moved about between the fences the composition of blue spots on the 'live canvas' made of sheep's wool constantly changed.

In this environmental project in which the traditional boundaries between the various arts and between art and reality became blurred, the artist went back to his youth when he was a shepherd in the kibbutz and a pathfinder for an archaeological expedition which explored the copper deposits in the Negev. This project is different in spirit from his large sculptures of metal and plate glass which create the illusion of massive weight suspended in mid-air and held aloft by unseen forces. These sculptures link him to the international tendencies of minimal art, and are the result of his protracted stay in today's metropolitan art centres and his fascination with the world of technology.

144. Menashe Kadishman, *The Altar*, 1959. Bronze, $8\frac{1}{2} \times 8\frac{1}{2} \times 4\frac{3}{4}$ in ($21.5 \times 21.5 \times 12$ cm). Collection of the artist.

In *Trees in the Ocean* (Plate XI), Kadishman harmonizes the tension between his pastoral organic creations and technological structural ones. Large rectangular metal sheets are perforated by the shape of a tree and 'planted' on the shoreline. They break the incoming waves, letting them flow through. The sculpture metaphorically unites the natural world of tree and the flow of tide with unyielding metal sheet. The iron sheets stand there as firm barriers, while the cut-out trees are windows through which the sky and the sun can be seen. They convey a sense of freedom. Romantic feelings stirred by the setting sun, the distant horizon, and the stormy sea are reinforced by an industrially produced object. The work is rooted in contemporary artistic tendencies explored by Caro, Segal, Christo, Haacke, Andre and Beuys. Like them, Kadishman moves from the self-contained work into the surrounding space and uses at will steel, glass, curtains, animals, trees, and flowing water. *Trees in the Ocean* is charged with romantic Zionist echoes. The hero returns home from afar on a battered ship, plants trees, rejuvenates the country, protects it, and becomes a free man.

Yechiel Shemi, a student of Danziger and since his youth a member of a kibbutz and deeply rooted in his country, uses other visual metaphors. Many of his early iron sculptures bear the marks one associates with Israeli conditions. *Standing Sculpture* (fig. 145) is a steel plate torn from the hull of a ship. It is

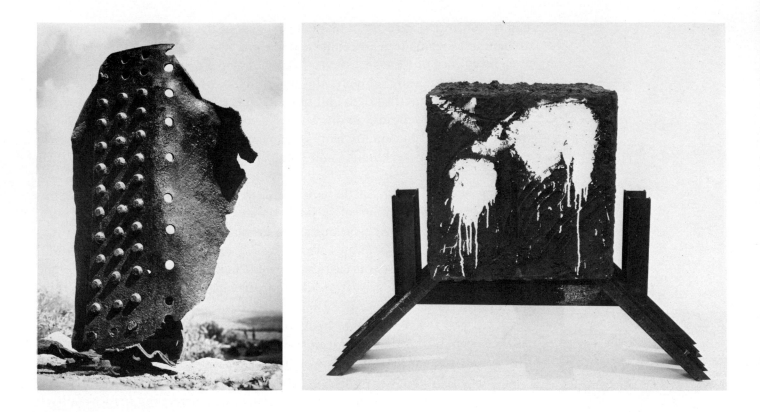

transplanted from the harbour to the hillside. The associations it evokes are many. It is a shield which protects, a defiant and triumphant figure robed and winged, like a Nike, it is a marker in the field. It bears the signs of violence and scarcity. It reveals a capacity often observed in Israeli life for improvisation, imagination and inventiveness. The physical and social landscape of Israel is an integral part of its content.

Ygael Tumarkin combines steel and earth when he reverts like many of his contemporaries to the archetypal image of the altar. It is a twentieth-century altar constructed of steel beams and a cube of dried soil, which evokes the conflicting claims over the land. In this work he responds to the central religious and political issues which beset the country. Restless, pugnacious, resourceful, Tumarkin's boldness may have been encouraged by Bertolt Brecht, with whom he worked as stage designer. In his work he uses scraps of metal, concrete, and discarded armour, helmets, photographs, prints and polyester, and anything which comes to hand to meet his expressive needs. (figs. 146, 147).

Danziger after the Second World War also developed a concept of environmental art, already implicit in his *Nimrod*. Probably this was a natural outcome of his previous work as it expressed his feelings for the landscape. His teaching responsibility at the School of Architecture of the Technion in Haifa reinforced his tendency to combine the object of his compositions with its geographical, archaeological and historical context, and nurtured his ever-widening conception of art. He began to take note of local shrines which abound in the country: sacred trees and sacred groves and the various rites connected with them—the hanging of cloths, rags and lamps from branches and the burning of incense. He noticed also the dense orchards surrounded by walls, the cisterns and irrigation

145. (LEFT) Yechiel Shemi, *Standing Sculpture*, 1963. Wired metal, $43\frac{5}{8}$ in high (110 cm). Collection of the artist.

146. (RIGHT) Ygael Tumarkin, *Earth Sculpture*, 1979 (model). Corten and soil, $38\frac{1}{2} \times 44\frac{3}{4} \times 24\frac{1}{2}$ in ($97 \times 138 \times 62$ cm). Tel Aviv Museum of Art.

147. Ygael Tumarkin,
Sculpture in Arad, 1963.
Reinforced concrete,
52 ft 9 in × 26 ft 4 in × 33 ft
(16 × 8 × 10 m). Arad, Israel.

methods; the small tombstones which served as signposts in the landscape; and connected them with the Biblical concept of Makom, literally God, but also a holy place.

He became involved in the ecological aspects of the landscape and conservation as well, and in co-operation with scientists devised draining systems and rehabilitation projects on the slopes of Mount Carmel devastated by quarrying and mining. Rather than a concrete monument, he designed a sacred grove as a memorial for soldiers who fell in the War of Independence.[12]

A tragic source for memorial sculptures arose from the frequent Israeli wars. Sometimes destroyed armoured vehicles are planted near the site of battle, sometimes obelisks serve as markers. Dani Karavan in his memorial for the Negev brigade clearly crossed the boundary of sculpture toward environmental design, the outdoor stage set and architecture. The monument, which is constructed on a hill south-west of Beer Sheba and overlooks the desert end of the city, does not overpower by cold formality or by overwhelming monumentality which keeps the viewer at a respectful distance. Its size is calculated so that it is neither overwhelmed by the vastness of the desert nor does it dwarf its viewers (fig. 148).

One is aware at first of rough, concrete shapes which seem to be scattered at random over the crest of the hill. A cylindrical tower rises over the varied shapes of concrete. The monument intrigues us by the choreography of its plastic forms. Their unique shape and informal arrangement evoke the partisan character of the brigade which it commemorates. It invites the viewer to approach and walk among the strange masses. Different plastic forms arise from the desert ground, gloomy and grand. Some resemble a bird, a cut-up snake, a

concrete sail moving through the air, the sloping canvas of a tent, the dropped wing of a plane. Some shapes curl and wind on the ground and abruptly rise into the air. There are sloping walls advancing toward the viewer or moving away from him. A long aqueduct carries water from the spring: one follows it and reaches a narrow passage bounded by large inclined walls leading toward a split memorial dome. Narrow passages resemble communications trenches and bunkers or the odd shapes of desert wadis. The monument can be visually comprehended in its totality only from its tower. Its parts are grouped around two axes: north–south and west–east. Merging into architecture, the sculpture is designed to evoke an intense spatial experience. The viewer is made to squeeze through a narrow path or to stoop low in order to advance into one of the spaces, only to be turned back in frustration by an ever-descending ceiling. One is led to act out and feel the rhythm of movement in one of the beleaguered lonely settlements, with their rising watchtowers which dot the landscape in border areas; the rhythm and experience of advance and retreat, of surprise and anxiety, and of taking cover. The wind howls through the pipes placed in the perforations of the tower. The water that flows through the aqueduct and falls into a well provides an ever-present sound. The concrete shapes are heavily textured with the songs of the period, graffiti of soldiers, military maps and battle reports. Among the surrealistic shapes a romantic mood of siege prevails.

The work of Naftali Bezem and Abraham Ofek, who came to Israel as youths, is saturated with the experience of emigration and settlement. The lives of both were affected by the apocalyptic events of mass migration following World

148. Dani Karavan, *Monument to the Negev Brigade*, 1965. Reinforced concrete, ground area 325 × 325 ft (100 × 100 m), tower 65 ft high (20 m). Beer Sheba, Israel.

166

War II. These events transformed Israel from an intimate, pioneering society, bent upon the creation of a national culture, into a melting pot of Jews from North Africa and Asia; a haven for refugees and survivors of concentration camps in Europe; and finally into a beleaguered nation. Bezem is haunted by the trauma of the emigrants arriving in small boats with their meagre belongings. In his paintings, newly arrived refugees step from the boat, and kiss the earth or embrace a stinging cactus plant (fig. 149).

While many of the younger generation of Israeli artists have chosen to enter the mainstream of modern art, and thus, like others in international art centres, have largely been preoccupied with formal problems, Bezem and Ofek have rooted their art in the landscape and life of the people which they have intimately experienced.

Ofek creates compositions with figures commonly referred to in Israel as 'the other Israel' or 'the second Israel'—the underprivileged oriental section of the population. In his paintings, people are like plants which have been uprooted from their native habitat but have not yet struck new roots (fig. 150). They do not seem to belong to their new country. They are unwilling settlers who do not love the earth. They are disoriented, inarticulate and grotesque. Their gestures, like their bodies, are heavy, slow, and out of proportion. They are people who have struggled all their lives to exist. Now their struggle is with authority, with the soil, with their neighbours, with their family and with themselves. These conflicts distort their posture and their gait. Their strength seems to lie in their patient submission to fate, in being rooted in themselves, in their limited awareness of the world. They are a silent people. They speak the language of instinct and substitute gaze, touch, and inarticulate gesture for words. Their needs are basic, they seem at their best when they turn to ancient rituals, still potent and imbued with a serious primitive religious force which guides them through a confused, insecure world.

In contrast to an earlier generation, Ofek paints life as he experienced it when he arrived in Israel on a fully packed boat from his native Bulgaria during a time

149. (LEFT) Naftali Bezem,
Man with Plant, 1960.
Oil on canvas,
39½ × 39½ in (100 × 100 cm).
Collection of the artist.

150. (RIGHT) Abraham Ofek,
Settlers Conversing, 1970.
Detail of mural, west wall,
10 × 14 ft (3 × 4.26 m).
K'far Uriah, Community Centre.

of extreme hardship following the War of 1948. He represents Israel as a crude network of brutal necessities, and bares life at its nodal points: birth, marriage, death, departure, wandering and arrival. There is a strong awareness of the solitariness of man and the ambivalence of human relations—a strong sense of closeness and distance. He paints man in relation to other men, in relation to his neighbour, his cat, his cow, his hut, his yard, his table, his chair, and his bread. There are influences of Picasso, Diego Rivera and Jankel Adler, as well as traces of Jean Dubuffet and Candido Portinari. There is also simple humour in the treatment of his figures and the love with which he depicts the domesticated animals, suggesting the influence of Bulgarian folk tales and the stories of the Yiddish writers like Sholom Aleichem and Mendele Mocher Sefarim. Like the disfigurement and stunting we often encounter in their characters, Ofek's grotesque figures manifest severe incongruities.

Ofek's most important work to date has been his large mural paintings in the

151. Abraham Ofek,
The Return, 1970.
Detail of mural, east wall,
10 × 38 ft (3 × 11.58 m).
K'far Uriah, Community Centre.

community centre of K'far Uriah, an isolated village on a hilltop settled mostly by immigrants from Morocco. The murals are unique in Israel because of their large size and the coherence with which the work is integrated with the experience of the villagers. There, on three walls facing the stage, Ofek painted the central motifs of the recurring epic of modern Jewish history—migrating toward the promised land, settling, and building a new life. On the eastern wall, 10×38 feet large, groups of men, women, children and animals walk along an uninhabited landscape. On the northern wall, 13×35 feet, the immigrants, with common effort, construct an ark near the sea. A city rises nearby. On the western wall, 10×38 feet, the growth and development of communal life is shown in three scenes, a wedding, a service in the synagogue and settlers seated at the table and conversing with each other (fig. 150).

Ofek depicts a process of painful dislocation and efforts of individual and group adjustment to a new place. He does not show this to be a heroic effort by

idealizing the figures, their faces or their postures. There is a sober matter-of-factness about the people. They are driven by forces they hardly understand; their family, their group and their mutual dependence keep them together. The statement is refreshingly anti-heroic. But as in others of his paintings, he attempts to understand the condition of their situation and to fathom the character of men and women by their gait, their body posture, their gestures, and their relation to one another.

Ofek, in his patient search to understand their conditions, hardships and unexpressed longings, and in his effort to make his art intelligible to the whole community, while drawing from their life-style, links his art with that of David Bomberg, Joseph Herman, Ben Shahn, Jack Levine, and the Soyers.

Migration and return are also the central theme of Yosl Bergner's mural at Haifa University. Here we are confronted with a critical evaluation of the central theme in modern Jewish and modern Israeli history.

Bergner, whom we have discussed earlier among those whose perception has been deeply influenced by the Holocaust (p. 118), is the son of the Yiddish poet Melech Ravitch. He left his father's home in Warsaw in 1938, one year before the outbreak of World War II, and emigrated to Australia. There he studied art and became known as a social realist. Yet in his subsequent migrations he also turned toward a visionary, surrealist form of expression.

The mural, which covers an area of 1,600 square feet, is divided into five

152. Yosl Bergner, *Migration and Return*, 1973. Mural, central section 25 × 25 ft (7.56 × 7.56 m), each outer section 9 ft 8 in × 27 ft 8 in (3 × 8.5 m). Haifa University.

sections: one large central area covering the height of two floors, and four horizontal sections, two on the upper level and two on the lower level of the main building of the University of Haifa. These sections are situated on the right and left of the central area and flow into it. Thus, the mural's composition can be regarded as a large triptych, the wings of which are horizontally divided by the floor and exist on different levels of the building. In the upper left wing, pots, pans, graters, and other kitchen utensils fly over the sea toward the centre section of the mural. In the upper right wing, pointed spice boxes and square and round alms boxes coming in over the ocean descend against a dark sky on a deserted coast.

The lower part of the left wing is dominated by the façade of a white horizontal building with doors and windows blocked by wild bulls, roots and plants, all of which point like threatening fingers toward the centre. One doorway is filled with the head of a lonely man.

In the lower part of the right wing, a boat packed with masked people, fierce dogs, one-eyed giraffes and many-eyed men with pointed caps or crowns is gently steered by an angel toward the centre wall. This part of the mural is 25 feet high and 25 feet wide. It contains a large façade of a white-walled building, punctuated irregularly with doorways and windows from which masked figures of men, women, and animals emerge.

The composition is overflowing with details—heads, crowns, flags, fool's caps, soldiers, many-eyed faces, bare women's breasts, horned masks of bulls, protruding jaws of giraffes, images of birds and dogs, all of which are metamorphosed into images of men. We are confronting a masquerade on the ladders and steps, windows and doorways of a white stage set. There is a feeling of restlessness in the mural which is heightened by the artist's swift brush strokes, by the distortions of people and objects, and by the multiple transparent overlapping of green, ochre, red and black, freely applied. The surface is activated by the dominant silver-grey and blue tones contrasting sharply with white, black and occasional orange-red. The colour is like a visceral stew, applied sometimes with heavy impasto and at other times with nervous, thin brush strokes. It is always sensuously felt, activating the surface.

The painting, especially in its large centre section, seems whipped into a state of frenzy by the multiplicity of eyes which stare in all directions, and by its strange array of masks. One looks in vain for a point of rest. One grasps at the white of the building only to be caught again by the frenzied brush strokes, the thicket of branches and roots, the open-mouthed faces, moving in packed groups across the wall.

The artist chose not to work in the traditional fresco technique. The irregular concrete surface, with its visible lines created by the wooden mould into which the concrete was originally poured, the left-over marks, incisions and nails suited him perfectly. He applied acrylic paint directly onto the wall.

The question of the overall meaning arises. While the various compositions seem to be independent of each other, it is evident from their themes, their style and location and certain formal links that they belong to each other. They are not connected by any particular causal relation but by hidden parallels and by threads of association. The medieval composition of the triptych points to a quasi-religious meaning.

The Holocaust had haunted this artist for many years. His ceaseless wanderings often brought him to Spain, where the impressions he gathered from the deserted Toledo synagogues of Santa Maria la Blanca and El Transito created an intimate connection in his mind between the recent Holocaust and an earlier one, the Spanish Inquisition. The periodicity of these catastrophic events, the migrations, deaths and resurrections of communities, of ways of life and of cult objects became an integral part of his artistic vision. The weird became grounded in historical reality. The Inquisition and the Holocaust became one recurring event, a cycle of expulsion and return.

The return of the persecuted and the wretched to the country of their prayers seems to be indicated by the sacred and home-like objects, their tribal signs, which point toward the deserted sandy coast on which they gather. It is further indicated by means of the crowded boat and the divine guidance of the angel. It is suggested as well by the desolation of homes reclaimed by nature and the carnival-like atmosphere of violence and make-believe established by the 'redeemed'. Their screaming, posturing, and parading, the perpetual excitement and continuous happening seem to contain the essence of their own being and of the situation in which they find themselves. Man is a born fool and bound to join a community of fools. Also, there is never a dull moment in a company of fools. These are allusions in the painting to contemporary Israel.

The artist who has conjured up the Inquisition has himself been witness to the Holocaust and the Return, and does not view the return of the people to the land of their prayers as heroic and radiant with the aura of a romantic nationalism. They return with pots and pans and pretensions to a country which devours its inhabitants. Doubt, sarcasm and the grotesque prevail and mark the people as well as the objects. The consequences of the Holocaust are all around us. The inner transformation which the prophets of the Return had envisaged, and which has been at least partially realized, is discounted or ignored. The centre wall could be the location of any ghetto around the world. Israel is but another version of the Jewish ghetto. In this mural Bergner sees Israel as a circus at the seashore.

Man's foolishness and pretence do not depend on his geographical location; the *Ship of Fools* by Hieronymus Bosch comes to mind. Bergner's work has a self-flagellating quality and a great deal of Jewish self-deprecating humour. In its style and its bold conception the artist conveys a highly personal view of the world and of Israel. It is the work of an artist fully at home both in twentieth-century painting and in the worldwide outlook of modern Yiddish literature. In its anguished and Kafkaesque ambivalence it echoes, however faintly, well-known works by European masters. There are the sharp-pointed forms of Sutherland and Picasso, and echoes of Ensor's masks, the flayed skin in the portraits of Soutine and Bacon, and the bats of Goya's etchings and his paintings from the House of the Deaf.

The saga of the Israeli pioneer intrigued Bergner in a significant series of works created in the late 1970s. He had an uncle who had come to Palestine in 1910 as a pioneer. Like others who came, he dried swamps, planted trees, built roads and stood guard. Later he studied art at Bezalel, went to Vienna to continue his art studies, and there, in 1921, he shot himself, leaving his paint box and colours and an old photograph of himself dressed as a bedouin shouldering a rifle. The colours became the playthings of Yosl Bergner the child, and the photograph a source of wonder and puzzlement to this very day. Who was this uncle? Who were those pioneers? What did they want and what did they come for? These are the questions which intrigue the painter. But he really has no answer. In his paintings they are visionaries, frenzied, living in groups, burnings with an inner fire, living in a reality of their own making, always restless and, like the painter himself, animated by dreams and ideas only, whose meaning is unclear even to themselves (Plate XII).

Beyond the romantic dream, and beyond the harsh realities there remains in many artists a strong emotional, atavistic tie to the idea of Israel which remains an integral part of their identity. Hanna Orlof, who resided in Paris, made the sculpture *Mother and Child* (fig. 153) for Kibbutz Ein Gev on the eastern shore of Lake Kinnerth. In its compact form the sculpture expresses a tower of hope, continuity and offering. The mother extends her reach by lifting the child toward the sky.

George Segal, who visited Israel in 1973, felt his encounter with the rocks in the desert landscape as a soaring, almost metaphysical experience. He sensed the intimate relation between the harshness of the physical surroundings, the history of the people and the way they live and behave. The Akedah seemed to

153. (OPPOSITE) Hanna Orlof, *Mother and Child*, 1949. Bronze, 54¾ in high (239 cm). Kibbutz Ein Gev, Israel.

154. (RIGHT) George Segal, *Abraham and Isaac*, 1973. Plaster and metal, 84 × 120 × 5 in (211 × 305 × 126 cm). Tel Aviv Foundation for Literature and Art, Mann Auditorium.

him a natural theme for the landscape he found in Israel.

Segal cast a nine-foot-square rock, not far from the site where, according to tradition, the Akedah had taken place, and made it the base and the stony environment, integral to the Biblical scene (fig. 154). The composition is restrained, built on a vertical versus horizontal axis. The artist synthesized in the composition both the formal and descriptive character of the situation, stressing the psychological aspect of the Akedah rather than the outward dramatic moment of great physical exertion interrupted by divine intervention.

Before approaching his task Segal immersed himself in Kirkegaard's variety of interpretations of the thoughts that went through Abraham's mind as he approached Mount Moriah: 'But Abraham prepared everything for the sacrifice, calmly and quietly; but when he turned and drew the knife, Isaac saw his left hand was clenched in despair, that a tremor passed through his body—but Abraham drew the knife.'[13] In the sculpture the son, still a boy, is unbound, lying on the flat rock, calm and trusting, observing his father's actions closely. The son looks at Abraham, Abraham does not look at the son. The right hand of the father holds the knife; the left hand is clenched. The action is frozen at the moment of decision.

The sculptor has turned the religious event into an everyday story. Abraham is middle-aged and pudgy, dressed in jeans and naked from the waist up. The sculpture, a mummified and calcified image, is felt to be both near to and removed from everyday life. It is a haunting metaphor of reality and a twentieth-century echo of an ancient legend.

CHAPTER SIX

The Evocation of the Religious Tradition

However free and liberal Jewish people tend to be in their religious practices, at the core of their cohesiveness and collective consciousness exists a common religious tradition shared for centuries. It is this tradition which shaped them and made a people scattered all over the world feel a common identity. Whatever their adjustment to the diverse demands made on them by the different environments in which they made their home, there are common rituals, objects and garments around which their religious life revolves.

Artists may deal with Jewish religious subject-matter because they are attracted by the inherent picturesqueness of ceremonial rites and ceremonial objects and dress. Often they are fascinated by the variety of religious emotion, by the enthusiasm of Hassidic dance, the intensity of communal worship, the inwardness of solitary prayer, or the quiet dignity of the Rabbi. The evocation of the religious life may stem from a need of personal identification; by transporting the artist back to his own childhood it reunites him with his family and the home he came from. All this accounts for the basic unity which pervades the treatment of Jewish religious subject-matter in works of art, although created in different countries, under different circumstances and often under the influence of different local traditions.

The expression of the religious theme in the works of Chagall, Ryback, Lissitzky and other artists from the Pale was marked by a certain folk-like quality rather than by personal religious emotion. These artists painted Jews who were still living in an environment that was dominated by religious observances as manifested in custom and dress. Their work revealed a strong folkloristic conception often endowed with a touch of humour, even of the grotesque.

In the art of Jewish artists working in the West, religious life is recalled with nostalgia, as an experience that touches the artist deeply. Prayer is perceived as an individual act of devotion and introspection, as in the etchings of Herman Struck (fig. 158) or the paintings of Ben Zion or Marvin Cherney (figs. 157, 162). A mood of intimate reverence prevails in the blessing of the candles with the arrival and departure of the Sabbath and in the act of carrying the Torah.

Some works deal with everyday communal prayer, as in the ink and wash drawing of Jacob Steinhardt (fig. 156), or with childhood memories of fervent rituals, colourful services and fear-inspiring sacred days.

Invocation (fig. 155) by Max Weber makes us think of Cézanne, of Cubist forms, of the art of the Incas, the Aztecs, the Mayas and also some African sculpture. Weber synthesizes these diverse influences and infuses them with a highly personal and emotional expression.

The composition possesses a solid architectural quality. Although the forms are grossly distorted the massive figures seated around the table are kept in a tense equilibrium by strongly expressive gestures. A primitive and religious

155. Max Weber, *Invocation*, 1919. Oil on canvas, 48 × 41 in (121 × 103 cm). Rome, Vatican Museums, Modern Galleries.

feeling pervades the canvas. The woman on the right, her head supported by her arm, is in a trance. The man on the left side of the table motions her and points with his right arm to the central figure seated at the head of the table, who lifts both his arms as he communicates with the beyond. The solid forms, the strong colours and expressive distortions fuse the spiritual and formal qualities of primitive art with the peculiar fervour of Hassidic prayer.

156. Jacob Steinhardt, *In the Synagogue*, 1923. Ink and wash, $4\frac{1}{2} \times 7$ in (11.4 × 17.7 cm). Collection of Mrs Olga Bineth, Jerusalem.

The painting was done in 1919 when the artist had departed from pure abstraction and veered toward expression and representation in which the religious theme has a marked place. It is probable that his association with the group of Jewish painters and poets around David Ignatoff and the Yiddish magazine *Schriften* (see above, p. 62), to which Weber contributed poems, essays, woodcuts and paintings, relieved him from the intense loneliness which he experienced in America as a modern painter. The very modernity of his paintings intensified his sense of loneliness and reactivated memories of New York's East Side and his boyhood in Bialystock.

From that time Jewish religious themes appear frequently in his work. The Rabbi, discourses around the Torah, family reunions, prayer, and ecstatic Hassidic dances become important motifs. In his Jewish subject-matter he often painted the exaltation of religious rapture and recaptured the transcendent ecstasy of the Hassidic experience. 'Art has a higher purpose', he said, 'than the mere imitation of nature. It transcends the earthly and measurable. It

157. (LEFT) Ben-Zion,
Friday Evening, before 1956.
Oil on canvas, 42 × 25⅛ in
(106.5 × 64 cm). Washington
D.C., Hirshhorn Museum and
Sculpture Garden, Smithsonian
Institute.

158. (RIGHT) Herman Struck,
Separation (Havdalah), 1902.
Etching, 10 × 15¾ in
(25.4 × 40 cm).
New York, Jewish Museum.

has its own scale and destiny. It is concerned with the informing spirit that emanates only from spiritual and mystical realms, from the nether and astral. A work may be ever so anatomically incorrect or "distorted" and still be endowed with the miraculous and indescribable element of beauty that thrills the discerning spectator. On the other hand the world is full of "works of art" utterly barren, unevocative and worthless.'[1]

In *Invocation* the quest for the spiritual brings Weber to fuse Hassidic prayer with primitive art. In *The Talmudists* (fig. 159), painted in 1934, he discovers an intense spirituality and aliveness in the traditional Jewish study group where learning is considered a form of religious activity, as significant as prayer. 'What are they', remarked Philo already in the first century when he spoke about synagogues, 'but schools of wisdom and temperance and justice and piety and holiness, even virtue, by which human and divine things are appreciated and placed upon a proper footing?'[2]

The painting is a homage to the synagogue as a house of learning. Plain people engage seriously and enthusiastically in the most rational and educational aspects of Jewish communal prayer, the study of the Torah and its commentaries. They are gathered in a vaulted room, a man-made cave which has become a world of study, where the artist explores the various attitudes of the participants. There he finds those who study in solitude, who meditate and quietly absorb what they have read, those who express astonishment at certain

passages, and those who argue with others over the meaning and fine points of the commentaries. Weber's distortions are not to be seen as caricature, they arise out of keen observation and subtle discernment. 'I was prompted to paint this picture', the artist said, 'after a pilgrimage to one of the oldest synagogues of New York's East Side. I find a living spiritual beauty emanates from, and hovers over and about a group of Jewish patriarchal types when they congregate in search of wisdom in the teaching of the great Talmudists of the past. The discussions of the Talmudists are at times impassioned, inspired, ecstatic, and at other moments serene and contemplative . . . To witness a group of such elders bent on and intent upon nothing but the eternal quest and interpretation of the ethnical, significant and religious content of the great Jewish legacy—the Torah—is for me an experience never to be forgotten.'[3]

The Adoration of the Moon (Plate V), which properly should be called *The Blessing of the Moon* since it depicts the traditional Jewish ceremony which blesses the rise of the new moon, recalls a scene the artist had witnessed as a five-year-old child in Bialystock, Russia. He stood then near a group of Hassidim who were blessing the moon, and thought at that moment of his father who had left for distant New York to establish there a foothold for the family which was to follow him. The five-year-old thought that he and his father could see that evening the same moon in the sky.

In the canvas the light of the moon spreads through the sky and infuses the picture with translucent tones of great subtlety—mysterious silver grey and pale blue and violet—and at the same time the canvas is lit up with brightly glowing reds. The light gnaws at the figures and lends them a grotesque, hallucinatory appearance. Weber has substituted for his former strong architectonic compositions a much looser one in which a capricious linear rhythm animates the composition and suggests a state of spiritual abandon and intoxication. The three figures on the left chant their prayer and bless the rising moon while the figure on the right seems actually moonstruck, staring upward in adoration.

Although one can detect in the painting a gently teasing attitude and a touch of grotesqueness in the enactment of an ancient ritual against the background of a modern city, Weber senses the poetry and mystery of the rite and aims at the expression of an authentic religious emotion. This is the experience of the utterly other, which is also manifest in the intensity of Hassidic prayer and the ecstatic excitement of Hassidic dance, which the artist also often painted. The out-of-door prayer at night, the moon rising above the clouds, pulling, lifting, stretching, eating away and corroding and dematerializing the bodies of the praying men and turning them into otherworldly creatures, gives the scene a haunting pantheistic air.

In his painting *Day of Atonement* (fig. 160), Jacob Kramer, who had come to England as a child with his parents from Russia and had been a student at the Slade Art School together with David Bomberg, Mark Gertler and Isaac Rosenberg, conveys intense religious devotion. In its powerful design the painting reflects the strong influence of Vorticism, a combination of Cubist and Futurist forms which emerged in England under the influence of Wyndham Lewis. For Kramer, painting was a spiritual activity. By means of a decisively structured rhythm and sparse colours he penetrates the transcendent essence of the Day of Atonement. Although aiming to express deep emotion, he foregoes the violence and tumultuous feeling which so often mark expressionistic painting; he achieves his imaginative insight instead by discipline and restraint. The pervasive rhythm he creates by his choreography of close-knit forms is symbolic of the Day of Atonement. The most dramatic moment of the day is chosen. The

159. Max Weber,
The Talmudists, 1934.
Oil on canvas, 50 × 33¾ in
(127 × 85.8 cm).
New York, Jewish Museum.

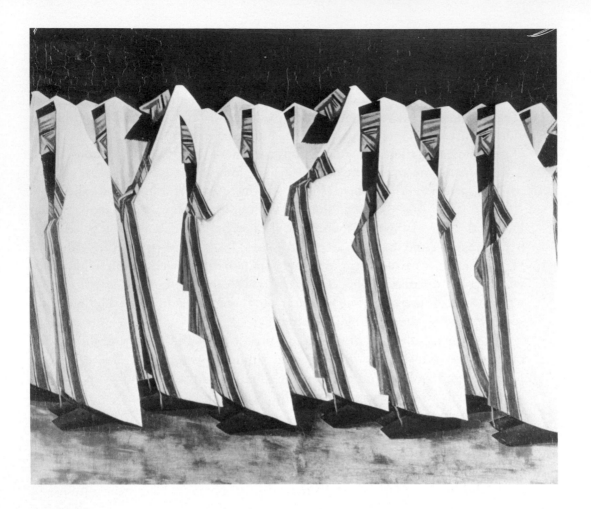

congregation stands in silent prayer, repenting; and with their swaying, slightly inclined bodies, they plead before their God whom they address as the King of the Universe. According to the medieval prayers of Yom Kippur, chanted in synagogues to this very day, alternately by the reader and the congregation, the Host of Heaven on this day sits in judgement. The congregation passes under his crook like a flock of sheep, while He records the deeds and the destiny of each man and seals his fate:

> Behold the Day of Judgement. The Host of Heaven is to be sitting in judgement. For in thine eyes they are not pure, and all who enter the world dost thou cause to pass before thee as a flock of sheep. As a shepherd seeketh out his flock, and causeth them to pass beneath his crook, so dost thou cause to pass and number, tell and visit every living soul, appointing the measure of every creature's life and decreeing their destiny. [4]

Kramer resolved the rival demands of abstraction and representation by omitting all unnecessary details. By placing the figures against a dark background, he lifted them out of any literal context. And by repetition of the abstracted, stern-faced, bearded figures wrapped in their prayer shawls, strongly marked at their edge by a slim vertical stripe, he condensed the Day of Atonement into a stark image of the sacred ritual.

For Sigmund Menkes, the painting *The Uplifting of the Torah* (fig. 161) was an expression of identification with home and family. Living in Paris during the 1920s, he was known for his colourful and sensuous still-lifes, landscapes and women combing their hair before the mirror. One day he was suddenly over-

160. (LEFT) Jacob Kramer, *Day of Atonement*, 1919. Oil on canvas, $39\frac{1}{4} \times 48\frac{1}{8}$ in (99.6×122.4 cm). Leeds City Art Galleries.

161. (OPPOSITE) Sigmund Menkes, *The Uplifting of the Torah*, 1928. Oil on canvas, 86×65 in (218.4×165.1 cm). Private collection.

182

come by the haunting memory of his youth in Poland:

> About 1927, I decided to take stock of myself, of my youth, of my family, of
> my race and the way I was brought up. I did the *Torah* . . . This was a kind
> of confession on my part, a homage to my people . . . I worked at it for five
> or six weeks. It seems to me I did not leave my studio, nor did I eat, drink or
> sleep.[5]

The Torah scroll is lifted and unrolled. A tribal feeling emanates from the
canvas as the figures round the scroll and the worshipper who lifts it respond
with enthusiasm to their most sacred object. The centrality of the Torah in the
life of the congregation is manifest in the circular composition; the figures
crowd around the sacred scroll, which they guard while it guards them. There is
agitated movement as the people press forward to touch the Torah. The concept
of the Brith, the covenant between God and his people, and the divine origin of
the book, which by tradition represents the words of God as spoken through
Moses, are expressed intimately, but with full grasp of the historical dimensions
of the relationship. Menkes shows us a yearning and suffering people pressing
toward the light of the Torah.

The painting is fundamentally expressionistic. Its texture is dazzlingly
sensuous. The religious paintings of Rembrandt and Nolde come to mind. The
brushwork is rough and deft. Its overall dark hue is lit up dramatically to reveal
the exaggerated expressions of the homely congregation. Details are sacrificed
for the sake of vivid expression. Hands, eyes and foreheads are especially
accentuated. There is no hierarchy or distinction between priests and laymen.
All are simple, suffering humanity. Only the Torah itself has a crown which
swings on one of its staffs. It reigns supreme and is accessible to all. The
pervasive mood is of a primitive tribal rite.

The boy in the foreground, who resembles the artist, stretches his hand in
amazement and completes the circle around the Torah. By closing the circle, he
symbolically conveys a sense of historic continuity and also affirms his own
identity.

While the *Torah* presents a major effort on the part of Menkes to come to
grips with himself and bears the marks of inner turmoil, *Les Talmudistes*
(fig. 163), painted about the same time, is more restrained. Here, the faculties of
reason and emotion are more balanced, producing a work of a quieter but no less
intense expressiveness. A group of children, with their teacher or parent in the
background, hold a large open book. There is no table. The heads of the
children contrast with their small bodies and echo the large, bright, open pages
of the book. The book is felt in its whole weight as a tiresome burden and a
source of deprivation. The wide-open eyes of the children peer into the
distance; the burdensome book acts as ballast against the lure of the world of
games, the jumping ball and the flying arrow.

The composition, firm and stable, forms a triangle. At its apex is the head of
the figure who stands quietly in the background. At the base is the book. The
teacher's presence is hardly felt; he from one side and the open book from the
other encompass the children in a tightly knit group. The absence of gestures or
environment lifts the subject above the realm of the implied narrative. The
painting symbolizes the grave importance of the book in Jewish childhood. It is

162. (LEFT) Marvin Cherney, *Man with Torah*, c.1957–8. Oil on canvas, 36 × 25⅞ in (91.4 × 65.5 cm). Washington D.C., Hirshhorn Museum and Sculpture Garden, Smithsonian Institute.

163. (RIGHT) Sigmund Menkes, *Les Talmudistes*, 1928. Oil on canvas. Location unknown.

a burden children must bear to ensure the survival of the religious community.

Marvin Cherney's many paintings of Jewish religious themes are somewhat traditional compositions but are marked by an unusually rigorous and austere style in which the artist explores the inward aspects of faith. The painting *Man with Torah* (fig. 162) is worked in muted, velvety dark blues and reds, colours traditionally used in the synagogue, with a limited palette and a softened focus. The Torah, wrapped in a mantle embroidered in white, stripped of its shiny appurtenances, without silver ornament, breastplate or pointer, itself assumes a pensive aspect, as reticent and brooding as the man who carries it. He is doubtlessly a Jewish worker whom Cherney must have encountered in the Jewish Ghettos of Baltimore or the Lower East Side of New York. He carries the Torah tenderly like a child whom he wants to protect. To him the Torah is an anchor in an unfriendly world. This unassuming figure draws the spectator into the orbit of his apprehension. He is not a Rabbi or an office-holder in his congregation but one of the multitudes who find consolation in religious ritual. It was Ernst Troeltsch who observed that genuine religious sentiment is to be found only in the lower classes, and it was Karl Marx who stated that religion is the heart of the world in a heartless world.

In *The Synagogue* (fig. 164) Abraham Ofek, observing Moroccan immigrants

assemble for prayer in an Israeli village, also conveys the semblance of order and anchorage the synagogue introduces into their disjointed lives. The grotesque expressions of the congregation mirror their confusion and the incongruity which they feel in their new surroundings. By its pre-established order, the service introduces a measure of balance into their uprooted lives. This balance is expressed in the clear horizontal and vertical groupings of the figures and in the clearly defined simple architectural scheme that contains them. One senses a passive listening and the close tie that unites the people. The religious service is seen as a cementing force without which neither the group nor the individual can exist.

Hyman Bloom painted his *Synagogue* (Plate IV) in a festive mood. The voice of the cantor and the ardent prayer of the congregation seem to fill the air and even move the gigantic chandeliers which sway above them. Dark blue dominates, but the painting scintillates with brilliant lights which are reflected in the Torah breastplates, the pomegranates, and the Torah crowns. Bright reds make the canvas vibrate like a Byzantine mosaic. The oversized figure of the cantor and the dense crowd of worshippers create colourful patterns which fill the nearly flat composition and bring to mind images of medieval Christian art.

In the gouache painting *Rabbi* and the large drawing *The Rabbi* (figs. 166 and 167), Bloom gives us portraits of penetrating insight and compassion. In both, the artist discovers a close unity between the face of the Rabbi and the design of the Torah and prayer shawl. The furrowed lines of the Rabbi's face echo the intricately ornamented prayer shawl and Torah mantle. In the drawing, the spiritual authority of the Rabbi is underlined by the strict frontality, the noble head and the alert, finely cut face. The expressive hands that hold the book and the Torah convey Bloom's perception of the Rabbi as both spiritual leader and scholar.

164. (LEFT) Abraham Ofek, *The Synagogue*, 1971. Oil on canvas, 40 × 52 in (101.5 × 132 cm). Collection of the artist, Jerusalem.

165. (RIGHT) Leonard Baskin, *The Blind Rabbi*, 1971. Ink drawing, 40 × 27 in (101.5 × 68.5 cm). New York, Kennedy Galleries, Inc.

Leonard Baskin's large ink drawing *The Blind Rabbi* (fig. 165) renders a physically powerful figure who inhabits his own space and conveys a disciplined, far-sighted intelligence. The vigorous posture, the unfocused eyes that seem to be directed both inward and outward, and the resolute arm reveal a self-assured character. The entire figure is girded by a cross-like silhouette within which fluid and dry brushwork and continuous and broken lines, fine and wondrously delicate, merge into smudges and flecks which build and destroy form, mirroring the vigour of a scholarly life and imbuing the drawing with a pulsating rhythm.

Rabbis are teachers who know the Torah, its commentaries, and the intricacies of the law. They provide spiritual leadership, and their influence and authority rest on knowledge and scholarship.

Reder's large sculpture, *Aaron* (fig. 168), however, points to magic rather than scholarship as the source of authority. Aaron, the brother of Moses, brings us back to Egypt. He was a magician, a master of arcane knowledge, a cult figure, the high priest who wore special vestments and a peaked cap. He wore a breast plate and was master of the mysterious Urim and Tumim through which he received divine counsel. He alone was allowed to enter behind the curtain into the Holy of Holies. He had the power to influence the fate of events; he could cause plagues and avert them.

Reder's art is an open, boisterous, baroque art. It is rich in fantasy, and

166. (LEFT) Hyman Bloom, *Rabbi*, 1957. Gouache on paper, $19\frac{1}{2} \times 17\frac{1}{2}$ in (49.5 × 44.4 cm). Collection of Mr and Mrs Jacob Schulman, Gloversville, New York.

167. (RIGHT) Hyman Bloom, *The Rabbi*, 1955. Drawing, pencil on paper, 72 × 53 in (183 × 135 cm). Collection of Mr and Mrs Jacob Schulman, Gloversville, New York.

marked by a hybrid iconography of Hassidic and Rabelaisian images; it is filled with satyrs, Minotaurs and Jewish wedding canopies, trumpets, bells, Amazons, fruit trees, and playing cards; with goats, telescopes, and pyramids.

Aaron is a personal prayer, the offering, as it were, of an artist deeply rooted in Jewish tradition and believing, as artists often do, in the hidden powers of their work. The figure of Aaron resembles a blooming tree, reminiscent of Aaron's staff. The sculptor offers Aaron, Aaron offers the tabernacle. The sculpture is not the representation of a specific ritual. The artist, here, becomes a magician like Aaron.

In his life Reder was often a refugee, forced to relocate his studios many times, from Czernowitz to Prague to Paris to Havanna and finally to New York. When his wife was in hospital for several months in 1959, Reder created *Aaron*. He commented: 'I knew that I had to create a centre of discipline and morale and I had to bring her everyday, to the hospital, news about this centre—positive news. I chose Aaron because it was he who kept the Jews together when Moses was on Mount Sinai.'[6]

John Baur, observing the sculpture, sees the 'robes flow out, tier over tier, the outer ones completely separated from the body and affording vistas that pierce the solidity of the trunk'.[7] The figure itself is like the trunk of a tree and the upper branches are like a Menorah.

The sculptor Elbert Weinberg, although born and educated in the United States, draws heavily on Jewish religious ritual, which has impressed him since

168. (LEFT) Bernard Reder, *Aaron with Tabernacle*, 1959. Bronze, 97 in high (244 cm). Jerusalem, Israel Museum.

169. (RIGHT) Elbert Weinberg *Procession no.1*, 1957. Bronze, each figure, toe to head top, 60 in (152.4 cm). New York, Jewish Museum.

170. Elbert Weinberg,
Ritual Figure, 1953.
Beechwood, 60¼ in high (153 cm).
New York, Museum of Modern
Art, A. Conger Goodyear Fund.

childhood. This is evident in such works as *The Scribe*, *The Opening of the Ark*, *Reading from the Torah* and *Abraham, Isaac and the Angel*.

Ritual Figure (fig. 170), carved of soft-brown beech wood, is marked by a series of expansive, interlaced curves which carry the figure aloft. The rhythm of the upward sweep is resolved within the space and volume as defined by the head and the curiously displaced arms that hold the Shofar. The draped figure, which reveals the influence of Armitage, Barlach and Marini, combines a supple elegance with the intensity and distortion of primitive sculpture.

Procession (fig. 169) is related to *Ritual Figure* by its simplified and abstract forms. Here, Weinberg created a group of four monumental, heavily draped figures who, in solemn measured steps, carry the Torah, the book and the Menorah, the three central objects of Jewish tradition. As in Kramer's *Day of Atonement*, the accent is not on the individuality of the figures but on their being bearers of an impersonal sacred tradition. The faces of the figures are ceremonial masks, their bodies are bell-shaped liturgical robes, their gestures are invocations. The Torah is a standard held high as it is carried among the people. Like the Menorah, it is a tree of life; the figures who carry the book symbolize prayer and scholarship.

The significance of this group of sculptures lies in the bold conception of its form. The sculptures express an image of a confident Jewish community that is rare in Jewish history; they convey the sense of security and acceptance the Jewish community has found in the New World. The Torah as presented in art is often held close to the body, a precious possession of individuals or groups in flight. Weinberg's figures are firmly rooted in the ground. He contributes a supple elegance and expressive intensity of a particular personal character. Without consciously intending to, he has also succeeded in creating an intelligible public image rare in modern art.

CHAPTER SEVEN

Reaching for the Absolute

There is a Jerusalem which is an idea and not a specific location, which embodies ascent and the quest for redemption. A Jerusalem which is in the heart, in dreams, in the sky—not of this earth. A Jerusalem which vanishes and is built, vanishes again, and is built again, until it resembles heaven.

Leopold Krakauer and Anna Ticho express in their landscapes the yearning for the ideal Jerusalem. Their Jerusalem is outside the city, in the barren, gently curved hills that evoke the unspoiled dreams of their youth. In Krakauer's drawing, thistles which grow in the parched fields in late summer are transformed and elevated into suns. They are reality encountered and dreams remembered and pursued. They are symbols of pain and sources of solace and warmth. They are dry and twisted, tenacious and unyielding like the thorny path to the sun (fig. 1).

Mordechai Ardon, once a pupil at the Bauhaus in Weimar, carried Jerusalem in his heart and could not rid himself of it. He personifies that peculiar blend of rationalism and mysticism which Jewish tradition so often produces. Like his father, a Hassid, Ardon searches for the hidden sparks that dwell in the most humble objects, and seeks to unite them with the heavenly light. He admired Rembrandt and El Greco, and felt a strong affinity to Klee, the mystic, and to Feininger, the metaphysician. Ardon spiritualizes physical matter. The sources he draws from are varied: the rich vocabulary of modern art transmitted through Otto Doerner and his teachers at the Bauhaus, the dramatic sense of Max Reinhardt and the spiritual ferment of Weimar, Berlin and Paris during the 1920s. All this is filtered through and fused with the rich store of childhood memories and Jewish learning he gathered at his home in Tuchov, Galicia. In his father's workshop the hands of the different clocks used to show different hours, and as a child Ardon marvelled that occasionally they all struck at the same time. The mature Ardon brings the past, the present, and the future together. From 1933, when he intended to go to Paris, but landed shipwrecked in Jerusalem, he has drawn from the literature and art of Sumer and Babylonia, the Bible, the Cabbala, Hebrew illuminated manuscripts, and the dry rocks of the desert.

Ardon's problem has been defined as that of a European painter who decided to remain a Jew. Always admiring and attracted to Apollonian and Dionysian Athens, he found Jerusalem 'ascetic with sackcloth on its head'. Jerusalem, the overbearing, with its moral injunctions and demands about widows, orphans and the oppressed, did not let him accept the concept of the absolute autonomy of art.

> No getting away from it! Queer Jerusalem always has some orders to give!
> 'Thou shalt . . .', 'Thou shalt not . . .'—like a black woodpecker Jerusalem
> always knocks at your bark:—thou . . . thou . . . thou . . . Thou—thou and

171. Anna Ticho,
Jerusalem Hills, c. 1963.
Charcoal on paper, $20\frac{3}{8} \times 27\frac{1}{2}$ in
(51.3 × 69.8 cm).
Tel Aviv Museum of Art.

the orphan—thou and the widow—thou and the distressed—thou and the oppressed. Never is one alone! As if life could only be lived in the 'thou' and as if being alive could only manifest itself in conjunction with the 'thou' . . . That's the problem: the 'you' does not play any part in modern art. Artists are suns revolving on their own axes.[1]

172. Mordecai Ardon,
Homage to Jerusalem, 1965.
Triptych, oil on canvas.
Left, *Night of Ascents*
58¾ × 77 in (148 × 193.4 cm);
centre, *Parchments and Scrolls*
59 × 76¾ in (146.6 × 193.4 cm);
right, *Lament of Nails*
59½ × 76¾ in (151 × 195cm).
Collection of the Israel Discount
Bank of New York.

Ardon looks at the universe through a filter tinted by the Jewish mystic tradition. He uses the vocabulary of abstract art, but he is not satisfied with formal problems alone. His work touches that of Barnett Newman, Mark Rothko, and Adolph Gottlieb. They too do not restrict themselves to formal problems, since subject-matter is crucial to them. Is it possible that because they are related to the Hebraic tradition, they look for a moral frame of reference and that the 'thou' is essential to them?

Ardon's shapes and signs suggest something that exists potentially. In *Train of Numbers* (fig. 100) and *In the Beginning* (Plate XIV), he makes visible what one does not see. He is on the track of the timeless, the numinous, and is conscious that he works under the Biblical sky in the Biblical land. But as we have said, being a European artist who has decided to remain a Jew, Ardon found it difficult to paint the daily life of Palestine. He also could not paint symbols because they divest the unknown of its secret. His paintings are the pilgrimage of a modern mystic, who attempts to lift the veil, to reach the Gates of Light, although he is not sure if there is anything to be found beyond them. Search and creation are the substance of his pilgrimage; therefore, the process of his work is long, a slow unfolding of ideas, associations, a slow lifting of the veil. They are not religious pictures in the traditional sense; they breathe a pantheistic

humanistic spirit, but they remain centred in the Biblical landscape. They are the work of a modern Jew who went through assimilation, Enlightenment, and nationalism, but decided to remain a Jew and take from tradition that with which he could live.

Homage to Jerusalem, one of several large triptychs Ardon has created, places Jerusalem at the centre of religious experience. Jerusalem is the place where ladders were erected which stood on the ground but reached to heaven, a place where ladders fell and parchments and scrolls of ancient teaching were written, a place of lamenting nails which allude to the Crucifixion. The painting is a poem about Jerusalem. Ladders are related to the ladder of Jacob, to heavenly ascent. The paintings can be seen as parables of the fate of man, his effort to rise and his unavoidable fall, his illusions and disillusions. The ladder also has an intense personal meaning for Ardon. When he returned to Tuchov after having finished his studies, an uncle came to congratulate him: 'What did you study?' he asked. When Ardon answered that he had become a painter, the uncle looked around the room and inquired: 'So, where is your ladder?'

The Cabbalistic Sphere by Luise Kaish (fig. 173) evolves from a personal mystical attitude nourished by the Psalms and the cosmic imagery of the Zohar, and from her form-giving energy which constantly interprets, elaborates, and shapes her spiritual experience. In the cabbalistic literature, the spheres are manifestations of the hidden process of divine life, which flow directly from the *Ein Sof* (infinite), and mediate between God and the Universe.

According to the Zohar, the thirteenth-century 'Book of Splendour' central to the Cabbala, God emerges not out of chaos, but out of nothingness—out of the hidden hiddenness—and creates the world according to the Torah, which

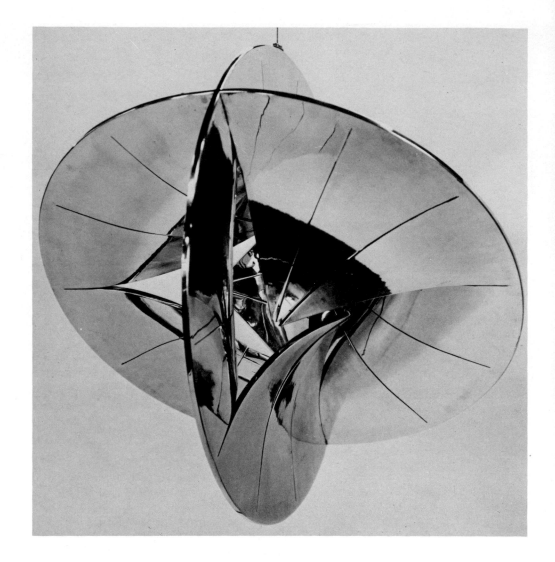

preceded the creation of the world. God is equated with the *Ein Sof*, the Absolute, Infinite, Boundless, the First Cause which the cabbalists also called *Or Ein Sof* (the unending light). Like a seed this great light contains the potential energy and plan of all the physical and intellectual world—the entire plan of the universe. The cabbalists call the power which resides in the First Cause *Kav*, the line which runs through the whole universe, giving it form and being. The letters of the Hebrew alphabet, developed out of the 'Sefirot', constitute a bridge between the world of the divine and the human. In the words of Gershom Scholem, the cabbalists saw Judaism as 'a symbolic transparency through which the secret of the cosmos could be discerned'. [2]

Kaish's spherical sculptures do not represent hermetically closed spheres, but seem rather to be formed of organically evolved reflecting elements. They constitute a self-developing and self-revealing dynamic world of becoming: centres of transcendental energy. Their parts are partially overlapping, dissected by the mystical line called *Kav* in the Cabbala, and appear to be growing, spreading fruit. Their convex planes spread, arch, meet and intersect. Some of these spherical structures can even be opened. They reveal a mysterious, labyrinthine interior. Allusions to cosmic and lunar voyages abound.

Yehoshua Kovarsky, in *Temple Above the Moon* (Plate XV), approaches the mythological domain of the Biblical world, and establishes contact with its spirits. In his other paintings, Kovarsky re-creates the world in which Baal and Astarte, Avatar and Jezebel, Lillith and the White Goddess held sway. He does not present these mythological figures in an allegorical manner but rather seems intent on revitalizing their ancient myths. For him the Bible is a doorway to the mythical world from which its tales of creation and the tree of knowledge emerge. He paints the days of creation as if the images of Genesis were guiding him, but also resurrects the ancient myths of the Near East and pays homage to their gods and heroes. For him painting itself is a ritualistic, myth-producing act in which he re-enacts the process of creation by turning chaos, that is the unformed void of the bare canvas, into an ordered universe.

Penetrating through the act of painting into the world of ancient myth, Kovarsky embodies in his art the central metaphysical human need for a discernable cosmic pattern in the moral and physical universe, a need which links both ancient and modern man. The act of painting becomes for the artist a self-revealing instrument serving his longing for the eternal, the numinous and the transcendent, as well as his craving for omnipotence and magical power. At the same time it establishes a sense of unity in his own life experience, ridden with conflicts and discontinuities, by ever enlarging his own consciousness and by constantly re-examining the conditions of the self. The act of painting links Kovarsky's personal life history to the mythical, archetypal figures of a particular cultural area, providing the background of feelings and associations with the ancient Biblical world in which the artist felt his innermost self rooted.

To give form to ancient myths Kovarsky relies heavily on introspection and the unconscious. This brings him close to the Surrealists, whom he may have encountered during his stay in Paris between 1931 and 1935, and also to the American Abstract Expressionists whose work he saw when he moved to the United States in 1951. Like many of them he embraces the world of mythology and strives toward a visualization of an interior image: 'The image', he says,

> is somewhere hidden inside. You try to connect and try to get very close to what you have hidden inside of you. Sometimes you get very near, sometimes you never reach it. It comes after a long time. It is a kind of atavistic spirit that you have hidden . . . there is something in you and you are trying to get after it. You come close to your very deep vision inside and it comes to the surface, and you bring it to a visual state. . . . But there is more in you than you can express and therefore you come back and you want to put in more, and every time you see it deeper. There is in theology the idea that you never come close to the Lord, because the higher you go the higher He is. You never come close to Him. It's the same with this. The deeper you get into yourself, the more you can come back to the canvas.[3]

There is a strong romantic and mystical element in Kovarsky, who grew up in Vilna, 'the Jerusalem of Lithuania', a centre of rabbinic rationalism and of a thriving Jewish secular culture. A student of the Yiddish Gymnasium, a pioneer in Palestine in the early 1920s, paving roads through Galilee and listening with fascination to the miraculous stories of the Yemenite stonemasons with whom

173. Luise Kaish
The Cabbalistic Sphere, 1975. Polished aluminum, 39 × 39 in (99 × 99 cm). Collection of the artist, New York.

he worked, he rolled like many of his generation several life stories into one. He painted altars, fires, temple stones, lintels, steps, moons, half-moons, the charred and burned flesh of consumed offerings. The images are sharply defined by colour and line as if to assure their existence before an outside threat. He thereby connects the search after the archaic and primitive we have seen among Israeli painters who were fascinated by the desert with the myth-makers and myth-worshippers among the Surrealists in Paris of the 1930s and their descendants in New York in the following decades.

Barnett Newman, Adolph Gottlieb and Mark Rothko, painters of the New York School, react in their mature work, created after World War II, to the crisis of faith. Like other American painters, they felt that the ideas and ideologies which shaped the form and content of American art of the previous decade were obsolete. The war and its aftermath had shattered the very foundations upon which their art was built. By exposing the limits of human rationality, the war had shown the irrational to be a constant and powerful presence in human nature. The artists now rejected the ideas and attitudes of Social Realism, Regionalism, Geometric Abstraction and all styles derived from faith in technology and the values of mass culture. To construct a meaningful universe, the artists turned to themselves and their private visions. The presence in New York during World War II of major European artists and leaders of the Surrealistic movement opened new avenues of exploration to American artists. Automatism and Metamorphism, because of their organic and

174. (LEFT) Barnett Newman, *Zim Zum*, 1969.
Corten steel, 8 ft × 6 ft 6 in × 15 ft (2.44 × 1.98 × 4.59 m).
Collection of Annalee Newman, New York.

175. (RIGHT) 'Separation of Day from Night', from the *Haggadah of Sarajevo*, Spanish manuscript, mid-14th century. Sarajevo, Yugoslavia, National Museum.

therefore human-like formal aspects, became a basis from which they could move. For these artists, subject-matter was of utmost importance, and they considered abstract art practised for its own sake a futile exercise, built on a slogan of purism. 'There is no such thing as good painting about nothing,' declared Gottlieb and Rothko in a letter Newman helped to draft to the *New York Times*. 'We assert that the subject is crucial and only that subject-matter is valid which is tragic and timeless.'[4]

For these painters, art was an adventure into an unknown world. They attempted to transcend the here and now, to approach the absolute. Their paintings are religious in that through them they aim to touch elemental cosmic forces and to penetrate the universe.

Newman's paintings consist of a single flat colour divided by one or more bands of contrasting or complementary colours which transform the canvas into two or more rectangles that have a definite scale, expanse, and proportion, but are devoid of imagery. They have been called colour field paintings. The canvas—its shape, its height and length, its colour field—offers a sacred environment which engulfs the viewer and summons him to an act of contemplation.

By their stern quality, their lack of atmosphere or tactile details, by their strict intellectual approach, by their quest for the absolute with its inherent antagonism to the image, these paintings attack the sensuous nature of Western art at its very roots, and seek to divorce the act of painting from its European tradition. A theoretician of considerable originality, Newman wrote during the War years,

> . . . the new painter desires to transcend the plastic elements in art. He is declaring that the art of Western Europe is a voluptuous art first, an intellectual art by accident. He is reversing the situation by declaring that art is an expression of the mind first, and whatever sensuous elements are involved are incidental to that expression. The new painter is therefore the true revolutionary, the real leader, who is placing the artist's function on its rightful plane of the philosopher and the pure scientist, who is exploring the world of ideas, not the world of senses. Just as we get a vision of the cosmos through the symbols of a mathematical equation, just as we get a vision of truth in terms of abstract metaphysical concepts, so the artist is today giving us a vision of the world of truth in terms of visual symbols.[5]

In his stubborn search for a grand theme for modern art, which should express the sublime, pure ideas, and abstract philosophical concepts, Newman was impelled toward an abstract art. In his search, he focused on the creative action of nature, and equated the creation of a new art with the process of creation itself. He fell back on Biblical and cabbalistic ideas with which he was familiar, and which offered him a ready source for his intellectual and metaphysical speculations. Newman worked in the classic 'no graven image' tradition of Judaism not because images are forbidden, but because the absolute cannot be rendered by an image. It is a purely abstract conception, imageless, like the Jewish God.

If there were a Jewish style Newman's work would be regarded as its most authentic and classic expression.

It is not accidental that the stark simplifications of Newman's canvas have a precedent in the fourteenth-century Spanish Haggadah of Sarajevo, where the separation of day from night in Genesis is realized by a similar abstract colour field (see fig. 175). Thomas B. Hess points to the deep attachment which Newman felt for the Cabbala, and the crucial part it played in the formation of his art and subject-matter.[6] Thus, the *Onement* series suggests completion, harmony, and also 'at onement'—the day of remembering the dead, which was for the cabbalists the ideal moment for meditation on the secrets of the messianic act of redemption and resurrection. The *Onement* paintings intimate also the separation of day from night, the creation of Adam and the creative union of Adam and Eve.

Titles of Newman's work suggest the measure of his involvement with Biblical and cabbalistic lore: *Day One, Day Before One, Zim Zum* (fig. 174), *Primordial Light, Uriel, White Fire, Black Fire, Cathedra, Gate, Word, Here, Voice, Abraham, Joshua* (fig. 176). The titles are metaphors of ideas and feelings which preoccupied Newman during the process of their creation.

Unlike Ardon, whose mysticism is centred on Jerusalem, Newman, who was born in New York City and was at home in the community of New York artists, echoes in his paintings the Jewish mysticism of the Zohar, and of the Ari Hakadosh, and Rabbi Isaac Luria of Safed. His work relates to the cosmology of *Or Ein Sof*, to open and hidden symmetries, contraction and expansion and the breaking and repairing of vessels. Hess writes:

> Being Jewish was a part of his past and of his present; he was heir to a culture, and took delight in studying it—more delight than he did in studying other religions. One could say that all civilizations and sciences were like an enormous museum through which he loved to wander, and among his favorite galleries were those devoted to Jewish myths and customs, philosophers and artists, and especially to that remarkable fusion of mysticism and logic that is known as the Cabbala, and to the men who for over two thousand years contributed to its insights.[7]

Barnett Newman is closely connected, artistically, socially and philosophically, with Adolph Gottlieb and Mark Rothko. Gottlieb, who has executed significant commissions for American synagogues, takes us in his work on a journey into the unknown regions of myths, dreams and distant planets. His work has strong universal and pantheistic overtones (fig. 177).

In Mark Rothko's work we are confronted with a highly personal statement that brings us close to the world of ritual and icons (Plate XIII). Rothko's diffuse, rectangular configurations float in a hazy colour field and echo the edges of the canvas. Their soft, blurred contours melt into ambiguous space, rather than setting themselves off against a distinct background. The thinly painted shapes vibrate and breathe, advance and recede as if moved by an unseen hand, and leave an after-image. By eliminating line, movement, and imagery from these paintings and by reducing them to shape, colour and space, the artist has dematerialized them. The paintings induce an atmosphere of silence, solemnity, meditation, and transcendence; they mirror the thoughts and feelings which the spectator brings to them. In their bright yellow, deep red, dark blue or grey variations, these paintings evoke the mysterious and the numinous; they create

176. Barnett Newman,
Joshua, 1950.
Oil on canvas, 36 × 25 in
(91.4 × 63.5 cm). Collection of
Mrs Samuel Weiner, New York.

sombre, repetitive spaces of otherness—abstract icons of sacred pathos.

Rothko's art has been interpreted in terms of withdrawal from the affairs of the world, from involvement in social and political issues, an escape from the noise of the media. It has also been seen as being influenced by the wide-open landscapes, clouds and mist-filled spaces the artist experienced in his native Oregon. His paintings have evoked for many the Orphic cycles of death and resurrection, entrances to tombs and open sarcophagi. However, most critics agree that Rothko's paintings convey a world in which the numinous and the spiritual experience dominate. While these are generalized in Rothko's work, it

177. Adolph Gottlieb,
Tints, 1971.
Oil on canvas, 90 × 48 in
(228.6 × 121.9 cm). Collection
of Mrs Adolph Gottlieb, New
York.

is interesting to note that the German art historian Werner Haftmann points to Rothko's Jewish background as a major factor in the emergence of the artist's style. He compares the advancing and receding planes of his canvases to doors and corridors, which at one moment invite one to look and then, immediately, draw the veil. He likens them to 'silently animated, stirring, concealing drapery', which are ancient Jewish metaphors for the hidden God of whom it was forbidden to make an image; to veils in the Biblical tent of meeting; to the Temple curtain before the Holy of Holies (which existed only as emptiness); and to the woven canvas of the Mosaic tent. 'The painter in his imagination renewing itself daily, undertook the erection of that tent which the Jews, a nomadic people, raised around their ark in order to establish a space for the Holy in which there existed only the void and the word. From these images derive his pictures.'[8] Haftmann continues,

> Clearly we do not confront real 'pictures' in our classic humanistic terms. They are meditation veils, icons, tablets of contemplation, decorated tent canvases, which shelter the Numinous. With his 'image', Rothko created a new type of votive picture which in its mythic religious space is the counterpart of the aesthetic icon of Mondrian. In the face of these works, an amazing fact should become clear to historians, namely that Judaism, which for 2,000 years remained 'imageless', has found in our century—with the help of the meditative process of modern art—a pictorial expression of its own, a Jewish art of its own. And this at the same time when Israel was re-established as their ancient home.[9]

Haftmann's statement may have to be qualified by additional considerations. He may be overstating his point by reducing Rothko's work to Jewish sources. Yet it is interesting that this interpretation comes from a German scholar, who might be particularly sensitive to Jewish aspects of modern art. Rothko himself never gave us any clues concerning his work. In this vein it is interesting to consider Leo Steinberg's attempt to find common ground between Jewish life and modern art:

> Both Jewry and modern art are masters of renunciation, having at one time renounced all the props on which existence as nation, or art, once seemed to depend. Jewry survived as an abstract nation, proving, as did modern art, how much was dispensable. I would add also that, like modern painting, Jewish religious practices are remarkably free of representational content, the ritual being largely self-fulfilling, rather than the bearer of a detachable meaning. Lastly, both Judaism and contemporary art established themselves by uncompromising exclusiveness.[10]

Notes

Notes to the Introduction

1. Chagall is not the first Jewish artist to deal with Christ as a Jew. This tendency appears in the 1870s as a result of the rise of political anti-Semitism. Mark Antokolsky carved *Christ before his Judges* in 1874 wearing a skullcap (now in Leningrad). Mauricy Gottlieb painted *Christ before Pilatus* in 1877 (coll. D. Hartenstein, Vienna), and *Christ in the Temple* in 1879 (coll. H. Lowenthall, Warsaw). In both paintings Christ is wrapped in the traditional Jewish prayer shawl. In Max Liebermann's *Christ in the Temple*, 1879 (Kunsthalle, Hamburg), the young Christ supports his argument with strong gestures of his hand. In all these works, Christ's Jewishness is marked by garment, headdress or gesture. At the beginning of the twentieth century, Samuel Hirszenberg portrayed the head of Christ as a rabbi (reproduction in *Ost und West*, 10 (Berlin, Oct. 1904), p. 683).

2. U. Z. Greenberg, 'Drachim Bamaarav' ['Roads in the West'], in *Rimon* [Hebrew journal for arts and letters], 6 (Berlin, 1924), pp. 19–21.

3. L. V. Snowman, *Tchernichovski and his Poetry* (London, 1929), p. 41.

Notes to chapter 1

1. For a broad discussion of the issue, and various views on Jewish art, see Joseph Gutmann, 'Jewish Art, Fact or Fiction?' *Central Conference American Rabbis Journal* (Apr. 1964); Bezalel Narkiss, 'Ha'im kajemet omanuth jehudith?' (Does Jewish Art Exist?), *Journal of the Hebrew University* (Jerusalem, October, 1965), Hebrew. The issue is not only a theoretical one but has preoccupied many artist groups and Jewish communal institutions whose cultural activities have spread into the field of art, and is particularly felt in the programmes of various Jewish museums. Henryk Berlevi writes: 'Thirty-six years ago . . . when we organized, in Warsaw, the first Jewish exhibition, we discussed at great length its title. And later, when we founded a 'society for the Promotion of Art' we were careful not to speak about 'Jewish Art'. This caution was determined by a certain need for linguistic precision. We did not like to appear pretentious and we limited ourselves to purely artistic considerations. and not national ones. We wanted, first of all, to spread art among the Jews. In all modesty we did not want to appear pretentious about Jewish art—so sacred were these words to us.' 'Der Zigzag fun der Yiddischer Kunst', *Almanach* (Paris, 1955), published by the Association of Jewish Writers and Journalists in France. With the movement of Jewish artists from Eastern Europe to the West, they were often grouped together and the term 'Jewish Art' was often attached to their work. See introduction in catalogue of exhibition, 'Jüdische Künstler', in the Galerie für alte und neue Kunst, Berlin (Nov.–Dec. 1907). See also the critical appraisal of this show by G. Kutna, 'Zur Ausstellung Jüdischer Künstler', *Ost und West*, 1 (Berlin, Jan. 1908). For a discussion of the issue as it arises in recent times, see Avram Kampf, 'The Jewish Museum—An Institution Adrift', *Judaism* (summer 1968).

2. 'According to a list which the English Jewish painter Frank L. Emanuel compiled, there are now in Europe more than four hundred Jewish artists who have made a name for themselves.' Alfred Nossig, 'Austellung Jüdischer Künstler', *Ost und West*, 12 (Berlin, Dec. 1907).

3. Hans Kohn, *Martin Buber: Sein Werk und sein Zeit* (Hellerau: Verlag Jacob Hegner, 1930), p. 301.

4. Martin Buber, 'Lesser Ury', *Ost und West*, 2 (Berlin, Feb. 1902). 'Is a Jewish art possible today? There is only one answer, a clear and hard one: No!' For an almost identical but less definitive denial of the existence of Jewish art, and a broad discussion of the problem, note Buber's speech at the Fifth Zionist Congress in Basel in December 1901. At this forum Buber spoke as a political, cultural leader rather than as a historian of art. He defined the term 'Jewish art' as the 'awakened longing for the beautiful . . . the birth of the power to create . . . What we call national art is not that which exists but what develops and may come into being. Not fulfilment but a beautiful possibility.' The speech is noteworthy because of its early date and because in it Buber mentions the possibility of using folk art as a foundation for national art, and also because it sharply differentiates between Zionist cultural directions and its political, philanthropic ones. For that Fifth Zionist Congress, Buber prepared, together with Ephraim Lillien, an exhibition of paintings, lithographs, pen drawings, photographs and architectural plans by artists such as Samuel Hirszenberg, Isidore Kaufman, Ephraim Lillien, Lesser Ury, Max Liebermann, Josef Israels, Oscar Marmorek and others. See *Stenographisches Protocoll der Verhandlungen des V. Zionist Kongresses in Basel* (Vienna, 1901).

5. The Palestine Exploration Fund was established in 1865.

6. Chernichevsky was a writer and champion of the 'Wanderers'. 'Reality is more beautiful than its representation in art,' 'the true function of art is to explain life and comment on it,' quoted in Camilla Gray, *The Great Experiment, Russian Art 1865–1922* (London, 1962), p. 10.

7. Quoted from Ilya Günzburg, 'Jüdische Nationalkunst (Gedanken eines gelehrten Russischen Kritikers)', *Ost und West*, 10, 11, 12 (Berlin, Oct., Nov., Dec. 1905). About Vladimir Stassof's role in nineteenth-century Russian art criticism, see Elizabeth Valkenier, *Russian Realist Art, The State and Society, the Peredvizhniki and their Tradition* (Ann Arbor, 1977), pp. 56–62. Stassof's powerful influence extended even into Jewish music. It

was because of him that Joel Engel, a graduate of the Moscow Imperial Conservatory in 1895, who became music critic of the *Russkia Vedomosti* and won broad recognition in the artistic and academic circles of St. Petersburg and Moscow, turned suddenly to Jewish music. 'It happened on the eve of the Russian Easter in 1897 in Moscow when the young Russian music critic Engel met his friend, the sculptor Mark Antokolski, who was to introduce him to Vladimir Stassof, the champion of Russian national art. Stassof lived in St. Petersburg and usually visited Moscow for his Easter vacation. When Engel and Antokolski arrived, they found Stassof in the company of the painter Ilya Repin, both absorbed in Stassof's beloved topic, nationalism in the arts. Stassof, a genuine Slav, was a great admirer and student of the Bible. He felt the inner profound relationship between the Bible and Western culture. Thereupon, Yuli Dmitrevich Engel was introduced by Mark Matveyevich Antokolski. Stassof immediately started a vigorous attack on both men, as Jews who used Russian names instead of their Hebrew ones. "Look here," he shouted at Antokolski, "what is the idea of calling yourself 'Mark' a genuine Roman, Latin name? What have you in common with Mark? Certainly nothing. Are you ashamed of your own Mordehai? I simply cannot understand it. Where is your national pride in being a Jew? Can you not see the magnificent biblical splendour, the nobility of that Mor-de-hai? Yes, yes you should forget Mark and become proud of your ancient aristocratic forefather Mordehai. The great Mordehai!" ' Jacob Weinberg, 'Joel Engel, Champion of Jewish Music', in Lucy S. Davidowicz, *The Golden Tradition* (New York, 1967).

8. The effect of Ansky's activities cannot be overrated. He was a pivotal figure in creating an awareness of the cultural significance of Jewish folklore as a creation of the Jewish people. In his many-sided literary, political, social and scientific activities, and in his very personality, he connects different groups, parties and points of view. He was at home with Russian, Yiddish and Hebrew writers, with historians, ethnographers, people of the theatre, with Bundists, Zionists, revolutionaries, folklorists and a wide network of Jewish welfare agencies.

9. According to the historian Jacob Shatsky, the expedition cost 23,000 roubles, of which Baron Horace Ginzburg donated 10,000. The expedition gathered 2,000 photographs, 1,800 folktales and legends, 1,500 folk songs and mystery plays (500 with Jewish folk music), 1,000 melodies with lyrics and without, 100 historic documents, 500 manuscripts and 700 antique articles (on which 6,000 roubles were spent and which were collected to form a Jewish National Museum). All this material was given to the Jewish Historic Ethnographic Society at the end of 1916. 'S. Ansky, the folklorist', in *Vitebsk Amol*, ed. H. A. Abramson (New York, 1956). For eyewitness accounts of the expedition, see Abraham Rechtman, *Jewish Ethnography and Folklore* (Argentina: YIVO, 1958), Yiddish; P. Graubard, *An ander Leben* (Warsaw: Kulturlige, 1928), Yiddish; and S. Ansky, *Dos Yiddische Ethnografische Program* (St. Petersburg, 1914), Yiddish.

10. These objects are locked in storage in the Ethnographic Museum of the People of the U.S.S.R. in Leningrad (verbal communication, Zussia Ephron, 1977).

11. It is interesting to note that included at the Academy were courses in Jewish art taught by Ilya Günzburg. Zalman Shazar, who was a student there, leaves an interesting description of

Günzburg's course: 'Among the visiting teachers there was a sculptor Elyahu Günzburg, student of the great sculptor Antokolski, the "favoured child" of the Baron Ginzburg. The academic sculptor Günzburg was of small stature, and his work adorned the Hermitage in St. Petersburg. Thin and vibrant like quicksilver, he reminded me of one of the descriptions of N. Sokolov of Israels, and of Hanokh Glitzenstein, whom I met later in New York. In his excitement there was something of the aliveness of the bronze figure of a Jewish boy who dips his toe into a broad river. This was a very popular figure with the visitors of the Hermitage. Now, there stood before us the creator of this boy and talked with us about Jewish art. He believed that his teacher Antokolski was a classic representative of Jewish art, the very essence and very soul of Jewish art. He saw in Antokolski's work the celebration of the superiority of spirit over matter. Examples? Jesus, whom Antokolski fashioned with his bound back, Nestor weak and feeble, and Socrates condemned to die. A celebration of the spirit overcoming matter—that is the character of Jewish art. I remember how fascinated I was by the effort of this Jewish teacher from Vilna at the Russian Academy at St. Petersburg, who aimed at discovering the specific Jewish quality in the art of our generation, and especially in the work of Antokolski, recently singled out by Ahad Ha'am as an example of the denial of Jewishness . . . Among the frequent guests at the Institute was S. Ansky who recruited students for his expedition.' Zalman Shazar, 'Our Teachers at the Institute of Baron Ginzburg', *Heavar*, 6 (Tel Aviv, 1958), Hebrew.

12. David Ginzburg and Vladimir Stassof, *L'Ornement hébraïque* (Berlin, 1905).

13. See George Margoliouth, 'Hebrew Illuminated Manuscripts. *L'Ornement hébraïque* par D. Ginzburg et V. Stassof', *The Jewish Quarterly Review*, 18 (London, 1906), and also 'Hebrew Illuminated Manuscripts', *The Jewish Quarterly Review*, 20 (London, 1908).

14. Thus Joseph Klausner writes: 'In this book they laid the foundation for Hebrew arts.' 'The Baron David Ginzburg', *Heavar*, 16 (Tel Aviv, 1958). See also G. Kutna, 'Zur Ausstellung . . .' (note 1 above): 'Since the founding of Zionism there arose, together with the longing for the re-establishment of a Jewish people (*volkstum*), a longing for Jewish art. With the strong emphasis on the national and the rising interest in art in our time, this was a natural phenomenon.'

15. In Darmstadt, Lissitzky undoubtedly became familiar with the famous fifteenth-century Hebrew illuminated manuscript the *Haggadah of Darmstadt*. It is also known that he travelled frequently to Worms to study the oldest synagogue in Europe, dating from the eleventh century. See Sophie Lissitzky-Küppers, *El Lissitzky* (London, 1968), p. 12.

16. The paintings of the synagogue of Mohilev were first mentioned in the literature of 1914, and even then knowledge about the synagogue paintings was very limited. See Rachel Wischnitzer, 'The Ornaments of the Mohilev Synagogue', *Heavar*, 15 (Tel Aviv, 1968). This article also contains significant iconographic information.

17. Eliezer Lissitzky, 'The Synagogue of Mohilev, Reminiscences', *Rimon*, 3 (Berlin, 1923), Hebrew.

18. Ibid.

19. Ibid. Shlomo Yudovin and M. Malkin made a similar observation: 'Jewish art had to be decorative. Religion permitted decoration but not illustration. The paintings in synagogues, communal books, paper cut-outs, gravestone carvings, and carvings on holy arks are all purely decorative. They all serve as ornament. They are all the products of the artist's imagination, the artist who preferred a secular rather than a religious content. For instance, the synagogue of Mohilev contains twelve figures of the zodiac, various birds, serpents, cities, trees, etc. Without the possibility of presenting the human figure, the artist carried the human into beasts and birds. These are really not beasts but symbols of Jewish life. The way they stand or move is completely human. Many remind us of the Hassidic tales of transformation (*gilgul*).' Shlomo Yudovin and M. Malkin, *Yiddisher Folksornament* (Vitebsk: Y. L. Peretz Society, 1920).

20. Rachel Wischnitzer, 'Modern Art and Our Jewish Generation', *Rimon*, 1 (Berlin, 1922), Hebrew.

21. M. Etkind, *Nathan Altman* (Moscow, 1971), Russian. I would like to thank Mrs. Luba Schapiro for her help in translating the Russian texts.

22. Ibid.

23. See M. Diamant, *Jüdische Volkskunst* (Vienna, 1937), pp. 39–40, for information about Jewish painted gravestones.

24. See introduction of Nathan Altman, *Jüdische Graphik*, text by Max Osborn (Berlin, 1923). Diamant comes to similar conclusions in regard to the tradition of Jewish gravestones in Eastern Europe.

25. Marc Chagall, 'Bletlach', *Shtrom*, 1 (Moscow, 1922), Yiddish. Chagall returns to this theme later in his article 'Mein Arbeit in Moscawer Yiddischen Kamerni Theater', *Die Yiddische Welt*, 2 (Warsaw, 1928), Yiddish.

26. The general impression which the work of Jewish Russian artists left on the Western-trained eye can be deduced from Kutna's review of the large Exhibition of Jewish Artists held in Berlin in 1907: 'How do these artists look at the world? How do these artists look at Jews? What means do they use and what effect does their art have? As in the total world feeling of Jews, we recognize here also a trend from East to West, a trend to becoming freer, brighter, to progressive liberation. Of course this is not a dogma without any exceptions. But one can make the following observation: in the east, there clings to the object, to the conception, to the artistic development, a sorrowful, depressing and gloomy element. Subject-matter plays an important role. The effect aims at our mood, and pure sensuous artistic delight plays an almost secondary role. In the West, the conception is an artistic one, the treatment more objective and freer. Line, colour, composition and space have an artistic autonomous function and the result is artistic beauty and sensuous delight. To reach the beautiful so freely cannot be done by those who are so weary from the hardships of the day. They are also people whose whole art is a pensive glance back at the misery of their home and childhood. Through art they regain the life-time of their youth and lift the bitterness of their existence into a sphere which transforms pain into pensive melancholy. A solemn and silent promise emanates from their work. This world of sorrow is the realm of our art and we are the messengers of its mute agony. Thus, their work is enveloped in a veil of sadness and fatigue; there is no brightness in it, no sun, no joyous Greek spirit. Absent are the bright meadows, the free and open spaces, the cheerful colours and the carefree sensuality.' G. Kutna, 'Zur Austellung' (note 1 above).

27. Issachar Ryback and Boris Aronson, 'Di Vegen fun der Yiddisher Malerei' ['Paths of Jewish Painting'], *Oifgang* (Kiev: Kulturlige, 1919).

28. Ibid.

29. Ibid.

30. The Bezalel School of Art was established in Jerusalem in 1906.

31. Ryback and Aronson, 'Di Vegen . . .'

32. Dobrushin's inventory includes: the painted synagogues, carved gravestones, carved arks, the *bimoth* (tables from which the Torah is read), Torah crowns, Torah ornaments, pointers, covers, ark curtains, jars, *menorot*, chairs of Elijah, *shofars*, *seder* plates, Passover cups, Sabbath table-cloths, embroidered pillows, marriage canopies, marriage contracts (*ketubot*), Torah mantles, Torah curtains, embroidered pouches for phylacteries, ritual washstands, *almemars*, synagogue lecterns, embroidered pouches for prayer-shawls, signs of the zodiac, pulpits, fixtures and paper cut-outs marking the east wall, embroidered skull caps, covers for the Sabbath bread, snuff boxes, illuminated manuscripts, rattles, tops, title pages, spice boxes, booths for *Succah*, Holy Day cookies, *Purim* pastry, *haggadot*, kerchiefs, bow and arrows, flags for *Simhat Torah*, candlesticks. Yechezkel Dobrushin, 'Kunst Primitiv un Kunst Buch far Kinder', *Gedankengang* (Kiev: Cooperativer Verlag Kulturlige, 1922).

33. S. Ansky, 'Di Yiddische Volksschaffung' (1908), *Gesammelte Schriften*, 15 (1925). See also 'Der Yiddische Volksgeist un sein Schaffen' (Lecture) (Vilna, 1918).

34. Dobrushin, 'Kunst Primitiv'.

35. Ibid.

36. Boris Aronson, *Sovremmenaya Evreiskaya Grafika* (Berlin, 1924). See also Elias Lippiner, *Ideologie fun Yiddishen Aleph Beis* (Argentina: YIVO, 1967), for information about the significance of the Hebrew letter.

37. Dobrushin, 'Kunst Primitiv'.

38. Ryback and Aronson, 'Di Vegen . . .'

39. Ryback and Aronson strongly echo some general ideas about the nature of abstract art then widely current among avant-garde Russian artists. See for instance their writings in *Russian Art of the Avant-Garde: Theory and Criticism 1902–1934*, ed. John E. Bowlt (New York, 1976).

40. Ryback and Aronson, 'Di Vegen . . .'

41. Ibid.

42. Ibid.

43. Ibid.

even became fierce and savage, their sadness fanatical and their joy rapture. They were Dionysian Jews.

'This was a play of a genuine community, with consciousness of the events on the stage and of the reality of our world . . . a theatre which fully expresses communal feelings and which is an expression of the Jewish masses and where actors are equals. . . . It is not a Jewish theatre in the vulgar sense. It is a real world theatre.'

65. The Habimah theatre was organized on a strictly collective basis with expenses as well as income equally shared among the actors. Once being admitted to membership, the actor had to pledge not to treat its director as owner or supervisor of the theatre but as teacher and guide, and not to engage in any class struggle against him. Actors signed a statement written by the founder of the group in which they pledged to see the theatre as a temple of the Hebrew Arts in which they were about to serve. 'In ancient times the people and its prophets—tomorrow the people and its theatres.' Habimah was seen as a branch of the eternal Hebrew culture, a means for spiritual redemption. The actors had to sacrifice their personal well-being for that of the theatre. Their pledge said in part: 'The problems of the theatre I see as my own, its goals as my goals. I promise not to treat my work as a trade, a job or profession but as a highest personal commitment. The idea demands a personal, spiritual, ascetic attitude and the goal is reached like all truth by special talent, long preparation and terrible suffering.' Quoted from Haklai (note 53 above), p. 76.

66. M. Chagall, 'Bletlach', *Der Shtrom* (Moscow, 1922).

67. Ziva Amishai-Maisel sees Chagall as 'a perfect example of the newly emancipated Jew caught midway between the culture of his childhood, which shaped his memory and his personality, and the culture of St. Petersburg and Paris, which shaped his art and mode of life. The constant oscillations in Chagall's self-image are themselves symptomatic of his position: he was a Jew in St. Petersburg and a Russian in Paris (1807–1914); he fully reintegrated within the Jewish revival movement in Russia between 1914–22, and returned to full assimilation within the French world in 1923–35, only to revert to full Jewish consciousness in the late 1930s, and during World War II, finally he has returned to full affirmation of his French nationality and stresses the universality and the non-Jewish character of his art.' See 'Chagall's Jewish In-Jokes', *Journal of Jewish Art*, 5 (1978). See also Amishai-Maisel's article, 'Chagall and Jewish Art', *Gazith*, 32, no. 12 (1978, in Hebrew).

68. Camilla Gray sees Kiev as the centre of the Jewish artistic avant-garde and the book illustrations emanating as decisively influencing modern typography: 'It was from this Jewish tradition that the first post-revolutionary experiment in typographical design was done.' *The Great Experiment: Russian Art, 1863–1922* (London, 1962).

69. Chimen Abramsky has already indicated some connection between Lissitzky's illustrations for Yiddish books and the development of the *proun* ('El Lissitzky as Jewish Illustrator and Typographer', *Studio International*, 172, no. 382 (Oct. 1966)). However, he puts the date for *Yingl Zingl Chwatt* as 1919, Kiev-Petersburg. I refer to another edition published by the *Kulturlige* in Warsaw in 1922 in which Lissitzky introduces on the title page, as part of the design, his name and the date 1918, that is, one year before he was appointed Professor of Architecture at the Vitebsk School of Art, and before he came under the influence of Malevich. It seems that Lissitzky was already moving independently into the direction toward the proun and that Malevich's joining the Art School of Vitebsk in 1919 only reinforced this tendency. Abramsky's article gives a full bibliography of the Hebrew and Yiddish books illustrated by Lissitzky.

70. Alan C. Birnholz, 'El Lissitzky and the Jewish Tradition', *Studio International*, 186, no. 959 (Oct. 1973).

71. Personal communication from Boris Aronson.

72. Alan C. Birnholz, 'El Lissitzky. . .' Up to this point one is indeed indebted to Birnholz's analysis of Lissitzky's Jewish sources. However, he overplays his hand when he conceives of Lissitzky's conversion to an abstract Suprematist and Constructivist style not as a negation of Jewish folk art or a negation of the quest for a national Jewish art but as a transcendence thereof and as being actually derived from 'the status of Jewish art in Russia in 1919 and from the basic tenets of the Jewish attitude towards art'. According to Birnholz, Lissitzky considers the *proun* to be more in accord with Jewish tradition than his prior efforts had been, and he turned to a literal acceptance of the Second Commandment as a means of defining modern art and modern Jewish art. This argument as presented by Birnholz is complex and emerges from an ambiance close to that of the New York School in which a relationship between the abstract art of the late 1940s, 1950s and 1960s and the Jewish background of some of its leading figures has in recent years frequently been suggested. (Robert Pincus-Witten, 'Six Propositions on Jewish Art', *Arts Magazine* (Dec. 1975); George Hamilton, 'Painting in Contemporary America', *Burlington Magazine*, 102 (May 1960), p. 193; Robert Rosenblum, *Modern Painting and the Northern Romantic Tradition: Friedrich to Rothko* (London, 1975), p. 212; W. Haftmann, *Mark Rothko* (Düsseldorf städtische Kunsthalle, 1971); T. B. Hess, *Barnett Newman* (New York, 1971).) The argument in the case of Lissitzky essentially rests on Birnholz's own ingenious interpretation, in which he freely uses the cabbalistic method which invests letters and their numerical equivalents and their myriad combinations with a mystical power. Thus, he brings the word *proun*, an acronym for 'the new art' into relation with certain Hebrew and Yiddish words, and also establishes far-fetched relationships between the 'common' negative attitude of Constructivism and Suprematism and Jewish tradition toward the image. Not only Lissitzky but also people who were in close personal contact with Lissitzky would have disagreed most vehemently with Birnholz's thesis.

Thus Rachel Wischnitzer: 'For him they [these ideas] already represented a past thoroughly overcome. He had joined wholeheartedly the movement of abstract non-objective art inspired by technology, and of an acute sense of social change.' ('Berlin in the Early 1920s', *Studies in Jewish History*, Raphael Mahler Jubilee Volume, ed. by S. Yeivin (Merhavya, 1974). The whole generation of Jewish artists, even Chagall, was assimilationist to begin with, and only World War I and its pogroms turned their interest toward Jewish art (Gabriel Talpir, editor of *Gazith*, in a personal interview). A careful reading of Lissitzky's statements makes it clear that he wholeheartedly accepted the new era and that in the name of creativity he sought to abolish the differentiation between art and work. (See *Dos Gower* and *Suprematism in World Reconstruction*.)

73. For his entire development, see Sophie Lissitzky-Küppers, *El Lissitzky* (London, 1968).

74. Lissitzky, 'The Synagogue of Mohilev', *Dos Gower*, and *Suprematism in World Reconstruction*.

75. Lissitzky, 'The Synagogue of Mohilev'.

76. Ibid.

Notes to chapter 2

1. Saul Raskin, 'An Exhibition of Jewish Artists, A Proclamation', *Dos Neie Land* (New York, 17 Nov. 1911), Yiddish.

2. B. Liber, 'About the Art Exhibition', *Dos Neie Land* (24 Nov. 1911), Yiddish.

3. Saul Raskin, 'The Future of Jewish Art', *Dos Neie Land* (15 Sept. 1911), Yiddish.

4. Ibid.

5. Martin Buber, *Jüdische Künstler* (Berlin: Jüdischer Verlag, 1903).

6. Jacob Epstein, *Let There be Sculpture*, the autobiography of Jacob Epstein (London, 1942), p. 2.

7. Ibid., p. 8.

8. Hapgood Hutchins, *The Spirit of the Ghetto* (New York: Funk & Wagnall, 1902).

9. Epstein, *Let There be Sculpture*, p. 8.

10. Ibid, p. 10.

11. David Ignatoff, 'Abraham Walkowitz', *Zukunft* (New York, Dec. 1949), Yiddish.

12. B. Kopman, *Abraham Walkowitz* (Paris: Editions Le Triangle, 1927), Yiddish.

13. Fishman, William J., *East-End Jewish Radicals, 1875–1914* [Camden Town], in association with the Acton Society Trust, 1975).

14. William Lipke, *David Bomberg* (London, 1967), p. 40.

15. Richard Cork, *Vorticism and Abstract Art in the First Machine Age* (London, 1976), reproduces *Ezekiel's Vision* (1912), *The Mud Bath* (1914) and *In the Hold* (1913–14), and a study for *Reading from the Torah* (1914) (the original is lost).

16. David Bomberg, from The catalogue of his one-man exhibition at the Chenil Gallery in July 1914, London.

17. See Joseph Leftwich, 'Jewish London—Fifty Years Ago', in *Ben Uri Commemorative Volume* (London: Ben Uri Society, 1966).

18. See David Bomberg, 'Songs of War', *Renaissance*, 2, no. 2 (London, May 1920), Yiddish.

19. *Broom*, an international magazine of the arts, appearing in Rome, Berlin and New York between 1921 and 1924.

20. Daniel Ignatoff (the son of David), in his essay 'A Brif Zu di Einiklech', in David Ignatoff, *Obgerissene Bletter* [*Drifted Leaves*] (Buenos Aires, 1957), Yiddish.

21. Weichsel Papers, Archives of American Art, New York.

22. Weichsel Papers. People's Art Guild, Prospectus, Archives of American Art.

23. John Weichsel, 'To the East Side and its Friends', Foreword to the 26th Exhibition of the People's Art Guild, in the Jewish Daily Forward Building, May 1917, John Weichsel Papers, Archives of American Art.

24. Ibid.

25. John Weichsel, The Society of the Jewish Museum, A Prospectus, 28 Dec. 1917. John Weichsel Papers, Archives of American Art.

26. Raphael Soyer, *Self-Revealment: A Memoir* (New York, 1969), pp. 50–2.

27. J. Tofel. 'The Jewish Art Center', *Der Hammer* (New York, Mar. 1927), Yiddish.

28. Ibid.

29. Moses Rischin, *The Promised City, New York Jews, 1870–1914* (Harvard University Press, 1962), p. 140.

30. Louis Lozowick, 'Jewish Artists of the Season', *Menorah Journal* (New York, July, 1924).

31. Ibid.

32. Louis Lozowick Papers, Archives of American Art, New York. Ryback stuck to his views (see pp. 28–9) about Jewish art even after the Russian Revolution had disappointed his hopes. (It is interesting to note that Boris Aronson also continued to hold the same views even in the 1960s when I had the opportunity to speak with him in New York.) Lozowick, however, who discusses in his notes his meetings with Ryback and other Jewish artists in Berlin, makes it clear that he does not share the views of Ryback. His views are closer to Lissitzky's, after the Russian Revolution, who felt that to use the past as a source of art in order to prove that like other nationalities Jews have a tradition, is anachronistic.

33. Louis Lozowick, 'Three Phases in the Development of a Proletarian Artist', *BODN*, 2, no. 1 (New York, April, June 1935), Yiddish.

34. Lozowick, introduction to the catalogue of the Machine Age Exposition, May 1927, Steinway Gallery, New York, sponsored by the *Little Review*.

35. Ibid.

36. The Babylonian Talmud, Hagigah, fol. 14b.

37. Leonard Baskin, 'Of Roots and Veins', address at Dickinson College, 17 Oct. 1963, Dickinson College Office of Information Services in Cooperation with the Fine Arts Department.

38. See Irma B. Jaffee, *The Sculpture of Leonard Baskin* (New York, 1980).

39. Karl Jay Shapiro, 'The 151st Psalm', in *Poems of a Jew* (New York, 1958).

40. For an insight into the home-life of George Segal see Martin Freedman, 'George Segal: Proletarian Mythmaker', *Art International*, 23/9 (Jan.–Feb. 1980).

41. Using the Biblical theme of Abraham and Isaac, Segal may have hoped to overcome the objections of conservative groups to the obvious allusions his sculpture evokes, and still be understood by a wide public. But this was not to be; the sculpture was rejected and later acquired by the Princeton University Art Museum.

42. Soyer, *Self-Revealment*, p. 63.

43. Quoted from Albert Elsen, *Seymour Lipton* (New York 1970), p. 53.

44. For a detailed account of this development see Rachel Wischnitzer, *Synagogue Architecture in the United States* (Philadelphia: The Jewish Publication Society, 1955); Avram Kampf, *Contemporary Synagogue Art* (Philadelphia: The Jewish Publication Society, 1965).

45. Chagall, *Bible* (Paris: Verve, 1965); Ben Shahn, *Haggadah for Passover* (London: MacGibbon and Kee, and Paris: Trianon, 1965); Oscar Kokoschka, *Saul and David* (Lucerne: C. J. Bucher, 1970); Leonard Baskin, *Passover Haggadah* (New York: Viking Press, 1974).

Notes to chapter 3

1. M. Wheeler, *Soutine* (New York, 1950), p. 37.

2. G. Waldemar, 'The School of Paris', in C. Roth, *Jewish Art* (Greenwich, Conn., 1971), pp. 229–60.

3. E. Faure, *Soutine* (Paris, 1928), pp. 8–9.

4. M. Raynal, *Modern French Painters* (New York, 1928), p. 152.

5. Ibid., p. 151.

6. G. Waldemar, *Soutine* (Paris, 1928), pp. 15–18.

7. M. Tuchman, *Chaim Soutine* (Los Angeles, 1968), pp. 11f.

8. R. Talpir, 'Jewish Painters of Paris', *Gazith*, 7, no. 10 (June 1945), pp. 19–24; continued in nos. 11–12 (July, August 1945), pp. 35–44, Hebrew.

9. Communication with Hanna Orlof, July, 1961, Paris.

10. Communication with Hanna Orlof, July, 1961, Paris.

Notes to chapter 4

1. See H. Fenster, *Unzere Farpainikte Kinstler*, [*Our Persecuted Artists*] (Paris, 1951), Yiddish.

2. Erich Hancke, *Max Liebermann* (Berlin 1923), pp. 131–42.

3. Thomas Grochowiak, *Ludwig Meidner* (Recklinghausen, 1966).

4. Christian von Lenz, 'Max Beckmanns "Synagogue" ', *Städel Jahrbuch*, Neue Folge 4 (Frankfurt-am-Main, 1973).

5. Meyer, *Marc Chagall* (New York, 1964), p. 416.

6. Ibid.

7. E. Roditi, 'The Jewish Artists in the Modern World', in C. Roth, ed., *Jewish Art* (New York, 1971), p. 301.

8. A. Klapheck, *Jankel Adler* (Recklinghausen, 1966), p. 24.

9. Personal Communication from Joseph Herman, London, March 1974.

10. E. Brauer, *Malerei des Fantastischen Realismus* (Munich, 1968), p. 16.

11. Personal Communication from the artist, Vienna, Feb. 1974.

12. W. Schmied, *Hundertwasser* (Auckland, 1973), p. 68.

13. 'Ariel' 42, Feb. 1977, album published by Galerie Ariel, Paris.

14. Nelly Sachs, 'Oh the Chimneys', in *Selected Poems*, translated from the German by Michael Hamburger (Philadelphia: Jewish Publication Society, 1968).

15. Paul Celan, 'Todesfuge', in *Mohn und Gedächtnis, Gedichte* (Stuttgart: Deutsche Verlags Anstalt, 1952).

16. Harold Paris, *The California Years*, ed., P. Selz, (Berkeley, 1972), p. 28.

17. Ibid, p. 29.

18. 'I was hiding with a painter friend. We ran out of food and had no money left. We did not know what to do and decided to go to Picasso. He asked how we were doing. I answered, "What can we do?" He said "I do what I want to do." He looked at our paintings and bought two from each of us.' Personal communication from Aberdam, Paris, July 1961.

19. Alfred H. Barr, Jr., *Picasso: Fifty Years of his Art* (Museum of Modern Art, New York, 1946), p. 250.

20. Jacques Lipchitz with H. H. Arnason, *My Life in Sculpture* (London, 1972), p. 160.

21. Personal communication from the artist, New York, Dec. 1980.

22. Personal communication from Mrs. Siporin, New York, Oct. 1980.

23. Albert Elsen, *Seymour Lipton* (New York, 1970), p. 27.

Notes to chapter 5

1. R. Rubin, *My Life and My Art* (New York, 1970), p. 43.

2. Ibid., p. 53.

3. See Ahron Amir, *Kadim*, poems (Tel Aviv, 1949), Hebrew; Jonathan Ratosh, *Black Canopy* (1941), Hebrew; the journal

Adelph (Tel Aviv, 1948); Moshe Shamir, *Milchemet B'nai Or* [*War of the Sons of Light*], Kamerni Theatre, Tel Aviv, 1956.

4. Louis Ginzburg, *The Legends of the Jews* (Philadelphia: Jewish Publication Society, 1937), vol. 1, p. 177.

5. Ben Ami Sharfstein, 'Alone together in a Place', *Yediot Aharonot* (22 July 1977), Hebrew.

6. Excerpts from an interview with Itzhak Danziger, 1963, in *Siman Kria* (*Literary Quarterly*), 8 (Tel Aviv, 1977), p. 365, Hebrew.

7. William C. Seitz, *Art Israel, 26 Painters and Sculptors* (Museum of Modern Art, New York, 1964), p. 43.

8. Taken from a lecture by the artist at the symposium 'The Myth of Canaan', University of Haifa Art Gallery, 12 June 1980.

9. Moshe Castel, catalogue of the retrospective exhibition, 1928–1973, the Tel-Aviv Museum, 1973.

10. Store cities which the Israelites built for the Pharaoh in Egypt (Exodus 1:11).

11. Nathan Sach, 'Toward the Sea Shore', in *Early Poems* (Jerusalem, 1955), Hebrew.

12. Danziger moved consistently to a conception of environmental art and aimed for the integration of the artist into contemporary society. See Itzhak Danziger, 'The Rehabilitation of the Nesher Quarry' Feb–Nov. 1971, project Israel-Portland Cement Work, Nesher Ltd., sponsored by the Israel Museum, Jerusalem. Danziger is quoted in an interview with Amnon Barzel in the July 1977 *Ha'aretz Supplement*: 'The responsibility of the artist in society is that of an educator, philosopher, Rabbi, father, prophet at the gate, preacher. He has to conserve the things which have been accomplished here. Yes, romanticism is an unusual force. The artist has to initiate ideas, to point into a direction, to flow like a stream within society, to overcome all the difficulties. The artist is a politician, and that was always so. There were manifestos; but an artist who claims: 'all my activity is concentrated on the canvas, from the distressing water bill to the expression of the Tel Aviv light, is an artist who turns around his own navel. This is a standard, average good artist. If the goal is only to create objects of art, the artist will be left with the steering wheel in his hands like in the cartoons of Walt Disney.'

13. Soren Kierkegaard, *Fear and Trembling and the Sickness to Death*, translated by Walter Lowrie (Princeton University Press, 1974), p. 29.

Notes to chapter 6

1. Max Weber, 'Distortion in Modern Art', *The League* [Art Students League], 6, no. 2 (New York, 1934).

2. Philo, *Life of Moses*, III.27, translated by C. D. Young (London, 1854).

3. Lloyd Goodrich, *Max Weber*, catalogue, Whitney Museum of American Art, New York, 1949, p. 47.

4. Translation of a prayer for the Day of Atonement (Yom Kippur).

5. Personal communication from the artist, New York, April 1956.

6. John I. H. Baur, *Bernard Reder* (New York, 1961), p. 27.

7. Ibid., p. 33.

Notes to chapter 7

1. Letter to W. Sandberg, Jerusalem, 15 Aug. 1960, in Mordechai Ardon, exhibition catalogue. Neuer Berliner Kunstverein, Berlin, 1979.

2. Gershom G. Scholem, *On the Kabbalah and its Symbolism* (New York: Schocken Books, 1969).

3. From an interview with the artist, 15 Feb. 1966, in *Paintings of Yehoshua Kovarsky*, catalogue of an exhibition at the University of Haifa, 1976.

4. *New York Times*, 13 June, 1943, section 2, p. 9.

5. T. B. Hess, *Barnett Newman* (New York, 1971), p. 39.

6. Ibid., p. 57.

7. Ibid., p. 53.

8. W. Haftmann, *Mark Rothko*, catalogue of an exhibition at the Städtische Kunsthalle, Düsseldorf, 1971. Haftmann relates how he arrived at his insight. He came to New York City to invite Rothko to participate in *Documenta*, 1959. Rothko refused, on the grounds that he did not want to exhibit in a group show and that his work needed its own space. When Haftmann promised that this would be done. Rothko still refused and said that as a Jew he would not even think of exhibiting in Germany which had committed so many crimes against Jews. However, during the conversation, Rothko remarked that he would be willing to paint, without fee, a 'Chapel of Repentance' to honour the Jewish victims in hateful Germany, even if that Chapel were only a tent. This set Haftmann on the trail of his interpretation. He adds that Rothko saw in the isolated painting an example for a special conception which was to surround and absorb the whole person.

9. Ibid.

10. Leo Steinberg, 'The New York School, Second Generation', article in the catalogue of the exhibition at the Jewish Museum, New York, March 1957.

Artists' Biographies

Alfred Aberdam (1894–1963)
B. in Lvov, Poland. Studied painting at the Munich Academy (1913–14). Served in the Austrian Army during World War I, wounded on the Russian front and captured. Stayed in Russia, where he participated in the Revolution, and when the Red Army conquered Irkutzk he was appointed Director of the local museum. In 1920, he studied at the Cracow Academy and then in Berlin with Archipenko. He remained in Paris in hiding during the Nazi occupation. In 1949 and 1952 he visited Israel and exhibited in Tel Aviv, Haifa, and Jersusalem.
Aronson, C., *Art polonais moderne* (Paris, 1929).

Achiam (b. 1919)
B. in Bayit Vagan, a village in Galilee. In 1934 was sent to study at the Mikve-Israel Agricultural School. During that period, started to sculpt. In 1945 moved to Jerusalem. In 1947 he went to Paris. After being rejected by the Academy of Fine Arts and Zadkin's studio, he commenced working on his own and exhibited in the Salon de Paris. Lives in Paris.
Flament, A., *Achiam, sculptures et poèmes* (Paris, 1979).

Jankel Adler (1895–1949)
B. in Lodz, Poland. Lived in Germany from 1913 to 1933. He had trained in Poland to be a goldsmith and engraver. His international reputation was established in 1926 with his decoration of the Düsseldorf Planetarium. Fleeing Germany in 1933, Adler lived precariously in various European capitals, finally settling in England in England in 1941.
Klapheck, A., *Jankel Adler* (Recklinghausen, 1966).

Nathan Altman (1889–1970)
B. 1889 in Vinnitza, Ukraine. Studied in Odessa Art School (1902–7). Visited Vienna, Munich, and Paris (1910–11), and then settled in St. Petersburg. From 1913 he was strongly influenced by Jewish folk art. In 1916 he organized a Jewish art exhibition in St. Petersburg. After the October revolution he actively participated in the Russian avante-garde movement, developing the Constructivist style. He headed the Petrograd section of the Department of Fine Arts and organized mass outdoor scenes in Leningrad 1918–20. Drew and sculpted portraits of Lenin and other Soviet leaders. Designed stages for *The Dybbuk* at the Habima Theatre in Moscow, and for *Uriel Accosta* and *The Ten Commandments* at the Jewish State Theatre in Moscow. Published book on Jewish graphics in Berlin (1923). Between 1924 and 1931 lived in France, then returned to Russia, conforming to the artistic demands of the regime.
Lozowick, L., 'The Art of Nathan Altman', *Menorah Journal*, 12, no. 1 (Feb. 1926).

Mordecai Ardon (b. 1896)
B. in Tuchow, Poland. In 1920–5 studied at the Bauhaus in Weimar and later in Dessau, and in 1926 at the Staatliche Kunstakademie in Munich. In 1929 taught at the Itten-Kunstschule in Berlin. In 1933 arrived in Palestine and settled in Jerusalem. From 1935 to 1952 was teacher and director at the Bezalel School of Arts and Crafts, Jerusalem.
Grohmann, W., *Ardon* (New York, 1967).

Boris Aronson (1900–1980)
B. in Kiev. Before emigrating to New York in 1923, Aronson studied at the State Art School of Kiev; the School of Theatre, Kiev; in Berlin with Herman Struck; and in Paris. Known primarily as a theatrical stage designer, Aronson's first one-man show of designs, models, and costume drawings was at the Anderson Galleries, New York (1927). Died in New York.
George, W., *Boris Aronson et l'art du théâtre* (Paris, 1928).

Samuel Bak (b. 1933)
B. in Vilna, Lithuania. Corralled into the Vilna Ghetto in 1940, Bak and his mother escaped only to be recaptured. Two years later Bak had his first exhibition of drawings there. His formal art education included classes at the Vilna Academy (1945); with Professor Blocherer in Munich (1946–8); at the Bezalel School of Arts and Crafts, Jerusalem (1952–3); and at the Beaux Arts Atelier, Paris (1956–9). Lives in Israel.
Nagano, P., *Bak, Paintings of the Last Decade* (Aberbach Fine Art, New York, 1974).

Leonard Baskin (b. 1922)
B. in New Jersey. Grew up in Brooklyn where as the son of an orthodox rabbi he was sent to a yeshiva. He studied at the Educational Alliance Art School, New York; New York University; and at Yale University where he founded the Gehanna Press in 1942. Of the many one-man exhibitions of his evocative figurative sculpture and graphics, the most significant were held by the Museum of Modern Art, New York (1962), and the Borgenicht Gallery (1953–69). Lives in England.
Leonard Baskin: Recent Sculpture and Drawing (Kennedy Galleries, New York, 1975).

Max Beckmann (1884–1950)
B. in Leipzig, Germany. His art education included studying at the Weimar Art School in 1899 and a trip to Paris (1903–4). Settling in Berlin in 1906, he was an immediate success as a member of the Berlin Secession. His characteristic deformed Expressionist imagery, termed 'the new objectivity', was not fully developed until after his service in the Army Medical Corps (1914–15). Beckmann taught art at the Frankfurt Art School from 1915 until 1933, when he was dismissed by the Nazi authorities; he taught subsequently at Washington University, St. Louis (1947–9), and at the Brooklyn Museum. Died in New York.
Fischer, F., *Max Beckmann* (London, 1973).

Ben-Zion (b. 1897)
B. in the Ukraine. A painter and a sculptor, he studied in Vienna and came to the United States in 1920. An amateur artist until

1933, Ben-Zion was self-taught. He taught painting at Cooper Union, New York (1943–50). Lives in New York.
Kayser, S., *Ben-Zion* (Jewish Museum, New York, 1959).

Zeev Ben Zwi (1904–1952)
B. in Ryki, Poland. Studied at Warsaw Academy of Art. Went to Palestine in 1923 and studied at Bezalel School of Art. In 1936 appointed there as teacher of sculpture. From 1947 to 1949 taught art to illegal immigrant groups detained in Cyprus by the British. Many of his works and especially portraits are in private collections.
Israel Museum, Jerusalem, artist file.

Yosl Bergner (b. 1920)
B. in Vienna. Lived in Warsaw until 1937. He is the son of the Yiddish poet and essayist Melech Ravitch. He emigrated to Australia in 1937, where he studied art. During World War II he joined the Australian Army, and later continued his art studies. In 1948 he left Australia to travel and exhibit in Paris, Montreal, and New York. He emigrated to Israel in 1950. He lives in Tel Aviv.
Fischer, Y., *Bergner* (Paris, 1971).

Naftali Bezem (b. 1924)
B. in Essen, Germany. Went to Palestine in 1939 with Youth Aliyah. Studied under Ardon at the Bezalel School of Arts and Crafts, Jerusalem (1943–6). In Paris between 1949 and 1951, he absorbed current European transformations of Surrealism. He lives in Tel Aviv.
Seitz, W., *Art Israel* (Museum of Modern Art, New York, 1964).

Hyman Bloom (b. 1913)
B. in Bounoviski, Lithuania. Emigrated to Boston where he studied with Jack Levine under Denman Ross. Worked for the WPA Federal Arts Project in Boston (1933–6). Currently exhibits at the Dintenfass Gallery, New York.
Hyman Bloom Retrospective (Institute of Contemporary Arts, Boston, 1954).

David Bomberg (1890–1958)
B. in Birmingham, England. Attended Walter Sickert's classes at the Westminster School (1908–10) and studied under Wilson Steer, C. W. Nevinson, and Roger Fry at the Slade School of Fine Arts (1911–13). Had his first one-man show at the Chenil Gallery, Chelsea, in 1914. In 1924 he travelled to Palestine. Died in London.
Lipke, W., *David Bomberg* (London, 1967).

Erich Brauer (b. 1929)
B. in Vienna. From 1942 to 1945 was in a slave labour camp in Vienna. Studied at the Academy of Fine Arts, Vienna (1945–51), and travelled extensively in Europe, Africa, Israel and the United States. Lives and works in Paris, Vienna, and Ein Hod, Israel.
Brauer, E., *Brauer* (Salzburg, 1973).

Moshe Castel (b. 1909)
B. in Jerusalem to a Sephardic family which came to Palestine from Castille in 1492. From 1922 to 1925 he studied at the Bezalel School of Arts and Crafts, Jerusalem. Went to Paris in 1927 and studied at the Julien Academy and at the École du Louvre. In 1940 he returned to Israel and settled in Safed. In 1948, joined the 'New Horizons' art movement. Since 1959 he has lived intermittently in Israel, New York, and Paris.
Tapie, M., and Sachar, H., *Castel* (Neuchatel, 1968).

Marc Chagall (b. 1887)
B. in Vitebsk, Russia. Grew up in an orthodox home in the Jewish quarter. Before leaving for Paris in 1910, he studied painting at the St. Petersburg Academy with Leon Bakst. Living in Paris until 1914, came under the influence of Cubism and Orphism. He exhibited at the Salon des Indépendants and the Salon d'Automne in 1912. From 1915 to 1922 he lived in Russia, and directed the Vitebsk Academy (1918–20), and was a stage and costume designer (1920–2). In 1923 he moved to Paris. Throughout his career, Chagall has worked in various media, including theatre decorations, book illustrations, stained glass windows, and print-making. Currently lives in Venice.
Meyer, F., *Marc Chagall* (New York, 1964)

Marvin Cherney (1925–1967)
B. in Baltimore, Maryland. Studied at the Maryland Institute of Art, the School of Art Studies, New York, and in France and Italy. Died in New York City.
Wilson, S., *Marvin Cherney* (Morgan State College, Philadelphia, 1968).

Itzhak Danziger (1916–1977)
B. in Berlin, Germany. Came to Jerusalem with his family in 1923. From 1929 to 1933 studied at the Bezalel School of Arts and Crafts, Jerusalem. In 1934 went to London where he studied at the Slade School of Fine Art. In 1939 settled in Tel Aviv, where he worked and taught sculpture. In 1945 went to Paris and worked with the sculptor Ossip Zadkin. He joined the 'New Horizons' group. In 1948 went to London, studied landscape and garden planning at London University. Returned to Israel in 1955, when he was appointed professor at the Architecture Department at the Technion. Died in Israel.
Itzhak Danziger, ed. Rina Valero (Tel Aviv, 1981).

Koso Elul (b. 1920)
B. in Mourom, in the Urals. Arrived in Israel with his family in 1924. Studied drawing with Hendler and sculpture with I. Danziger. In 1939 went to the USA and studied at the Chicago Institute of Art. In 1944 joined the American Navy. Returned to Israel in 1946. From 1947 to 1949 lived at Kibbutz Ein Harod. In 1948 joined the art movement 'New Horizons'. Participated at the Venice Biennale (1958). Initiated and worked at 'Form in Space', the International Sculpture Symposium, in the Negev Desert, 1962. Lives in Canada.
Museum of Modern Art, New York, artist file.

Jacob Epstein (1880–1959)
B. in New York. Studied at the Art Students League (1893–1902). Before moving to London in 1905, studied in Paris at the École des Beaux-Arts and the Julien Academy. In 1952 he published his autobiography, *Let There Be Sculpture*.
Buckle, R., *Jacob Epstein, Sculptor* (New York, 1963).

Naum Gabo (1890–1977)
B. Naum Pevsner in Briansk, Russia. In 1910, he entered the University of Munich to study medicine and engineering, and he also attended Wölfflin's lectures. Becoming increasingly interested in art, he travelled to Paris (1912–14). At the beginning of World War I he travelled to Oslo via Copenhagen. Returning to Russia (1917–22) he and his brother issued the 'Realist Manifesto'—a proclamation of the Constructivist programme in 1920. In Berlin from 1922 to 1932, he propagated Constructivist ideas through international exhibitions of his work, lectures (at the Bauhaus), and participation in the 'Abstraction–Creation' group. Before settling permanently in the United States in 1952, he worked in England with the 'Circle' group. He died in Middlebury, Connecticut.
De La Motte, M., *Naum Gabo* (Hanover, 1971).

Mark Gertler (1891–1939)
B. in 1891 in London. Attended Slade School of Art (1908–12). Early work strongly influenced by life of Whitechapel ghetto. Established close relations with Bloomsbury group of intellectuals. Exhibited at Chenil Gallery, Chelsea (1912), at Whitechapel Gallery and Leeds Art Gallery (1914), and at Goupil Gallery (1921). His works are represented at the Fitzwilliam Museum, Cambridge, Ashmolean Museum, Oxford, Tate Gallery and Ben Uri Gallery, London. Committed suicide in 1939.
Woodeson, J. *Mark Gertler: Biography of a Painter* (London, 1972.)

Adolph Gottlieb (1903–1971)
B. in New York. A student at the Art Students League in New York, and worked under John Sloan and Robert Henri in 1920. He also studied at the Académie de la Grande Chaumière, Paris (1921–3), and at the Parsons School of Design in New York (1923). Worked with the WPA Federal Arts Project (1936). Has been honoured at numerous retrospectives in New York. Died in New York.
Doty, R., and Waldman, D., *Adolph Gottlieb* (New York, 1968).

Leopold Gottlieb (1883–1934)
B. in Galicia, Poland. The younger brother of the well-known painter Moritz Gottlieb, he studied at the Academy of Art in Cracow, continued his studies in travel to Munich and Vienna, and finally settled in Paris. He showed his Expressionist portraits at the Salon d'Automne (1908–13) and Salon des Indépendants. During World War I he joined the Polish Legion and described the war in numerous paintings. He returned to Paris in 1929, where he lived until his death.
Salmon, A., *Leopold Gottlieb* (Paris, 1927).

William Gropper (1897–1977)
B. in New York. Studied art at the National Academy of Design and the School of Fine and Applied Art, New York. Like other Social Realists, Gropper was a staff member of several New York newspapers and contributed illustrations and cartoons to various periodicals in the 1920s and 1930s. He travelled to the Soviet Union with Theodore Dreiser and Sinclair Lewis in 1927. Died in New York.
Freundlich, A., *William Gropper* (Los Angeles, 1968).

Chaim Gross (b. 1904)
B. in Galicia. Studied in Budapest and Vienna. After emigrating to New York (1921), he studied at the Educational Alliance Art School, New York, and at the Art Students League of New York. Early in the 1930s he exhibited at galleries in New York. From 1933 to 1935 he worked for the WPA Federal Arts Project, Sculpture Division. Lives in New York City.
Getlein, F., *Chaim Gross* (New York, 1974).

Shamai Haber (b. 1922)
B. in Lodz, Poland. In 1919 went to Paris and attended several schools. In 1935 came to Palestine. Had his first one-man show at the Stedelijk Museum, Amsterdam (1951). Works on a town-planning project for the Negev. Lives in Paris.
Israel Museum, Jerusalem, artist file.

Minna Harkavy (b. 1895)
B. in Estonia. After her emigration to New York, her art education included classes at the Art Students League, New York, and frequent travel and study in Europe. In Paris she worked under Antoine Bourdelle. Currently lives in New York.
Whitney Museum of American Art, New York, artist file.

Josef Herman (b. 1911)
B. In Warsaw. From 1930 to 1932 studied at the Warsaw School of Art, and in 1932 had his first exhibition in Warsaw. He emigrated to Belgium in 1938 and escaped to London in 1940. His subject-matter is largely drawn from a small Welsh mining village, Ystradgynlair, where he lived from 1944 to 1953. Has lived in London since 1953.
Mullins, E., *Josef Herman* (London, 1967).

Samuel Hirszenberg (1865–1908)
B. in Lodz, Poland. Studied in Cracow, Munich, and Paris. In 1907 went to Jerusalem. His genre compositions, based on Jewish contemporary and historical events, were popular in Poland during his lifetime. Died in Jerusalem.
Naphtalie, B., *Samuel Hirszenberg* (Berlin, 1929).

Fritz Hundertwasser (b. 1928)
B. in Vienna. Studied at the Vienna Academy (1948) and travelled to Tuscany, Paris, Morocco, and Tunisia. He has had retrospectives at the Moderne Museet, Stockholm (1965), and at the University Art Museum, Berkeley (1968).
Chipp, H., and Richardson, B., *Hundertwasser* (University Art Museum, Berkeley, 1968).

Marcel Janco (b. 1895)
B. in Bucharest. Completing his training as an architect at the Polytechnique, Zurich (1915), he participated in Dada activities. He worked on a Dada magazine, *Zurich* (1919), designed posters and decorations for Cabaret Voltaire, and created abstract relief works. Lived in Paris 1921–2. In 1923 he returned to Bucharest as an architect and joined the radical artists' group 'Contemporanul'. In 1941 he went to Palestine where in 1948 he helped to found the 'New Horizons' artists' group, Tel Aviv. In 1953 he founded the artists' community, Ein Hod, Israel.
Seuphor, M., *Marcel Janco* (Bodensee, 1963).

Menashe Kadishman (b. 1932)
B. in Tel Aviv. Studied sculpture with Moshe Sternschus (1948), and with Rudi Lehmann (1953). In 1959 arrived in London. Studied at St. Martin's School of Art and at the Slade School of Art. Lives in Tel Aviv.
Selz, P., 'Kadishman – Planting Trees, Making Sculpture', *Arts Magazine* (New York, Dec. 1976).

Aharon Kahana (1905–1967)
B. in Stuttgart, Germany. Studied at the Stuttgart Academy of Art (1922–5), and in Berlin and Paris (1925–8). Arrived in Israel in 1934 and settled in Ramat-Gan. In 1948 joined the 'New Horizons' group. Since 1950 lived in Paris and Israel.
Gamzu, H., *Kahana* (Tel Aviv Museum, 1970).

Morris Kantor (1890–1974)
B. in Minsk, Russia. Kantor came to New York with his parents in 1911. He studied with Robert Henri and Homer Boss at the Art Students League, New York. Kantor showed regularly with the Rehn Gallery, New York (1930–59). Other one-man exhibitions were held at the Bertha Schaefer Gallery, New York (1959, 1962, 1965, 1967, 1971), and Davenport Municipal Art Gallery, Iowa (1965). He taught painting at The Art Students League and Cooper Union. His work spans the artistic movements from Cubism to Abstract Expressionism. Died in Nyack, New York.
Kantor, M., 'Ends and Means, Autobiography', *Magazine of Art* (March 1940), pp. 138–47.

Luise Kaish (b. 1925)
B. in Atlanta, Georgia. Studied at Syracuse University (1941–51) with Ivan Mestrovic. Received commissions for synagogue sculpture. She lives in New York City.
Kampf, A., *Luise Kaish* (Jewish Museum, New York, 1973).

Dani Karavan (b. 1930)
B. in Tel Aviv. Studied at the Avni Studio of Painting and Sculpture, Tel Aviv, with Yeheskiel Streichman, Avigdor Stematsky, and Mordecai Ardon, and learned fresco and mural techniques at the Accademia di Belle Arti, Florence (1956). Lives in Tel Aviv.
Kampf, A., *Dani Karavan* (Florence, 1971).

Yehoshua Kovarsky (1907–1967)
B. in Vilna, Lithuania. Sent to Palestine (1924), he studied painting with an older Yemenite friend while working on a kibbutz near Jerusalem. Before returning to Vilna in 1928 to attend the Academy of Fine Arts, he stayed briefly in Paris, becoming familiar with the modern tradition. From 1935 to 1949 he lived in Israel—first in the artistic community of Safed, then as an art teacher in Zichron Ya'akov. Resided in New York City from 1951. Died in Los Angeles.
Kayser, S., *Yehoshua Kovarsky* (New York, 1956).

Leopold Krakauer (1890–1954)
B. in Vienna. Trained as an engineer and architect and graduated from the Imperial Academy of Fine Arts, Vienna. In 1929 he went to Palestine and settled in Jerusalem, where he died.
Cohen, E., *Leopold Krakauer: Drawings* (Jerusalem, 1974).

Jacob Kramer (1892–1962)
B. in Klintsky, Ukraine. With his family, he emigrated to England and settled in Leeds where he spent most of his life. He attended the Leeds School of Art (1907–11) and the Slade School of Art, London (1912). Honoured as an artist and educator, in a retrospective exhibition of his work at the Leeds City Art Gallery (1960), and in the renaming of the Leeds College of Art in his name.
Kramer, M., ed., *Kramer Memorial Volume* (London, 1969).

Joe Lasker (b. 1919)
B. in New York City. Graduated from Cooper Union Art School, New York (1939), and studied at Escuela Universitaria de Bellas Artes, San Miguel de Allende, Mexico. His commissions include murals for Post Offices in Calumet, Michigan and Millbury, Massachusetts, and the Henry Street Settlement Playhouse, New York. Lives in South Norwalk, Connecticut.
Kraushaar Galleries, New York, artist biography.

Jack Levine (b. 1915)
B. in Boston. Grew up in the immigrant slums. He studied art with Hyman Bloom under Denman Ross at Harvard. Worked with the WPA Project (1935–40). He lives in New York.
Getlein, F., *Jack Levine* (New York, 1966).

Max Liebermann (1847–1935)
B. in Berlin. Spent his student years in Berlin in the studio of the animal painter Karl Steffeck. Studied and travelled in Paris and Holland (1872–8). In 1898, he became a foundling member and later President of the Berlin Secession. He died in Berlin.
Scheffler, K., *Max Liebermann* (Munich, 1923).

Jacques Lipchitz (1891–1973)
B. Chaim Jacob in Druskienki, Lithuania. Moved to Paris (1909) where he studied at the École des Beaux-Arts and the Julien Academy. Fleeing Paris in 1940, he settled in New York City. He died in Capri and was buried in Jerusalem.
Hammacher, A. M., *Jacques Lipchitz* (New York, 1960).

Seymour Lipton (b. 1903)
B. in New York. Studied at City College, New York (1922–3) and Columbia University (1923–7). He taught at the New School for Social Research (1940–64). He lives in New York.
Elsen, A., *Seymour Lipton* (New York, 1970).

El Lissitzky (1890–1941)
B. Lazar Markowich in Smolensk, Russia. An architecture student in Darmstadt (1909–14), he worked as an architect in Moscow and from 1916 contributed to art exhibitions. With Ryback, he explored Jewish folk art on the Dnieper River. In 1919 he developed his *prouns*. He died in Moscow.
Lissitzky-Kuppers, S., *El Lissitzky* (London, 1968).

Louis Lozowick (1892–1973)
B. in Kiev, Russia. Emigrated to New York City in 1906. He

studied at the National Academy of Design, New York (1912–15), and at Ohio State University, Columbus (1915–18), as well as in Paris and Berlin. Known primarily as an American Precisionist, Lozowick has exhibited prints, drawings, and paintings in numerous one-man and group exhibitions in the United States, Russia, and Europe. He died in New Jersey.
Solomon, E., *Louis Lozowick* (Whitney Museum of American Art, New York, 1972).

Abraham Manievich (1881–1942)
B. in Mstislav, Russia. Studied at the Art School of Kiev, at the Munich Academy of Art, and travelled throughout Europe. His first one-man show was held at the Kiev State Museum of Art in 1910. Elected to a Professorship at the Ukraine Academy of Art, Kiev (1917). After his arrival in America (1922), he had numerous exhibitions. He died in New York.
Ein Harod Museum, Israel, artist file.

Maryan S. Maryan (1927–1977)
B. in Poland. Interned in Auschwitz, Maryan arrived in Israel (1947) after two years in displaced persons' camps in Germany. He attended the Bezalel School of Arts and Crafts, Jerusalem, where his first one-man show was held at the YMCA in 1949. In 1950 he moved to France and studied at the École des Beaux-Arts until 1953. He regularly showed in Paris, New York and Chicago. He died in New York.
Allen Frumkin Gallery, New York, artist biography.

Hava Mehutan (b. 1925)
B. in Philadelphia, U.S.A. Studied at the Pennsylvania Academy of Fine Art. In 1946 arrived in Israel and joined Kibbutz Chazor. In 1950 settled in Beer Sheba and in 1956 travelled in Europe and the U.S.A.
Goldfine, G., *Hava Mehutan* (Tel Aviv, 1978).

Abraham Melnikov (1892–1960)
B. in Bessarabia, Romania. After a short period of medical studies in Vienna, he went to the U.S.A. and studied sculpture at the Art Institute in Chicago. He became friendly with Jack London, and together they travelled across the U.S.A. During World War I, he joined the Jewish Brigade and served in Palestine, where he settled after his release from the Army. In 1959 he returned to Israel, but died shortly thereafter.
Israel Museum, Jerusalem, artist file.

Sigmund Menkes (b. 1896)
B. in Lvov, Poland. Studied at the Higher Institute of Decorative Arts of Lvov (1914), and at the Academy of Cracow (1919); he moved to Paris in 1919, where he lived until his move to the United States in 1936. He lives in Riverdale, New York.
New York Public Library, Art Division, artist file.

Abraham Mintchine (1898–1931)
B. in Kiev. In 1921 he began his career as a goldsmith's apprentice while studying painting and drawing. He left Russia in 1923 to go to Berlin, where he remained until going to Paris in 1926. He participated in the Salon d'Automne, and the Salon des Indépendants while living in Paris. He died during a visit to Provence.
Waldemar, G., 'School of Paris', in *Jewish Art, an Illustrated History*, ed. C. Roth (New York, 1971), pp. 229–60.

Amedeo Modigliani (1884–1920)
B. in Livorno, into a distinguished Italian-Jewish family. Before moving to Paris in 1906 he studied painting and sculpture in Florence and Venice. He died in Paris and was subsequently honoured at numerous retrospectives.
Ceroni, A., *Amedeo Modigliani*, 2nd edn. (Milan, 1965).

Louise Nevelson (b. 1899)
B. in Kiev, Russia. Moved with family to Rockland, Maine, in 1905. Studied at the Art Students League in New York and briefly in Germany with Hans Hofmann. Known primarily as a sculptor, she was included in the Young Sculptors exhibition at the Brooklyn Museum (1935). Since then, she has had many one-woman shows in the United States and Europe. Lives in New York City.
Friedman, M., *Nevelson* (New York, 1973).

Barnett Newman (1905–1970)
B. in New York City. Studied at City College, New York (1927), and also at the Art Students League with Duncan Smith and John Sloan, 1922–4 and 1929–30. Initially known as a polemicist. Regularly contributed to *Tiger's Eye* (1947–9). Linked to New York Abstract Expressionists, he was a colour-field painter and sculptor. His first one-man show was at Betty Parsons Gallery, New York (1950). He died in New York City.
Hess, T., *Barnett Newman* (Museum of Modern Art, New York, 1971).

Abraham Ofek (b. 1935)
B. in Bourgas, Bulgaria. In 1949 he came to Israel and joined Kibbutz Ein-Hamifratz. From 1958 to 1960 he studied at the Accademia di Belle Arti in Florence. In 1962 he was appointed teacher at the Bezalel School of Arts and Crafts, Jerusalem. In 1965, he worked at the Arts Centre in Paris. Head of art workshops at Haifa University Art Department.
Kampf, A., *Ofek* (Jewish Museum, New York, 1973).

Hanna Orlof (1888–1968)
B. in the Ukraine. In 1905 came with her family to Palestine. After 1910 lived in Paris, studied art and then devoted herself to sculpture. Friends with Picasso, Modigliani and other artists of the Paris School. During World War II found refuge in Switzerland. Exhibited in numerous group shows and had one-woman shows in Europe, the U.S.A. and Israel. She died in Tel Aviv.
Gamzu, H., *Hanna Orlof* (Tel Aviv Museum, 1969).

Harold Paris (1925–1979)
B. in Edgemore, New York. With his father, a member of the Yiddish Art Theatre, he worked as a make-up man and actor (1941–3). In the US Army Corps of Engineers, and as *Stars and Stripes* artist-correspondent in the United States, England, France, and Germany (1943–6). Lived in San Francisco.

Selz, P., ed., *Harold Paris: The California Years* (University Art Museum, Berkeley, 1972).

Jules Pascin (1885–1930)
B. Jules Pincas in Vidin, Bulgaria. Studied in Munich (1903–4). First known as a cartoonist and illustrator for German periodicals, *Simplicissimus* and *Jugend*, he moved to Paris in 1905 and was associated with the Montmartre and Montparnasse painters. In 1914 he emigrated to New York. Died by suicide in Paris.
Warnod, A., *Pascin* (Monte Carlo, 1954).

Antoine Pevsner (1886–1962)
B. in Orel, Russia. Studied at the School of Fine Arts, Kiev (1902–9); the St. Petersburg Academy (1910), and then in Paris (1912, 1913–14). In Paris he was introduced to Cubism by his friends Archipenko and Modigliani and was greatly impressed by the Eiffel Tower. Pevsner returned to Russia (1914) before joining his brother Naum Gabo in Oslo (1915–16), where he turned from abstract painting to sculpture. When Pevsner returned to Russia in 1917, he taught at the Moscow Academy of Fine Arts, with Kandinsky and Malevich. In 1920 he and Gabo conceived the *Realist Manifesto* in which they argued that void (not mass) is the fundamental element of sculpture. Pevsner left Russia in 1923 and settled permanently in Paris. He became a French citizen in 1930 and received the French Legion of Honour (1961). In Paris he joined the *Abstraction-Création* group with Gabo, Herbin, Kupka, and Mondrian (1931) and co-founded *Réalités-Nouvelles* (1946). Pevsner and Gabo have been given a joint retrospective at The Museum of Modern Art, New York (1966). Pevsner had a retrospective at Musée National d'Art Moderne, Paris (1957), and a special room for his work at the Venice Biennale (1959). D. in Paris.
Peissi, P., and Giedion-Welcker, C., *Antoine Pevsner* (Neuchâtel, 1961).

Nathan Rappoport (b. 1911)
B. in Warsaw, Poland. Studied art at the Academy of Art, Warsaw; the École des Beaux-Arts, Paris; and in Italy and France. The recipient of numerous awards since his youth in Poland, he achieved notoriety for refusing to allow his sculpture *Tennis* to enter the Olympics Exhibition in Berlin (1936). Resides in New York and Israel.
Glass, A., 'Never to Forget', *The Jewish Standard* (15 May 1972), pp. 1–4.

Abraham Rattner (1895–1978)
B. in Poughkeepsie, New York. From 1913 to 1914, studied at George Washington University and the Corcoran School of Art in Washington, D.C. After World War I, he resumed his education at the École des Beaux-Arts in Paris, settling there until 1940. Forced to flee Paris, he returned to the United States and toured the country with Henry Miller. Since his first one-man show at the Galerie Bonjean, Paris (1935), he has had numerous exhibitions. He died in New York.
Leepa, A., ed., *Abraham Rattner* (New York, 1974).

Bernard Reder (1897–1963)
B. in Bukovina, Austria. At the Academy of Fine Arts, Prague, in 1919, he studied graphic art with Peter Bromse and sculpture with Jan Stursa. Returning to Bukovina in 1922, he worked as a stonemason. Not until 1930, two years after his first one-man exhibition of watercolours in Prague, did he devote his entire efforts to sculpture. Lived and worked in New York from 1958.
Baur, J., *Bernard Reder* (New York, 1961).

Larry Rivers (b. 1923)
B. in the Bronx, New York. Studied at the Julliard School of Music, New York (1944) and played jazz saxophone in New York. He studied painting at the Hans Hofmann School of Art (1947–8) and at New York University (1948–50). He lives in New York City.
Hunter, S., *Larry Rivers* (New York, 1970).

Mark Rothko (1903–1970)
B. in Dvinsk, Russia. Rothko's family emigrated to Portland, Oregon, in 1913. He studied at Yale University (1921–32), and at the Art Students League, New York, with Max Weber in 1925. His formative years include such activities as co-founding the Ten with Ilya Bolotowsky and Adolph Gottlieb (1935); working on the WPA Federal Arts Project, New York (1936–7). Rothko reached his general format—colour rectangles floating on a colour ground—by 1950. He died by suicide in New York.
Selz, P., *Mark Rothko* (Museum of Modern Art, New York, 1961).

Reuven Rubin (1893–1975)
B. in Galatz, Romania. Studied at the Bezalel School of Arts and Crafts, Jerusalem (1912), in Paris at the École des Beaux-Arts and the Académie Colarossi (1913–14), and in Italy. His reputation as a painter of Jewish folk themes was established during his stay in Romania (1916–19). Since his first one-man show, sponsored by Alfred Stieglitz at the Anderson Gallery, New York (1920), he has had numerous international exhibitions, which include the inaugural show at the Tel Aviv Museum of Art (1932). He died in Israel.
Wilkinson, S., *Reuven Rubin* (New York, 1974).

Issachar Ryback (1897–1935)
B. in Elisabethgrad, Russia. Studied art in Kiev and in 1917 was appointed drawing teacher by the Jewish Cultural League. He associated with the Constructivists while in Moscow (1919–21) and with the Russian Jewish artists living in Paris (1926). He died in Paris.
Cogniat, R., *Ryback* (Paris, 1935).

Shalom Seba (1897–1973)
B. in Tilsit, Russia (then Germany). Served in the German army during World War I. After the war studied architecture in Danzig, specialized in lithography and etching at the Königsberg Academy of Art. From 1920 to 1933 travelled extensively in Berlin, the Far East, the Balkan States, southern France and North Africa. In 1933 he left Germany and went to Switzerland and Sweden where he worked in films. In 1936 arrived in Israel.

He moved to Germany in the early 1960s.
Tel Aviv Museum of Art, artist file.

George Segal (b. 1924)
B. in New York City. Grew up in the Bronx, and moved in 1940–1 to South Brunswick, N.J., where he worked part-time on his father's poultry farm while attending Rutgers University (1948–9). Studied briefly at the Pratt Institute in New York (1947) and New York University (1948–9). Lives in New Jersey.
Marck, J. van der, *George Segal* (New York, 1976).

Lasar Segall (1891–1957)
B. in Vilna, Lithuania. Emigrating to Berlin in 1906, he studied at the Academy of Fine Arts in Berlin (1907–9). Since his first one-man exhibition at the Gurlitt Gallery, Dresden (1910), he worked within a German Expressionist style. His paintings, engravings and sculpture have been internationally exhibited since 1926. In 1923 he emigrated to Brazil.
Bardi, P. M., *Lasar Segall* (São Paulo, 1959).

Kurt Seligman (1900–1961)
B. in Basel, Switzerland. After studying at the Geneva Academy of Art, he lived in Paris (1929–39), and was a member of the Surrealist and Abstraction–Creation groups. Since his first one-man show at Galerie Bucher, Paris (1932), he has had numerous exhibitions, notably at the Ruth White Gallery, New York (1960), and the D'Arcy Galleries, New York (1964). He died in Sugar Loaf, New York, where he had lived since 1939.
Myers, B., 'Puppets of Kurt Seligman—an Homage', *Craft Horizon* (Dec. 1970), pp. 33–5.

Ben Shahn (1898–1969)
B. in Kovno, Lithuania. His parents emigrated to New York. Apprenticed to a lithographer (1911–17), he worked intermittently as a lithographer until 1930. Studied at the National Academy of Design, The Art Students League, and the Educational Alliance Art School, all in New York. He lived in Hightstown, New Jersey.
Shahn, B., *Ben Shahn* (New York, 1972).

Yechiel Shemi (b. 1922)
B. in Haifa. In 1938 joined Kibbutz Beit H'aarava near the Dead Sea (deserted during the War of Independence). Under the desert's influence started to sculpture mainly in basalt and sandstone. In 1948 came to the U.S.A., and worked with the sculptor Chaim Gross. Returned to Israel via Paris in 1949 and joined Kibbutz Cabri.
Fisher, Y., *Yechiel Shemi: Sculptures* (Tel Aviv, 1965).

Johanan Simon (1905–1976)
B. in Berlin. Studied at the Berlin Art Academy (1924), the Bauhaus (1925), Munich Art Academy (1926) and in Frankfurt with Max Beckmann. Living in Paris (1928–36), he joined the circle of painters around Derain. He travelled to New York (1935), before settling permanently in Palestine (1936). He died in Israel.
Correspondence with artist.

Mitchell Siporin (1910–1976)
B. in New York City. Siporin studied at the Art Institute of Chicago School. A participant in the WPA Federal Arts Project, Mural Division, he received commissions for Post Offices in Decatur, Illinois (1935) and in St. Louis, Missouri (1939). He was Professor of Painting at Brandeis University, Waltham, Massachusetts. Died in Boston.
Whitney Museum of American Art, New York, artist file.

Chaim Soutine (1893–1943)
B. in Smilovitchi, near Minsk, Lithuania. With Michael Kikoïne, he attended the Vilna Academy of Fine Arts (1910–13). He continued his studies in 1913 at the École des Beaux-Arts and at the Atelier Cormon. There he met Chagall, Laurens, Lipchitz, and Modigliani. He lived in Paris (1925–39), and went into hiding until 1943. He died in Paris.
Tuchman, M., *Chaim Soutine* (Los Angeles, 1968).

Moses Soyer (1899–1974)
B. in Borisoglebsk, Russia. He came to New York in 1913. Like his twin brother, Raphael, he studied in New York at Cooper Union, The National Academy of Design, and the Educational Alliance Art School. He participated in the WPA Federal Arts Project, and taught at the New School for Social Research, New York, for many years. His works were exhibited regularly from 1944 at the ACA Gallery, New York. He died in New York.
Willard, C., *Moses Soyer* (New York, 1962).

Raphael Soyer (b. 1899)
B. in Borisoglebsk, Russia, twin of Moses Soyer. Emigrated to New York in 1913. He studied and later taught at the Art Students League of New York. His work has been included in the Whitney Museum of American Art Annual (1934–72). In 1953 he co-founded *Reality* magazine. He lives in New York.
Goodrich, L., *Raphael Soyer* (New York, 1972).

Jacob Steinhardt (1881–1968)
B. in Zerkow, Russia. Studied at the Museum of Arts and Crafts in Berlin (1906), with Louis Corinth and Herman Struck. In 1909, he moved to Paris where he worked with Laurens, Steinlen, and Matisse. He returned to Germany and together with Ludwig Meidner and Richard Janthus founded the Pathetiker group in 1912. Settling in Jerusalem (1933), he was the Head of the Graphic Department of the Bezalel School of Arts and Crafts and its Director (1953–7). He died in Jerusalem.
Pfefferkorn, R., *Jacob Steinhardt* (Berlin, 1973).

Herman Struck (1876–1944)
B. in Berlin. Studied etching at the Berlin Academy with Max Kone. He visited Palestine in 1903, and settled there in 1923. Struck was known in Germany as a master craftsman, teacher, illustrator and author of a popular book on graphics, *The Art of Etching*. He taught Chagall, Liebermann, Israels, and Corinth. He died in Haifa.
Donath, A., *Herman Struck* (Berlin, 1920).

Joseph Tchaikov (1888)
B. in Kiev. Studied in Paris 1910–14 in the studio of the sculptor Aronson, in the École des Beaux-Arts and École des Arts decoratifs (1910–14). Passionately involved in 'Machmadim', a group of Jewish artists—among them Indenbaum and Orlof—bent on the creation of a Jewish national style. Moved into the circles of Archipenko, Lipchitz, Modigliani, and Zadkine. Returned to Kiev, engaging simultaneously in the work for the Revolution and the Jewish national movement (1917). Illustrated Yiddish books for children and executed monuments of Marx and Liebknecht. Moved toward a Constructivist style (1919). Published, in Yiddish, a book on sculpture (1921). Resided in Berlin (1922–3). Returned to Moscow. Moved toward social realism (1925). Active in the art life of Moscow. Professor at the Art Institute of Moscow and Dean of the Faculty of Sculpture.
Ternovetz, B., *Edition de la Société des Relations Culturelles avec l'Etranger* (Voks) comp. 9–10 (Feb. 1935).

Anna Ticho (1894–1980)
B. in Brno, Moravia. Spent her childhood in Vienna, where she studied painting and drawing. Emigrating to Palestine in 1912, she settled in Jerusalem. She died in Jerusalem.
Cohen, E., *The Drawings of Anna Ticho* (Jewish Museum, New York, 1969).

Jennings Tofel (1891–1959)
B. in Poland. Emigrated to America in 1905 and lived in New York City the rest of his life. He began his career within the Stieglitz circle. Active in the circle of David Ignatoff and his Yiddish journal *Schriften*. He died in New York City.
New York Public Library, Art Division, artist file.

Ygael Tumarkin (b. 1933)
B. in 1933 in Dresden, Germany. In 1935 came to Israel. In 1954 studied sculpture with Rudi Lehmann. From 1955 to 1957 worked as an assistant in stage designing with the Berliner Ensemble. Travelled extensively in Europe, the U.S.A., the Far East, Africa and Australia. Lives in Tel Aviv.

Tumarkin, Y., *Tumarkin by Tumarkin: 1957–1970* (Tel Aviv, 1970).

Abraham Walkowitz (1878–1965)
B. in Tyumen, Russia. Emigrated to New York in 1886 where he studied at Cooper Union and later taught at the Educational Alliance Art School. Lived in Paris (1906–9). His broad range of subject-matter, from the well-known Isadora Duncan drawings to scenes of the Lower East Side, gained a reputation through various exhibitions including a major retrospective at the Jewish Museum, New York (1949). He died in New York.
Hunter, S., *American Art of the Twentieth Century* (New York, 1972).

Max Weber (1881–1961)
B. in Bialystok, Russia. Emigrated to New York in 1891. Before moving to Paris to study with Henri Matisse, he had studied art at the Pratt Institute, New York. Returning to New York in 1909, he taught at the Art Students League through the 1920s. He was a member of the Stieglitz circle and also associated with David Ignatoff's Yiddish journal *Schriften*. He died in Great Neck, New York.
Werner, A., *Max Weber* (New York, 1975).

Elbert Weinberg (b. 1928)
B. in Hartford, Connecticut. Graduated from the Rhode Island School of Design (1951), and Yale University (1955). Lives in Hartford, Conn.
Borgenicht Gallery, New York, artist biography.

William Zorach (1887–1966)
B. in Eurburg, Lithuania. Emigrated with his family to Ohio in 1891. Studied at Cleveland Museum School of Art from 1902 to 1905; in New York at the Art Students League, and the National Academy of Design (1907–10) and in Paris at La Palette (1910–11). In 1917 he turned to sculpture. He died in Bath, Maine.
Baur, J., *William Zorach* (New York, 1959).

Select Bibliography

Note: Entries marked with a (C) are exhibition catalogues.

Abramsky, C., 'El Lissitzky as Jewish Illuminator and Typographer', *Studio International*, 172, no. 882 (Oct. 1966), pp. 182–3.

Adler, H., 'Das Christus Bild im Lichte Jüdischer Autoren', *Symbolon, Jahrbuch für Symbol Forschung*, 2 (Basle, 1961).

Altman, N., *Jüdische Graphik*, Text by Max Osborn (Berlin: Razum-Verlag, 1923).

Amishai-Maisels, Z., 'Lipchitz – Themes within a Jewish Context', *Jacques Lipchitz at Eighty* (Israel Museum, Jerusalem, Aug.–Sept. 1971). (C)

Ansky, S., 'Di Yiddische Volksschaffung' [Jewish Folk Art, 1908], in *Gesammelte Schriften* [Collected Writings], vol. 15 (Vilna–Warsaw–New York, 1925). (Yiddish)

Ansky, S., *Dos Yiddische Ethnografische Program* [The Jewish Ethnographic Programme], report of the Baron G. H. Ginzburg Jewish Ethnographic Expedition (St. Petersburg, 1914). (Yiddish)

Aronson, B., *Sovremmenaya Evreiskaya Grafika* [Contemporary Hebrew Graphics]. (Berlin: Petropolis, 1924).

Ballas, G., *New Horizons: Modern Israeli Painting, 1948–1963* (Tel Aviv: Tel Aviv University and Reshafim, 1979). (Hebrew)

Bardi, P., *Lasar Segall* (São Paulo: Museum of Art, 1959).

Baur, J. I. H., *Bernard Reder* (New York: Praeger, 1961).

Baur, J. I. H., *William Zorach* (New York: Praeger, 1959).

Berckelaers, F. L. (M. Seuphor), *Marcel Janco* (Bodensee: Amriswill Verlag, 1963).

Beresniak, D., *Aspects de l'art juif* (Paris: Presses du Temps Present, 1960).

Berlevi, H., 'Jewish Artists in Russia', *Rimon*, 3 (Berlin, 1923). (Hebrew)

Bialik, Ch. N., and Osborn, M., *Leonid Pasternak: His Life and Work* (Berlin: A. Stiebel, 1924). (Hebrew)

Birnholz, A. C., 'El Lissitzky, the Avant Garde and the Russian Revolution', *Art Forum*, 2, no.1 (Sept. 1972), pp. 70–6.

Birnholz, A. C., 'El Lissitzky and the Jewish Tradition', *Studio International*, 186, no.959 (Oct. 1973).

Birnholz, A. C., 'For the New Art: El Lissitzky's Prouns', *Art Forum*, 8, no.2 (Oct. 1969), p. 66.

Birnholz, A. C., 'Lissitzky's Writings on Art', *Studio International*, 183, no.942 (Mar. 1973), pp. 90–2.

Bowlt, J. E., *Russian Art of the Avant-Garde: Theory and Criticism 1902–1934* (New York: Viking Press, 1976).

Brown, M. W., *American Painting from the Armory Show to the Depression* (Princeton, N.J.: Princeton University Press, 1955).

Buber, M., *Jüdische Künstler* (Berlin: Jüdischer Verlag, 1903).

Cahill, H., *Max Weber* (New York: Downtown Gallery, 1930).

Carter, H., *The New Theatre and Cinema of Soviet Russia* (New York: International Publishers, 1925).

Ceroni, A., *Amedeo Modigliani* (Milan: Edizioni del Milione, 2nd edn., 1965).

Chagall, M., 'Bletlach', *Shtrom*, 1 (Moscow, Feb. 1922). (Yiddish)

Chagall, M., *My Life* (New York: Orion Press, 1960).

Chagall, M., 'Mein Arbeit in Moscawer Yiddischen Kamerni Theater', *Di Yiddische Welt*, 2 (Warsaw, 1928). (Yiddish)

Chipp, H., and Richardson, B., *Hundertwasser* (University Art Museum, Berkeley, 1968). (C)

Cogniat, R., *Soutine* (Paris: Éditions du Chêne, 1945).

Cohen, E., *Leopold Krakauer: Drawings* (Israel Museum, Jerusalem, 1974). (C)

Cohen, E., *The Drawings of Anna Ticho* (Jewish Museum, New York, 1969). (C)

Cohn-Wiener, E., *Die Jüdische Kunst* (Berlin: M. Wasservogel, 1929).

Cork, R., *Vorticism and Abstract Art in the First Machine Age* (London: Gordon Fraser, 1976).

Cusin, S., *Art in the Jewish Tradition* (Milan: Adei-Wizo, 1963).

Diamant, M., *Jüdische Volkskunst* (Vienna: Löwit, 1937).

Dinur, B., *Days of War and Revolution* (Jerusalem: Mossad Bialik, 1960). (Hebrew)

Dinur, B., 'From February to October', *Heavar*, 15 (Tel Aviv, May 1968). (Hebrew)

Dobrushin, Y., 'Kunst Primitiv un Kunstbuch far Kinder' [Primitive Art and the Children's Art Book], in *Gedankengang* (Kiev: Cooperativer Verlag Kulturlige, 1922). (Yiddish)

Doty, R., and Waldman, D., *Adolph Gottlieb* (New York: Praeger, 1968).

Eichenbaum, P., *Memorial Exhibition: Jewish Artists who Perished in the Holocaust* (Tel Aviv Museum of Art, Tel Aviv, 1968). (C)

Elsen, A., *Seymour Lipton* (New York: Abrams, 1970).

Epstein, J., *Let there be Sculpture* (London: Readers Union Ltd., 1942).

Etkind, M., *Nathan Altman* (Moscow: Sovetskii Khudoznik, 1971). (Russian)

Ettinger, S., 'The Jews in Russia at the Outbreak of the February Revolution', *Heavar*, 15 (Tel Aviv, May 1968). (Hebrew)

Fenster, H., *Unzere Farpainikte Kinstler* [Our Persecuted Artists] (published by the author, Paris, 1951). (Yiddish)

Fischer, F., *Max Beckmann* (London: Phaidon, 1973).

Fischer, Y., *Expressionism in Eretz–Israel in the Thirties and its Ties with the École de Paris* (Israel Museum, Jerusalem, 1971). (C)

Fishman, J. W., *East-End Jewish Radicals, 1875–1914* (London: Camden Town, in Association with the Acton Society Trust, 1975).

Freedman, M., 'George Segal: Proletarian Mythmaker', *Art International*, 23. 9 (Jan.–Feb. 1980).

Gamzu, H., *Painting and Sculpture in Israel* (Tel Aviv: Eshcol, 1951).

Getlein, F., *Chaim Gross* (New York: Abrams, 1974).

Ginzburg, D., and Stassof, V., *L'Ornement hébraïque* (Berlin: S. Calvary & Co., 1905).

Glazer, N., *American Judaism* (Chicago: University of Chicago Press, 1972).

Goldfine, G., *Hava Mehutan* (Tel-Aviv: Hakibbutz Hameuchad, 1977).

Goodrich, L., *Raphael Soyer* (New York: Abrams, 1972).

Goodrich, L., *Max Weber: Retrospective Exhibition* (Whitney Museum of American Art, New York, 1949). (C)

Granil, A., *Jennings Tofel*, introduction by Alfred Werner (New York: Abrams, 1976).

Graubard, P., *An ander Leben* [Another Life] (Warsaw: Kulturlige, 1928). (Yiddish)

Gray, C., *The Great Experiment: Russian Art, 1863–1922* (London: Thames and Hudson, 1962).

Grochowiak, T., *Ludwig Meidner* (Recklinghausen: Verlag A. Bongers, 1966).

Günzburg, I., 'Jüdische Nationalkunst (Gedanken eines Gelehrten russischen Kritikers)' *Ost und West*, 10, 11, 12 (Oct., Nov., Dec. 1905).

Gutfeld, L., *Jewish Art from the Bible to Chagall* (New York: T. Yoseloff, 1968).

Gutman, J., 'Jewish Art: Fact or Fiction?', *Central Conference American Rabbis Journal* (New York, Apr. 1964).

Haftmann, W., *Mark Rothko* (Städtische Kunsthalle, Düsseldorf, 1971). (C)

Hancke, E., *Max Liebermann, sein Leben und seine Werke* (Berlin: Bruno Cassirer, 1923).

Haklai, U., *The Life Work of Nachum Zemach against the Background of the Revival of Jewish Culture in the Soviet Union* (Ph.D. Dissertation, Hebrew University, Jerusalem, 1974). (Hebrew)

Hammacher, A. M., *Jacques Lipchitz* (New York: Abrams, 1960).

Hamilton, G. H., 'Painting in Contemporary America', *Burlington Magazine*, 102 (May 1960), p. 193

Hapgood, H., *The Spirit of the Ghetto* (New York: Funk & Wagnall, 1902).

Herman, J., 'On Being a Jewish Artist', *Jewish Quarterly* (London: autumn 1964).

Herman, J., *Paintings and Drawings* (London: Adams & Mackay, n.d.).

Hess, T., *Barnett Newman* (New York: Museum of Modern Art, 1971).

Hunter, S., *American Art of the Twentieth Century* (New York: Abrams, 1972).

Hunter, S., *Larry Rivers* (New York: Abrams, 1970).

Ignatoff, D., *Drifted Leaves* (Buenos Aires: YIVO 1957). (Yiddish)

Jaffee, I. B., *The Sculpture of Leonard Baskin* (New York: Viking Press, 1980).

Jewish Artists of Great Britain, 1848–1945 (Exhibition at the Bedgrave Gallery, London, 15 Nov.–16 Apr. 1978); essay by Irving Grose. (C)

Jüdische Künstler (exhibiton at the Galerie für alte und neue Kunst, Berlin, Nov.–Dec. 1907). (C)

Kampf, A., *Contemporary Synagogue Art* (Philadelphia: Jewish Publication Society, 1955).

Kampf, A., *Jewish Experience in the Art of the Twentieth Century* (Jewish Museum, New York, 1975). (C)

Kampf, A., 'The Jewish Museum – An Institution Adrift', *Judaism* (New York, summer 1968).

Kampf, A., *Luise Kaish* (Jewish Museum, New York, 1973). (C)

Kampf, A., *Dani Karavan* (Florence: C. G. Editrice, 1977).

Kampf, A., *Maryan, The Fate of an Artist* (Haifa University Art Gallery and Tel Aviv Museum, 1979). (C)

Kampf, A., *Ofek* (Jewish Museum, New York, 1973). (C)

Kayser, S., *Ben-Zion* (Jewish Museum, New York, 1959). (C)

Kayser, S., 'Visual Art in American Jewish Life', *Judaism*, 3, no.4 (1954).

Kayser, S., *Yehoshua Kovarsky* (Jewish Museum, New York, 1956). (C)

Klaphek, A., *Jankel Adler* (Recklingausen: Verlag A. Bongers, 1966).

Kopman, B., *Abraham Walkowitz* (Paris: Éditions Le Triangle, 1927). (Yiddish)

Kozloff, M., 'Jewish Art and the Modern Jeopardy', *Art Forum* (April 1976).

Kutna, G., 'Zur Ausstellung Jüdischer Künstler', *Ost und West* (Berlin, Jan. 1908).

Landsberger, F., *History of Jewish Art* (Cincinnati: Union of American Hebrew Congregations, 1946).

Langer, L., *The Holocaust and the Literary Imagination* (New Haven: Yale University Press, 1975).

Leftwich, J., 'Jewish London – Fifty Years Ago', *Ben-Uri Commemorative Volume* (London: Ben-Uri Society, 1966).

Lenz, C. von, 'Max Beckmanns "Synagogue"', *Städel Jährbuch*, Neue Folge 4 (Frankfurt-am-Mein, 1973).

Lipchitz, J., with H. H. Arnason, *My Life in Sculpture* (The Documents of Twentieth Century Art) (New York: Viking Press, 1972).

Lipke, W., *David Bomberg* (London: Evelyn, Adams & Mackay, 1967).

Lissitzky, E., 'The Overcoming of Art', *Ringen*, 10 (Warsaw, 1922). (Yiddish)

Lissitzky, E., 'The Synagogue of Mohilev, Reminiscences', *Rimon*, 3 (Berlin, 1923). (Hebrew)

Lissitzky-Küppers, S., *El Lissitzky* (London: Thames and Hudson, 1968).

Lozowick, L., 'The Art of Nathan Altman', *Menorah Journal*, 12, no.1 (Feb. 1926).

Lozowick, L., 'Eliezer Lissitzky', *Menorah Journal*, 12, no.2 (Apr.–May 1926).

Lozowick, L., *100 Contemporary American Jewish Painters and Sculptors* (New York: YKUF [Yiddisher Kultur Farband], 1947).

Lozowick, L., 'Survivor from a Dead Age', unpublished autobiography, n.d. Courtesy of Mrs. Adele Lozowick, New York City.

McCabe, C. Jaffee, *The Golden Door, Artists Immigrants of America, 1876–1976* (Hirshhorn Museum, Washington D.C., 1976). (C)

Mark, Van der J., *George Segal* (New York: Abrams, 1975).

Mayer, L., *Bibliography of Jewish Art* (Jerusalem: Magnes Press, 1967).

Meyer, F., *Marc Chagall, Life and Work* (New York: Abrams, 1964).

Nagano, P., *Bak, Paintings of the Last Decade* (Aberbach Fine Art, New York, 1974). (C)

Naimenyi, E., *The Essence of Jewish Art* (New York: Yosselof, 1960).

Narkiss, B., 'Does Jewish Art Exist?', *Journal of the Hebrew University* (Jerusalem, Oct. 1966). (Hebrew)

Nossig, A., 'Austellung Jüdischer Künstler', *Ost und West*, 12 (Berlin, Dec. 1907).

Pincus-Witten, R., 'Six Propositions on Jewish Art', *Arts Magazine* (Dec. 1975).

Rechtman, A., *Jewish Ethnography and Folklore* (Buenos Aires: YIVO, 1958). (Yiddish)

Rischin, M., 'The Jewish Labor Movement in America', *Labor History*, 4, no.3 (New York, Fall 1963).

Rischin, M., *The Promised City, New York Jews, 1870–1914* (Cambridge: Harvard University Press, 1962).

Rodman, S., *Portrait of the Artist as an American, a Biography with Pictures* (New York: Harper and Row, 1954).

Rosenau, H., *A Short History of Jewish Art* (London: J. Clarke, 1948).

Rosenberg, H., 'Is there Jewish Art?', *Commentary* (July 1966).

Rosenberg, H., *Barnett Newman* (New York: Abrams, 1970).

Rosenblum, R., *Modern Painting and the Northern Romantic Tradition, Friedrich to Rothko* (London: Thames and Hudson, 1975).

Roth, C., ed., *Jewish Art, an Illustrated History* (New York: McGraw–Hill, 1971).

Ryback, I., and Aronson, B., 'Di Vegen fun der Yiddisher Malerei' [The Paths of Jewish Painting] *Oifgang* (Kiev: Kulturlige, 1919).

Schapiro, M., 'The Liberating Quality of Avant Garde Art', *Art News* (June 1957).

Schatz, B., '*Bezalel': Program und Zweck* (Jerusalem, Aug. 1906).

Schazar, S., 'Our Teachers at the Institute of Baron Ginzburg', *Heavar*, 6 (Tel Aviv, 1958). (Hebrew)

Schoener, A., ed., '*The Lower East Side: Portal to American Life' (1870–1924)* (Jewish Museum, New York, 1966). (C)

Schwartz, K., *Jewish Artists in the 19th and 20th Centuries* (New York: Philosophical Library, 1949).

Schwarz, K., *Jewish Sculptors* (Jerusalem: Art Publishers, 1954).

Seitz, W. C., *Art Israel: 26 Painters and Sculptors* (Museum of Modern Art, New York, 1964). (C)

Selz, P., ed., *Harold Paris, The California Years* (University Art Museum, Berkeley, 1972). (C)

Shahn, Ben, *Love and Joy about Letters* (New York: Grossman, 1963).

Shapiro, D., *Social Realism: Art as a Weapon* (New York: Frederick Ungar, 1973).

Shechori, R., *Art in Israel* (Tel Aviv: Sudan Publishing House, 1974).

Shmeruk, C., and Sand, M., *Jewish Culture in the Soviet Union* (Jerusalem: Hebrew University, 1973. (Hebrew)

Slutsky, Y., 'Russian Jewry during the Years of the Revolution', *Heavar*, 15 (Tel Aviv, May 1968). (Hebrew).

Soby, J. T., *Ben Shahn Paintings* (New York: George Braziller, 1963).

Solomon, E., *Louis Lozowick* (Whitney Museum of American Art, New York, 1972). (C)

Soyer, Raphael, *Self-Revealment: A Memoir* (New York: Maecenas Press of Random House Inc., 1969).

Strauss, H., *Die Kunst der Juden im Wandel Der Zeit und Umwelt – Das Judenproblem im Spiegel der Kunst* (Tübingen: Verlag Ernst Wasmuth, 1972).

Szjeklocha, P., and Mead, I., *Unofficial Art in the Soviet Union* (Berkeley: University of California Press, 1964).

Tammuz, B., Levite, D., and Ofrat, G., *The Story of Art in Israel* (Ramat-Gan (Israel): Massada Ltd., 1980). (Hebrew)

Tapie, M., and Sacher, H., *Castel* (Neuchatel: Griffon, 1968).

Tchaikov, J., *Sculpture* (Kiev: State Publishing House, 1921). (Yiddish)

Tofel, J., 'The Jewish Art Center', *Der Hammer* (New York, Mar. 1927). (Yiddish)

Toller, E., Roth, J., and Goldschmidt, A., *Das Moscauer jüdische akademische Theater* (Berlin: 'Die Schmiede', 1928).

Tscherikover, A., *Issachar Ryback, His Life and Work*, memorial volume published by A. Tscherikover for the Committee of the Friends of the Artist (Paris, 1937). (Yiddish)

Tuchman, M., *Chaim Soutine* (Los Angeles: Los Angeles County Museum of Art, 1968).

Valero, R., *Itzhak Danziger* (Tel Aviv: Hakibbutz Hameuchad, 1981).

Valkenier, E., *Russian Realist Art, The State and Society: The Peredvizhniki and their Tradition* (Ann Arbor: Ardis, 1977).

Vishny, M., *Mordecai Ardon* (New York: Abrams, 1975).

Waldemar, G., and Ehrenburg, I., *Nathan Altman* (Paris: Éditions Le Triangle, 1937). (Yiddish)

Waldman, D., *Mark Rothko, 1903–1970* (New York: Abrams, 1978).

Walkowitz, A., *Faces from the Ghetto* (New York: Machmadim Art Editions Inc., 1946).

Weinberg, L., 'Jewish Artists in America, Abram Walkowitz', *The American Hebrew* (New York, 31 Aug. 1917).

Werner, A., *Amedeo Modigliani* (New York: Abrams, 1966).

Werner, A., *Max Weber* (New York: Abrams, 1975).

Wilkinson, S., *Reuven Rubin* (New York: Abrams, 1974).

Wilson, S., *Marvin Cherney* (Morgan State College, Philadelphia, 1968). (C)

Wischnitzer, R., 'Berlin in the Early 1920s', in *Studies in Jewish History*, ed. S. Yeivin, Raphael Mahler jubilee volume (Merhavya: Sifriyat Poalim, 1974).

Wischnitzer, R., 'Modern Art and Our Jewish Generation', *Rimon*, 1 (Berlin, 1922). (Hebrew)

Wischnitzer, R., 'The Ornaments of the Mohilev Synagogue', *Heavar*, 15 (Tel Aviv, May 1968). (Hebrew)

Wischnitzer, R., *Symbole und Gestalten der jüdischen Kunst* (Berlin: Verlag Siegfried Scholem, 1935).

Wischnitzer, R., *Synagogue Architecture in the United States* (Philadelphia: The Jewish Publication Society, 1955).

Yudovin, S., and Malkin, M., 'Yiddischer Folksornament' [Jewish Folk Art] (Vitebsk: Y. L. Peretz Society, 1920).

Chronology

Date History	Culture	Publications
1870		Leopold Löw, *Graphische Requisiten und Erzeugnisse bei den Juden*
1872		Vladimir Stassof (art historian), 'On the Occasion of the Construction of the Synagogue of St. Petersburg', and 'A Jewish Generation in the Creation of a European Art', in *Evreiskaia Biblioteka: istoriko-literaturnyi sbornik* (periodical)
1875	Founding of Art Students League, New York	
1876	Abraham Goldfaden establishes Yiddish theatre in Jassi, Romania	Heinrich Graetz completes *Geschichte der Juden* (History of the Jews) George Eliot completes *Daniel Deronda*
1878	Exhibition of Jewish ceremonial art from the collection of Joseph Strauss at the Universal Exhibition at the Trocadéro, Paris	
1881	Wave of pogroms in southern Russia followed by mass emigration which brought over 2,000,000 Jews to U.S., 350,000 to Western Europe, and 60,000 to Palestine (to 1914) Am Olam (Eternal People), organization founded in Odessa to settle Jews in American communes		Laurence Oliphant, *The Land of Gilead*
1882	Am Olam establishes New Odessa, Jewish socialist commune near Portland, Oregon Bilu, first organized group of pioneers, established in Russia, settles in Palestine	First Yiddish play, *Machashefa* (The Witch), performed in New York, by The Hebrew Opera and Dramatic Co.	Leon Pinsker, *Autoemanzipation* Emma Lazarus, *Epistle to the Hebrews*
1883		L.Pasternak goes to Munich and enrolls in the Academy of Art	
1886		A.Walkowitz, age 8, moves with family from Russia to U.S.	
1887		The Jewish Theological Seminary of America established in New York	
1888	The United Hebrew Trades (Vereinigte Yiddishe Gevergschaften) founded, parent institution of Jewish labour movement		Jewish Publication Society of America established

Date History	Culture	Publications
1889	Educational Alliance Art School founded in New York, on the Lower East Side	Founding of the *Jewish Quarterly Review* (England)
1890	Art Nouveau spreads throughout European centres (1890–1900)	
1891 Expulsion of Jews from Moscow	Bernard Berenson, art historian, converted to Catholicism M.Weber, aged 10, arrives in U.S. with family, from Bialystock, Russia W.Zorach, aged 4, emigrates to U.S. from Lithuania with family	
1892	Yehuda Pen opens art school in Vitebsk	Israel Zangwill, *Children of the Ghetto*
1893	Hadji Ephraim Benguiat Collection of Jewish ceremonial objects exhibited at the World's Columbian Exposition, Chicago	
1894 Start of Dreyfus affair in France	E.M.Lilien arrives in Munich from Cracow	Discovery of Sarajevo Haggada, 14th-century illuminated manuscript; published with commentary by Mueller and Schlosser, with first survey of Hebrew illuminated manuscripts by David Kaufmann
1896	M.Gertler emigrates with family from Przemysl, Galicia, to London	Discovery of Cairo Genizah, storehouse of literary and historical documents Theodor Herzl, *Der Judenstaat* (The Jewish State)
1897 Bund founded (general Jewish workers' union) in Lithuania, Poland and Russia First Zionist Congress, Basle	Establishment of Jewish Museum, Vienna	
1900	J.Kramer, aged 8, emigrates with family from Ukraine to Leeds, England	Sigmund Freud, *Die Traumdeutung* (The Interpretation of Dreams) *Jewish Daily Forward* begins publication in New York under editorship of Abraham Cahan *Ost und West*, an illustrated monthly for modern Jewry with contributions by artists, scholars and writers (Berlin)
1901 Founding of Poalei Zion, socialist Zionist organization, active in Russia, Europe, Palestine and U.S.	The Jewish Museum and the Society for Exploration of Jewish Antiquities established in Frankurt	
1903 With pogroms in Kishinev, new wave of pogroms in Russia begins	Moshe Oved arrives in London from Poland and founds Cameo Corner, a shop for antique jewellery	Vladimir Stassof and David Ginzburg, *L'Ornement hébraïque*
1904 Russo-Japanese War (1904–5)		
1905 Abortive revolution in Russia	Edward Steichen and Alfred Stieglitz jointly found New York's Little Gallery of the Photo-Secession, later known as 291 Gallery Warburg Bibliothek founded in Hamburg by Aby Warburg Expressionist group Die Brücke established in Dresden	Albert Einstein publishes essay, 'The Spatial Theory of Relativity'

Date History	Culture	Publications
	Fauve movement in Paris J.Pascin goes from Munich to Paris J.Epstein leaves U.S. and settles in London M.Weber leaves U.S. for Paris A. Modigliani settles in Paris L.Nevelson, aged 6, and her family emigrate from Kiev to U.S. E.M.Lilien moves from Berlin to Jerusalem J.Tofel moves from Poland to U.S.	
1906 Peak of immigration to U.S.; 642,000 Jews arrive (1906–9)	Founding of the Jewish Museum, Prague	Martin Buber, *Die Geshichten des Rabbi Nachman* (The Tales of Rabbi Nachman)
	The Bezalel School of Arts and Crafts founded in Jerusalem under direction of sculptor Boris Shatz B.Shahn emigrates with family from Kovno to U.S. A.Walkowitz leaves New York for Paris L.Lozowick, aged 14, emigrates to U.S. from Kiev Picasso paints *Les Demoiselles d'Avignon* (1906–7); start of Cubism	Hayim Joseph Brenner, Yiddish and Hebrew writer, publishes *Ha-Meorer* (The Awakener) (periodical), London
1907	Writer Shmuel Agnon goes to Palestine S.Hirszenberg joins faculty at Bezalel School of Arts and Crafts Artists Georges Kars and Louis Marcoussis go to Paris Meyer Schapiro, art historian, brought by his family from Lithuania to U.S.	Heinrich Kohl and Carl Watzinger publish results of their excavation of ancient Galilean synagogues, which uncovered sculpted friezes
1908	Establishment of Jewish Historical and Ethnological Society in St. Petersburg headed by S. Ansky Exhibition of Ashcan School paintings by The Eight, at Macbeth Gallery, New York	
1909 First collective workers' settlement (kibbutz) founded in Palestine Founding of Tel Aviv	Leon Bakst, theatre designer, arrives in Paris J. Lipchitz, aged 18, arrives in Paris from Lithuania	Louis Ginzberg, *The Legends of the Jews*, a collection from the Talmudic literature *Evreiskaia Starina* (Jewish Antiquity), journal published in St. Petersburg (1909–16)
1910	Establishment of Jewish Museum in Warsaw First issue of *Der Sturm*, published in Berlin by Herwarth Walden M. Chagall arrives in Paris from Vitebsk, via St. Petersburg Moise Kisling arrives in Paris	
1911	Expressionist Blue Rider group in Munich	

Date History	Culture	Publications

1912	Ansky leads Jewish Ethnographic Expedition through the villages of Wholinia and Podolia in the Ukraine D.Bomberg, J.Kramer, M.Gertler, and I.Rosenfeld students at the Slade School of Art, London A.Pevsner arrives in Paris from Russia R.Rubin goes from Romania to Jerusalem to study at Bezalel School of Arts and Crafts A.Ticho arrives in Jerusalem from Vienna Three brothers, Moses, Raphael and Isaac Soyer, arrive with their family in U.S. from Russia M. Chagall paints *Calvary* in Paris Benno Schotz goes from Lithuania to Glasgow, via Darmstadt	Yiddish journal *Schriften* started in New York by David Ignatoff *Machmadim*, Hebrew art magazine published in Paris
1913	P.Kremegne, M.Kikoïne, Mané-Katz and C.Soutine arrive in Paris and live at La Ruche M. Rothko, aged 10, arrives in Portland, Oregon, from Russia with his family H.Leivick, Yiddish poet, arrives in U.S.	First literary publications of Franz Kafka Else Lasker-Schüler, lyric poet, *Hebräische Balladen* (Hebrew Ballads)
1914 World War I begins		Ansky publishes 'Dos Yidische ethnographische program' in *Jewish Academy of Petrograd* concerning his Jewish Ethnographic Expedition *Blast*, manifesto of Vorticist movement, published in England
1915	Establishment of Ben Uri Society in London John Weichsel establishes People's Art Guild in New York M.Chagall returns to Vitebsk via Berlin M.Janco arrives in Zurich from Bucharest	
1916	Sholom Aleichem dies in New York E.Lissitsky and I.Ryback explore folk art in the synagogues along the Dnieper River, and copy wall paintings of Mohilev Synagogue	*Der Jude*, a monthly magazine founded by Martin Buber Herman Struck, *Skitzen aus Litauen Weissrussland und Kurland* (Sketches from Lithuania, White Russia and Kurland)
1917 Russian Revolution followed by the abolishment of restrictions affecting the Jews Balfour Declaration	Yiddish State Theatre and Habimah Theatre founded in Moscow Constructivist movement in Russia Sculptor Abraham Melnikov arrives in Palestine and joins Jewish Brigade Painter David Sterenberg returns from Paris to Russia and assumes Directorship of Soviet Commission on Culture	

Date	History	Culture	Publications
1918	World War I ends	M.Chagall appointed Commissar and Director of Vitebsk Art Academy	Literary magazines *Baginnen* and *Eigenes* appear in Kiev
1919	Pogroms in the Ukraine and Poland	C.Soutine paints in Ceret S. Menkes arrives in Paris from Poland M.Beckmann paints *Synagogue* E.Lissitzky appointed Professor at Vitebsk Art Academy N.Altman, Art Commissar of Petrograd, designs the festivities for first anniversary of Russian Revolution M.Chagall paints murals for Yiddish State Theatre, Moscow Bauhaus established in Weimar	Hermann Cohen, *Die Religion der Vernunft aus den Quellen des Judentums* (The Religion of Reason, from the Sources of Judaism), published posthumously I.Ryback and B.Aronson publish in *Oifgang* (Kiev) their programmatic article 'Di Vegen fun des Yiddischer Malerei' (The Paths of Jewish Painting)
1920	Histadrut (general federation of Jewish labour) founded in Palestine	M.Ardon enters the Bauhaus M.Lieberman elected President of the Berlin Academy of Art Painter Avigdor Steimatsky arrives in Palestine Ben-Zion emigrates to U.S. from the Ukraine via Vienna	N.Gabo and A.Pevsner publish Realist Manifesto in Moscow Herman Struck, *Das Ostjuedische Antlitz* (The Eastern European Jewish Portrait) *Renaissance*, Yiddish literary magazine starts publication in London
1921		E.Lissitzky moves to Berlin M.Levanon arrives in Palestine from Hungary C. Gross emigrates from Galicia to U.S. Chaim Bialik, Hebrew poet, leaves Odessa with the help of Maxim Gorky and goes to Berlin	Ludwig Wittgenstein, *Tractatus Logico-philosophicos* H. Leivick, *Der Goylem* (The Golem)
1922		Berlin becomes a centre for Jewish artists and writers—A.Aberdam, N.Altman, B.Aronson, M.Band, M.Chagall, N.Gabo, I.Kulvianski, L.Pasternak, I.Ryback arrive from the east; L.Lozowick comes from the U.S.; Saul Tchernichovski (Hebrew poet), Vladimir Mayakovsky (Russian poet) move to Berlin A.Manievich emigrates from Kiev to U.S. E.Lissitzky engages in propagandistic activity and publishes, with Ilya Ehrenburg, *Vesh, Gegenstand, Object* Performance of Ansky's *The Dybbuk* by Habimah Theatre in Moscow; N.Altman designs sets M.Band moves from Berlin to Paris	Gershom Scholem, *Das Buch Bahir* (The Book Bahir) The Yiddish art and literary magazines *Shtrom* (Moscow), *Ringen* and *Chaliastra* (Warsaw), and *Albatross* (Warsaw and Berlin) start publication
1923		L.Segall emigrates to Brazil A.Aberdam, M.Chagall and L.Pasternak go from Berlin to Paris J. Zaritsky arrives in Palestine from Russia D.Bomberg visits Palestine	E.Lissitzky, 'The Synagogue at Mohilev, Reminiscences', in *Rimon* Henryk Berlewi, 'Jewish Artists in Contemporary Russian Art, The Russian Art Exhibition in Berlin, 1922,' in *Rimon*

Date	History	Culture	Publications
		I.Danziger, aged 7, arrives in Jerusalem with his parents	Nathan Altman, *Jüdische Graphik* (Hebrew Graphics)
		B.Aronson arrives in U.S. from Kiev via Germany and France	
		Tower of David exhibition in Jerusalem includes work of R.Rubin, Nahum Gutman, Israel Paldi, Pinhas Litvinovsky and J.Zaritsky	
1924	Jewish Immigration to U.S. limited by Johnson Act	Chaim Bialik arrives in Tel Aviv	Boris Aronson, *Sovremmenaya Evreiskaya Grafika* (Contemporary Hebrew Graphics)
		L.Pasternak visits Palestine	
		Y.Kovarsky moves to Palestine from Vilna	
		L. Krakauer moves to Palestine from Vienna	
		Jacques Chapiro arrives in Paris	
1925	YIVO founded (Yiddisher Vissenshaftlicher Institut/Yiddish Scientific Institute)	A.Melnikov creates the monument *Roaring Lion* at Tel Khai in memory of its defenders	
1926		Salo Baron, historian, emigrates to U.S. from Vienna	
		L.Gottlieb and A.Mintchine arrive in Paris from Poland and Russia	
		I.Ryback moves to Paris	
		J.Simon studies in Frankfurt with M. Beckmann	
1927		M.Castel moves to Paris from Jerusalem	Richard Krautheimer, *Mittelalterliche Synagogen* (Medieval Synagogues)
1928		E.Lissitzky returns to Russia	Rudolf Hallo, *Jüdische Volkskunst in Hessen* (Jewish Folk Art in Hessen)
		S. Menkes paints *The Torah* in Paris	
1929	Beginning of the Great Depression in U.S.	The Museum of Modern Art opens in New York	Ernst Cohen Wiener, *Die Jüdische Kunst* (Jewish Art)
		Discovery of mosaic floor of ancient synagogue of Beth Alpha	
1930		B.Shahn executes drawings for a Haggadah; published in U.S. in 1965	
		Art dealer Ambroise Vollard commissions M.Chagall to illustrate the Bible	
		J.Pascin commits suicide	
1931		M.Chagall arrives in Palestine with Jewish writers Chaim Bialik and Edmond Fleg	Founding in Berlin of Schocken Verlag, Jewish oriented publisher
1932		Founding of the Tel Aviv Museum of Art	*Gazit*, journal for literature and art, published in Tel Aviv
		Discovery of ancient synagogue of Dura Europas by American-French expedition	
1933	Hitler rises to power; establishment of first concentration camp in Nazi Germany—Dachau	Warburg Bibliothek transferred to London and renamed Warburg Institute	Rudolf Hallo, *Jüdische Kunst aus Hessen und Nassau* (Jewish Art from Hessen and Nassau)
	Public burning in Germany of Jewish books and books by opponents of Nazism	M.Liebermann ousted from Presidency of the Berlin Academy of Art; his paintings removed from all German museums	

Date	History	Culture	Publications
1934		Establishment of Jewish Museum in Berlin Erwin Panofsky, art historian, arrives in the U.S. from Germany M.Ardon, J. Budko and J.Steinhardt setttle in Jerusalem J.Adler escapes from Düsseldorf to Paris J.Simon works with Diego Rivera in New York	
1935	Nuremberg Laws proclaimed Works Progress Administration (WPA) sponsored by the U.S. Government; participating American artists include H. Bloom, A.Gottlieb, J.Levine, L.Lozowick, M.Rothko, B.Shahn, M.Siporin, M.Soyer	J.Adler goes to Warsaw A.Naton moves from Romania to Palestine Richard Krautheimer, art historian, arrives in U.S.	Rachel Wischnitzer, *Gestalten und Symbole der Jüdische Kunst* (Forms and Symbols of Jewish Art)
1936		Aharon Avni establishes Studio for Painting and Sculpture in Tel Aviv J.Simon and S.Seba emigrate to Palestine; Simon settles in Kibbutz Gan-Shmuel J.Adler visits U.S.S.R.	
1937	Buchenwald Concentration Camp established Establishment of 'Aliya Beth', illegal immigration to Palestine	Nazi exhibition Entartete Kunst (Degenerate Art) Y.Bergner moves from Warsaw to Australia Pablo Picasso paints *Guernica* L.Pasternak goes to England	Salo Baron, *A Social and Religious History of the Jews*
1938	Kristallnacht ('Night of Broken Glass'), Nazi anti-Jewish riots in Germany and Austria	Hans Tietze and E.Conrat Tietze, art historians, emigrate from Austria to U.S. Stephen Kayser, art historian, emigrates to U.S.	
1939	Soviet-German Pact Poland invaded; World War II begins Establishment of ghettos in Poland Beginning of destruction of European Jewish communities	Guido Schoenberger, art historian, emigrates to U.S. N. Bezem emigrates to Palestine from Germany I. Danziger carves *Nimrod*	
1940	Himmler directive to establish concentration camp at Auschwitz Western Europe invaded by the Nazis	Mark Gertler commits suicide Rachel Wischnitzer emigrates to U.S. J.Herman flees to England M.Maryan inmate at Auschwitz J.Lipchitz arrives in New York from Paris S.Bak, aged 7, flees Vilna and spends four years hiding in a monastery, and in displaced persons' camps in Germany after the War Ossip Zadkine flees from Paris for U.S.	
1941	Nazis invade Russia; Japan and U.S. enter World War II	M.Janco settles in Palestine J.Adler arrives in England E.Lissitzky dies in Moscow	Gershom Scholem, *Major Trends in Jewish Mysticism*
1942	Germany adopts policy of 'Final Solution' for systematic annihilation		

Date	History	Culture	Publications

of European Jews
Armed resistance in the ghettos of
Mir, Lehava and Nieswiecz, all in
Western Byelorussia
The *Struma* sinks in Black Sea with
769 refugees

Date	History	Culture	Publications
1943	Uprising of Warsaw Ghetto Resistance and revolt in ghettos of Vilna, Bialystock and Czestochova WPA disbanded in U.S.	Otto Freundlich dies in Lublin Concentration Camp O. Ritterband transported to Auschwitz F. Hundertwasser, aged 14, makes first crayon drawings; 69 of his maternal relatives are deported to Eastern Europe and killed B. Reder emigrates to U.S. from Prague C. Soutine dies in Paris	
1944		Picasso paints *Charnel House* (1944–8)	Jacob Leveen, *The Hebrew Bible in Art*
1945	Germany surrenders; World War II ends in Europe	H.Paris enters Buchenwald Concentration Camp as artist- correspondent for *Stars and Stripes* newspaper; starts Buchenwald series of graphics Else Lasker-Schüler, German poet, dies in Jerusalem	H.Leivick, Yiddish poet, *In Treblinke bin ikh nit geven* (I was not in Treblinka)
1946		Rise of Abstract Expressionism in U.S.	Franz Landsberger, *A History of Jewish Art*
1947	Start of mass migration to Israel by Holocaust refugees	Establishment of the Jewish Museum in New York Discovery of Dead Sea Scrolls J.Lipchitz creates *Miracle* Artist Ben-Zwi creates monument for the children of the Diaspora in Kibbutz Mishmar Haemek, Israel	Helen Rosenau, *A short History of Jewish Art*
1948	Establishment of State of Israel; War of Independence begins Actor-director Michoels murdered by Russian Secret Police	Architect Percival Goodman with assistance of artists Robert Motherwell, Herbert Ferber and Adolph Gottlieb introduces contemporary art in the Synagogue B'nai Israel in Milburn, New Jersey Establishment of New Horizons group in Tel Aviv under leadership of J.Zaritsky and M.Janco N.Rappoport creates *Ghetto Monument* on the site of the Warsaw Ghetto S.Bak goes to Israel B.Newman paints *Onement I*	Rachel Wischnitzer, *The Messianic Theme in the Painting of the Dura Synagogue*
1949	Year-long air transfer of *c*. 50,000 Jews from Yemen to Israel	Y.Kovarsky moves to New York from Israel Fima emigrates to Israel from Shanghai A.Ofek arrives in Israel from Bulgaria	Karl Schwarz, *Jewish Artists of the 19th and 20th centuries*
1950	Air transfer of 123,000 Jews from Iraq to Israel	J.Adler dies at Aldbourne, near London	

Date	History	Culture	Publications
1951	Over 30 Russian-Jewish writers executed	M.Moreh goes from England to Israel	M.D.Cassuto, *The Goddess Anat Canaanite Epics of the Patriarchal Age*, translated [into Hebrew] from the Ugaritic
1952	Prague trials		Kurt Weitzman, *The Illustration of the Septuagint*
1953	'Doctors' Plot' in USSR	Rudolph Wittkower, art historian, arrives in U.S.	Erwin Goodenough *Jewish Symbols in the Greco-Roman Period* (13 vols., 1953–65)
1954			B. Shahn, *Alphabet of Creation*
1956		Rico Lebrun paints Buchenwald Series E.Brauer entertains Israeli troops during the Sinai campaign	Carl Kraling, *The Synagogue*, an investigation of the architecture of wall paintings of Dura-Europos Chagall's Bible illustrations published in Paris
1957		M.Chagall and J.Lipchitz are commissioned to work on the Church of Assy	Ernst Naimenyi, *L'Esprit de l'art juif* (The Spirit of Jewish Art)
1959		J.Epstein sculpts *Saint Michael Killing the Devil* for Coventry Cathedral	
1961			Cecil Roth, *Jewish Art, an Illustrated History*
1962		Spread of Pop Art movement in U.S.	
1963		Monumenta Judaica—an exhibition of 2,000 years of Jewish history and culture on the Rhine, at The Stadtmuseum, Cologne Artist Boris Penson arrested and sent to hard labour in U.S.S.R.	
1964		Opening of the Israel Museum in Jerusalem Moshe Barasch establishes art history department at Hebrew University, Jerusalem	Kurt Weitzman, *The Question of the Influence of Jewish Pictorial Sources on Old Testament Illustration*
1965	Immigration Act liberalizes quota system in U.S.	D.Karavan creates *Memorial Monument for Negev Brigade* near Beer Sheba	Trianon Press in Paris publish Haggada with drawings by Ben Shahn
1967	Six Days War		L.A.Mayer and Otto Kurz, *Bibliography of Jewish Art*
1968		L.Klapish moves to Jerusalem from Paris	
1970	Leningrad Trials; Russian Jews agitate for the right to emigrate		
1972		M.Rothko commits suicide	Heinrich Strauss, *Die Kunst Der Juden im Wandel der Zeit und Umwelt* (The Art of the Jews in differing Periods and Environments)
1973	Yom Kippur War	E.Brauer acts as war correspondent in Golan Heights L.Baskin illustrates *A Passover Haggadah* J.Lipchitz dies in Capri, Italy, and is buried in Jerusalem	Mendel Metzger, *La Haggada Enluminée. Étude iconographique et stylistique des manuscrits enluminés et décorés de la Haggada du XIIIe au XVIe siècle* (The illuminated Haggadah. Iconographical and Stylistic Study of Illuminated and Decorated Manuscripts of the

Date	History	Culture	Publications
			Haggadah from the 13th to the 16th Century)
1974		J.Gurvich dies in New York, buried in a kibbutz in Israel Y.Bergner paints mural, *Cycle of Expulsion and Return*, at Haifa University	Bezalel Narkiss starts publication of *Journal of Jewish Art* at Spertus College, Chicago Yosef Yerulshami, *Haggadah and History*
1975		M.Ardon completes triptych on Yom Kippur War: *Kol Nidrai, Sacrifice, Requiem* H.Paris completes environment *Kaddish for the Little Children*	Gabrielle Sed-Rayna *L'Art juif* (Jewish Art)
1977		M.S.Maryan dies in New York I.Danziger dies in traffic accident in Israel	
1978		Retrospective exhibition of Maryan's works at Haifa University Art Gallery and Tel Aviv Art Museum	
1980		B.Aronson dies in New York	Colette Sirat, *La Lettre hébraïque et sa signification* (The Hebrew Letter and its Significance) Leila Avrin, *Micrography as Art*

Illustrations

Plates

I. Chaim Soutine, *Woman in Profile*, 1937.
II. Marc Chagall, *Calvary*, 1912.
III. Marc Chagall, *Time is a River Without Banks*, 1930–9.
IV. Hyman Bloom, *The Synagogue*, 1940.
V. Max Weber, *Adoration of the Moon*, 1944.
VI. Ben Shahn, *Ram's Horn and Menorah*, 1958.
VII. Jankel Adler, *Two Rabbis*, 1942.
VIII. Fritz Hundertwasser, *Blood Garden—House with Yellow Smoke*, 1962–3.
IX. Max Beckmann, *The Synagogue*, 1919.
X. Samuel Bak, *Thou Shalt Not*, 1977.
XI. Menashe Kadishman, *Trees in the Ocean*, 1975–7 (model).
XII. Yosl Bergner, *Excursion to the Kinnereth*, 1980.
XIII. Mark Rothko, *Green and Maroon*, 1953.
XIV. Mordecai Ardon, *In the Beginning*, 1970.
XV. Yehoshua Kovarsky, *Temple Above the Moon*, 1958.
XVI. Maryan S. Maryan, untitled, 1973.

Figures

1. Leopold Krakauer, *Sun and Thistles*, 1952.
2. Ben Shahn, *Identity*, 1968.
3. Samuel Hirszenberg, *Funeral of the Zadik*, 1905.
4. Mitchell Siporin, *Endless Voyage*, 1946.
5. Marc Chagall, *The Praying Jew*, 1914.
6. Jewish *lubok*.
7. Anonymous working drawing for a gravestone.
8. *Lion*, from a wall painting in the Mohilev synagogue.
9. *Lion*, from a wall painting in the Mohilev synagogue.
10. *Birds of Paradise*, from the Mohilev synagogue.
11. Artist's inscription, from the ceiling of the Mohilev synagogue.
12. Issachar Ryback, *The Old Synagogue*, 1917.
13. Issachar Ryback, *The Synagogue of Chiklov*, 1917.
14. Issachar Ryback, *The Old Jew*, 1917.
15. Issachar Ryback, *Portrait of a Jew*, c.1917.
16. Nathan Altman, *Eve*, 1923.
17. Nathan Altman, *Two Birds Flanking a Vase*, 1923.
18. El Lissitzky, study for the cover of *Chad Gadya*, 1917.
19. Boris Aronson, untitled, 1920.
20. Marc Chagall, *Over Vitebsk*, 1914.
21. Marc Chagall, *Green Violinist*, 1923–4.
22. Nathan Altman, calligraphy page, 1922.

23. Nathan Altman, *Head of a Young Jew* (self-portrait), 1916.
24. Boris Aronson, untitled, no date.
25. Joseph Tchaikov, *Self-Portrait*, 1920.
26. Joseph Tchaikov, *A Young Jew*, 1921.
27. Nathan Altman, stage design for *Uriel Accosta*, 1922.
28. Nathan Altman, stage design for the *Dybbuk*,
29–32. Nathan Altman, four of the costume designs in the *Dybbuk*, 1920.
33. Marc Chagall, *Introduction to the Yiddish Theatre* (detail), 1921.
34. Nathan Altman, portrait of the Michoels.
35. Marc Chagall, cover of *Shtrom*, 1922.
36. El Lissitzky, illustration for the *Prager Legende*.
37. El Lissitzky, design of title page for *Yingl Zingl Chwatt*, 1918.
38. El Lissitzky, illustration for *Yingl Zingl Chwatt*, 1918.
39. El Lissitzky, illustration for *Der Ber*, 1919.
40. El Lissitzky, poster, *Beat the Whites with the Red Wedge*, 1919.
41. El Lissitzky, 'A Journey to America', illustration, 1922.
42. Jacob Epstein, *East Side People*, 1900–1.
43. William Gropper, *Tailor*, 1940.
44. Abraham Walkowitz, *East Side Crowd*, 1903.
45. David Bomberg, *Jewish Theatre*, 1913.
46. Mark Gertler, *Jewish Family*, 1913.
47. David Bomberg, *Vision of Ezekiel*, 1912.
48. David Bomberg, *The Mud Bath*, 1914.
49. David Bomberg, *Ghetto Theatre*, 1920.
50. Chaim Gross, *East Side Girl*, 1948.
51. Jack Levine, *The Passing Scene*, 1941.
52. Louis Lozowick, *Autobiographic*, 1967.
53. Naum Gabo, *Column*, 1923.
54. Antoine Pevsner, *Twinned Column*, 1947.
55. Louis Lozowick, *The Concrete Mixer*, 1939.
56. Louis Lozowick, *Minneapolis*, 1926–7.
57. Ben Shahn, *New York*, 1947.
58. Ben Shahn, *East Side Soap Box*, 1936.
59. Leonard Baskin, *The Four Mystics*, 1952.
60. Larry Rivers, *Bar Mitzvah Photograph Portrait*, 1961.
61. Joe Lasker, *Scissor Grinder*, 1954.
62. Joe Lasker, *Memo*, 1954.
63. George Segal, *Abraham and Isaac*, 1978.
64. Morris Kantor, *Farewell to Union Square*, 1931.
65. Jack Levine, *Tombstone Cutter*, 1947.
66. Jack Levine, *Planning Solomon's Temple*, 1940.
67. Raphael Soyer, *Artist's Parents*, 1932.
68. Raphael Soyer, *The Bridge*, 1926–7.

69. Raphael Soyer, *Dancing Lesson*, 1926.
70. Moses Soyer, *Old Man in Skull Cap*, after 1913.
71. Jennings Tofel, *Family Reunion*, 1928.
72. Joseph Herman, *The Discussion*, 1940–1.
73. Seymour Lipton, *Eternal Light*, 1953.
74. Seymour Lipton, *Menorah*, 1953.
75. Seymour Lipton, *Manuscript*, 1961.
76. Amedeo Modigliani, *Portrait of Jacques Lipchitz and his Wife*, 1916–17.
77. Leopold Gottlieb, *Plasterers*, 1928.
78. Abraham Mintchine, *Self-Portrait*, 1926.
79. Jules Pascin, *Young Girl Sitting*, 1921–2.
80. Chaim Soutine, *Hanging Turkey*, 1926.
81. Chaim Soutine, *Fish and Tomatoes*, 1925.
82. Chaim Soutine, *The Old Mill*, c.1922–3.
83. Chaim Soutine, *Portrait of Moise Kisling*, c.1925.
84. Chaim Soutine, *Self-portrait*, 1917.
85. Abraham Manievich, *The Destruction of the Ghetto, Kiev*, 1919.
86. Marc Chagall, *Solitude*, 1933.
87. Marc Chagall, *White Crucifixion*, 1938.
88. Jankel Adler, *Two Orphans*, 1942.
89. Yosl Bergner, *Flying Spice Box*, 1966.
90. Erich Brauer, *The Rainmaker of Carmel*, 1964.
91. Page from the 'Autobiography' by Maryan S. Maryan, 1976.
92. Maryan S. Maryan, *Figure with Upraised Arms*, 1963.
93. Maryan S. Maryan, *Personage, Man with Donkey Ears*, 1962.
94. Maryan S. Maryan, *untitled*, 1961.
95. Samuel Bak, *Father and Son*, 1972–3.
96. Samuel Bak, *The Family*, 1974.
97. Samuel Bak, *Smoke*, 1977.
98. Alfred Aberdam, *Deportation*, 1941–2.
99. Harold Paris, *Torah Soul*, 1975.
100. Mordecai Ardon, *Train of Numbers*, 1963.
101. Jacques Lipchitz, *The Prayer*, 1943.
102. Pablo Picasso, *The Charnel House*, 1944–5.
103. Kurt Seligman, *Sabbath Phantoms—Mythomania*, no date.
104. Minna Harkavy, *The Last Prayer*, 1949.
105. Siegmund Menkes, *Uprising of Ghetto Warsaw*, 1943.
106. Jack Levine, *To an Unknown German*, 1969.
107. Naftali Bezem, *The Binding of Isaac*, 1968.
108. Abraham Rattner, *Ezekiel's Valley of the Dried Bones*, 1963.
109. Luise Kaish, *Holocaust*, 1975.
110. Louise Nevelson, *Homage to Six Million I*, 1964.
111. William Zorach, *Man of Judah*, c.1957.
112. William Zorach, *Head of Moses*, 1956.
113. Lasar Segall, *Emigrant Ship*, 1939–41.
114. Lasar Segall, *Exodus*, c. 1940.
115. Seymour Lipton, *Exodus no. 1*, 1947.
116. Jacques Lipchitz, *Mother and Child II*, 1941–5.
117. Jacques Lipchitz, *Mother and Child*, 1930.
118. Jacques Lipchitz, *Miracle II*, 1947.
119. Jacques Lipchitz, *Hagar*, 1971.
120. Ben Zwi, *Memorial to the Children of the Holocaust*, 1947.
121. Nathan Rappoport, *Scroll of Fire*, 1971.
122. Nathan Rappoport, *Scroll of Fire* (detail).
123. Reuven Rubin, *First Fruits*, 1923.
124. Reuven Rubin, *Early Morning in Galilee*, 1937.
125. Reuven Rubin, *Portrait of Ahad Ha'am*, 1926.
126. Reuven Rubin, *Meal of the Poor*, 1920.
127. Johanan Simon, *Sabbath in the Kibbutz*, no date.
128. Johanan Simon, *In the Shower*, 1952.
129. Marcel Janco, *Maabaroth in Grey*, c.1950.
130. Marcel Janco, *The Wounded Soldier*, no date.
131. Abraham Melnikov, *The Roaring Lion*, monument of Tel Khai, 1926.
132. Itzhak Danziger, *Nimrod*, 1939.
133. Itzhak Danziger, *Negev Sheep*, 1964.
134. Shalom Seba, *Shearing of Sheep*, 1947.
135. Aharon Kahana, *Dialogue at Night*, 1950.
136. Achiam, *Adam and Eve*, 1955.
137. Achiam, *Pregnant Woman*, 1952.
138. Shamai Haber, *Altar*, 1957.
139. Hava Mehutan, *Offering*, 1963.
140. Koso Elul, *Horizon*, 1963.
141. Moshe Castel, *Sephardic Wedding Feast*, 1942.
142. Moshe Castel, *Basalt of Galilee*, 1964.
143. Moshe Castel, *Basalt Relief*, 1959.
144. Menashe Kadishman, *The Altar*, 1959.
145. Yechiel Shemi, *Standing Sculpture*, 1963.
146. Ygael Tumarkin, *Earth Sculpture*, 1979.
147. Ygael Tumarkin, *Sculpture in Arad*, 1963.
148. Dani Karavan, *Monument to the Negev Brigade*, 1965.
149. Naftali Bezem, *Man with Plant*, 1960.
150. Abraham Ofek, *Settlers Conversing*, 1970.
151. Abraham Ofek, *The Return*, 1970.
152. Yosl Bergner, *Migration and Return*, 1973.
153. Hanna Orlof, *Mother and Child*, 1949.
154. George Segal, *Abraham and Isaac*, 1973.
155. Max Weber, *Invocation*, 1919.
156. Jacob Steinhardt, *In the Synagogue*, 1923.
157. Ben-Zion, *Friday Evening*, c. 1956.
158. Herman Struck, *Separation (Havdalah)*, 1902.
159. Max Weber, *The Talmudists*, 1934.
160. Jacob Kramer, *Day of Atonement*, 1919.
161. Sigmund Menkes, *The Uplifting of the Torah*, 1928.
162. Marvin Cherney, *Man with Torah*, c.1957–8.
163. Sigmund Menkes, *Les Talmudistes*, 1928.
164. Abraham Ofek, *The Synagogue*, 1971.
165. Leonard Baskin, *The Blind Rabbi*, 1971.
166. Hyman Bloom, *Rabbi*, 1957.
167. Hyman Bloom, *The Rabbi*, 1955.
168. Bernard Reder, *Aaron with Tabernacle*, 1959.
169. Elbert Weinberg *Procession no. 1*, 1957.
170. Elbert Weinberg, *Ritual Figure*, 1953.
171. Anna Ticho, *Jerusalem Hills*, c.1963.
172. Mordecai Ardon, *Homage to Jerusalem*, 1965.
173. Luise Kaish *The Cabbalistic Sphere*, 1975.
174. Barnett Newman, *Zim Zum*, 1969.
175. 'Separation of Day from Night', from the *Haggadah of Sarajevo*.
176. Barnett Newman, *Joshua*, 1950.
177. Adolph Gottlieb, *Tints*, 1971.

Index

Numbers in italics indicate illustrations

Aaron, 187–88
Aaron with Tabernacle, see Reder
Aarons, George, 86
Aberdam, Alfred, 131, 212;
  Deportation, 131, *131*
Abraham, 134, 175
Abraham, see Newman
Abraham and Isaac, see Segal, George
Abraham, Isaac and the Angel, see
  Weinberg
Abstract Expressionism, 77, 124, 195,
  214, 216
Abstraction-Creation group, 214,
  217–18
Achiam, 156–57, 212; *Adam and Eve*,
  157, *158*; *Pregnant Woman*, 157, *158*
Adam and Eve, see Achiam
Adler, Jankel, 116–17, 168, 206, 212;
  Two Orphans, 117, *117*; *Two Rabbis*,
  103, 116
Adoration of the Moon, see Weber
Akedah, see Segal, George
Akiba, (R.), 74
Albatross, 34–35, 66
Albers, Anni, 86
Alechinsky, Pierre, 124
All That Remains, see Paris, Harold
Altar, see Haber
Altar, The, see Kadishman
Altman, Nathan, 16, 18, 22–23, 33,
  37–39, 43, 62, 207, 212; calligraphy,
  30; *Anna Achmatova*, 33; *Dybbuk*,
  design for, *38*; *Eve*, 23; *Head of a
  Young Jew*, 30; portrait of Michoels,
  42; *Two Birds Flanking a Vase*, 23;
  Uriel Accosta, design for, 37
American art, 70
Anat, 150
Andre, Carl, 163
Anisfeld, Boris, 62, 65
Ansky, S., 17, 28–29, 38, 204, 205
Antokolski, Mark, 15–17, 28–29, 35,
  38, 51, 203, 204, 206, 208; *Christ
  before His Judges*, 203
Appel, Karel, 124
Ardon, Mordechai, 131, 134, 191–93,
  212; *Homage to Jerusalem*, 192–93;
  In the Beginning, 110, 192; *Lament
  of Nails*, 193; *Night of Ascents*, 192;
  Parchments and Scrolls, 192–93;
  Train of Numbers, 131, *132*, 192
Ari Hakadosh, 198
Armitage, Kenneth, 189
Aronson, Boris, 16–17, 25, 28–33, *31*,
  35, 47, 62, 64, 86, 205–208, 212;
  Contemporary Hebrew Graphics, 16,
  30
Art Autre, 123
Art Brut, 123
Art Informel, 123
Artist's Parents, see Soyer, Raphael
Art Students League, 54, 214–19
Ashcan School, 63, 83
Ashtoret, 150

Astarta, 159
Atlan, Jean-Michel, 124
Auschwitz, 121–22, 134, 216
"Autobiography," see Maryan
Avant-garde art, see Modern art
Avni Studio of Painting and Sculpture,
  215
Aztecs, art of, 124, 177

Baal, 150, 159
Baar, Alfred H., 132
Babel, tower of, 154–55
Babylon, 163
Bacon, Francis, 173
Baginnen, 34
Bak, Samuel, 125–28, 130, 212; *The
  Family*, 126–27, *127*; *Father and Son*,
  126, 128; *Landscapes of Jewish
  History*, 106, 128, *128*; *Smoke*, 128,
  128; *Thou Shalt Not*, 106
Bakst, Leon, 25
Band, Max, 89, 134
Barlach, Ernst, 189
Bar Mitzvah Photograph Portrait, see
  Rivers
Basalt of Galilee, see Castel
Basalt Relief, see Castel
Baskin, Leonard, 70, 74–76, 86, 134,
  212; *The Blind Rabbi*, 186, *187*; *The
  Four Mystics*, 74–75, *75*
Bauhaus, 191, 212
Baur, John, 188
Beardsley, Aubrey, 29
Beat the Whites with the Red Wedge,
  see Lissitzky
Beckmann, Max, 147–48, 212; *The
  Synagogue*, 105, 113–14
Beginning, In The, see Ardon
Bellow, George, 54
Belluschi, Pietro, 86
Ben Ari, Raiken, 207
Ben, Ben, 62
Ben Azzai, 74
Bendemann, Edward, 51
Ben Uri Society, 50, 61
Ben-Zion, 177, 212; *Friday Evening*,
  179
Ben Zoma, 174
Ben Zwi, 142–43, 213; *Memorial to the
  Children of the Holocaust*, 142–43,
  142
Der Ber, see Lissitzky
Berdichevsky, Joseph Micha, 152
Bergelson, David, 36
Bergner, Yosl, 118, 170–73, 213;
  Excursion to the Kinnereth, 108;
  Flying Spice Box, 119; *Migration and
  Return*, 170–72, *170–71*
Berlevi, Henryk, 35, 203
Berlin, 12, 35, 47, 62, 66, 68, 156, 191,
  212–18
Bernstein, Theresa, 65
Beth Alpha synagogue, 74, 156

Beth Shearim, Israel, 142
Beuys, Joseph, 163
Bezalel Art School, 29, 122, 145–46,
  173, 213, 216–18
Bezem, Naftali, 134, 166–67, 213; *The
  Binding of Isaac*, 135; *Man with
  Plant*, 167
Bialik, Ch.N., 28
Bialystock, Russia, 178, 181, 219
Bible, in art, 80, 86–87, 134, 138, 140,
  145, 152, 156–57, 159, 175, 191–93,
  195
Binding of Isaac, The, see Bezem
Birds of Paradise, see Segal, Haim B.
  Isaac
Birnholz, Alan C., 46
Black Fire, see Newman
Blind Rabbi, The, see Baskin
*Blood Garden—House with Yellow
  Smoke*, see Hundertwasser
Bloom, Hyman, 186, 213; *Rabbi*, 186,
  187; *The Rabbi*, 186, *187*; *The
  Synagogue*, 100, 186
Bloomsbury group, 214
Bomberg, David, 57–58, 61, 149, 170,
  181, 213; *Ghetto Theatre*, 60, 61; *In
  the Hold*, 58; *Jewish Theatre*, 57, 58,
  61; *The Mud Bath*, 58, 60; *Reading
  from the Torah*, 58; *Vision of
  Ezekiel*, 58, 60
Bosch, Hieronymus, *Ship of Fools*, 173
Brauer, Erich, 118–20, 125, 130, 213;
  Destruction of the Temple, 119;
  Israel Besieged, 119; *The Kishiniev
  Pogrom*, 119; *The Martyr*, 119;
  Masada, 119; "Persecution of the
  Jewish People," 119; *The Rainmaker
  of Carmel*, 121; *Slaves Were We in
  Egypt*, 119
Brauner, Victor, 124
Brecht, Bertolt, 164
Bridge, The, see Soyer, Raphael
Broderson, Moshe, 44, 206
Broom, The, 62, 66
Buber, Martin, 15, 52, 203, 209
Buchenwald, 128, 132

Cabbala, 30, 95, 117, 161, 191, 193–94,
  197–98
Cabbalistic Sphere, The, see Kaish
Calligraphy, 123, 161; Jewish, 18, *30*,
  72, 74, 137
Calvary, see Chagall
Camera Work (Stieglitz), 63
Canaan, 150, 155–56, 163
Caro, Anthony, 163
Castel, Moshe, 146, 160–62, 213;
  Basalt of Galilee, 161; *Basalt Relief*,
  161; *Sephardic Wedding Feast*, 160
Cathedra, see Newman
Catullus, 62
Celan, Paul, 128
Central School of Arts and Crafts, 58

Cézanne, Paul, 33, 58, 62, 177
Chad Gadya, see Lissitzky
Chagall, Marc, attraction to the West, 12; biography of, 213; and folk art, 25–28; and Jewish culture, 33, 47, 86, 116, 208; in Paris, 62, 89–90, 206; religious theme in, 177; in Russia, 16, 40, 46–47; in theatre, 40, 42–43; work of, 52, 91, 93, 161; *Calvary*, 11–12, 98; *The Falling Angel*, 115; *Green Violinist*, 27; *Introduction to the Yiddish Theatre*, 40–41, 41; *Over Vitebsk*, 26; *The Praying Jew*, 14, 33; *Shtrom*, cover of, 44; *Solitude*, 114, 115–16; *Time Is a River without Banks*, 99; *White Crucifixion*, 115–116, 115
Chai, see Paris, Harold
Chaliastra, 34–35, 206
Chapiro, Jacques, 91
Charnel House, see Picasso
Cherney, Marvin, 177, 185, 213; *Man with Torah*, 185, 185
Chernichevsky, Nikolai, 15
Chicago Art Institute, 213, 216, 218
Chorazin, synagogue of, 161
Christ, in art, 12, 115–16, 203
Christo Javachev, 163
Circle group, 214
Cobra Group, 124
Colour, in Jewish art, 32–33
Column, see Gabo
Comfuturists, 37
Concrete Mixer, The, see Lozowick
Constructivism, 16, 37, 40, 44, 47, 68, 208, 212, 214, 217–18
Contemporanul group, 214
Contemporary Hebrew Graphics, see Aronson
Cooper Union Art School, 213, 215, 218–19
Cubism, 20, 28, 33, 37, 89, 138, 143, 177, 181, 214, 217
Cubo-Futurism, 38–39, 44, 46

Dachau, 132, 134
Dadaists, 149
Daedalus, 128
Dancing Lesson, see Soyer, Raphael
Danziger, Itzhak, 150, 152–56, 163–65, 211, 213; *Negev Sheep*, 154; *Nimrod*, 152, 153, 154–55, 164
Daumier, Honoré, 54
David, in art, 80, 86, 138, 152
David and Goliath, see Lipchitz
Day of Atonement, see Kramer
Day Before One, see Newman
Day One, see Newman
Dead Sea scrolls, 85, 156
Degas, Edgar, 82; *The Absinthe Drinkers*, 82
Deportation, see Aberdam
Depression, 66, 70, 80
Derain, André, 147–48
Desert, 150, 154–56, 159, 162, 173, 191, 196, 218
Desnos, Robert, 132
Destruction of the Ghetto, The, see Manievich
Destruction of the Temple, see Brauer
Dialogue at Night, see Kahana
Discussion, The, see Herman

Dobrovna, synagogue of, 20
Dobrushin, Yekhezkel, 29–32, 205, 206
Doerner, Otto, 191
Donatello, 152
Drancy camp, 132
Dreyfus affair, 71
Dubuffet, Jean, 124, 168
Dura Europos synagogue, 74
Dybbuk, 37–39, 38, 39, 207

Early Morning in Galilee, see Rubin
Earth Sculpture, see Tumarkin
East End, London, 52, 57
East Side Crowd, see Walkowitz
East Side Girl, see Gross
East Side, New York, 50–55, 63–64, 68, 80, 178, 180, 185
East Side People, see Epstein, Jacob
East Side Soap Box, see Shahn
East Side Street, see Soyer, Raphael
École des Beaux-Arts, 213, 215–18
Educational Alliance, 49–50, 54, 212, 214, 218–19
Effross, N., 40
Ehrenburg, Ilyah, 46, 207
Eigenes, 34, 206
Ein Hod, Israel, 214
Ein Gev, Israel, 173
Ein Sof, 193–94, 198
Eisner, Kurt, 114
Elisha Ben Avuyah, (R.), 74, 76
Elsen, Albert, 137
Elul, Koso, 150, 156–57, 213; *Horizon*, 159
Emigrant Ship, see Segall
Endless Voyage, see Siporin
Engel, Betty, 64
Engel, Joel, 43, 204
Enlightenment, 11–12, 29, 49, 193
Ensor, James, 173
Epstein, Henry, 34
Epstein, Jacob, 52–54, 58, 65, 213; *East Side People*, 53; *The Spirit of the Ghetto*, 65
Eternal Light, see Lipton
Eve, see Altman
Excursion to the Kinnereth, see Bergner
Exhibitions, 58, 62–65, 113, 203, 205, 212–19
Existentialism, 123
Exodus, see Lipchitz; Segall
Exodus no. 1, see Lipton
Expressionism, 42, 44, 116, 124, 137, 143, 184, 212, 218
Exter, Alexandra, 39, 207
Ezekiel's Valley of the Dried Bones, see Rattner

Falk, Robert, 16, 33
Family, The, see Bak
Family Reunion, see Tofel
Fantastic Realism, 118
Farewell to Union Square, see Kantor
Father and Son, see Bak
Faure, Eli, 94
Fauvism, 89
Feder, Adolph, 65
Feininger, Lyonel, 191
Figure with Upraised Arms, see Maryan

First Fruits, see Rubin
Fish and Tomatoes, see Soutine
Flying Spice Box, see Bergner
Folk art, in Chagall, 26–27; colour in, 21; form in, 30; Hebrew letter in, 31, 38; idea of, 18–19, 28–29, 36–37, 47; and modern art, 16, 23–24, 34–35; motifs of, 24, 38, 205; sources of, 16–18; see also Gravestone art; Manuscripts; Synagogues, art of
Four Mystics, The, see Baskin
Friday Evening, see Ben-Zion
Frug, Shimon, 29
Fry, Roger, 58
"Fugue of Death" (Celan), 128
Funeral of the Zadik, see Hirszenberg
Futurism, 181

Gabo, Naum, 68, 213; *Column*, 69
Gate, see Newman
Geometric Abstraction, 196
Germany, 113–14, 135, 147, 212; see also Holocaust
Gertler, Mark, 57, 181, 214; *Jewish Family*, 59
Ghetto Theatre, see Bomberg
Ginzburg, David, 18
Ginzburg, Horace, 18, 204
Giotto, 51
Glitzenstein, Hanoch, 35
Goldfaden, Abraham, 29
Goodman, Percival, 86
Gottlieb, Adolph, 86, 192, 196–98, 214; *Tints*, 200
Gottlieb, Leopold, 89, 149, 214; *Plasterers*, 90
Gottlieb, Mauricy, 17, 203; *Christ before Pilatus*, 203; *Christ in the Temple*, 203
Goya, Francisco, 54, 125, 173
Granovsky, Alexander, 36, 40, 42–43
Gravestone art, 16, 17, 22–24
El Greco, 80, 191
Greenberg, Uri Zvi, 12, 35, 203, 206
Green and Maroon, see Rothko
Green Violinist, see Chagall
Gropius, Walter, 86
Gropper, William, 54, 64, 70, 149, 214; *Tailor*, 55, 149
Gross, Chaim, 62, 214; *East Side Girl*, 62
Guernica, 132
Günzburg, Ilya, 35, 203, 204
Gutman, Nahum, 146
Gutzkov, Carl, 39

Haacke, Hans, 163
Haber, Shamai, 156–57, 214; *Altar*, 157, 158
Habimah Theatre, see Hebrew Habimah Theatre
Haftmann, Werner, 201
Hagar, see Lipchitz
Haggadah of Sarajevo, 196, 198
Haifa, 218; School of Architecture in, 164
Haifa University, 170–71
Halpert, Samuel, 64
Der Hammer, 64–65
Hanging Turkey, see Soutine

Hapgood, Hutchins, 54
Harkavy, Minna, 64, 214; *The Last Prayer*, 134, *134*
Harriton, Abraham, 62, 64
Hassidic motifs, 90–91, 177–78, 181, 188
Hatzor, 156
Hazaz, Chayim, 152
Head of a Young Jew, see Altman
Hebrew Habimah Theatre, 36–37, 42–43, 206, 208, 212
Hebrew Technical Institute, 63
Hebrew theatre, 36; see also Jewish theatre; Yiddish theatre
Henry, Robert, 54
Here, see Newman
Herman, Joseph, 84, 117, 170, 214; *The Discussion*, 85
Hess, Thomas B., 198
Hillel (R.), 11, 71, 80
Hiram, (king), 80
Hirschbein, Peretz, 62, 206
Hirzenberg, Samuel, 17, 203, 214; *Funeral of the Zadik*, 10, 11
Hodler, Ferdinand, 147
Hofmannsthal, Hugo von, 62
Hofstein, David, 36
Holocaust, 8, 70, 80, 86, 96, 152, 156; Jewish artists of, 113–43, 170, 172–73
Holocaust, see Kaish
Homage to Jerusalem, see Ardon
Homage to Six Million I, see Nevelson
Horizon, see Elul
Horn, Milton, 86, 134
Hundertwasser, Fritz, 119–20, 125, 130, 214; *Blood Garden—House with Yellow Smoke*, 104, 119; *Jew's House in Austria*, 119
Hundred Drawings of Abraham Walkowitz, A, 57

Icarus, 128
Icon painting, 25, 28
Identity, see Shahn
Ignatoff, David, 56, 62, 64, 178, 209
Immigration and immigrants, 7–10, 12, 49, 70, 78, 87, 137, 149, 162, 169, 185; see also Israel, migrations to
Impressionism, 16
Incas, art of, 177
Indenbaum, Leon, 34
Introduction to the Yiddish Theatre, see Chagall
Invocation, see Weber
Israel, artists in, 145–75, 212–19; building of, 8, 140, 143, 149; landscape of, 149–50, 152; migrations to, 118, 121–22, 135, 149–50, 160, 162, 166–67, 169–70, 172; in War of Independence, 123, 155; wars of, 165
Israel Besieged, see Brauer
Israels, Joseph, 51, 203, 204, 206

Jacob, in art, 134, 138
Jacob, Max, 132
Janco, Marcel, 149, 214; *Maabaroth in Grey*, 149, *149*; *The Wounded Soldier*, 149, *149*
Jerusalem, 146, 160, 191, 193, 198, 212–16, 219

Jerusalem Hills, see Ticho
Jewish Academy, 18
Jewish art, 43–44, 49, 51–52, 65–66, 203–205; definition of, 15; and Israel, 145–75; modern, 7–8, 23–24, 34–35, 70, 152, 218; and religious tradition, 177–89; and Russian revolution, 35, 37, 40, 47; themes of, 134; see also Folk art
Jewish Art Center, The, 64–65
Jewish Artists (Buber), 52
Jewish community, 22, 43, 49, 66, 71, 177; Eastern European, 11, 23, 28, 49, 80; in Israel, 150, 156; in New World, 189; Sephardic, 160; see also East Side, New York; Religious tradition, in art
Jewish culture, Chagall and, 33; in Eastern Europe, 10, 49; in Israel, 150, 161; in New York, 50–55, 57, 64; in Russia, 35–36, 47; secular, 28, 195; see also Religious tradition, in art
Jewish Daily Forward, 63
Jewish Educational Aid Society, 58
Jewish Ethnographic Expedition, 17–18, 38
Jewish Ethnographic Society, 18
Jewish Family, see Gertler
Jewish Morning Journal, 83
Jewish Museum, New York, 66
Jewish School of Paris, 89, 147
Jewish theatre, 36–43, 57, 121, 124, 152, 207, 212; see also Yiddish theatre
Jewish Theatre, see Bomberg
Jew's House in Austria, see Hundertwasser
Jezebel, 159
John, Asger, 124
Johnson, Philip, 86
Joshua, see Newman
"Journey to America, A," see Lissitzky
Jugendstil movement, 29
Jules, Mervin, 70
Di Junge, 61–62

Kadishman, Menashe, 163, 215; *The Altar*, 163; *Trees in the Ocean*, 107, 163
Kahana, Aharon, 156, 215; *Dialogue at Night*, 156, *157*
Kahn, Louis, 86
Kaish, Luise, 86, 134, 193, 215; *The Cabbalistic Sphere*, 193–94, *194*; *Holocaust*, 134, *136*
Kalavalla, 62
Kamerni Theatre, see Moscow Yiddish Kamerni State Theatre
Kantor, Morris, 65, 215; *Farewell to Union Square*, 78
Karavan, Dani, 165, 215; *Monument to the Negev Brigade*, 165–66, *166*
Kars, Jiri, 89
Katznelson, I., 206
Kaufman, Isidore, 17, 203
Kav (Cabbala), 194
Kepes, Gyorgy, 86
Kent State University, 78–79
Kesalon, Israel, 143
Khorsabad, 152

Kibbutz Ein Gev, 173
Kibbutzim, 147–48, 213, 216, 218
Kibbutz Mishmar Haemek, 142–43
Kienholz, Edward, 131
Kiesling, Moshe, 89
Kiev, 34–36, 206, 208, 212, 215–16, 218
Kiev Art School, 66, 212, 216–17
Kikoïne, Michael, 89, 91
Kirchner, Ernst, 114
Kirkegaard, Soren, 175, 207
Kishinev Pogrom, The, see Brauer
Klausner, Joseph, 204
Klee, Paul, 117, 191
Klimt, Gustav, 120
Knave of Diamonds movement, 37
Koenig, Leo, 34, 206
Kohn, Hans, 203
Kokoschka, Oscar, 86
Kopman, Benjamin, 57, 62, 64
Kovarsky, Yehoshua, 195–96, 215; *Temple Above the Moon*, 111, 195
Krakauer, Leopold, 191, 215; *Sun and Thistles*, 2
Kramer, Jacob, 57, 181–82, 215; *Day of Atonement*, 181, *182*, 189
Kremegne, Pinkus, 34, 89, 91
Kulturlige (Kiev), 29, 34–35, 206
Kutna, G., 203, 204, 205

Lam, Wilfredo, 124
Lament of Nails, see Ardon
Landau, Sishe, 62
Landauer, Gustav, 114
Landscapes of Jewish History, see Bak
Lasansky, Mauricio, 131
Lasker, Joe, 77, 215; *Memo*, 77, 78; *Scissor Grinder*, 77, 77
Lassaw, Ibram, 86
Last Prayer, The, see Harkavy
Lebrun, Rico, 131
Léger, Fernand, 124, 148
Leib, Mani, 62
Lelwick, Halper, 62
Lenin, V. I., 37
Lestschinsky, Joseph, 36
Lethaby, W. R., 58
Letter(s), Hebrew, 31, 38, 44, 128, 194
Leviathan, I., 51–52
Levine, David, 149; *The Pressers*, 149
Levine, Jack, 70, 79–80, 170, 215; *The Passing Scene*, 67, 79; *Planning Solomon's Temple*, 80, 81; *Tombstone Cutter*, 79–80, 81; *To an Unknown German*, 134, 135
Lewis, Wyndham, 181
Lichtenstein, Itzhak, 34, 206
Lie, The, 42
Liebermann, Max, 51, 203, 206, 215; *Christ in the Temple*, 113, 203
Lilien, Ephraim Moses, 17, 29, 203
Lillith, 159
Lion, see Lissitzky
Lion of Tel Khai, see Melnikov
Lipchitz, Jacques, 65, 89, 132–34, 138, 140–42, 215; *David and Goliath*, 138; *Exodus*, 138; *Hagar*, 140, 141; *Miracle II*, 140, 141, 142; *Mother and Child*, 138, 141; *Mother and Child II*, 140, 141; *The Prayer*, 132, 133, 134; *Prometheus Strangling the Vulture*, 140; *The Rape of Europa*, 140; *Theseus and the Minotaur*, 140

Lipton, Seymour, 70, 84–86, 137, 215; *Eternal Light*, 86, *86*; *Exodus no. 1*, 137, *140*; *Manuscript*, 87; *Menorah*, 87; *Panorama of Judea*, 137

Lissitzky, Eliezer, biography of, 215; and folk art, 24, 44–45, 177, 215; as modern artist, 65, 68, 208; on national art, 49; in Berlin, 62; synagogue studies of, 18–20, 47; in Russia, 16, 44, 46; *Der Ber*, illustration for, *45*; *Chad Gadya*, 24, 24–25, 46; "A Journey to America," 48; *Krasnim Klinom Bye Byelikh* (Beat the Whites with the Red Wedge), 46, *47*; *Lion*, *18, 19*; *Prager Legende*, illustration for, 44, *45*; *Yingl Zingl Chwatt*, illustration for, 44–46, *45*

Lodz, Poland, 11, 212, 214

London, 12, 162, 214; see also East End, London

Lozowick, Louis, 35, 62, 64–65, 68–70, 149, 215; *Autobiographic*, 66, *69*; *The Concrete Mixer*, *71*, 149; *Minneapolis*, *71*

Lubok, Jewish, 16, *16*, 30, 32

Lubomirsky, O., 43

Luftmensch, 41–42

Luitpold, Prince, 113

Lunatcharsky, Anatoly, 37, 206, 207

Luria, Rabbi Isaac, 198

Luxemburg, Rosa, 114

Maabaroth in Grey, see Janco

Machmadim group, 34, 206, 218

Madrid, 128

Maimonides, Moses, 80

Malevich, Kasimir, 39, 46, 207, 208

Man of Judah, see Zorach

Man with Torah, see Cherney

Mane-Katz, 89

Manievich, Abraham, 64, 215; *The Destruction of the Ghetto*, 114–15, *114*

Manuscript, see Lipton

Man with Plant, see Bezem

Marini, Marino, 189

Martyr, The, see Brauer

Marx, Karl, 185

Maryan, Maryan S., 112, 121–25, 130, 216; Autobiography, page from, *122*; *Figure with Upraised Arms*, *123*; *Personage, Man with Donkey Ears*, *123*; (untitled, *112, 125*)

Masada, see Brauer

Matisse, Henri, 55, 62

Matta, Robert Echaurrent, 124

Mayas, art of, 177

Mazel Tov, 42

Meal of the Poor, see Rubin

Mehutan, Hava, 157–60, 216; *Offering*, *158*, 159–60

Meidner, Ludwig, 113–14

Melnikov, Abraham, 152, 216; *The Roaring Lion (Lion of Tel Khai)*, *151*, 152

Memorial to the Children of the Holocaust, see Ben-Zwi

Mems, see Paris, Harold

Mendel, Menachem, 43

Mendele Mocher Sefarim, 28, 62, 79, 168

Mendelsohn, Eric, 86

Menkes, Siegmund, 89, 134, 182–84, 216; *Les Talmudistes*, 184, *185*; *The Uplifting of the Torah*, 182, *183*, 184; *Uprising of Ghetto Warsaw*, 134, *135*

Menorah, see Lipton

Menorah in art, 74, 77, 85–86, 138, 140, 142, 189

Menorah Journal, 65

Meyer, Franz, 41, 115, 116, 207

Meyerowitz, William, 65

Michaux, Henri, 124

Michelangelo, 51, 58, 152

Michoels, Solomon, 40, 42–43, *42*

Migration and Return, see Bergner

Minchah, concept of, 159

Minkovsky, Mauricy, 17

Minneapolis, see Lozowick

Mintchine, Abraham, 89, 216; *Self-Portrait*, *91*

Miracle II, see Lipchitz

Mir Iskutswa, 16

Modern art, 35–37, 40, 51, 58, 197, 201; form in, 8, 32, 34; in Paris, 89, 123–24; see also Folk art, and modern art; Jewish art, modern

Modigliani, Amedeo, 8, 89, 216; *Portrait of Jacques Lipchitz and His Wife*, *88*

Mohilev synagogue, 18–20, 25, 47, 204–205

Moment in M., see Paris, Harold

Montparnasse, 123

Monument to the Negev Brigade, see Karavan

Mooney, Tom, 71

Moscow Yiddish Kamerni State Theatre, 36–37, 39–41, 43, 207–208

Moses, see Zorach

Mother and Child, see Lipchitz; Orlof

Mother and Child II, see Lipchitz

Motherwell, Robert, 86

Mud Bath, The, see Bomberg

Munich, 12, 22, 28, 128

Museums, 37, 212–19; Jewish, 18, 36, 66, 206

Mysticism, Jewish, 91, 191–201

Nabateans, 154

Nagy, Moholy, 68

Nathan, Fritz, 86

National Academy of Design, 68

National art, see Jewish art

Naton, Abraham, 149

Nazis, see Holocaust

Near East, 152, 162–63, 195; deities of, 195

Negev, 150, 156–57, 159, 165

Negev Sheep, see Danziger

Dos Neie Land, 51

Nevelson, Louise, 134, 216; *Homage to Six Million I*, 134, *137*

New Horizons group, 162, 213–15

Newman, Barnett, 192, 196–98, 216; *Abraham*, 198; *Black Fire*, 198; *Cathedra*, 198; *Day Before One*, 198; *Day One*, 198; *Gate*, 198; *Here*, 198; *Joshua*, 198, *199*; *Onement* series, 198; *Primordial Light*, 198; *Uriel*, 198; *Voice*, 198; *White Fire*, 198; *Word*, 198; *Zim Zum*, *196*, 198

New York, artists in, 12, 61–66, 68, 70, 121, 123–24, 146–47, 162, 188, 196, 198, 212–19; Jewish culture in, 50–55, 57, 64; see also East Side, New York

New York, see Shahn

New York University, 63

Night of Ascents, see Ardon

Nimrod, 150, 152, 154–55

Der Nister, 28, 36

Nolde, Emil, 184

Nossig, Alfred, 203

Ofek, Abraham, 166–70, 185–86, 216; *The Return*, 168–69; *Settlers Conversing*, 167; *The Synagogue*, 185–86, *186*

Offering, see Mehutan

Oifgang, 34, 204, 206

Old Jew, The, see Ryback, Issachar

Old Man in Skull Cap, see Soyer, Moses

Old Mill, The, see Soutine

Old Synagogue, The, see Ryback, Issachar

Opatasho, J., 62

Opening of the Ark, The, see Weinberg

Orlof, Hanna, 89, 95, 173, 216; *Mother and Child*, 173, *174*

Ornamentation, Jewish, 18, 24, 31; see also Folk art; Synagogues, art of

L'Ornement hébraïque, 18

Osborn, Max, 23, 205

Ost und West, 203

Ostrowsky, Abbo, 62

Over Vitebsk, see Chagall

Paldi, Israel, 146

Pale of Settlement, 12, 15, 28, 177

Palestine, 126, 145–47, 149, 155–56, 173, 192, 195

Palestine Exploration Fund, 15

Panorama of Judea, see Lipton

Parchments and Scrolls, see Ardon

Paris, artists in, 12, 22, 25, 28, 37, 58, 62, 89–90, 94–96, 121, 123–24, 161–62, 182, 191, 195–96, 212–19; German occupation of, 131, 138, 212; modern art in, 89, 123–24; trends in, 155; World Exhibition in 1878, 15

Paris, Harold, 128–30, 216; *All That Remains*, 130; *Chai (Life)*, 128; *Mems*, 128; *Moment in M.*, 130; *Souls*, 130, *131*; *Torah Soul*, 130, *131*

Pascin, Jules, 8, 89, 217; *Young Girl Sitting*, *91*

Passing Scene, The, see Levine, Jack

Pasternak, Leonid, 51

Pathetiker group, 218

People's Art Guild, The, 62–63

Peredvizhniki (Wanderers), 15–16, 28

Peretz Y.L., 28, 62

"Persecution of the Jewish People," see Brauer

Personage, Man with Donkey Ears, see Maryan

Petrograd Academy of Art, 37

Pevsner, Antoine, 68, 217; *Twinned Column*, *69*

Philo, 179

Picasso, Pablo, 62, 117, 132, 168, 173; *Charnel House*, 132, *133*

Pilichovsky, Leopold, 17
Pissarro, Camille, 51–52
Planning Solomon's Temple, see
Levine, Jack
Plasterers, see Gottlieb
Podolia, 17
Pop Art, 78, 127–28
Popova, Liubov, 39, 207
Portinari, Candido, 168
Portrait of Ahad Ha'am, see Rubin
*Portrait of Jacques Lipchitz and His
Wife*, see Modigliani
Portrait of Jew, see Ryback, Issachar
Portrait of Moise Kisling, see Soutine
Post-Cubist Abstraction, 123
Prager Legende (Sichot Chulin), see
Lissitzky
Prayer, The, see Lipchitz
Precisionism, 216
Pregnant Woman, see Achiam
Pressers, The, see Levine, David
Primitive art, 28; see also Folk art
Primordial Light, see Newman
Procession no. 1, see Weinberg
Prometheus Strangling the Vulture, see
Lipchitz
Proun, 44, 46, 208, 215

Rabbi, see Bloom
Rabbi, The, see Bloom
Rabbis, 74–75, 177–78, 186–87
Rainmaker of Carmel, The, see Brauer
Ram's Horn and Menorah, see Shahn
Rape of Europa, The, see Lipchitz
Raphael, 80, 94
Rappaport, Nathan, 134, 143, 217;
Scroll of Fire, 143, *143*
Raskin, Saul, 51, 64
Rattner, Abraham, 217; *Ezekiel's
Valley of the Dried Bones*, 134, *135*
Ravitch, Melech, 170, 206, 213
Raynal, Maurice, 94
Rayonism, 16
Reading from the Torah, see Weinberg
Realism, 28, 32
Realist Manifesto, 214, 217
Réalités-Nouvelles, 217
Reality magazine, 218
Reder, Bernard, 187–88, 217; *Aaron
with Tabernacle*, 187–88, *188*
Reinhardt, Max, 36, 191
Reisen, Abraham, 51
Religious tradition, in art, 134, 177–89;
see also Bible, in art; Synagogues, art
of
Rembrandt, 54, 80, 184, 191
Renaissance, 34, 61, 206
Return, The, see Ofek
Riegel, Alois, 15
Rimon, 34, 203, 204, 205, 206
Ringen, 34, 206
Rischin, Moses, 65, 209
Ritterband, Olly, 132
Ritual Figure, see Weinberg
Rivera, Diego, 147–48, 168
Rivers, Larry, 76, 217; *Bar Mitzvah
Photograph Portrait*, 76–77, *76*
Roaring Lion, The, see Melnikov
Romantic nationalism, 145–47, 162
Rosenberg, Isaac, 57, 181
Rosenthal, Bernard, 86
Rothko, Mark, 70, 192, 196–99, 201,

211, 217; *Green and Maroon, 109*
Rouault, Georges, 161
Rousseau, Henri, 62, 145
Rubin, Reuven, 89, 145–47, 156, 217;
*Early Morning in Galilee, 146; First
Fruits, 144, 145; Meal of the Poor,
147; Portrait of Ahad Ha'am, 147*
La Ruche, 34, 37, 206
Russia, 12, 15–18, 22, 33–36, 47, 68,
204–208, 212–19
Russian Revolution, 8, 15–16, 20,
35–37, 40, 42–43, 46–47, 66
Ryback, Issachar, 16, 18–22, 28–33, 35,
47, 177, 205–207, 217; *The Old Jew,
20, 22, 22; The Old Synagogue, 20,
21; Portrait of a Jew, 22; The
Synagogue of Chiklov, 20, 21*
Ryback, Louis, 62, 64

Sabbath in the Kibbutz, see Simon
Sabbath Phantoms—Mythomania, see
Seligman
Sacco and Vanzetti, 71
Sach, Nathan, 211
Sachs, Nelly, 128
St. Petersburg, Art Academy of, 15, 18;
artists in, 12, 20, 25, 212; Imperial
Library of, 18; research in, 17;
University of, 18
Santa Maria la Blanca synagogue,
Toledo, 172
Sargent, John Singer, 57
Sargon, King, 152
Sartre, Jean Paul, 123
Saul, 80, 86
Schiele, Egon, 120
Schlemmer, Oskar, 35
Scholem, Gershom, 194
Schriften, 34, 62, 64, 178, 206, 219
Schüler, Else Lasker, 117
Schwarz, Marek, 34–35
Scissor Grinder, see Lasker
Scribe, The, see Weinberg
Scroll of Fire, see Rappaport
Sculpture (Tchaikov), 34
Sculpture in Arad, see Tumarkin
Seamstress, see Soyer, Raphael
Seba, Shalom, 149, 156, 217; *Shearing
of Sheep, 155, 156*
Sefad, Galilee, 161
Segal, George, 70, 78, 134, 163, 173,
217–18; *Abraham and Isaac, 78–79,
79, 175; Akedah, Tel Aviv, 79, 173,
175*
Segal, Haim B. Isaac, 25; *Birds of
Paradise, 20*
Segall, Lasar, 132, 135, 137, 218;
Emigrant Ship, 139; Exodus, 137, 139
Seifert, David, 91
Self-Portrait, see Mintchine; Soutine;
Tchaikov
Seligman, Kurt, 132, 218; *Sabbath
Phantoms—Mythomania, 132, 133*
Separation, see Struck
"Separation of Day from Night," *196*
Sephardic Wedding Feast, see Castel
Seroya, H., 95
Settlers Conversing, see Ofek
Shahn, Ben, 64, 70–74, 78, 86, 170, 218;
*East Side Soap Box, 72, 73; Identity,
9, 11, 72; New York, 72; Ram's Horn
and Menorah, 72, 74, 102*

Shapiro, Karl, 77
Shatz, Boris, 145–46
Shazar, Zalman, 204
Shearing of Sheep, see Seba
Shemi, Yechiel, 150, 163–64, 218;
Standing Sculpture, 163–64, 164
Ship of Fools, see Bosch
Sholom Aleichem, 28, 40–42, 62, 152,
168
Shor, Ilya, 86
Shower, In the, see Simon
Der Shtrom, 43, 45, 206
Sickert, Walter Richard, 58
Simon, Johanan, 147–49, 218; *In the
Shower, 148; Sabbath in the
Kibbutz, 148*
Siporin, Mitchell, 70, 86, 135, 218;
Endless Voyage, 13, 135
Six Stories with Light Endings
(Ehrenburg), *48*
Slade School of Fine art, 57–58, 181,
213–15
Slaves Were We in Egypt, see Brauer
Sloan, John, 83, 214, 216
Smoke, see Bak
Social Realism, 78–79, 135, 148, 170,
196, 214
Solitude, see Chagall
Solomon, King, 80
Solomon, Solomon J., 58
Soulages, Pierre, 124
Souls, see Paris, Harold
Soutine, Chaim, 52, 80, 89–96, 124,
173, 206, 218; *Fish and Tomatoes,
93; Hanging Turkey, 92; The Old
Mill, 95; Portrait of Moise Kisling,
96; Self-Portrait, 96; Woman in
Profile, 99*
Soyer, Isaac, 70, 83, 149, 170;
Employment Agency, 149
Soyer, Moses, 64, 70, 83, 170, 218;
*Lover of Books, 83; Old Man in Skull
Cap, 83, 83*
Soyer, Raphael, 64, 70, 80–83, 149, 170,
218; *Artist's Parents, 80, 81, 82; The
Bridge, 82, 83; Dancing Lesson, 82,
83; East Side Street, 83; Seamstress,
149*
Spinoza, 95
Spirit of the Ghetto, The (Hapgood), 54
Spirit of the Ghetto, The, see Epstein,
Jacob
Standing Sculpture, see Shemi, Yechiel
Stanislavsky, K., 36, 38–39
Stars and Stripes, 128
Stassof, Vladimir, 15–16, 18, 29,
203–204
Steinberg, Leo, 201
Steinhardt, Jacob, 177, 218; *In the
Synagogue, 178*
Stematsky, Avigdor, 147
Stepanova, Varvara, 39
Sterenberg, David, 37
Stern, Maurice, 64
Stieglitz, Alfred, 63
Strauss Judaica Collection, 15
Streichman, Yehezkiel, 147
Struck, Herman, 177, 218; *Separation
(Havdalah), 179*
Sun and Thistles, see Krakauer
Suprematism, 16
Surrealism, 118, 124, 195–96, 218
Sutherland, Graham, 173

Synagogue, The, see Beckmann; Bloom;
Ofek
Synagogue, In The, see Steinhardt
Synagogue of Chiklov, The, see
Ryback, Issachar
Synagogues, 179–80, 186; art of, 16,
18–20, 74, 85–86, 152, 161; see also
names of specific synagogues

Tachism, 123–24
Tagore, R., 62
Tailor, see Gropper
Les Talmudistes, see Menkes
Talmudists, The, see Weber
Talpir, G., 208
Tapies, Antoni, 161
Tatlin, Vladimir, 39, 46, 207
Tchaikov, Joseph, 16, 34–35, *34–35*,
206, 218–19; *Self-Portrait, 34; A
Young Jew*, 35
Tchernichovski, Saul, 13, 152, 203
Tel Khai, 152
Temple Above the Moon, see Kovarsky
Temple Beth El, Gary, Indiana, 85–86
Temple Israel, Tulsa, 85
Temple Oheb Shalom, Nashville, 74
Theatre, see Jewish theatre; Yiddish
theatre
Theresienstadt camp, 132
Theseus, 120
Theseus and the Minotaur, see Lipchitz
Thou Shalt Not, see Bak
Ticho, Anna, 191, 219; *Jerusalem Hills,
190*
Tiger's Eye, 216
Time Is a River without Banks, see
Chagall
Tintoretto, 51
Tints, see Gottlieb, Adolph
Tofel, Jennings, 62, 64–65, 84, 219;
Family Reunion, 84, 84
Tohu Vabohu, 150, 156
Toledo, Synagogue of, 172
Tombstone Cutter, see Levine, Jack
Torah Soul, see Paris, Harold
Train of Numbers, see Ardon
El Transito synagogue, Toledo, 172
Trees in the Ocean, see Kadishman
Troeltsch, Ernst, 185
Trumpeldor, J. 152
Tuchman, Maurice, 94

Tumarkin, Ygael, 164, 219; *Earth
Sculpture, 164; Sculpture in Arad,
165*
Twentieth Century Art exhibition,
Whitechapel, 58
Twinned Column, see Pevsner
Two Birds Flanking a Vase, see Altman
Two Orphans, see Adler
Two Rabbis, see Adler
Tyshler, Alexander, 207

Ugaritic language, 156
Ukraine, 35, 38, 42, 66, 114, 212,
215–16
United States, 49, 65, 68, 138, 140, 188,
195
Unknown German, To an, see Levine,
Jack
Uplifting of the Torah, The, see
Menkes
Uprising of Ghetto Warsaw, see
Menkes
Uriel, see Newman
Uriel Accosta, 37, 39

Van Doesburg, Theo, 68
Van Gogh, Vincent, 114
Vechtangov, Yevgeny, 36, 38, 43
Verrocchio, Andrea del, 152
Vesnin, Alexander, 39, 207
Vienna, 22, 28, 118–20, 173, 213–15
Vilna, Lithuania, 124–25, 135, 195, 212,
215, 218
Da Vinci, Leonardo, 127
Vitebsk, Russia, 40, 46, 213
Vision of Ezekiel, see Bomberg
Voice, see Newman
Vorticism, 181

Waldemar, George, 89, 94
Walkowitz, Abraham, 54–57, 62, 64–65,
219; *East Side Crowd, 55–57, 56;*
"The Kiss," 57
Wanderers group, 15–16, 28, 203
War of Independence, 123, 155–56, 162;
memorial of, 165
Warsaw, 35, 134, 143, 170, 214, 217
Weber, Max, 62, 65–66, 177–81, 219;
*Adoration of the Moon, 101, 181;
Invocation, 176, 177–79; The
Talmudists, 179–81, 180*

Weichsel, John, 62–64
Weil, Shraga, 134
Weinberg, Elbert, 134, 188–89, 219;
*Abraham, Isaac and the Angel, 189;
The Opening of the Ark, 189;
Procession no. 1, 188, 189; Reading
from the Torah, 189; Ritual Figure,
189, 189; The Scribe*, 189
Whitechapel, London, 57–58, 61, 214
White Crucifixion, see Chagall
White Fire, see Newman
Wholinia, 17
Wickhoff, Franz, 15
Wiethuechter, Gustav, 116
Wilansky, Anna, 134
Wischnitzer, Rachel, 20, 204, 205, 208
Wolpert, Ludwig, 86
Woman in Profile, see Soutine
Word, see Newman
Works Progress Administration, 72, 80,
213–15, 217–18
World War I, 8, 28, 68, 114, 149
World War II, 8, 11, 70, 86, 113, 123,
128, 135, 155–56, 162, 167, 170, 196
Wounded Soldier, The, see Janco
Wright, Frank Lloyd, 86

Yakulov, Giorgi, 39, 42
Yamasaki, Minoru, 86
Yevsektsiya Commissariat, 34, 36, 206
Yiddish Art Theater, 128
Yiddish language, 29, 36, 51–52, 57,
62–63, 206
Yiddish theatre, 17, 36, 41–42, 57, 61,
207, 216; see also Moscow Yiddish
Kamerni State Theatre
Yingl Zingl Chwatt, see Lissistzky
Young Girl Sitting, see Pascin
Young Jew, A, see Tchaikov
Yudo'win, Shlomo, 18
Yung Yiddish, 34, 206

Zaritsky, Josef, 147
Zemach, Nachum, 36, 43, 206, 207
Zim Zum, see Newman
Zionist movement, 29, 57, 145, 203
Zohar, see Cabbala
Zorach, William, 64, 70, 134, 219; *Man
of Judah, 137–38, 138; Moses*, 137,
138